Reading Now

Amy E. Olsen
Argosy University

Longman

Boston   Columbus   Indianapolis   New York   San Francisco   Upper Saddle River
Amsterdam   Cape Town   Dubai   London   Madrid   Milan   Munich   Paris   Montreal   Toronto
Delhi   Mexico City   São Paulo   Sydney   Hong Kong   Seoul   Singapore   Taipei   Tokyo

Editor in Chief: Eric Stano
Director of Development: Mary Ellen Curley
Development Editor: Janice Wiggins-Clarke
Senior Marketing Manager: Thomas DeMarco
Senior Supplements Editor: Donna Campion
Senior Media Producer: Stefanie Liebman
Production Manager: Savoula Amanatidis
Project Coordination and Electronic Page Makeup: Electronic Publishing Services Inc., NYC
Text Design: PreMediaGlobal
Cover Design Manager: Wendy Ann Fredericks
Cover Photo: Copyright © digitalskillet/iStockphoto
Photo Researcher: Connie Gardner
Manufacturing Manager: Mary Fischer
Printer and Binder: Courier Kendallville
Cover Printer: Coral Graphic Services, Inc.

For permission to use copyrighted material, grateful acknowledgment is made to the copyright holders on pp. 513–514, which are hereby made part of this copyright page.

2 3 4 5 6 7 8 9 10—CKV —13 12 11

Longman
is an imprint of

www.pearsonhighered.com

Student Edition:
ISBN-13: 978-0-205-63994-6
ISBN-10: 0-205-63994-1

Annotated Instructor's Edition:
ISBN-13: 978-0-205-75530-1
ISBN-10: 0-205-75530-5

Reading
Now

To Gerry and his love of books. Readers Unite!
—*Amy E. Olsen*

Brief Contents

Detailed Contents

Reading well is an essential skill for success in college, in the workforce, and in daily life. Students need to be able to easily understand what they read and to convey their understanding in a variety of ways. One of the principal goals of *Reading Now* is to make the reading process enjoyable so that students will want to read, and thereby improve their reading skills. Another key goal of the text is to get students actively involved in the reading process by helping them establish connections to material they are reading. The text combines exciting and diverse readings, eye-catching photographs and other visuals, and stimulating questions to involve students with what they read.

The text uses a holistic and a specific-skill approach. Because the skills involved in successfully reading articles, essays, textbooks, and short stories are connected, it is important to present those skills as a whole early in a reading textbook. The first three chapters provide an overview of the skills needed to be a proficient reader. Chapter 1 covers questions an active reader needs to ask, Chapter 2 presents ways to answer those questions, and Chapter 3 examines vocabulary-building skills. The next six chapters each focus on a specific reading skill—main ideas, supporting details, organization, purpose and tone, inferences, and critical thinking—with exercises tied to six readings per chapter. With this form of organization, students can learn each skill in depth while they still use all the skills needed to fully comprehend a piece of writing. The repeated exposure that comes from introducing all the skills holistically in Chapter 1, and then focusing on specific skills in Chapters 4 through 9, serves to reinforce each skill for the students. The final chapter reviews the essentials of each skill that have been introduced in the preceding six chapters. Students can use the readings in this last chapter as mastery tests.

The text can be used in various ways. Instructors can begin with the first chapter and continue on through the text picking as many readings per chapter as they have time for. Or they can introduce Chapter 1, most of Chapter 2, and Chapter 3, and then read the essays, articles, and textbook excerpts in the following chapters as they focus on specific reading skills. When instructors are ready for students to read the short stories, they can finish covering Chapter 2. Another alternative is to cover Chapters 1, 2, and 3 and then move to each skills chapter, but only do three or four readings in each and come back to the readings that were skipped once all six skills have been covered in more depth. Using any of these approaches gives instructors the opportunity to show students the big reading picture and then let them work on the various elements that make up that picture.

Content Overview

Reading Now is divided into ten chapters. After the three introductory chapters, the remaining chapters contain the following sections:

Before You Read The first activity provides questions to get students thinking about the topic before they start reading. By asking questions, a reader begins to make connections to a reading and becomes more involved in the reading process. No write-on lines are provided in the text in order to focus students on answering the questions in their heads as one would normally do if reading the newspaper or an article in a magazine. The goal is to build a skill students will use outside of the classroom. Instructors may at times want to ask students to write answers to the questions on a separate sheet to monitor their progress in responding to the questions. The student is occasionally asked, especially in the later chapters, to create a question (a write-on line is supplied in these cases), so he or she can move to the stage of being able to foresee ways of connecting with a reading.

Vocabulary Preview Ten vocabulary words that are used in the Vocabulary section are presented here. By pointing out these words to the students before the reading, they can be on the lookout for them and use their context-clue skills as they encounter each word.

About the Writer This section gives a brief background on the writer's life and other works and includes information on where the reading originally appeared. This section gives the reader some insight into the writer and the reading, which can help in making connections to a reading.

The Reading The first four readings in each chapter are articles or essays taken from a variety of sources, including newspapers, magazines, and books. The first three readings are usually contemporary (within the last 5 years). The fourth essay or article is more of a "classic," usually by a well-known writer. The fifth reading is a textbook excerpt. The excerpts come from various disciplines and cover information that will apply to most students. The final reading is a short story. The short stories give students the chance to make more inferences and build other reading skills.

The Visual Each chapter contains one or more photographs or other visual (cartoon, chart, graph, or map) within the reading. The visuals help students to read texts other than the written word. With the photographs, students learn to look closely at a picture to see how it connects to a reading and decide what it adds to the reading's message. Learning to interpret information provided by cartoons, graphs, and maps also makes students more resourceful readers. A second purpose of the visuals is to attract students to the readings and excite their curiosity about the reading's topic. A third purpose is to serve as a memory aid for visual learners. Sometimes by recalling a photograph or other visual, a student can remember an important point in a reading.

Getting the Message The first activity after the reading contains ten multiple-choice questions and five short-answer questions that cover the essential reading skills. Question 14 asks students to share the information they have annotated in the reading. This question keeps students on track in their annotating and aids instructors in seeing what students find important or confusing in the readings. Question 15 always covers a recording skill, such as having students write a summary, paraphrase a sentence, make or complete an outline, or create a visual aid.

Vocabulary The Vocabulary section includes three parts. Parts A and B provide various vocabulary questions. Among the exercises in this section are sentence completions; clozes exercises; matching words to synonyms, antonyms, definitions, or examples; writing one's own sentences; and recognizing if words are used correctly in sentences. Students are encouraged to refer back to the reading to discover the meanings through the use of context clues, though referring to a dictionary is an option. Part C focuses on word parts. Again various types of exercises are employed, including supplying missing word parts or meanings and creating words with the word parts. Students can always refer to Chapter 3 to review a word part's meaning. The word parts used in these exercises can be found in either the vocabulary words used in Parts A and B or in other words in the reading. The goal in learning the word parts is to help students figure out the meanings of unfamiliar words they may later encounter.

The Reading and You This section has different headings depending on the type of reading: The Essay and You, The Article and You, The Textbook and You, and The Short Story and You. This section contains four questions. The first three questions ask students to make connections between themselves and the reading. Write-on lines are provided for the students' answers. These questions also lend themselves well to small-group or whole-class discussion. The fourth question asks students to write a paragraph related to material in the reading. Some of the prompts ask for analytical responses and some ask for more imaginative replies. If instructors would like longer answers, most of the prompts can be used as is or adapted for essay-length responses.

Take a Closer Look The student is referred back to the photograph or other visual to look at it more closely. By looking at the photograph or other visual again, after having read about the topic related to it, the student is given the opportunity to see if his or her response to the image has changed or been enhanced in some way.

Internet Activities The final section offers two questions that ask students to use the Internet to find further information on an aspect of the reading. Sometimes the Web address is given for a student to use, and other times the student is given words to do a search on and asked to pick sites that appear useful. This section helps to build students' Internet savvy, helps students further connect to the topic, creates more reading experiences, and works on recording skills through additional writing of summaries, creating outlines, and making graphs. This section also takes advantage, when possible, of the Internet's ability to give visual and auditory learners a chance to watch videos, search for photographs, or listen to music.

Additional Features

In addition to the nine chapters that either holistically or individually present the essential reading skills, the text includes a chapter on vocabulary development, a Using the Internet section, a review of skimming and scanning, various forms for photocopying, and a Glossary.

A Word about Words Chapter 3 covers the main points of vocabulary acquisition. It is divided into three parts: context clues, dictionary use, and word parts. The first part explains what context clues are and provides practice exercises on finding different types of clues. The section on dictionary use includes methods of marking unknown words, information on how to read a dictionary entry, a discussion on the pros and cons of online and paper dictionaries, suggestions on how to make flash cards, and explanations of multiple meanings and denotations and connotations. The final part explains what word parts are and provides the meanings for more than eighty prefixes, roots, and suffixes.

Using the Internet This section provides tips on how to effectively use the Internet. It would be helpful for students to review this section before doing their first Internet Activities. Issues covered here include deciding on one's purpose for using the Internet, checking Web sites for reliability, and using one's search time wisely.

Skimming and Scanning This section gives a brief description on how to skim and scan and when it is most appropriate to use each technique. A few exercises are provided to practice these skills.

Forms for Photocopying Several forms are provided here for students to make photocopies as needed. The Reading Review Form provides an additional opportunity for students to review and record their findings and impressions for each reading. On the form, students answer the main reading questions, record their reactions to the reading, pick vocabulary words they especially want to study, and reflect on the reading. With the Evidence Chart students analyze and evaluate the supporting details in a reading. The Checklist Forms cover the skills introduced in Chapters 2 and 4 through 9. Answering the questions on the forms will assist students in internalizing each of the reading skills. Instructors can use the forms to see how students are progressing as they apply the essential reading questions. The forms can also be used for pair and small-group activities. See the Instructor's Manual for suggestions on collaborative ways to use the forms.

Glossary The Glossary supplies definitions for key words introduced in the text. The words in the Glossary appear in bold when they are introduced in the text.

The Teaching and Learning Package

Each component of the teaching and learning package for *Reading Now* has been carefully created to extend the value of the main text.

Annotated Instructor's Edition An annotated instructor's edition is available for this text. It provides answers to the activities and exercises in the text printed on the write-on lines that follow each exercise.

Instructor's Manual and Test Bank The Instructor's Manual includes additional activities and practice exercises. Among the activities are questions that ask students to make connections between readings in a chapter and directions on how to take Cornell notes and create study maps. The practice exercises include more vocabulary building for Chapter 3 and exercises for each of the reading skills covered in Chapters 4 through 9. The Test Bank includes quizzes for all seven reading skills covered in the text, as well as tests of combined skills. The tests are formatted for easy copying.

For Additional Reading and Reference

The Longman Basic Skills Package In addition to the book-specific supplements discussed above, many other skills-based supplements are available. All of these supplements are available either at no additional cost or at greatly reduced prices.

The Dictionary Deal Two dictionaries can be shrink-wrapped with *Reading Now* for a nominal fee. *The New American Webster Handy College Dictionary* is a paperback reference text with more than 100,000 entries. *Merriam-Webster's Collegiate Dictionary,* eleventh edition, is a hardback reference with a citation file of more than 14.5 million examples of English words drawn from actual use. For more information on how to shrink-wrap a dictionary with your text, please contact your Pearson publishing representative.

MyReadingLab (www.myreadinglab.com) MyReadingLab is the first Web site that combines diagnostics, practice exercises, tests and powerful assessment to help improve student reading skills and reading level. Student reading skills are improved through a mastery-based format of practice exercises. Exercises include objective-based questions, open-ended questions, short-answer questions, combined-skills exercises and more. Student reading level is assessed through the Lexile Framework (www.lexile.com), the most widely adopted reading measure in use today. The Lexile Framework measures both reader ability and text difficulty on the same scale, called the Lexile scale. Based on a carefully developed diagnostic, students are assigned an initial Lexile number. Then, using a combination of cloze questions and combined skills exercises, MyReadingLab allows students to increase their Lexile number and realize their progress over time.

Acknowledgments

I want to thank the following reviewers for their helpful suggestions as the text took shape: Marilyn Black, Middlesex Community College; Morris Caspar, Vance-Granville Community College; Lisa Dadeppo, Pima Community College; Carrie Finestone, Middlesex Community College; Carol Fox, Middlesex County College; Gael Grossman, Jamestown Community College; Ellen Gruber, Ivy Tech Community College; Geraldine Gutwein, Harrisburg Area Community College; Nancy Hoefer, Central Carolina Technical College; Leo Hopcroft, Whatcom Community College; Windy Jefferson-Jackson, Montgomery College; Sandy Jones, Community College of Baltimore County; Barbara Ann Kashi, Cypress College; Tamara Kuzmenkov, Tacoma Community College; Linda Miller, South Plains College; Linda Mininger, Harrisburg Area Community College; Michele Peterson, Santa Barbara Community College; Carrie Pyhrr, Austin Community College; Laurel Severino, Santa Fe College; Eileen Steeples, Middlesex Community College; Melanie Ward, Tyler Junior College; Karen Whalen, Collin College; Susan Wickham, Des Moines Community College; and Dr. Marisol Varela, Miami Dade College.

Additionally, I am much obliged to Kate Edwards from Pearson Longman for her support of this project. I thank my editor Janice Wiggins-Clarke for her insightful comments and encouragement as the text came together. Thanks also to the Production, Marketing, and Supplement departments of Pearson Longman for their efforts on various aspects of the book. I am grateful to my colleagues for informative discussions. I warmly thank my family for their enduring support. And I heap loads of gratitude on my husband for being a guinea pig as I initially tried out exercises in the text on him.

I am pleased that *Reading Now* combines traditional and innovative approaches toward the reading process. I am proud to present a reader that is both visually appealing and mentally stimulating.

—AMY E. OLSEN

To the Student

Reading is a wonderful activity. It can bring much pleasure and knowledge into your life. For these reasons, being able to understand what you read is an essential life skill. This text is designed to make the reading process easy to comprehend and fun to employ. The following are a few points to keep in mind as you work through the text.

Have an open mind Approach each reading as a treasure chest to be opened. Get excited about the new information you will learn and the ways you will be entertained. If a subject doesn't interest you at first, give it time, and think of ways to make the subject relevant to your life. This text has several questions after each reading that will help to build your connection-making skills.

Devote time to reading Give each reading your full attention. Don't try to multitask when you read (e.g., watch television or talk on the phone). By giving your undivided attention to a reading, you will appreciate it more and derive more from it.

Welcome critical thinking into your life Sometimes a reading, or the exercises after it, will challenge your thinking skills. Welcome these challenges as brain enhancers. Every time you engage in a situation that forces you to push yourself, you have the opportunity to expand your critical-thinking skills. This text offers various types of questions and vocabulary-building exercises to develop diverse critical-thinking skills.

Enjoy new experiences Keep a positive attitude toward each new undertaking in your life whether it is a class, job, or reading assignment. Enjoying what you do and what you have to do will make each task more pleasant and fulfilling.

The joys of reading are yours to discover in *Reading Now*.

—AMY E. OLSEN

Overview of the Reading Process

CHAPTER 1

The Active Reader

Part One: Asking the Right Questions

The Big Picture

To get the most out of the reading experience there are important concepts you need to be aware of. This chapter gives a brief overview of the essential questions to ask to be an active reader. Chapters 4 through 9 provide more information and more detailed practice on each reading skill. This chapter gives you the big picture so that you can start using each skill with the earliest readings in this text. Don't be intimidated by the variety of skills in this chapter; you will have plenty of opportunities to focus your learning of each skill as you work through the book.

As you ask the following questions about what you read, picture yourself as a detective trying to solve a case or a reporter getting all the information to write a top-notch story.

- What is the main idea of the reading?
- How does the writer support the main idea?
- How is the reading organized?
- What is the writer's purpose?
- What is the writer's tone?
- What can I infer from the reading?
- What other critical-thinking skills do I need to use to fully appreciate the reading?

- Appreciate the skills needed to be an active reader.
- Ask the essential reading questions.

Essential Questions to Ask

By asking the seven questions introduced in this chapter you will be better able to comprehend and appreciate what you read. As you work through the activities and readings in this text asking these questions will become a familiar part of your reading process.

What Is the Main Idea of the Reading?

This question is essential to understanding a reading. The **main idea** is the point the writer wants to make. If you don't know what central idea the writer is trying to get across, then either the writer did not do a good job of presenting the information or you need to read more closely.

Your first step in determining the main idea is to establish the **topic** of the reading. Decide what the reading is about in general: college, exercise, sun tanning, Mongolia. Next decide what the writer is saying about this topic. In one essay, the writer wants to convey the point that exercising four times a week is good for you. In another essay, the writer explains that combining various types of exercise makes for a better workout, while a third essay, which still deals with the topic of exercise, wants to persuade you to include yoga with your other forms of exercise. The same topic can be covered in numerous ways. Your goal in finding the main idea is to decide what this writer wants to say about the topic.

There are two methods you can use to determine the main idea. First, you can look for a stated main idea. A stated main idea is often referred to as a **thesis statement**. A thesis statement is one or two sentences that explain the writer's point. You may especially hear the term *thesis statement* when you take a composition class. Your instructor may strongly encourage you to have one sentence in your essay that clearly explains the point you want to make. A thesis statement usually comes in the first or second paragraph of a reading, but it can come anywhere. It can be in the middle or even at the end of an essay. The thesis statements below clearly express the idea the writer wants to get across to his or her readers.

Sample Thesis Statements

The college needs more parking spaces to enable students to get to their classes on time.

It is easy to build a garden bench in a weekend if you have the right tools, instructions, and a bit of creativity.

The eating habits of Americans must change or the country will face a serious health crisis.

There are, however, many times when a writer does not supply a stated main idea, a thesis statement. In these situations, the main idea is **implied** or indirectly conveyed. Now you need to apply the second method to figure out the main idea: use the information in the reading. First, look for topic sentences. A **topic sentence** expresses the point of a paragraph (it is like a thesis statement, but for just one paragraph). The topic sentence can be anywhere in a paragraph, but it is often the first or second sentence. Sometimes there are two topic sentences in a paragraph. The writer will start with a topic sentence and add another topic sentence at the end of the paragraph to clarify or emphasize the point of the paragraph. If there isn't a topic sentence, you need to use the supporting details in the paragraph to establish what point the paragraph is making. Once you have decided on the point of each paragraph, put that information together to determine the main idea of the whole reading.

Example

One of the paragraphs below contains a topic sentence, and in the other the main idea of the paragraph is implied. As you read the paragraphs, see if you can decide which is which before you read the explanation below.

1. Cities like Paris, Hong Kong, Buenos Aires, and Cairo show that the world is filled with exotic and fascinating places to explore.[1] Challenging yourself to climb a mountain, to speak a few words in another language, to eat a food you've never heard of—these are a few of the adventures you can have when you explore new places.[2] Sitting down to coffee with strangers at a café or chatting with a local at a farmer's market lets you in on a new world of ideas and viewpoints.[3] Travel enables one to get to know oneself and others better.[4] To enjoy the benefits of travel, get a passport if you don't already have one, open a world map, and pick a place to visit (one you've always dreamed about or one you've never heard of).[5]

2. Pam was thirty pounds overweight until she got Buster.[1] Buster is an energetic terrier that loves his twice-daily walks.[2] He even picks his leash up and brings it to Pam to remind her it is time to get moving.[3] Harry was lonely after his wife died until he met Midnight.[4] Midnight is there in the morning to lick his face when it is time to get up.[5] The 3-year-old calico cat can also be found curled up on Harry's lap every night while he reads by the fire.[6]

Did you determine that paragraph 1 contains the topic sentence? Sentence 4, "Travel enables one to get to know oneself and others better," expresses the point of the paragraph. The first sentence introduces the idea that there are several exotic cites to visit, but it doesn't explain what this paragraph is about. Sentences 2 and 3 give examples of what travel has to offer a person. Sentence 5 calls on the reader to do something related to the point of the paragraph, but it doesn't express that point. Only sentence 4 sums up what the paragraph is about as a whole. Paragraph 2 then is the one with the implied main idea. There is no one sentence that specifically covers the point of the paragraph. The paragraph contains two examples (Pam and Harry) that make the point of the paragraph. You need to express the point in your own words, such as "A pet can contribute to improving a person's physical and mental health."

Identify the main idea in the following short essay either by writing the thesis statement or your own sentence if the main idea is implied. Also identify the topic sentences.

Sometimes we all yearn for a place where everyone knows our name.[1] We want a place where we can walk into a restaurant and get a "Hi, (fill in your name)!"[2] If you come from a big city, you will have to look beyond the limitations of the cultural-events calendar or the lack of dining options to appreciate small town life.[3] Living in a small town has benefits that may not be apparent at first.[4]

Living in a small town makes for a calmer life.[5] You don't have to worry about traffic jams when there are only a thousand folks or so in the whole town.[6] You don't have to wait in long lines at the movie theater, grocery store, or post office.[7] You can usually walk right up to the counter, and even enjoy a pleasant conversation with the clerk.[8] Small problems won't raise your blood pressure as they can in big cities.[9] If you forget your wallet at home, it isn't time to panic or get angry.[10] It is quite possible that the checker at the grocery will say, "Don't worry—drop off the money next time you're in town."[11]

If you have the flu and haven't been to the local café for a week, it feels good to have three or four people call to see if everything is all right.[12] This is the kind of attention one usually gets in a small town.[13] When you go to the town's annual picnic, you know you will see hundreds of familiar faces and be able to shout "hello" to dozens of people by name.[14] That kind of personal contact is rarely found in big cities.[15] You know if you are in trouble, there are people ready to help, just as you would be there for them.[16] For many people, this sense of belonging is an important aspect of small town life.[17]

Main idea: _____

_____

Topic sentence paragraph 2: _____

_____

Topic sentence paragraph 3: _____

_____

How Does the Writer Support the Main Idea?

To aid your understanding of the main idea, you need to find the supporting details (sometimes also referred to as evidence) the writer uses throughout the essay. There are four main types of support a writer can use to prove a point: examples, statistics, testimony, and reasons. Being able to identify the different types of supporting details will assist you in evaluating whether writers have effectively chosen and presented their details to defend the main idea. A description of each type of support follows with examples dealing with Antarctica.

Types of Supporting Details

- **Examples can come in four forms.**

    Personal examples come from observations the writer provides from events he or she has experienced. These are the type of examples not everyone would have access to.

    As I stood on the ship's top deck, I marveled at the size of the iceberg even though I knew I was only seeing a small portion of it.

    Public examples come from sources the writer has read or seen, such as newspaper articles, books, movies, and television shows. These sources may be contemporary or ancient history. These are the kinds of examples other people could research and also find.

    One of the dangerous conditions men faced in the early days of polar exploration is seen in the fate of Titus Oates. Oates was suffering from frost-bitten feet, and not wanting to slow his party's progress, he sacrificed his life by leaving the safety of their tent in the middle of a blizzard.

    Hypothetical examples are created by the writer's imagination, but they represent situations that could happen to real people. They may be introduced by words such as *if* or *imagine*.

    Imagine saving for years to take a cruise to Antarctica. You then take 400 photos of penguins in one afternoon. You could certainly be forgiven. For like any enthusiastic photographer in a new environment, you don't want to miss a shot.

    Facts are pieces of information regarded as true or real, and they can be verified through research. The writer will often find facts through research.

    On December 14, 1911, Roald Amundsen of Norway was the first man to reach the South Pole.

- **Statistics** are numerical comparisons.

    Antarctica contains more than 90 percent of the world's ice.

- **Testimony** (also known as quotations) presents the opinions or statements of experts on a subject, often given in their own words.

    Amundsen's success in reaching the South Pole may be partly attributed to his belief of how to use sled dogs: "Don't treat your men like dogs or your dogs like men."

- **Reasons** are sensible explanations that answer the question "Why?"

    Penguins are my favorite animal, and I have always dreamed of seeing them in their natural environment. (This reply answers the question "Why do you want to travel to Antarctica?")

ACTIVITY 2

Identify which category each of the following supporting details fits.

1.   I loved the movie because it took place in Mexico City, where two years ago I had a fabulous time studying Spanish for a semester. _Reason (personal)_

2.   Among Mexico City's attractions are the Museo Frida Kahlo and the Floating Gardens of Xochimilco. _facts_

3.   Dog trainer Andrea Arden recommends people wait a month to name a dog because "waiting allows you to choose a name that's well suited" to your pet. _Testimony_

4.   In the United States, 39 percent of the households own at least one dog and almost 34 percent own at least one cat. _Statistics_

5.   I'm eating healthier now that I read food labels. Last week I read the label on a frozen pot pie I often used to have for dinner, and I discovered that it contains all the calories I should eat in a day. I didn't buy it this time. _examples (personal)_

6.   Yesterday Diana ordered a chicken salad instead of a hamburger at a fast-food restaurant thinking she was making a healthy choice. It turns out that her salad had 200 calories more than a regular hamburger. There are thousands of Dianas out there every day making the same mistake about fast-food salads. _Hypothetical (example)_

7.   On a recent episode of *The Biggest Loser*, trainers Bob and Jillian took the contestants on a trip to a grocery store to show them how to buy healthy groceries on a budget. This is the type of training all Americans need. _example (public)_

Occasionally you may be uncertain as to which category a supporting detail fits into. You might find yourself asking, "Is it a hypothetical example or something that really happened to the writer?" Don't stress about always being able to label every detail as a specific type. You just want to be aware that there are different types of supporting details so that you can use that knowledge to help you decide if the writer has done a good job of using the details to defend the main idea.

When you are analyzing the writer's use of supporting details, you will also need to consider if the writer's statements are facts or opinions. Recognizing a fact from an opinion will help you decide how effective a statement is, whether it is relevant to the writer's point, and how trustworthy the statement is. A fact, as previously mentioned, is information that is considered true, and it can be verified through research. An **opinion**, on the other hand, is a view or feeling a person has about something that cannot be supported by objective measures. Sometimes it is easy to distinguish between the two. If you look around the park and say, "The grass is green," you have a fact. Someone may want to check that your statement is accurate by seeing if the grass has been watered and that it is not, in fact, dry and brown. But if you also state, "Green is the loveliest color," then you have expressed an opinion. Someone else may very well like blue or pink or magenta better. Sometimes facts and opinions aren't as obvious to tell apart. You may have to do research to resolve whether a statement is a fact or an opinion. Sometimes a statement may include a fact and an opinion, but the overall purpose of the statement fits in one category or the other.

Identify whether the following statements are a fact or an opinion by putting *F* for fact or *O* for opinion on the line after the statement.

1. Spring, which usually begins about March 20, is the loveliest season. ___

2. The Boston Red Sox won the 2007 World Series. ___

3. Penguins in the wild can only be found in the Southern Hemisphere. ___

4. Apple pie is the best dessert. ___

5. The Mojave Desert is located in the United States. ___

6. The 1904 World's Fair in St. Louis was the grandest one of all. ___

Besides recognizing types of supporting details and deciding whether a statement is a fact or opinion, you will need to evaluate the supporting details. The reader has four main goals when evaluating supporting details:

- Decide if the types of supporting details used are effective for the writer's purpose.
- Determine if there are enough details to make or prove the writer's point.
- Determine if a supporting detail is relevant to the point being made.
- Establish if a supporting detail is accurate or credible.

There will be more information on these goals and practice exercises in Chapter 5.

How Is the Reading Organized?

To help you understand an essay, look at its **organization**, how it is put together. Being able to recognize how the information is presented will help you understand the writer's main idea and judge whether the supporting details are used effectively. First, determine the order of the information presented. Then look for common patterns of organization. Finally, identify transition words or phrases to help you verify the order of the information and patterns of organization.

First, note how the information is arranged or ordered. Realizing how an essay is ordered can help you understand the writer's purpose and establish what points the writer sees as least and most important.

Common Methods of Ordering Information

■ **Chronological** puts information in time order.

■ **Least to most important** starts with points that are not as important and builds up to the most important point.

(continued)

- **Most to least important** starts with the most important point, often to grab the reader's attention, and then adds points that the writer does not consider as important. (This technique is often used in newspapers where readers tend to skim for information.)
- **Problem and solution** presents a problem and then offers one or more solutions.

Next, look for common patterns of organization. If you can identify that a writer is telling a story or explaining how to do something or looking at differences between items, you will have an easier time following the writer's points and deciphering his or her purpose. A writer may use a pattern of organization in one paragraph, for several paragraphs, or for a whole essay. It is not uncommon to find two or more patterns of organization used in an essay.

Common Patterns of Organization

- **Cause and effect** examines the causes (the why) and/or the effects (results) related to an event.
- **Classification** puts items into categories to clarify the characteristics of each item.
- **Comparison and contrast** looks at similarities and/or differences between subjects or items.
- **Definition** attempts to define a term that may have more than one meaning or has an emotional association attached to it, such as *love, patriotism,* or *art* (all of which are ripe for a definition essay because not everyone agrees what these words mean).
- **Example** uses one extended example or a series of examples to prove a point.
- **Narrative** tells a story (usually in chronological order).
- **Process** tells how to do something or how something is done (usually in chronological order).

Finally, pay attention to the **transition words** the writer uses to move from one point to another. Being aware of transition words and phrases can help you recognize the point the writer is trying to make. For example, if a writer uses "but" you know that a contrast is coming: Tricia wanted to go to the party, but she decided that it was wiser to stay home and study for tomorrow's exam. Transitions words can be placed at the beginning of a sentence to help connect ideas from one sentence to another or appear within a sentence. Some transition words fit in more than one category. Common transition words fall into groups related to some of the organizational patterns.

Common Transition Words and Phrases

Addition: also, and, another, further, furthermore, in addition, next, first, second, third, finally

Cause and effect: because, since, due to, as a result, hence, so, then, thus, therefore, subsequently, consequently

Comparison: also, likewise, equally, similarly, in the same way

Contrast: but, yet, however, nevertheless, in contrast, instead, on the other hand, unlike, conversely

Example: for example, for instance, such as, to illustrate

Importance: first, second, third, next, least, of lesser concern, greatest, major, most important, most importantly

Time: after, before, next, then, meanwhile, later, eventually, soon, suddenly, when, while, during, now, finally

Identify the method of ordering information, pattern of organization, and the transition words used in the following paragraphs.

1. The position of office manager is now open, and Tim and Eliza have applied for the job. Tim has worked at the company for 10 years, and he always promptly meets deadlines. However, he has gotten into arguments with several colleagues, usually over small matters. Similarly, Eliza has worked at the company for 10 years. She also usually meets her deadlines, but sometimes her reports are not as complete as Tim's. On the other hand, Eliza gets along well with everyone at the company. She is highly respected and is always friendly and professional. Tim has many good traits, but because the office manager must work well with others, Eliza is the best candidate for the job.

    Method of ordering information: _Problem + Solution_

    Pattern of organization: _Compair + contrast_

    Transition words: _Contrast; comparison_

2. Alfredo's moving into the apartment has been harmful to my health. First, Alfredo used the floor mat in the bathroom as a towel, so when I got out of the shower it wasn't there, and I slipped and hit my knee on the edge of the toilet. Consequently, I had a huge bruise and had to limp around for a week. Next, because Alfredo left his skateboard in the middle of the living room floor, I tripped over it when I came home late one night. I hit my head on the coffee table as I fell, and I had to get eight stitches. Most importantly, Alfredo plays his rock music loudly every night

and, as a result, I haven't gone to bed without a splitting headache since he moved in.

Method of ordering information: _least important to Most important_

Pattern of organization: _Cause + effect_

Transition words: _importence, addition; cause; effect_

3. I woke up at eight o'clock and made myself scrambled eggs for breakfast. Then I decided to take a quick walk before meeting my study group at eleven. I headed out the door at nine and ran into Millie. I thought that we only talked for a few minutes, but it was 10:30 by the time I got home. Before I jumped in the shower, I called Paul to tell him I'd be a bit late, but I only got his voice mail. Soon I remembered that I needed to get gas, so I'd be even later. After frantically getting dressed, I realized that by the time I drove to campus I'd only get there for the last 10 minutes of the session.

Method of ordering information: _Cronological_

Pattern of organization: _process narritive_

Transition words: _Time_

What Is the Writer's Purpose?

You need to decide on the writer's **purpose,** why the writer wrote the piece. To determine the writer's intention keep in mind the three main reasons people write: to inform, to persuade, and to entertain. One piece of writing can include all three purposes, but one of the three often stands out.

- **To inform:** When writers want to inform their readers, they may explain a concept, describe what happened, or investigate a situation. Common types of informative writing are recipes and instructions on how to put something together. Most newspaper articles are supposed to be informative and not take sides on an issue. If the writer is telling you something without any preference and looks at multiple sides of an issue equally, then the purpose is likely to inform.
- **To persuade:** When writers engage in persuasive writing, they have a side to take. They argue for or against a point. They celebrate or attack a person, place, or thing. Persuasion is the basis of advertising and pamphlets sent out by political candidates, for example. If the writer shows a preference for one side or encourages you to do something, then the purpose is most likely to persuade. Look for words like "should," "need to," and "must" to show persuasion: "If you want the best service and the lowest price, you *need to* subscribe to Magnetic's phone plan today" or "We *must* not let Mayor Thompson continue to ruin our community. Cast your vote for Greg Walsh for mayor and see our town prosper."

- **To entertain:** When writers want to entertain, they strive to give the reader some type of enjoyment. This enjoyment often comes in the form of humor. The reader is meant to smile, chuckle, or laugh at the material. Enjoyment, however, can come in other forms. Many people enjoy being scared. The popularity of horror movies and writers like Stephen King show that people like to be frightened. People also get enjoyment from romance, mystery, and science-fiction genres that may contain no amusing elements. For these different genres, people enjoy sympathizing with a character's problems, having a "good cry" that releases pent-up emotions, feeling the suspense of discovering who the killer is, and just escaping from their everyday lives.

ACTIVITY 5

Identify whether the writer's purpose in the following paragraphs is to inform, to persuade, or to entertain.

1. Journal writing is a great way to release pent-up emotions and solve problems. Many people find comfort in being able to express their feelings in a journal that doesn't judge them, try to offer unwanted help, or reveal their feelings to others. Journal writing also allows people to work through issues on their own terms. Often by writing down one's problems, solutions are easier to see. If you are having trouble confronting an emotion or problem, you should try starting a journal and seeing the wonderful results you can get from expressing your thoughts on paper. After all, a $6 journal is a lot cheaper than a $100-an-hour therapist.

   Purpose: _____

2. Pictograms were the first method of writing used by Native Americans. Pictograms use a drawing to present an idea or object. Today pictograms can be found on restroom doors with a picture of a man or woman used to symbolize who the restroom is intended for instead of using words. Native Americans used pictograms for numerous reasons, including to remember parts of oral tales, to share information on healing ceremonies, and to tell about bad or good hunting seasons. Depending on a region's resources, pictograms were carved on rocks, painted on buffalo hides, or drawn on scrolls made from birch bark.

   Purpose: _____

3. I had long dreamed of owning a cabin in the woods. When I read the ad for a "cozy cabin nestled in the trees," I thought my dream had come true. On the drive up to the cabin, I was enraptured by the smell of the pines, the sight of the sun's rays poking through the trees, and the sounds of the birds. Then we turned into the driveway and thump! Reality hit hard as I banged my head on the roof of the car. The pothole must

have been four feet deep. My first glimpse of the cabin left me confused. Was the roof actually caved in or was I dizzy from hitting my head? Noticing my disbelief, the realtor looked at me and smiled, "It does need a little work." After my foot fell through a board on the porch, the realtor commented, "One or two boards may need replacing." He opened the door, and a family of raccoons looked up from their position on a decaying couch. As I turned to leave, I heard the realtor say, "Isn't it nice—you won't need to get a pet."

Purpose: _____

What Is the Writer's Tone?

Understanding the writer's **tone**, the writer's attitude toward the subject, will help you uncover the writer's purpose and answer other questions about a reading. Ask yourself if the writer is angry, happy, sad, or expressing some other attitude or mood toward the subject. You experience tone of voice all the time. If a person is shouting, you can usually tell if the person is angry, excited, or just trying to get your attention from far way. Through careful reading, you can also figure out tone in written material. You need to look at the writer's choice of words and punctuation marks to decipher the tone. For example, exclamation points can be used to show excitement or anger.

By paying special attention to the writer's **diction**, choice of words, discovering the tone isn't too difficult. Sometimes writers are neutral or objective about a matter, especially when the purpose is to inform, so the piece won't have a strong tone. But if a person is upset, disgusted, or overjoyed, you can tell through the writer's choice of words. For example, imagine a man is given a new candy to taste test, and he doesn't like it. You can gauge his attitude toward the candy through his word choice: "This candy leaves an <u>unpleasant</u> taste in my mouth," "This candy is <u>awful</u>," "<u>Gross!</u>" "This is <u>repulsive!</u>" Each of the underlined words conveys a tone of disgust with the candy, but at different levels. As you read, look for words that signal how the writer feels about the topic. For a list of tone words, see page 256 in Chapter 7.

You should also be able to identify two general tones—formal and informal—by looking at the writer's diction. If writers want to keep their readers at a distance, then they will use a formal tone. This is the tone usually used in college research papers and essays, in legal documents, and in instructions. If writers want to draw their readers in, then they will use an informal tone. This tone is often used in persuasive writing, advertising, and letters to friends. In informal pieces, the writer will often address the reader by using the pronouns "you" and "your" to make the reader feel comfortable.

Finally, look for the following two techniques that can show tone and purpose: irony and exaggeration.

- **Irony** involves either the use of words to state the opposite of their precise meaning or a clash between what is expected to happen and what really does. For example, you spill mustard on your shirt, and your friend says, "I can't wait to take you to a fancy restaurant." You can tell by the situation that your friend's words are the opposite of what they literally mean. People are not usually excited to take friends who spill food on themselves to a swanky restaurant. If you envision your day at the beach as being a relaxing break from your studies and other responsibilities, but somehow you end up babysitting for the family that spread their blanket next to yours, then the situation is ironic. It might not seem amusing to you at the time, but when your friends hear your stories about changing diapers and being buried in the sand by a 10-year-old, they will likely laugh, and with time, you will probably laugh too. Irony often indicates a humorous tone and a purpose to entertain, but it can also be used to criticize and may be found in persuasive writing. You can detect irony through word choice and the situation in a reading, and it is important to be on the lookout for irony so you aren't fooled as to the writer's tone.

- **Exaggeration** involves enlarging or overstating a situation to usually unbelievable proportions. If a writer wants to show how disastrous a date was in a humorous way, the mishaps get bigger and bigger: he spills a bowl of hot soup in his date's lap, they discover that the only topic that sustains more than a minute of conversation is a fondness for fruit salad, he hits her with the car door when he tries to open it for her, and on it goes. Exaggeration is also often seen in action movies and stories. The hero successfully faces villains and weaponry that, in reality, no one person could possibly survive. When the hero single-handedly takes on twenty men and defeats them all with a few karate chops, kicks, or punches, it is the exaggeration that is part of the fun of the scene. Exaggeration then often reveals a humorous tone and is used to entertain readers. Exaggeration, however, can also be used in persuasive writing. There are several reasons a writer might exaggerate a situation: to persuade people to vote for someone, to urge people to clean up a park, to get someone fired. In these cases the exaggeration may be accompanied with an angry or alarming tone.

ACTIVITY 6

For the following excerpts, match the writer's tone to one of the choices below.

excited _____   concerned _____   objective _____   angry _____

1. A letter to a company

   Your Blender 3000 is a piece of crap. I bought it a week ago, and it has already quit working. When I went to make my energy shake this morning, not one button—not a single one—worked. It would not blend, purée, or chop. One week! I demand an immediate refund of my money. I will never buy another of your company's worthless appliances—you can be assured of that!

2. A note

   I was at the zoo this afternoon, and Remba did not look at all well. Could she not be eating enough? Or maybe the extreme heat we have been experiencing isn't suiting her. I have been visiting the zoo since I was six, and the elephants have always been my favorite animals. I am prepared to help in any way to restore Remba's health. Please let me know what I can do.

3.   An e-mail

It's going to be a girl! We just heard that we will be grandparents by Valentine's Day. Our youngest daughter, Claire, is expecting her first child then. I started knitting our granddaughter a blanket the second I hung up the phone after talking with Claire. Look for lots and lots of photos in my e-mails after February 14th!

4.   An invitation

The next meeting of the Evergreen Bicycle Club will be held Sunday, September 19, at 6:00 p.m. at the Community Center. It will be a potluck dinner. If your last name begins with A–H bring an appetizer, I–P bring a main dish, and Q–Z bring a dessert. Fred will give a presentation on his recent bike trip across the United States. If you have any questions, call Wilma at (805) 555-3636.

What Can I Infer from the Reading?

When writers do not directly come out and say what they mean, you need to make **inferences** to figure out the writer's real purpose. Making inferences involves analyzing the evidence presented and using your own prior knowledge to reach a conclusion on what the writer intends. You likely already make such deductions. Imagine you are sitting in your living room with the door open and an occasional breeze blows through. Your friend says, "I'm cold." She doesn't ask you to shut the door, but by using the evidence (the breeze blowing through the door) and your knowledge (a cool breeze can make a person cold), you can conclude that your friend would like the door shut in order to keep warm. Remember to consider all the elements in a reading when you make inferences, including tone. Your inference could be incorrect if you miss the ironic tone in a reading or in a person's voice.

Read the following paragraphs and see what inferences you can make from the evidence given.

1.   Marsha walked into Stan's office and saw he wasn't there. She picked up a glass paperweight on his desk and started to toss it from one hand to the other.

Jacob came in and said Stan wasn't feeling well and that he wouldn't be coming in today. Marsha rolled her eyes. She started to set the paperweight down, but dropped it. "Oops," she said with a smile as it shattered into pieces.

How does Marsha feel about Stan? What evidence did you use to reach this conclusion?

_____

_____

_____

_____

2. Alex slammed the front door as he entered the apartment, dropped his backpack with a thud, and stormed down the hallway. His roommate called after him, "Get your math test back?" Alex grunted, "Yeah."

How did Alex do on the math test? What evidence helps you reach this conclusion?

_____

_____

_____

3. The man pulled his hat down over his ears. The woman turned up the collar on her coat and crossed her arms. She looked down the street again. The man paced back and forth. He looked at his watch. They looked at each other, shrugged their shoulders, and shook their heads. The woman stepped to the curb and looked down the street once more.

What time of year is it? What are the two people doing? What evidence did you use to reach this conclusion?

_____

_____

_____

_____

Bias

Another area where your inference skills will be called on is looking for **bias** in a reading. Bias is a preference or prejudice that can hinder one's objective decision making. We all have biases in our life, which come from our upbringing and experiences. Areas biases may come from include our gender, economic standing, ethnic backgrounds, religious and political beliefs, where we live or grew up, and even our hobbies and interests. We may be aware of our biases, or we may not recognize them. The same is true for writers. They may try to be objective and not bring personal prejudices into their writing, especially if the writer's purpose is to inform. However, when writers want to persuade their audience, they may consciously or subconsciously introduce their biases.

As an active reader, you want to search for any type of bias that the writer may include in a work. To look for bias, you need to use several reading skills. Consider the supporting details the writer has chosen to use, and think about details the writer left out and why. Examine how the reading is organized. For example, if the writer uses the comparison and contrast pattern, are both sides equally represented? Look at the writer's diction. Do some words the writer has chosen show a preference for the subject? Do other words have negative associations? By using inference with the other reading skills, you can determine if the writer is being objective or showing a preference, and this knowledge will assist you in evaluating the merits of the writer's main idea.

What Other Critical-thinking Skills Do I Need to Use to Fully Appreciate the Reading?

Two other areas you need to consider as you evaluate a reading are faulty logic and figurative language.

Faulty Logic

Sometimes the points a writer makes are not well thought out or developed. It is your job to look for these flaws in thinking. The following are procedures you want to follow in your search for faulty logic:

- Check that the evidence used to support a proposal is relevant to the argument.
- Determine whether enough support is given to make a strong case.
- Decide if there are other outcomes besides the one(s) the writer presents.
- See if the organization clearly shows how one action leads to another and will produce the result the writer asserts.
- Look closely at the words chosen to support the argument. Ask yourself if they show any bias or try to manipulate the reader through emotional appeals.

One way to look for these problem areas is to be aware of logical fallacies. A **fallacy** is an argument that is based on faulty logic or perception. There are more than a hundred types of fallacies. You don't need to know all of them to be able to detect a flaw in the logic used by a writer, but knowing the names and characteristics of a few fallacies will remind you to keep an eye open for faulty thinking in the materials you read, the advertisements you see on television, and your own thinking. Below are the definitions of four common fallacies with examples.

- **Appeal to emotion:** The writer uses words or images to appeal to people's feelings instead of their minds. The appeal can be to any number of emotions, including anger, fear, envy, pity, or hatred. *Example:* Please don't charge Billy a late fee on his library books because his parents are getting a divorce.

- **False dilemma (also known as black and white thinking):** The writer presents a situation as having only two choices when there are other possibilities. *Example:* We either quit going to dinner once a week or we don't have the money to pay the rent.
- **Hasty generalization (also known as leaping to a conclusion):** The writer reaches a conclusion (usually a sweeping one) based on too small of a sample, too few situations, or an uncommon situation. *Example:* I saw a naked man walking down the street in the neighborhood where I am thinking of buying a house; people in that area must be quite open-minded.
- **Slippery slope:** The writer reasons that one action will lead to a chain reaction with the outcome usually being something horrible, but the path from action A to result D isn't clearly shown. *Example:* If we start letting the students wear shorts on warm days, the next thing you know they will be coming to school in swimsuits.

Match the following statements to one of the fallacies.

1. We either hire Liz or wait at least another six months for a qualified candidate. _____

2. If we let one tattoo parlor open downtown, soon the area will be overrun with bars, strip clubs, and biker gangs. _____

3. I just met two of the neighbor boys, and they were extremely rude. The kids in this neighborhood weren't brought up properly. _____

4. You should vote for Sam's plan. He has been having a really hard time with his mother's illness and his house flooding this year. _____

Figurative Language

A final point you want to consider as you read is the use of figurative language. **Figurative language** creates vivid images for the reader between unlike items by using direct or implied comparisons. Writers may make comparisons to people, places, events, actions, and feelings. Effective figurative language allows readers to see a scene in a new, fun, or fascinating way. Two common figures of speech are the simile and the metaphor. A **simile** is a figure of speech that compares two unlike things, introduced by the word *like* or *as*. A **metaphor** is a figure of speech that makes a direct comparison between things that are not literally alike. To understand a simile or metaphor, you may need to use your inference skills if the meaning of a comparison is difficult to detect.

Follow the steps below to understand a simile or metaphor:

- Determine what two items are being compared. In the examples above the items being compared are a man's look to a tarantula on a slice of angel food cake, life to an onion, and a woman to a butterfly.
- Think about the meanings or qualities associated with the item the first thing is being compared to. For example, tarantulas are large spiders, and they are tan, reddish brown, or black.
- Decide how the meanings or qualities can be applied to the item to which it is being compared. For instance, considering the large size of a tarantula, it would be easy to spot one on a slice of cake, and its dark coloring would sharply contrast with the white of an angel food cake. Therefore, it is easy to infer that the man was quite noticeable.

ACTIVITY 9

Identify the type of figurative language, what items are being compared, and briefly explain the meaning of each sentence below.

1. After dating several jalapeños and even a few habañeros, I married a mashed potato.

    _____

    _____

    _____

2. Claudia is as ordinary as a giraffe in a Mini Cooper.

    _____

    _____

3. Her eyes sparkled like sapphires.

_____

_____

_____

In Summary

And so the credits roll on the big picture of the reading process, but a wide world of reading possibilities now unfolds for you. This introduction to the seven essential questions to ask when you read has prepared you for the next chapter where you will learn ways to further answer these questions and better understand what you read. You will also have the chance to practice your active-reader skills by reading a newspaper article, a textbook excerpt, and a short story.

PEARSON myreadinglab **Objectives Check**

To check your progress in meeting chapter objectives, log in to www.myreadinglab.com, click on the Study Plan tab, and then on the Reading Skills tab. Choose Reading Skills Diagnostic PreTest from the list of subtopics. Read and view the resources in the Review Materials section, then complete the Practices and Tests in the Activities section. You can check your scores by clicking on the Gradebook tab.

CHAPTER 2

The Active Reader

Part Two: Answering Your Questions

Chapter 1 explained what questions you need to ask when you read. This chapter provides ways to answer those questions. You will also have your first chance to apply the reading questions and methods for answering those questions to an article, a textbook excerpt, and a short story. The following areas are covered in this chapter:

- Annotating: Annotating means making notes on what you read, usually in the margins. By annotating a reading, it becomes easier to find answers to your questions.
- Making Connections: This section explains ways to relate to a reading, such as through personal experiences, current events, or to something you have read or seen. When you make connections, your interest in a reading increases, and you are more committed to finding answers to your questions.
- Recording Your Findings: Three methods of documenting what you have learned are introduced—the paraphrase, summary, and outline. Learning how to use these methods will assist you in understanding a reading, remembering important points, and sharing what you have learned with others.
- Visual Aids: This section deals with ways to interpret and use a variety of visual techniques, including photographs, cartoons, diagrams, graphs, sketches, and maps.
- Special Considerations: Elements that particularly relate to reading textbooks and short stories are presented.

Learning Objectives

- Annotate a reading.
- Make connections with a reading.
- Use different methods to record your findings about a reading.
- Make use of visual aids to understand a reading.
- Recognize the organizational features found in textbooks.
- Apply the SQ4R reading method.
- Identify the special elements found in short stories.

Delivering the Answers

There are three important techniques to master as you seek answers to the essential reading questions.

Annotating

The first technique you want to learn is how to **annotate**. Annotating means making notes on what you read. Making notes actively involves you in the reading process. If you own what you are reading, you can make notes in the margins of the text or you can make notes on a separate piece of paper if you don't own the book or wish to mark it. There are many ways you can employ the annotating process:

- Highlight important sections, such as the thesis statement, with a marker or underline them so that they will be easy to see when you review the reading.
- Circle words whose definitions you want to look up or that are important to the main idea; also circle the names of important people or characters: dilettante
- Put stars next to important passages: ☆ ☆   Miss Havisham
- Number supporting points: 1. 2. 3. 4.
- Write notes in the margins: *"points here relate to ideas in par. 3," "strongest point,"* or *"check this fact."*
- Ask questions: *"Why does she do this?"* or *"How does this example apply to what we learned last week?"* or *"Who do I know who has a similar problem?"*

Examine the sample annotation that follows and note what points are highlighted or underlined, circled, starred, and numbered. Read the comments in the margins. Can you determine why the reader decided to make these annotations?

As you practice annotating, you will find the kinds of highlighting and comments that are most helpful to your understanding of a reading. What works for one person may not work for someone else, so you need to find the style of annotation that bests suits you.

Writing Tips

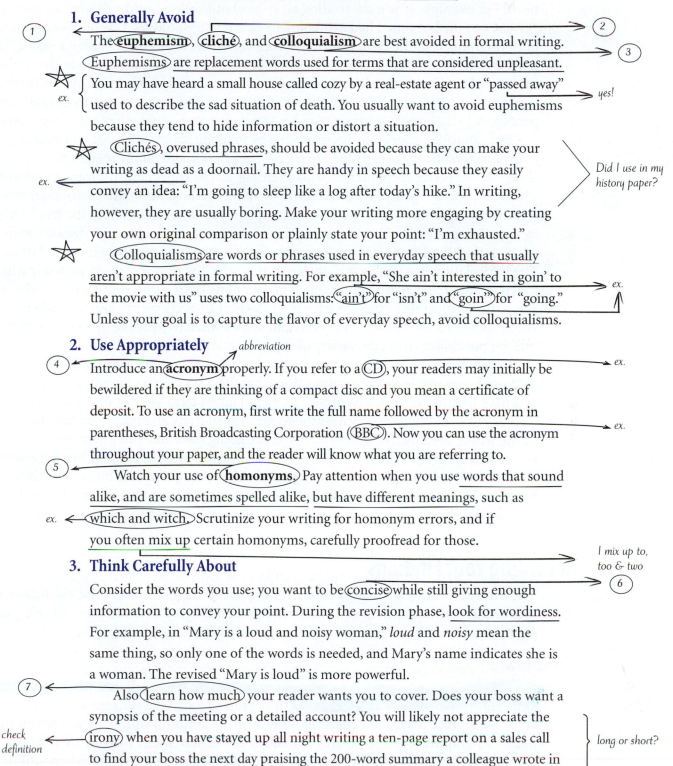

7 tips

When writing for school, work, or personal use, here are a few points to keep in mind that will make your writing more effective and interesting.

1. Generally Avoid

1

2

3

The euphemism, cliché, and colloquialism are best avoided in formal writing. Euphemisms are replacement words used for terms that are considered unpleasant.

ex. You may have heard a small house called cozy by a real-estate agent or "passed away" used to describe the sad situation of death. You usually want to avoid euphemisms because they tend to hide information or distort a situation.

yes!

Clichés, overused phrases, should be avoided because they can make your writing as dead as a doornail. They are handy in speech because they easily ex. convey an idea: "I'm going to sleep like a log after today's hike." In writing, however, they are usually boring. Make your writing more engaging by creating your own original comparison or plainly state your point: "I'm exhausted."

Did I use in my history paper?

Colloquialisms are words or phrases used in everyday speech that usually aren't appropriate in formal writing. For example, "She ain't interested in goin' to the movie with us" uses two colloquialisms: "ain't" for "isn't" and "goin'" for "going." Unless your goal is to capture the flavor of everyday speech, avoid colloquialisms.

ex.

2. Use Appropriately

abbreviation

4

Introduce an acronym properly. If you refer to a CD, your readers may initially be bewildered if they are thinking of a compact disc and you mean a certificate of deposit. To use an acronym, first write the full name followed by the acronym in parentheses, British Broadcasting Corporation (BBC). Now you can use the acronym throughout your paper, and the reader will know what you are referring to.

ex.

ex.

5

Watch your use of homonyms. Pay attention when you use words that sound alike, and are sometimes spelled alike, but have different meanings, such as ex. which and witch. Scrutinize your writing for homonym errors, and if you often mix up certain homonyms, carefully proofread for those.

I mix up to, too & two

3. Think Carefully About

6

Consider the words you use; you want to be concise while still giving enough information to convey your point. During the revision phase, look for wordiness. For example, in "Mary is a loud and noisy woman," *loud* and *noisy* mean the same thing, so only one of the words is needed, and Mary's name indicates she is a woman. The revised "Mary is loud" is more powerful.

7

Also learn how much your reader wants you to cover. Does your boss want a synopsis of the meeting or a detailed account? You will likely not appreciate the check definition irony when you have stayed up all night writing a ten-page report on a sales call to find your boss the next day praising the 200-word summary a colleague wrote in half an hour.

long or short?

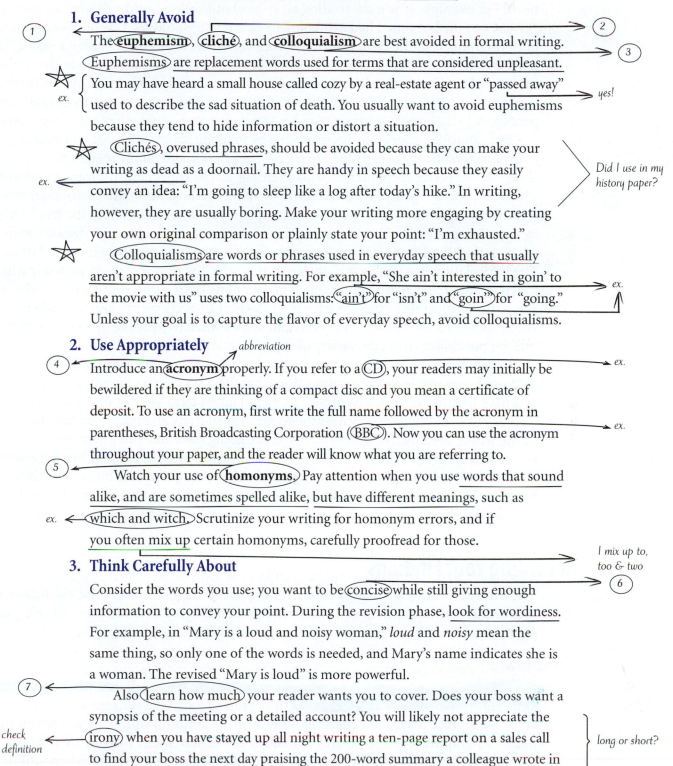

Making Connections

The second technique is making connections with what you read. By involving yourself in a reading you become more interested in it and invested in finding answers to your questions. For example, if you are reading an essay about eating healthy foods, ask yourself, "When was the last time I had broccoli?" Decide if you would try kale or pomegranates, both mentioned in the essay. The more connections you can make with a reading, the more meaningful it becomes for you. Put yourself in a situation presented in the reading to try to identify with the writer's point. If you have actually been in a similar situation, you can even better appreciate the writer's ideas. Also consider your experiences and compare them to the writer's statements and examples to test the strength of the writer's point.

You can widen your connection making by thinking about how what you read applies to experiences that have happened to friends, neighbors, and family members. You won't always have a personal connection with a reading, but by connecting the topic to someone you know, you can generate a greater interest in the reading. Additionally, consider how a reading may apply to world events. For example, if you are reading about the Black Death in your European history textbook, you can make connections to today's diseases, such as AIDS or the H1N1 virus. Also make connections to other materials you have read or seen. The information in a textbook chapter about World War II may connect perfectly with a movie about propaganda that you watch in your film class. Connecting the two media creates a stronger learning experience for both classes. Connections can also be made to television shows, songs, movies, and books and stories you have read. Be open to connection making possibilities from the variety of experiences you encounter.

Remember to pay attention to the writer's tone, so you don't make an incorrect connection. It is possible to make connections that the writer didn't intend, and sometimes you have to distance yourself from a reading to take a clear view of it. If you become so involved in a reading, you may miss the writer's use of irony and misunderstand the point of the whole reading. For example, if you are going bald and you are reading an essay about the effects of baldness, you may very well identify with the reading, but if the writer is exaggerating people's torment over going bald, you may miss the humor and irony in the essay. Finding the right balance in being connected to a reading, but still being able to be objective about the writer's ideas, is a skill that you will need to practice as you read.

Recording Your Findings

The third technique to employ is recording your findings. You may use the following recording methods to help you comprehend a reading, to assist in remembering important points, or to share what you have learned with other people.

Paraphrase

A **paraphrase** is a sentence where a person puts a writer's words into one's own words and retains the writer's original point. A person can also paraphrase a sentence. As a verb, paraphrase means to express in other words. Common situations where you may need to paraphrase are to convey a writer's thesis statement in your own words or to put a writer's words into your own instead of quoting a passage when you have already included several quotations in a paper. To write a paraphrase, carefully read the sentence you want to paraphrase and determine the main point of the sentence. Then look away from the original sentence so the words don't influence you when you write your own sentence. Now use your own words to express the same idea. A paraphrase usually only involves putting one sentence into your own words, but it can be used for two sentences next to each other that deal with closely related ideas.

Example

The following sentence is from paragraph 7 of "Sport or Not a Sport" by David Andriesen that begins on page 35 in this chapter.

Original: Mainstream newspaper sports sections report on hot dog eating world records.

Paraphrase: According to David Andriesen, the results of hot dog eating contests can be found in the sports pages of major newspapers.

Once you have written your own sentence, look back at the original and see if you have retained the writer's main point. Also see if you have used any of the writer's key words or the same sentence structure. For most key words you want to find synonyms that will make the sentence sound more like your writing. Other key words may be difficult or impossible to change. For example, in the paraphrase above, "hot dog eating" could be changed to "frankfurter consuming," but it would be silly and confusing to use such a term when most people know the contests as "hot dog eating." Likewise, trying to change "sports" and "newspaper" would not make much sense. Your goal with paraphrasing is to make the paraphrase fit into the rest of your paper in a natural way without stealing the writer's words or phrasing that make that writer unique.

When you use a paraphrase in an essay or research paper, you need to give credit to the original source. Because you are using the writer's ideas, it is fair to give him or her credit. You will either use lead-in words that include the writer's name or a parenthetical citation. In the example above, the words *According to* and David Andriesen's name are used to give credit to Andriesen. In a parenthetical citation, you give the writer's name and the page number where the original sentence can be found in parentheses after the paraphrase.

Example

It may be surprising to some people, but the results of hot dog eating contests can be found in the sports pages of major newspapers (Andriesen D3).

As with any new skill, learning to effectively paraphrase will take practice and become easier over time.

Read the paragraph below and find the thesis statement. Then express that sentence in your own words.

The scent of lavender fills the air, soft music plays in the background, and strong hands rub her back. Judith Simmons says, "I haven't felt this comfortable in years."

Judith is one of a growing number of people who are turning to alternative forms of medicine to help cope with daily stressors and the aches and pains they can bring. Natural alternatives to using drugs to deal with common problems have gained popularity in the last few years. People are turning to these alternatives to cure everything from headaches to depression. Among the most popular forms of alternative medicines are massages, aromatherapy, and mud baths.

Thesis statement: _____

_____

Your paraphrase: _____

_____

Summary

A **summary** is a condensing of a reading into a shorter version than the original. Writing a summary is a helpful way to extract the important information from what you read. Summarizing can be an especially useful tool for studying longer pieces of writing, such as textbook chapters. To write a summary, decide on the main points of the essay, textbook selection, or short story. Then use your own words to express those ideas in fewer words than the original. You will usually delete the examples a writer uses when you write a summary, and, depending on how short your summary is to be, you may delete the minor points a writer makes. A summary should be put into paragraph form on a separate sheet of paper. The information in a summary should keep the details in the same order as they were presented in the original work. Usually you want to aim to make your summary about 10 to 25 percent as long as the original.

Example

Below is a summary of the Paraphrase section. Without Activity 1, the Paraphrase section is 512 words. The summary in the box is 82 words, about 16 percent as long as the original.

> Paraphrasing is a process where you change the writer's words into your own, but keep the writer's main point. To paraphrase, cover the writer's sentence as you compose your own sentence. Then refer back to the sentence to check that you have kept the writer's meaning, but not used words that sound like the writer and not you. You also need to acknowledge the writer for using his or her ideas. With time and practice you will be able to paraphrase successfully.

When people first start writing summaries they tend to include too little or too much information. As you practice summarizing, you will find that balance between conveying enough information to help you review for a test or to let someone else know about a topic you have researched, but not so much information that you might as well reread the original or someone else might as well read your sources. You will have several chances to practice summarizing in a variety of activities that follow the readings in this text. To get started, do the activity below to assess your summarizing skills.

ACTIVITY 2

On a separate sheet of paper, write a summary of approximately 150 words on the information you read on pages 24–26 about annotating and making connections.

Outline

An **outline** is a numbered or lettered summary of a piece of writing that illustrates its major points. Outlines can be informal or formal. If your purpose for making an outline is to use it for future study sessions or to help you understand a reading, you can usually keep it simple, especially if the reading you are outlining is fairly short. You may want to use a formal outline to help you understand a longer piece of writing that has several major and minor points. An informal and formal outline for the full essay on alternative medicine introduced in Activity 1 above might look like the two outlines below. Note that the formal outline includes the minor points made in each paragraph. The informal outline uses the thesis statement from the introductory paragraph as the thesis, while the formal outline uses a paraphrase of the thesis statement. You can decide which is appropriate to use when you make your own outlines.

Sample Informal Outline

Thesis: Natural alternatives to using drugs to deal with common problems have gained popularity in the last few years.
1. An introduction to the popularity of natural alternatives instead of traditional drugs (par. 1)
2. Various uses of massage by athletes, doctors, and businesses presented (par. 2)
3. Different types of aromatherapy discussed (par. 3)
4. The popularity of mud baths for skin and general health examined (par. 4)
5. Conclusion sums up the trend of using natural alternatives to cure common pains (par. 5)

Sample Formal Outline

Thesis: People are increasingly using natural alternatives to deal with everyday health difficulties.
I. The introduction presents the popularity of using natural alternatives instead of traditional drugs.
II. The various uses of massage are discussed.
    A. An explanation of how athletes use massage is given.
        1. Massage can be used to prevent injuries.
        2. Massage can reduce soreness after exercising.

(continued)

     B. A few problem areas where doctors can use massage are presented.
        1. Doctors can treat arthritis with massage.
        2. Massages can help with back and neck pains.
     C. Why businesses have begun to hire massage therapists is explained.
        1. Massage has been shown to reduce a worker's stress level.
        2. Workers have proven to be more productive after receiving a massage.
 III. Different aromatherapy techniques are discussed.
     A. How oils are made from plants, flowers, and herbs is presented.
     B. Two problems that aromatherapy can provide aid in are described.
        1. Oils can be used to ease headaches.
        2. Oils can be used to relieve muscle pains.
     C. Different ways of using oils are shown.
        1. Oils can be used during a massage.
        2. Oils can be put in a bath.
        3. Oils can be inhaled.
 IV. The reasons people use mud baths is examined.
     A. Mud baths can help with skin problems.
     B. Mud baths can assist in relieving stress.
  V. The conclusion sums up the trend of using natural alternatives to cure common pains.

As you can see, outlines help you identify what each paragraph is about and allow you to easily return to a paragraph if you need to review part of the topic. Outlines also help in determining whether the writer has covered all the points mentioned in an introductory paragraph, and in deciding whether each paragraph is relevant to the main idea. You will have several opportunities to practice finishing and making outlines in the exercises after some of the readings.

Visual Aids

Visual aids can be photographs, cartoons, diagrams, graphs, charts, tables, sketches, or maps that are used to convey or enhance the meaning in a reading. They can also be created by readers to aid in comprehending a piece of writing. This section covers both aspects of visual aids.

Photographs and Cartoons   Photographs and cartoons often have an important role in conveying the writer's message. Magazines and newspapers have photographs of significant historical events, people, and places. Looking closely at these photographs can help you better understand what point the writer is trying to get across. As with reading written material, you want to ask questions about a photograph. Return to the seven essential reading questions and start with those.

- Ask yourself what the main idea of the photograph is. What message does the photograph present? What elements in the photograph support that idea? For example, if the photograph is supposed to show a scary costume party, look at the people's clothes. Are they wearing something other than everyday outfits? Can you recognize any of their clothing as representing monsters or characters from horror movies? Do the costumes look scary to you? If you can give "yes" answers to these questions, then you can agree that the photograph has expressed its intended message.

- Think about the purpose of the photograph. Why did the writer include the photograph? A photograph might be included to show something that is hard to explain, to create a mood, or to attract the reader.
- Look at the tone of the photograph. If the photograph is of a body of water, ask yourself if the scene looks inviting (a sunny sky and bright blue water) or mysterious (fog rolling in, gray water, and no one around).

- Use your inference skills to interpret photographs. Among the questions you can ask are why the photo was taken from a certain angle, why it is in black and white or color, and why people are dressed a certain way.
- Remember to consider other critical-thinking skills, such as deciding if the photograph is being used to appeal to your emotions.

Much of the above also applies to cartoons. Ask the same questions about a cartoon to determine why the writer included it in the essay, book, or story. Cartoons can say a lot with only a few words or no words at all. You will definitely need to use your inference skills to determine what a cartoon means. One place to practice your inference skills is with the cartoons that are usually found on the editorial pages in most newspapers. These cartoons often make statements about politics or other issues in the news. Most cartoons are humorous, but they do not always have to be so. Even funny cartoons, however, can convey an important message. Look at the cartoon below. Notice how the cartoonist is able to express a statement about summer with minimal words. Did you smile at the cartoon? Did you nod as you identified with the woman in the final panel or recognized the situation the cartoon is relating? The cartoon is not dealing with a major political issue, but it is sharing a slice of life that many people face each summer as they take vacations or travel to major events. The purpose of the cartoon could be to make us think about what we can do to ease these summer jams

or how to better cope with our emotional responses to them, or it might just serve to remind us that along with the good times come the bad.

Of the recording methods, creating your own photographs and cartoons will probably not be used as often as the other methods. Still, know that you have that option available to help you understand or remember an important point. Maybe going to tide pools near you and taking photographs of the sea creatures there would help you better remember what you are reading in an oceanography class. Or if you have talent in drawing and a humorous frame of mind, create your own cartoon for a political science or history reading. Creating your cartoon will surely help you remember the subject matter.

Diagrams, Graphs, Charts, and Tables Other visual ways of conveying information in a reading include diagrams, bar graphs, pie charts, and tables. All of these methods can be found in magazines, newspapers, and textbooks. Take the time to study these visual aids. They can sum up a point made in the reading or even introduce a new point. Look closely at all headings and any information to the side or at the bottom of a graph to help you understand what the graph means. For example, dollar amounts are sometimes abbreviated on the side of a graph, and at the bottom or top there will be an explanation

Venn Diagram

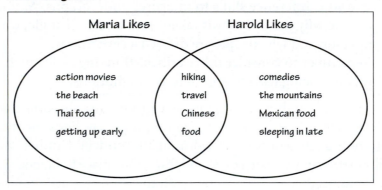

Bar Graph

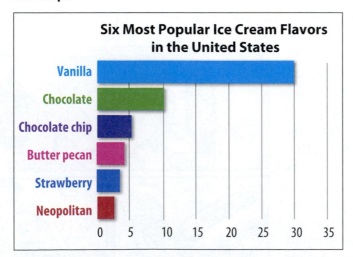

Adapted from information from the International Dairy Foods Association, 2007

Pie Chart

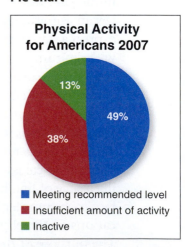

Adapted from information from the Centers for Disease Control, 2007

saying something like "in millions." This information lets you know that the "10," "20," and "30" on the side don't mean that the company only makes $10, $20, or $30 a year.

You can also create your own diagrams, graphs, charts, and tables. One especially helpful type of diagram when you want to compare and contrast items is the Venn diagram. In the sample diagram some of the characteristics of two people (Maria and Harold) are compared and contrasted. The overlapping area of the circles shows what they both like, the rest of the circle on the left shows what Maria likes, and on the right what Harold likes. Try this technique if you have two proposals in an essay, two characters in a story, or two theories in a textbook you want to compare. The diagram will help you see where ideas overlap and how they differ. Making diagrams, graphs, charts, or tables can be especially beneficial for visual learners who need to see something to best learn it. To familiarize yourself with some of the types of diagrams and graphs you will find when you read, examine the samples. You will find diagrams, graphs, charts, and tables in some of the readings in this text, and you will be asked to make a few of your own.

Sketches and Maps You may also find sketches and maps in the material you read. A sketch (a simple or rough drawing) might be used in a newspaper article or criminology textbook to show where objects and people were found at a crime. An interior decorating book or article might include a sketch of a room to show where items should be placed for best use of the space. Maps are used in a variety of reading environments. Among the many uses for maps are showing historical events (such as where battles took place), where people have traveled (such as Marco Polo's route), where countries are located, and where borders are in dispute. The writer Robert Louis Stevenson commented about maps: "I am told there are people who do not care for maps, and find it hard to believe. The names, the shapes of the woodland, the courses of the roads and rivers . . . here is an inexhaustible fund of interest for any man with eyes to see, or tuppenceworth of imagination to understand with!" Learning to appreciate maps can certainly expand your knowledge of the world and may even excite a desire to explore it.

You can create your own sketches and maps as learning aids. Drawing a small picture in the margin of a reading may jog your memory as to the content when you review an essay or chapter in a textbook. Some studies indicate that

Marco Polo and the Mongolian Empire, c. 1300
The map shows the route of Marco Polo from Venice to Cambaluc (modern Beijing) through the Mongolian Empire, ca. 1300.

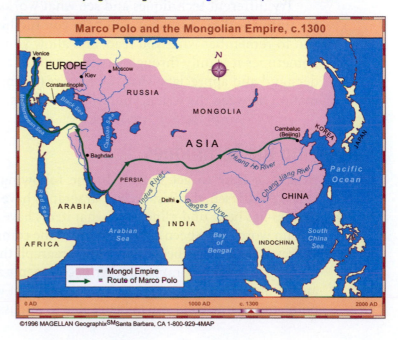

©1996 MAGELLAN Geographix℠Santa Barbara, CA 1-800-929-4MAP

Sketch of a Scene in a Mystery Story

Supposed locations of the characters at the time of the murder

those who doodle during phone conversations tend to remember more of what was said. You can experiment to see if making simple drawings help you remember more of what you read. If you know or discover that you learn better by creating drawings, then find ways to incorporate this learning method into your reading plans. When reading a story, if you aren't sure who is in the room or where the characters are located, reread the passage and make a sketch that indicates where each character is.

If a sequence in a reading is confusing you, a drawing of what happens at each stage (you could do it in panels as in the comic strips) may be the visual stimulus you need to understand the event. If you can't remember all of the characters in a story or novel, draw a map of the town indicating where each person lives and write down the names of the people in each house. If you are reading about a historical journey, such as Lewis and Clark's exploration of the West, make your own map of where the travelers went to reinforce your reading. Your artwork doesn't have to be a masterpiece—stick figures and simple shapes are fine. The goal of your sketch or map is to clearly grasp what is happening by using visual aids. There will be a few exercises later in the text that ask you to make a sketch or map to help you understand a reading.

Try different techniques and see what works for you. These recording methods are important because they will help you further comprehend what you read, help you to remember what you read, and allow you to share your ideas and knowledge. Sometimes it is only through writing or illustration that you will really come to understand and appreciate what you have read. Enjoy the process of transferring information between the writer, yourself, and others.

Applying the Techniques

Now it is time to get started. In the following article "Sport or Not a Sport" by David Andriesen, the first twelve paragraphs have been annotated. Look at what information has been underlined and what items have stars next to them. Think about why certain words have been circled, and read the comments in the margins. Then annotate the rest of the article beginning with paragraph thirteen. Underline, circle, and star the points you think are important. Write comments and ask questions in the margins. Try any of the techniques you have just learned that will help you understand the writer's point and that will aid you in being able to discuss and write about the article.

Sport or Not a Sport

by David Andriesen

Before You Read

1. Think of three activities you would define as being a sport.
2. What traits do these activities have in common?
3. What is your favorite sport? See if it is mentioned in the article.
4. Look at the two photographs. Do you consider these activities sports?

Vocabulary Preview

Look for these words in the reading. Exercises to reinforce the learning of new vocabulary using these words follow the reading. The paragraph number where the word appears is in parentheses.

agility (2)	**saturation** (10)	**parameters** (13)	**provision** (24)	**conveyance** (24)
constitutes (31)	**objective** (31)	**fallibility** (31)	**wayside** (35)	**muster** (37)

David Andriesen is a sports writer. He usually covered baseball for the *Seattle Post-Intelligencer* before the newspaper went to an online format in March 2009. From 1995 to 1999, Andriesen was a sports writer for the *Olympian* in Olympia, Washington. The following article was published in the *Seattle Post-Intelligencer* in January 2008.

1 **Search** for "cup stacking" on YouTube, and you can watch more than 1,000 videos of people taking nested stacks of plastic cups and arranging them into pyramids and back again so quickly the whole thing is almost a blur.

look up today

Wow!

2 It's impressive. It takes skill and agility. But is it a sport?

check definition

3 Stacking supporters think so. In 2005, the governing body changed the name officially to "sport stacking."

4 "When people challenge me on whether it's a sport, I usually turn it around on them," said Matt Reed, executive director of the World Sport Stacking Association. "I ask them, 'What's your definition of sport?' Invariably many of the things they mention are involved in our sport."

Good question

5 ESPN shows poker, cheerleading, arm wrestling and, yes, sport stacking.

who really thinks this is a sport?

WHAT'S CONSIDERED A SPORT?

Here's how some common sports—or nonsports—stack up in areas often included in debates on the matter.

✔ Yes   ? Opinions vary

SPORT OR NONSPORT	OBJECTIVE SCORING	MOSTLY HUMAN POWER	DIRECT HEAD-TO-HEAD	REQUIRES PHYSICAL STRENGTH	EMPLOYS A BALL
Auto racing	✔		✔	?	
Ballroom dancing		✔		?	
Baseball	✔	✔	✔	✔	✔
Basketball	✔	✔	✔	✔	✔
Bass fishing	✔	?			
Billiards	✔	✔			✔
Bobsled	✔	?			
Bowling	✔	✔		?	✔
Boxing		✔	✔	✔	
Competitive cheer		✔		✔	
Crew	✔	✔	✔	✔	
Diving	✔	✔		✔	
Cup stacking	✔	✔			
Downhill skiing	✔	✔		✔	
Competitive eating	✔	✔	✔	?	
Cycling	✔	✔	✔	✔	
Field events*	✔	✔		✔	✔
Figure skating		✔		✔	
Football	✔	✔	✔	✔	✔
Foot racing	✔	✔	✔	✔	
Golf	✔	✔		?	✔
Gymnastics		✔		✔	
Hockey	✔	✔	✔	✔	✔
Horse racing	✔	✔	✔	?	
Poker	✔	✔	✔		
Soccer	✔	✔	✔	✔	✔
Swim racing	✔	✔	✔	✔	
Synchronized swim.		✔		✔	
Table tennis	✔	✔	✔	?	✔
Tennis	✔	✔	✔	✔	✔
Weightlifting	✔	✔	✔	✔	

* (pole vault, high jump, discus, etc.)

6   ?   ⟨Bass fishing⟩ events offer million-dollar purses.

7   Mainstream newspaper sports sections report on ⟨hot dog eating⟩ *crazy competition* ⟨world records.⟩

8   The Olympics offer medals for kayaking and bobsled, but not for golf or football (at least not the American kind).

9   Some school districts classify ⟨chess⟩ as a sport.   → *I don't think so!*

10   So how, in this age of media saturation and fringe activities clamoring for legitimacy, can we define "sport"?

11   It's one of the great barroom debates, usually triggered by the sight of billiards or the X Games on TV at a watering hole. But while fans have argued over it for decades, there hasn't really been any official effort to define sport.

12   Rodney Fort, a professor of sport management at the University of Michigan who taught for more than two decades at Washington State University, uses a discussion about the definition of sport as an exercise to get students thinking about the field.

13   Fort has narrowed his definition to three parameters:

- It must use a "large motor skill."
- It must have an objective scoring system.
- It must use nothing more complicated than a "simple machine," such as a base-ball bat or vaulting pole.

14   "That's just me talking, my personal opinion," Fort said. "You'll never find a group of people who will reach total agreement."

15   There are many factors to consider, but most arguments end up centering on a few common factors.

Who's Got the Ball?

16   A ball helps a lot. Most things with a ball (or ball-like object, such as a puck) are generally considered to be sports. Heck, America's three top pro sports have "ball" right in the name.

17   If there are two people or teams on a playing surface at the same time competing with a ball, particularly the same ball, it's almost certainly a sport. Dozens of sports fit under this umbrella.

Who's Racing?

18   A footrace is the simplest form of sport, and most racing under human power is inarguably a sport. Whether people are racing over hurdles, through the woods or in a pool, they're engaged in sport.

19   The question becomes what level of human power you require, and what other implements you accept.

20   For instance, horse racing might be "the sport of kings," but is it a sport?

21   "It's a sport for the horse," Fort said. "They're the ones doing the racing. Certainly the jockey has something to do with it, but it's hard to conclude that that's a sport in the same way, say, the 100-meter dash is."

22   And in horse racing, at least it's the horse that gets the glory. Most people can name horses that have won the Triple Crown, but not jockeys who have done it.

23   But what about auto racing? NASCAR is one of the most popular sports in America, but it's the cars that are providing the power, and the fastest car usually wins, even if it's not driven by the most skilled driver on a particular day. Purists would reject all motorized racing, though they'd get a powerful argument south of the Mason-Dixon line.

24   What about human-powered racing in disciplines where differences in the equipment can affect the outcome, such as cycling and crew? Fort rejects these under his "simple machines" provision, but if you set the standard at the conveyance being primarily human powered, pedaling and rowing qualify.

Whose Turn Is It?

25   Then there is the question of whether participants must compete head-to-head. In a footrace, first one to the finish wins. But what about races like downhill skiing, in which competitors are theoretically racing each other but really just racing a clock?

26   Golf and bowling also are turn-based. In the case of bowling, it's to assure two competitors have the same lane conditions, but in golf a field of 144 can experience vastly different conditions on the same course—some might play a hole early or late, with or without wind or rain. People often complete the same round on different days.

27   Are the golfers truly competing against each other? And if you could get the same results by having golfers drop by and play four rounds at a certain course at their leisure, and then comparing scores to determine a winner, can a golf tournament be said to be a sporting event?

What's the Score?

28 When the results of a competition are a matter of opinion, it's tough for many to accept it as a sport.

29 If a judge scores an athlete higher or lower based on politics, or loving or hating a certain move, or, heaven forbid, whether he likes his outfit, the notion of competition goes down the drain quickly.

30 We like to know for certain whether someone won a contest. The ball went in the net or it didn't. The runner beat the throw to the plate or he didn't. Our most popular sports have this in common, even though human error is sometimes a factor.

31 "We have to all know what constitutes you getting a point," Fort said. "This causes a problem for some people, because they confuse the existence of an objective scoring definition with the human fallibility of recognizing it when they see it.

32 "They say, 'Well, what about when a ref blows a call in the end zone?' But that's not the point. We all know what constitutes a touchdown. We're just arguing about whether the ref saw it correctly or not."

33 Women often argue against the insistence on objective scoring, because it eliminates several sports most closely identified with women, or most popular when women are competing: figure skating, gymnastics, cheer.

34 But its sweep is much wider than that. Diving, out. Most extreme sports, out. Many rodeo events, out.

35 Even boxing, considered one of the most basic and pure sports, goes by the wayside if we insist on objective scoring. Are you ready to throw out boxing?

36 If you want boxing, you pretty much have to accept figure skating.

Getting Physical?

37 Even if you insist on humans doing the competing, head-to-head competition and objective scoring, you're still left with a lot of things that don't pass muster. Pinball. Poker. Darts. Which of your frat brothers can eat the most jalapeno poppers.

38 There has to be some level of physical effort. But where do you draw the line?

39 Golf looks pretty easy, but the average person might change his mind on that after playing 18 holes on foot carrying his own bag.

40   You could argue that throwing a 15-pound bowling ball for a few hours requires more physical strength than swinging a golf club, but a trip to the local bowling alley doesn't exactly turn up a lot of world-class athletes.

41   Tennis is a sport, but how about table tennis? It's pretty much the same thing, only on a smaller scale—and if you watch an international match you see that there's some physical effort involved.

42   Curling is an Olympic medal sport, but requires about the same level of effort as sweeping the back porch.

43   The question of what is or is not a sport will continue to be argued, and the only point of agreement likely to be reached is that we'll never agree.

44   What combination of factors must exist to make something a sport is up to you. Or maybe it's like the famous definition of art: You know it when you see it.

45   "Are we going to be in the Olympics? I don't know about that," cup stacking, er, *sport stacking* chief Reed said. "We're never going to be one of the major sports, but we feel like we're legit."

46   For Reed, whether sport stacking is classified as a sport is less important than people having fun doing it.

47   After all, that's the point, isn't it?

Getting the Message

____ **1.** The topic of the article is _____.

    a. cup stacking   c. sports

    b. unusual sports   d. sports that use a ball

____ **2.** The topic sentence in paragraph 30 can be found in

    a. sentence 1.   c. sentence 3.

    b. sentence 2.   d. sentence 4.

____ **3.** What is the main idea of the article?

    a. Some activities claim to be sports when they really are not.

    b. The definition of what constitutes a sport is up to the individual to decide.

    c. An activity is a sport if it is fun.

    d. An activity can only be defined as a sport if it uses a ball and has an objective scoring system.

____ **4.** Two types of supporting details used in the article are

    a. personal and hypothetical examples.

    b. statistics and testimony.

    c. examples and testimony.

    d. public examples and statistics.

____ **5.** Does the sentence "We like to know for certain whether someone won a contest" (par. 30) express a fact or an opinion?

    a. fact   b. opinion

____ **6.** In what order is the information presented?

    a. chronological   c. least to most important

    b. problem and solution   d. most to least important

____ **7.** The article uses the _____ pattern of organization.

    a. comparison/contrast   c. narrative

    b. cause and effect   d. definition

____ **8.** What does the transition word that begins paragraph 34 show?

    a. time   c. contrast

    b. comparison   d. importance

____ **9.** Andriesen's main purpose is to _____.

    a. persuade   c. inform

    b. entertain

____ **10.** It can be inferred from the line "You could argue that throwing a 15-pound bowling ball for a few hours requires more physical strength than swinging a golf club, but a trip to the local bowling alley doesn't exactly turn up a lot of world-class athletes" (par. 40) that

    a. all bowlers use 15-pound bowling balls.

    b. bowlers need to do more sit-ups.

    c. people can bowl while being overweight or out of shape in some other way.

    d. most golfers are in better shape than most bowlers.

11. When thinking about the supporting details, do you consider Rodney Fort a credible person whose testimony has some bearing on the topic (paragraphs 12–14, 21, and 31–32)? Explain why or why not.

_____

_____

_____

12. List three words or phrases that show whether the tone of the article is formal or informal.

_____

_____

_____

_____

13. What do you see as the purpose of the five headings, such as "Who's got the ball?"

_____

_____

_____

_____

14. Look at your annotations of the article. Which one of the questions you wrote in the margins or items you underlined or highlighted would you most like to bring up for discussion in class?

_____

_____

_____

15. On a separate sheet of paper, write a summary of the article in approximately 100 words.

Vocabulary

Use context clues to determine the meaning by looking back at the paragraph where the word is used (the paragraph number is in parentheses). If you need help, consult a dictionary for the definition.

A. Match each vocabulary word below to its synonym.

> **agility** (2)   **parameter(s)** (13)   **provision** (24)   **objective** (31)   **wayside** (35)

1. qualification _____
2. nimbleness _____
3. impartial _____
4. edge _____
5. guideline_____

B. Complete each sentence using the appropriate vocabulary word. Use each word once.

> **saturation** (10)   **conveyance** (24)   **constitutes** (31)   **fallibility** (31)   **muster** (37)

1. I usually expect so much of myself that I need to remember that _____ is a part of human nature, and we are all capable of making a mistake.

2. For my father, getting less than first place _____ failure in a race.

3. Hiding my stuff under the bed never passed _____ with my mother as cleaning my room.

4. I was sure downtown had reached the _____ point for coffee houses, but another one opened last week even though there are six others within two blocks.

5. During the busy tourist season, I found that the only _____ left to rent on the island was a donkey, but surprisingly I enjoyed our week of exploring the back country together.

The Article and You

1. What are three parameters you would have in creating your definition of a "sport"?

   _____

   _____

   _____

2. Pick two of the following activities that received only one or two checkmarks in the chart, and explain why you would or would not classify each as a sport: auto racing, ballroom dancing, bass fishing, bobsled, competitive cheer, cup stacking, figure skating, gymnastics, and synchronized swimming.

   _____

   _____

   _____

3. What activity wasn't on the chart that you would define as a sport? Explain why.

_____

_____

_____

4. On a separate sheet, write a paragraph where you give your definition of what makes an activity a sport.

 ## Take a Closer Look

Look at the photographs again. After reading the article and creating your own parameters, have you changed your mind about whether the activities are sports? Explain why or why not.

_____

_____

_____

Internet Activities*

If needed, use a separate sheet of paper to fully record your responses. Include the Web address of any sites from which you gather information.

1. Go to YouTube and look up "cup stacking." Watch three of the videos, and write a paragraph expressing your opinion on whether the activity is a sport or not.

2. Go to caloriecount.about.com/activities-sports or fitday.com and look up the calories burned for five sports/activities. Make a bar graph that shows five activities you consider sports from the least to the most strenuous in terms of calories burned per hour. Then consider how the amount of calories burned fits into the "requires physical strength" category in the chart in the reading. At the bottom of your graph explain whether the number of calories burned influences your decision on whether an activity is a sport or not.

_____

*If you haven't read the section "Using the Internet" on pages 492–493, now would be a good time to review the information on how to make your Internet searches productive.

Textbook Considerations

The questions to ask when reading a textbook are the same as those you want to ask when reading an essay or article. You still want to discover the writer's main point, look at the evidence presented to support that point, and understand how a chapter is organized. Two areas that are different in reading a textbook, however, are its length and its special features.

Organization

When you are assigned a textbook to read for a class, it is very rare that you would be expected to read the entire text at once. You will usually be assigned chapters or portions of chapters if the chapters are long. What this means is that you will need to be very careful in your annotating as you may need to review material from several reading sessions for a test.

The largest difference in reading a textbook selection compared to an essay or story is in the organization. Textbook chapters often provide materials that introduce you to a chapter, such as questions to consider before you read. Other organizational differences may include photographs and graphs scattered throughout a chapter, a concluding section that sums up the major points in a chapter, and questions at the end of a chapter to help you assess what you have learned. A good way to approach a textbook is to use the SQ4R method outlined below.

SQ4R Reading Method

To make reading a textbook productive, it is helpful to learn the SQ4R reading method. This method was developed by F. P. Robinson in the 1940s. There have been a few modifications to the process over the years, but as a whole it has proven to be an effective reading technique. The S stands for Survey, the Q for Question, and the first R for Read. The other three Rs can vary in name, but in general they have the same purpose. In this text they stand for Record, Recite, and Review.

Survey First, survey the pages you have been assigned to read. Look at the title of the reading for clues as to what it may be about. Read bold headings and subheadings for further ideas. Note any words in bold or italics; these are usually important to learn. Look at any photographs, cartoons, or other visuals, such as charts or graphs, to get an idea about the material the chapter will cover. Read any section with a name similar to "In Summary" or "In Conclusion" first so you know the important points to look for as you read the chapter. A textbook is not like a short story where the plot is going to be ruined if you read the end first. Also skim any questions at the end of the chapter so you have an idea of what the writer considers the important points. Taking about five minutes to survey a chapter can save you a lot of time as you read. Once you have a feel for what the reading is about move on to step two.

Question Ask questions about the reading to help you connect with the material. Questions to ask may be included in the introductory section in the textbook, but whether they are or are not, get used to asking some of your own questions to make the reading material pertinent to you. If you have questions that you are interested in finding the answers to, you will be more interested in the reading and pay closer attention to what you read. One way to form questions is to change the headings and subheadings into questions. If a heading is "Managing Money," you could ask "What is the best way to manage my money?" Or if a subheading reads "Building Better Relationships," then you could ask "How many ways are there to build better relationships?"

Read Now that you have an idea of what the chapter holds and you have questions to engage yourself with the reading, begin reading the chapter. You will usually own your textbooks, so have your pen ready to annotate: make comments, ask questions, underline or star important points, and circle words, people, or events that you think are important to know. If a section is confusing to you, reread it. And if some material is harder for you, slow down your reading speed for those sections. You may even want to read a section aloud if it is confusing for you. Hearing the words aloud may help you to understand the point. This technique can be especially useful if a writer uses dialogue that contains language that may be unfamiliar to you.

Record Write down what you have learned. Your annotating of what you read is the first step in recording. Make notes in the margins, ask questions, and highlight important points. It is helpful to read an entire paragraph before you highlight information, so you can focus on what really is important in the paragraph. You do not want to turn your whole textbook yellow (or whatever color highlighter you are using). Depending on the length of the chapter, you might want to stop and write a summary of what you have read after a few pages or answer questions posed in the book on a separate sheet of paper. If the chapter isn't that long, you can wait and write a summary once you have read the entire chapter. Summarizing is a great way to help you condense large sections of information into more manageable bits of information for future study or to discuss in class. You might also find that recording for you means to make charts, diagrams, or sketches. Try different methods to see what best helps you to understand and remember what you read.

Recite Repeat aloud what you have learned. Talking to yourself about what you have just read reinforces the ideas and can clarify points in your mind. After a few paragraphs, stop and summarize what you have read aloud. If you can't clearly express what you just read, that is a good indication that you need to reread the passage. You can also discuss the reading material with classmates informally before class begins, in a formal class discussion, or with a study group to further use the reciting step.

Review Once you are done reading, review what you have marked in the text to see if you have captured the important concepts. As you read, you may have come across an important idea that you may want to connect to an earlier part of the text. Reviewing the material while it is fresh in your mind will reinforce your learning, as well as show you if there are gaps that need filling. You should review your notes often so that studying for a test is not a major undertaking. For example, review your notes and annotations right after you finish reading, again the next day, and again the following week.

Two other *R*s that fit in the review step are reflect and relate. Stop and think about what you have just read. Ask yourself the following questions: "Why is this information important?" "How does it relate to me?" "How can I use it?" Connect the new information to information you already know. By making connections with previous knowledge you will find it easier to remember the new information. Think about ways to relate the new knowledge to your other classes and other aspects of your life. Making what you read relevant to your life will help you retain the information.

SQ4R Method Checklist

✓ **Survey:** Skim the pages you have been assigned to read looking at the title, headings and subheadings, **bold** and *italicized* words, visual aids, and any concluding sections.

✓ **Question:** Ask questions about the reading to help you connect with the material and generate interest in the reading.

✓ **Read:** Have your pen ready to annotate, reread confusing sections, and base your reading speed on the difficulty of the material.

✓ **Record:** Write down what you have learned.

✓ **Recite:** Repeat aloud what you have learned.

✓ **Review:** Review your annotations, summaries, and other notes often. Reflect on what you have just read and think of ways to relate the new knowledge to your life.

Applying the Techniques

What follows is a short excerpt on memory from a psychology textbook. The first section has been annotated. Look at the items that have been circled, starred, and underlined. Words that are in bold in a textbook are usually important to learn, and you should circle them and underline their definitions. Also answering any questions the book asks will help you remember important points. Note the comments in the margin that show the reader's involvement with the text: the connection to a vacation and the response to the "Try It!" exercise. Take advantage of every opportunity to use the learning tools a text provides, such as the "Try It!" exercise in this excerpt. After reading the "Memory as a Reconstruction" section, annotate the "Eyewitness Testimony" section yourself. Look for the important ideas and key words. Circle, underline, star, and number the ideas you think will be important to discuss in class or that might be asked on a test. Write comments and questions in the margins. Involve yourself with the reading.

Start using the SQ4R method by surveying the headings, looking at the notes in the margins, and studying the photograph and the "Try It!" The Before You Read questions presented in *Reading Now* introduce you to the questioning step of the SQ4R method. Later in the text you will be asked to create some of your own questions. Take the time to answer these questions in your head so that you begin to make connections with the readings.

After you read "The Nature of Remembering," the Getting the Message section will help you to record and review what you have learned. The Textbook and You section will assist in your recording and reviewing by asking you to make personal connections with the reading and to write a paragraph. This section can also be helpful with reciting if you discuss the questions with classmates. The exercises after all the readings in this text are designed to reinforce the SQ4R method so that later you will be able to automatically apply this process to everything you read.

The Nature of Remembering

from *Mastering the World of Psychology*

by Samuel E. Wood, Ellen Green Wood, and Denise Boyd

Before You Read

1. Survey the reading. Change the headings into questions.
2. Do you have a good memory?
3. Do you recall a time your memory played a trick on you?
4. Look at the photo. How do you think it will relate to the excerpt?

Vocabulary Preview

Look for these words in the reading. Exercises to reinforce the learning of new vocabulary using these words follow the reading. The paragraph number where the word appears is in parentheses.

fiction (2)	schemas (3)	frameworks (3)	subject (6)	perpetrator (7)
composition (8)	sequential (8)	simultaneously (8)	substantially (10)	erroneous (10)

Samuel E. Wood, Ellen Green Wood, and Denise Boyd have a combined 45 years of experience in teaching psychology. Between them they have taught in colleges in West Virginia, Missouri, and Texas. Besides traditional teaching experiences, they have been involved in developing distance learning programs, teaching seminars on critical thinking, and presenting papers at professional conferences. The following excerpt comes from their introductory psychology text *Mastering the World of Psychology*.

Memory as a Reconstruction

1　Wilder Penfield (1969), a Canadian neurosurgeon, claimed that experiences leave a "permanent imprint on the brain . . . as though a tape recorder had been receiving it all" (p. 165). Penfield (1975) based this conclusion on observations made while performing more than 1,100 operations on patients with epilepsy. He found that when parts of the temporal lobes were stimulated with an electrical probe, 3.5% of patients reported flashback experiences, as though they were actually reliving parts of their past.

2　After reviewing Penfield's findings, Ulrich Neisser and other memory researchers (Neisser, 1967) suggested that the experiences the patients reported were "comparable to the content of dreams," rather than the recall of actual experiences

(p. 169). Thus, today's memory researchers recognize that memory seldom works like a video cassette recorder, capturing every part of an experience exactly as it happens. Rather a memory is a reconstruction, an account pieced together from a few highlights, using information that may or may not be accurate (Loftus & Loftus, 1980). Put another way, remembering "is not so much like reading a book as it is like writing one from fragmentary notes" (Kihlstrom, 1995, p. 341). As a result, memory is quite often inaccurate, and recall is, even for people with the most accurate memories, partly truth and partly fiction.

highlights, puts pieces together

What is meant by the statement "Memory is reconstructive in nature"?

3   An early memory researcher, Englishman Sir Frederick Bartlett (1886–1969), suggested that memory is influenced by schemas—integrated frameworks of knowledge stored in long-term memory. Schemas aid in processing large amounts of material because they provide frameworks into which people can incorporate new information and experience. For example, if you have taken a course in the past that included discussion of psychoanalytic theory, the information about Freud and other psychoanalysts in this book will be easier for you to learn than it will be for students who have no prior knowledge of psychoanalytic theory. Your prior knowledge is organized into schemas that provide "shelves" on which to store the new information.

What are schemas, and how do they affect memory?

frameworks can "distort" memory

4   ☆ Schemas can also distort memory, though. When you witness an event, your schemas may cause you to omit some facts about what actually occurred or to add nonfactual details. Schema-based distortion can also occur when people alter the memory of an event or an experience in order to fit their beliefs, expectations, logic, or prejudices. The tendency to distort often causes gross inaccuracies in what people remember. For instance, people often distort memories of their own lives in the positive direction. Bahrick and others (1996) found that 89% of college students accurately remembered the A's they earned in high school, but only 29% accurately recalled the D's. *Try It! 6.2* demonstrates schema-based memory distortion.

like my view of summer vacation vs. Tim's view

5   *Try It! 6.2* shows that we are very likely to alter or distort what we see or hear to make it fit with what we believe should be true. All the words on the *Try It!* list are related to sleep, so it seems logical that *sleep* should be one of the words. In experiments using word lists similar to that one, between 40% and 55% of the participants "remembered" the key related word that was not on the list

reconstruction ☆
An account that is not an exact replica of a remembered event but has been pieced together from a few highlights, using information that may or may not be accurate.

schemas ☆
The integrated frameworks of knowledge about people, objects, and events, which are stored in long-term memory and affect the encoding and recall of information.

Try It! 6.2 Memory Distortion

Read this list of words aloud at a rate of about one word per second. Then close your book, and write down all the words you can remember.

| bed | awake | dream | snooze | nap | snore |
| rest | tired | wake | doze | yawn | slumber |

Now check your list. Did you "remember" the word *sleep*? Many people do, even though it is not one of the words on the list (Deese, 1959).

(Roediger & McDermott, 1995). If you "remembered" the word *sleep*, you created a false memory, which probably seemed as real to you as a true memory (Dodson et al., 2000).   *I did!*

Eyewitness Testimony

6   As the story at the beginning of this chapter suggests, eyewitness testimony is highly subject to error. In fact, most memory experts say that it should always be viewed with caution (Loftus, 1979).

What conditions reduce the reliability of eyewitness testimony?

Nevertheless, it does play a vital role in the U.S. justice system. Says Loftus (1984), "We can't afford to exclude it legally or ignore it as jurors. Sometimes, as in cases of rape, it is the only evidence available, and it is often correct" (p. 24).

7   Fortunately, eyewitness mistakes can be minimized. Eyewitnesses to crimes often identify suspects from a lineup. If shown photographs of a suspect before viewing the lineup, eyewitnesses may mistakenly identify that suspect in the lineup because the person looks familiar. Research suggests that it is better to have an eyewitness first describe the perpetrator and then search for photos matching that description than to have the eyewitness start by looking through photos and making judgments as to their similarity to the perpetrator (Pryke et al., 2000).

8   The composition of the lineup is also important. Other individuals in a lineup must resemble the suspect in age and body build and must certainly be of the same race. Even then, if the lineup does not contain the perpetrator, eyewitnesses may identify the person who most closely resembles him or her (Gonzalez et al., 1993). Eyewitnesses are less likely to make errors if a sequential lineup is used, that is, if the participants in the lineup are viewed

one after the other, rather than simultaneously (Loftus, 1993a). Some police officers and researchers prefer a "showup"—a procedure that involves presenting only one suspect and having the witness indicate whether that person is the perpetrator. There are fewer misidentifications with a showup, but also more failures in making positive identifications (Wells, 1993).

9   Eyewitnesses are more likely to identify the wrong person if the person's race is different from their own. According to Egeth (1993), misidentifications are approximately 15% higher in cross-race than in same-race identifications. Misidentification is also somewhat more likely to occur when a weapon is used in a crime. The witnesses may pay more attention to the weapon than to the physical characteristics of the criminal (Steblay, 1992).

10   Even questioning witnesses after a crime can influence what they later remember. Because leading questions can substantially change a witness's memory of an event, it is critical that the interviewers ask neutral questions (Leichtman & Ceci, 1995). Misleading information supplied to the witness after the event can result in erroneous recollections of the actual event, a phenomenon known as the *misinformation effect* (Kroll et al., 1988; Loftus & Hoffman, 1989). Loftus (1997) and her students have conducted "more than 20 experiments involving over 20,000 participants that document how exposure to misinformation induces memory distortion" (p. 71). Furthermore, after eyewitnesses have repeatedly recalled information, whether accurate or inaccurate, they become even more confident when they testify in court because the information is so easily retrieved (Shaw, 1996). And the confidence eyewitnesses have in their testimony is not necessarily an indication of its accuracy (Loftus, 1993a; Sporer et al., 1995). In fact, eyewitnesses who perceive themselves to be more objective have more confidence in their testimony, regardless of its accuracy, and they are more likely to include incorrect information in their verbal descriptions. (Geiselman et al., 2000).

Getting the Message

____ **1.** What is the topic?

    a. Freud's theories   c. memory

    b. how to improve one's memory   d. problems with the justice system

____ **2.** The main idea is stated in _____.

    a. paragraph 1   c. paragraph 4

    b. paragraph 2   d. paragraph 10

____ **3.** Which type of supporting detail can be found in the reading?

    a. statistics   c. expert testimony

    b. examples   d. all of the above

____ **4.** According to the reading, memory is like

    a. a tape recorder.   c. writing a book from disconnected notes.

    b. a VCR.   d. reading a book.

____ **5.** The statement "Eyewitnesses are more likely to identify the wrong person if the person's race is different from their own" (par. 9) is

    a. a fact.   b. an opinion.

____ **6.** The "Eyewitness Testimony" section uses _____ order to present the information.

    a. problem and solution   c. chronological

    b. least to most important   d. most to least important

____ **7.** How does paragraph 4 relate organizationally to paragraph 3?

    a. definition   c. examples

    b. narrative   d. comparison and contrast

____ **8.** The transition word *Furthermore* in paragraph 10 shows

    a. time.   c. comparison.

    b. addition.   d. contrast.

____ **9.** The writers' purpose is most likely to _____.

    a. inform   c. entertain

    b. persuade

____ **10.** It can be inferred from the sentence "The witnesses may pay more attention to the weapon than to the physical characteristics of the criminal (Steblay, 1992)" (par. 9) that witnesses

    a. may be interested in purchasing a similar weapon, which is why they are looking at the weapon.

    b. are distracted by how shiny knives and guns are.

    c. are always easily distracted.

    d. can be intimidated by a weapon and therefore distracted.

11. List an advantage and a disadvantage of schemas. Do you feel the schema system is more helpful or flawed?

_____

_____

_____

_____

_____

12. Why are the questions in green important to read?

_____

_____

13. List three methods mentioned in the reading that police can use with witnesses to identify a perpetrator. Which of the three methods seems like the best to use? Explain why you made your choice.

_____

_____

14. What are two points you highlighted in the excerpt? Why do you think these points are important?

_____

_____

15. Finish the informal outline of the excerpt.

Thesis: _____

1. Researchers have come to the conclusion that memories are _____
   _____ par. 1–2

2. Schemas are used to build memories, and they can be _____ par. 3–5

3. Eyewitness testimony is _____ par. 6

4. Eyewitness testimony _____ par. 7–9

5. Eyewitnesses must _____
   par. 10

Vocabulary

Use context clues to determine the meaning of each word by referring back to the paragraph where the word is used (the paragraph number is in parentheses). If you need help, consult a dictionary for the definition.

A. Match the word to its definition.

> framework(s) (3)   subject (6)   perpetrator (7)   sequential (8)   erroneous (10)

1. mistaken; incorrect; false _____

2. following in order _____

3. inclined; disposed _____

4. basic form or system; a fundamental structure _____

5. one who does, especially one who commits a crime _____

B. Put a *T* if the underlined vocabulary word is used correctly and an *F* if it is used incorrectly.

____ 1. I thought it was merely <u>fiction</u> (2) when Maya said Uncle Joe had been to see her last week. He hasn't visited Topeka for ten years, but I found out he really was in town.

____ 2. <u>Schemas</u> (3) can be helpful for building bits of information on top of each other.

____ 3. The <u>composition</u> (8) of the teams is important. We don't want all the best players on a couple teams and all the weaker players on the same team.

____ 4. My brother and I <u>simultaneously</u> (8) came up with the same idea of a gift for our father. I thought of it last week and he thought of it yesterday.

____ 5. Her account of the weekend was <u>substantially</u> (10) right. We did stay at a Hilton, but we were in Chicago not San Francisco, and we did not do any of the activities she said.

The Textbook and You

1. As mentioned in the reading, memory plays "a vital role in the U.S. justice system" (par. 6). Think of two areas in your life where memory plays an important part. Explain why memory is important to these areas.

_____

_____

2. Has your memory ever fooled you? For example, think of a time when you remembered a scene differently than a friend or family member or returned to a place and it was not the same as you had pictured it. Was your distorted memory in the "positive direction" as explained in paragraph 4? Was there a serious consequence to your memory distortion?

_____

_____

_____

3. Pretend you are a police officer at the scene of a robbery at a convenience store. Write a neutral question and a leading question you could ask of a witness.

_____

_____

4. On a separate sheet, write a paragraph where you explain how accurate you feel your memory is most of the time. Do people tell you that you usually remember events well or do you more often hear, "It wasn't like that"?

Take a Closer Look

Look at the photograph again. Now that you have read about police lineups, do you think this lineup looks like a fair one? Explain why or why not using information from the reading.

_____

_____

_____

_____

Internet Activities

If needed, use a separate sheet of paper to fully record your responses. Include the Web address of any sites from which you gather information.

1. Do a search for "false memories" or "false memory experiments." Read about a few of the experiments researchers have conducted. See if there are any experiments you can do online. Then make your own test similar to one that you read about or to the "Try It!" in the textbook excerpt. Have two classmates try your experiment. Discuss the results with each other.

_____

_____

2. Search for "eyewitness testimony" or "eyewitness testimony cases." List two cases where eyewitness testimony was important to the case. Write a summary of one of these cases.

_____

_____

_____

_____

Short Story Considerations

Reading a short story is not vastly different from reading an essay or article, except the events are fictional or imaginary. The people in the story are characters, not real life people, though they may often resemble people in real life or be based on real people. You will ask the same questions as you would when reading an essay or article, but some of the terminology will be different, and you will have a few extra areas to consider.

Plot

The **plot** is the storyline or the plan of the story. It is what happens in the story. Most stories use chronological order to develop the plot. Look for time transition words as you read to see if the writer uses this organizational method. Most short stories are also narratives, meaning they tell a story. Sometime writers may use a **flashback** where they look back on events that happened before the time of the current narration. Writers may also use **foreshadowing**, a technique where they subtly suggest what will happen later in the story. You may be aware of the foreshadowing as you read it, or you may not notice it until you have finished the story and then remember such a clue or suggestion. Then you can hear yourself making comments like "Oh, that's what that line meant," or "Now, I see why she bought that."

As you read look for the **climax**, the turning point or the point of highest intensity. Recognizing the climax will help you understand what point the writer is trying to get across. When you determine where the climax is, write a comment or put stars in the margin. After the climax comes the **resolution**, the outcome or closure to the events. Sometimes the resolution definitely ties up the story, but at other times it can leave the reader wondering what might happen, which is likely part of the writer's goal.

If you are ever confused about what happens in a story, make an outline of the events to help you see the order of what went on. Drawing a sketch of a scene is also a great way to visualize what happens and help you clarify a point that may be confusing you.

Characters and Dialogue

Central to a story are the **characters**: the people (or beings) who populate the story. The characters do not have to be human; for example, they can be animals, robots, or ghosts. As you read, it is helpful to write the names of the characters and their major traits on a separate sheet of paper or to circle the characters' names and write their traits in the margins. Among the qualities you should know about a character, if the writer indicates them, are the character's gender, age, and major personality traits (such as honest or dishonest, hard-working or lazy, brave or cowardly). Remember that a Venn diagram can be a useful way to understand the similarities and differences between characters. The main character is called the **protagonist**. This is the person who the action revolves around. The **antagonist** is the character who works against the main character. The antagonist does not have to a person. For example, it could be an animal, death, or an illness.

One area that makes fiction different from nonfiction is the use of dialogue. **Dialogue** is a vocal exchange between two or more characters. When characters talk to each other, you can learn a lot about how they feel and their personalities. Look at the diction each character uses to help understand their backgrounds. See if you can trust what the character says. Do the character's words match his or her actions? Also note how the characters respond to each other to help you make judgments on a character's personality. You may have to use your inference skills to understand why a character acts a certain way. Underline any lines of dialogue you think are important—characters often reveal themselves through what they say.

Conflict

If everything went perfectly fine in a story, it would not be exciting to read. There needs to be some kind of **conflict** or struggle to attract and hold the reader's attention. There are four major types of conflict a protagonist can face:

- Against the self: This conflict involves an internal struggle where the protagonist battles something within him- or herself, such as anger, jealousy, or madness.
- Against another character: The protagonist battles (fights with, schemes against) another character. Classic examples of this conflict include the shootout in a Western, the romantic triangle in a love story, and the knight rescuing the fair maiden from the evil wizard in a fantasy tale.
- Against society: In this case, the protagonist faces the hostility of the public, often for rebelling against accepted practices or beliefs. For example, when a well-respected lawyer chooses to take on a client the townspeople feel is unworthy of his help, he must face their anger though he feels he is doing the right thing. Or after a doctor discovers that the water to be used for the town's new spa is polluted, he and his family become outcasts when several townspeople fear that their livelihood will be destroyed.
- Against nature: Here the protagonist battles some aspect of nature, such as a river about to overflow, a treacherous mountain to climb, or attacking red ants. Battles with fate, gods and goddesses, or other all-powerful beings also usually fit in this category.

A story may have more than one type of conflict. The protagonist may be internally battling a fear of heights and combating nature by climbing a mountain and meeting obstacles such as snow and fog. Recognizing the conflicts in a story will help you to understand the plot and why a character behaves in certain ways. Put a star next to the key scenes in such struggles.

Setting and Tone

The **setting** is the time and place in which the story takes place. It is important to realize that a story may be taking place 700 years in the past or in the distant future. Pay attention to any clues the writer offers as to when a story is taking place. Not only the year is important, but also the season, day, or even hour. Also note where the story takes place. Knowing what country or city the story is set in can have consequences for what the characters say and do. The design of a house may play a role in what happens. Notice the colors and other descriptions of a room.

The setting can also add to the tone of a story. Remember that **tone** is the writer's attitude toward the subject. The tone expresses the mood the writer wants to convey. The difference in time of day and weather can affect the atmosphere of the story. You will likely react differently to a story if it takes place on a dark and stormy night than if similar circumstances happen on a sunny day. A writer can emphasize a scary tone by setting a story in a deserted house. Also continue to be aware of irony, so you don't miss the humor in a story, especially dark humor. Dark humor tackles a serious subject (such as death) in a light manner. It can be used to amuse readers, but also to get them to think seriously about the topic.

Symbolism

Symbols are items that on the surface appear to be what they literally are, but which also have another meaning or even many meanings. For example, in a story a man gives his girlfriend yellow roses. On the literal or factual level, they are roses. On the symbolic level, in the language of flowers popular in the Victorian period, yellow roses meant infidelity. By giving his girlfriend yellow roses, he could be showing her that he knows or suspects that she is cheating on him. Today, yellow roses are more often seen to mean friendship. If that is the symbolism the man's girlfriend attaches to yellow roses, she could think that he sees their romance as going in another direction. That is why as a reader you need to

pay attention to how the writer presents objects in a story. While some items have fairly well-known symbolic meanings, such as spring as a time of rebirth or midnight as the witching hour, other items take on the symbolic meanings the writer chooses to give them. To identify whether an item is symbolic think about how the item is used in the story, how characters react to the item, and how that item relates to points the writer is making.

Theme

The **theme** is the main idea the writer wants to convey. In fiction writers do not usually express the theme in one or two sentences as may be done in a thesis statement in an essay. In reading fiction, you will be called on to use your inference skills more often. A short story will rarely have a line that tells you this is the theme. You have to discover the theme by using the plot, the characters' actions, the conflicts, the setting and tone, and any other elements in the story. As you read and again once you have finished the story, ask yourself what idea the writer wants to get across. Sometimes it takes a while to mull over a story to discover the writer's theme. Use the SQ4R techniques of record, recite, and review to help you determine the writer's theme.

Short Story Checklist

✓ Determine what happens in the story to comprehend the plot.

✓ Know who the characters are and establish their personality traits through their actions and dialogue.

✓ Decide what kind or kinds of conflict the protagonist faces.

✓ Establish what impact the setting—time and place—has on the story, and how the tone may be developed through the setting.

✓ Decipher any symbols found in the story.

✓ Use the various literary elements to decide on the theme.

Applying the Techniques

In the "The Stolen Party" by Liliana Heker that follows about half of the story has been annotated. As you read the short story, look at the sections that are underlined or have stars next to them. What seems important about these parts? Note that the name of each character has been circled. Read the comments in the margins. Try to decide on the points the reader is looking at and determine why they may be important. When you get to paragraph 40, start annotating the story yourself. Mark important passages, and write notes in the margins on points you want to discuss in class or review later. Remember that asking questions about passages you don't understand is an important function of annotating. By writing your questions, you will likely take the time to contemplate those sections as you review the story, and you will remember to ask these questions in class discussions. You may even find a question answered by the time you finish a story.

The Stolen Party

by Liliana Heker

Before You Read

1. What do you think a "stolen party" could mean?
2. What do you remember about a favorite party you attended?
3. Were you excited about birthday parties when you were a child?
4. Look at the photo. What does it reveal about birthday parties?

Vocabulary Preview

Look for these words in the reading. Exercises to reinforce the learning of new vocabulary using these words follow the reading. The paragraph number where the word appears is in parentheses.

sneered (1)	pompously (11)	boisterous (19)	shrugged (26)
impatient (29)	instinctively (31)	bony (40)	unmanly (46)
chattering (52)	infinitely (73)		

Liliana Heker is an Argentine writer. She was born in Buenos Aires. She started as an editor of a literary magazine at age 17. Her first collection of short stories was published at age 23. She has since then written several novels and short stories. She has also explored the oppressive political regimes in Argentina in the 1970s and 1980s through her fiction and in her work as an editor and journalist. The following story was originally published in 1982.

1   **As soon** as she arrived she went straight to the kitchen to see if the monkey was there. It was: what a relief! She wouldn't have liked to admit that her mother had been right. *Monkeys at a birthday?* her mother had sneered. *Get away with you, believing any nonsense you're told!* She was cross, but not because of the monkey, the girl thought; it's just because of the party.

2   "I don't like you going," she told her. "It's a rich people's party."

3   "Rich people go to Heaven too," said the girl, who studied religion at school.

4   "Get away with Heaven," said the mother. "The problem with you, young lady, is that you like to fart higher than your ass." *meaning?*

5   The girl didn't approve of the way her mother spoke. She was barely nine, and one of the best in her class.

6   "I'm going because I've been invited," she said. "And I've been invited because Luciana is my friend. So there."

9 years old

7   "Ah yes, your friend," her mother grumbled. She paused. "Listen, Rosaura," she said at last. "That one's not your friend. You know what you are to them? The maid's daughter, that's what."

conflict between mother/ daughter

8   Rosaura blinked hard: she wasn't going to cry. Then she yelled: "Shut up! You know nothing about being friends!"

9   Every afternoon she used to go to Luciana's house and they would both finish their homework while Rosaura's mother did the cleaning. They had their tea in the kitchen and they told each other secrets. Rosaura loved everything in the big house, and she also loved the people who lived there.

10   "I'm going because it will be the most lovely party in the whole world, Luciana told me it would. There will be a magician, and he will bring a monkey and everything."

11   The mother swung around to take a good look at her child, and pompously put her hands on her hips.

12   "Monkeys at a birthday?" she said. "Get away with you, believing any nonsense you're told!"

13   Rosaura was deeply offended. She thought it unfair of her mother to accuse other people of being liars simply because they were rich. Rosaura too wanted to be rich, of course. If one day she managed to live in a beautiful palace, would her mother stop loving her? She felt very sad. She wanted to go to that party more than anything else in the world.

ambitious

14   "I'll die if I don't go," she whispered, almost without moving her lips.

15   And she wasn't sure whether she had been heard, but on the morning of the party she discovered that her mother had starched her Christmas dress. And in the afternoon, after washing her hair, her mother rinsed it in apple vinegar so that it would be all nice and shiny. Before going out, Rosaura admired herself in the mirror, with her white dress and glossy hair, and thought she looked terribly pretty.

16   Señora Ines also seemed to notice. As soon as she saw her, she said:

17   "How lovely you look today, Rosaura."

18   Rosaura gave her starched skirt a slight toss with her hands and walked into the party with a firm step. She said hello to Luciana and asked about the monkey. Luciana put on a secretive look and

whispered into Rosaura's ear: "He's in the kitchen. But don't tell anyone, because it's a surprise."

back to 1st ¶

19   Rosaura wanted to make sure. Carefully she entered the kitchen and there she saw it: deep in thought, inside its cage. It looked so funny that the girl stood there for a while, watching it, and later, every so often, she would slip out of the party unseen and go and admire it. Rosaura was the only one allowed into the kitchen. Señora Ines had said: "You yes, but not the others, they're much too boisterous, they might break something." Rosaura had never broken anything. She even managed the jug of orange juice, carrying it from the kitchen into the dining room. She held it carefully and didn't spill a single drop. And Señora Ines had said: "Are you sure you can manage a jug as big as that?" Of course she could manage. She wasn't a butter-fingers, like the others. Like that blonde girl with the bow in her hair. As soon as she saw Rosaura, the girl with the bow had said:

conflict with cousin

20   "And you? Who are you?"

21   "I'm a friend of Luciana," said Rosaura.

22   "No," said the girl with the bow, "you are not a friend of Luciana because I'm her cousin and I know all her friends. And I don't know you."

23   "So what," said Rosaura. "I come here every afternoon with my mother and we do our homework together."

24   "You and your mother do your homework together?" asked the girl, laughing.

25   "I and Luciana do our homework together," said Rosaura, very seriously.

26   The girl with the bow shrugged her shoulders.

27   "That's not being friends," she said. "Do you go to school together?"

28   "No."

29   "So where do you know her from?" said the girl, getting impatient.

30   Rosaura remembered her mother's words perfectly. She took a deep breath.

31   "I'm the daughter of the employee," she said.

32   Her mother had said very clearly: "If someone asks, you say you're the daughter of the employee; that's all." She also told her to add: "And proud of it." But Rosaura thought that never in her life would she dare say something of the sort.

33   "What employee?" said the girl with the bow. "Employee in a shop?"

34   "No," said Rosaura angrily. "My mother doesn't sell anything in any shop, so there."

35   "So how come she's an employee?" said the girl with the bow.

36   Just then Señora Ines arrived saying *shh shh,* and asked Rosaura if she wouldn't mind helping serve out the hotdogs, as she knew the house so much better than the others.

37   "See?" said Rosaura to the girl with the bow, and when no one was looking she kicked her in the shin.

38   Apart from the girl with the bow, all the others were delightful. The one she liked best was Luciana, with her golden birthday crown; and then the boys. Rosaura won the sack race, and nobody managed to catch her when they played tag. When they split into two teams to play charades, all the boys wanted her for their side. Rosaura felt she had never been so happy in all her life.

39   But the best was still to come. The best came after Luciana blew out the candles. First the cake. Señora Ines had asked her to help pass the cake around, and Rosaura had enjoyed the task immensely, because everyone called out to her, shouting "Me, me!" Rosaura remembered a story in which there was a queen who had the power of life or

death over her subjects. She had always loved that, having the power of life or death. To Luciana and the boys she gave the largest pieces, and to the girl with the bow she gave a slice so thin one could see through it.

40   After the cake came the magician, tall and bony, with a fine red cape. A true magician: he could untie handkerchiefs by blowing on them and make a chain with links that had no openings. He could guess what cards were pulled out from a pack, and the monkey was his assistant. He called the monkey "partner." "Let's see here, partner," he would say, "turn over a card." And, "Don't run away, partner: time to work now."

41   The final trick was wonderful. One of the children had to hold the monkey in his arms and the magician said he would make him disappear.

42   "What, the boy?" they all shouted.

43   "No, the monkey!" shouted back the magician.

44   Rosaura thought that this was truly the most amusing party in the whole world.

45   The magician asked a small fat boy to come and help, but the small fat boy got frightened almost at once and dropped the monkey on the floor. The magician picked him up carefully, whispered something in his ear, and the monkey nodded almost as if he understood.

46   "You mustn't be so unmanly, my friend," the magician said to the fat boy.

47   "What's unmanly?" said the fat boy.

48   The magician turned around as if to look for spies.

49   "A sissy," said the magician. "Go sit down."

50   Then he stared at all the faces, one by one. Rosaura felt her heart tremble.

51   "You, with the Spanish eyes," said the magician. And everyone saw that he was pointing at her.

52   She wasn't afraid. Neither holding the monkey, nor when the magician made him vanish; not even when, at the end, the magician flung his red cape over Rosaura's head and uttered a few magic words . . . and the monkey reappeared, chattering happily, in her arms. The children clapped furiously. And before Rosaura returned to her seat, the magician said:

53   "Thank you very much, my little countess."

54   She was so pleased with the compliment that a while later, when her mother came to fetch her, that was the first thing she told her.

55   "I helped the magician and he said to me, 'Thank you very much, my little countess.'"

56   It was strange because up to then Rosaura had thought that she was angry with her mother. All along Rosaura had imagined that she would say to her: "See that the monkey wasn't a lie?" But instead she was so thrilled that she told her mother all about the wonderful magician.

57   Her mother tapped her on the head and said: "So now we're a countess!"

58   But one could see that she was beaming.

59   And now they both stood in the entrance, because a moment ago Señora Ines, smiling, had said: "Please wait here a second."

60   Her mother suddenly seemed worried.

61   "What is it?" she asked Rosaura.

62   "What is what?" said Rosaura. "It's nothing; she just wants to get the presents for those who are leaving, see?"

63   She pointed at the fat boy and at a girl with pigtails who were also waiting there, next to their mothers. And she explained about the presents. She knew, because she had been watching those who left before her. When one of the girls was about to leave, Señora Ines would give her a bracelet. When a boy left, Señora Ines gave him a yo-yo. Rosaura preferred the yo-yo because it sparkled, but she didn't mention that to her mother. Her mother might have said: "So why don't you ask for one, you blockhead?" That's what her mother was like. Rosaura didn't feel like explaining that she'd be horribly ashamed to be the odd one out. Instead she said:

64   "I was the best-behaved at the party."

65   And she said no more because Señora Ines came out into the hall with two bags, one pink and one blue.

66   First she went up to the fat boy, gave him a yo-yo out of the blue bag, and the fat boy left with his mother. Then she went up to the girl and gave her a bracelet out of the pink bag, and the girl with the pigtails left as well.

67   Finally she came up to Rosaura and her mother. She had a big smile on her face and Rosaura liked that. Señora Ines looked down at her, then looked up at her mother, and then said something that made Rosaura proud:

68   "What a marvelous daughter you have, Herminia."

69   For an instant, Rosaura thought that she'd give her two presents: the bracelet and the yo-yo. Señora Ines bent down as if about to look for something. Rosaura also leaned forward, stretching out her arm. But she never completed the movement.

70   Señora Ines didn't look in the pink bag. Nor did she look in the blue bag. Instead she rummaged in her purse. In her hand appeared two bills.

71   "You really and truly earned this," she said handing them over. "Thank you for all your help, my pet."

72   Rosaura felt her arms stiffen, stick close to her body, and then she noticed her mother's hand on her shoulder. Instinctively she pressed herself against her mother's body. That was all. Except her eyes. Rosaura's eyes had a cold, clear look that fixed itself on Señora Ines's face.

73   Señora Ines, motionless, stood there with her hand outstretched. As if she didn't dare draw it back. As if the slightest change might shatter an infinitely delicate balance.

Getting the Message

____ 1. The story's plot is developed using the _____ pattern of organization.

    a. classification   c. example

    b. comparison and contrast   d. narrative

____ 2. Which of the following lines foreshadows what happens at the end of the story?

    a. "Rosaura was the only one allowed into the kitchen." (par. 19)

    b. "Just then Señora Ines arrived saying *shh shh*, and asked Rosaura if she wouldn't mind helping serve out the hotdogs...." (par. 36)

    c. "Señora Ines had asked her to help pass the cake around, and Rosaura had enjoyed the task immensely...." (par. 39)

    d. all of the above

____ 3. The major characters are

    a. Rosaura, Luciana, and the cousin.

    b. Rosaura, Herminia, and Señora Ines.

    c. Herminia, Señora Ines, and the magician.

    d. Rosaura, the magician, and the monkey.

____ 4. Rosaura is _____ years old.

    a. 5   c. 9

    b. 7   d. 11

____ 5. Three of Rosaura's traits that are central to the story are her

    a. courage, her honesty, and her worldliness.

    b. beauty, her vanity, and her intelligence.

    c. generosity, her honesty, and her enthusiasm.

    d. ambition, her naivety, and her pride.

____ 6. _____ says, "Thank you for all your help, my pet."

    a. Señora Ines   c. Herminia

    b. The magician   d. The fat boy

____ 7. The two main types of conflict in the story are struggles

    a. against the self and nature.

    b. against a character and society.

    c. against society and nature.

    d. against nature and a character.

____ 8. What is the setting for most of the story?

    a. a birthday party in a middle-class home

    b. a child's birthday party at the home of rich people

    c. an adult's birthday party in a house in Argentina

    d. a birthday party in a park

_____ **9.** It can be inferred from paragraphs 2–7 that Herminia doesn't want Rosaura to go to the party because

      a. she doesn't think rich people have good manners.

      b. she is worried about her daughter's manners.

      c. she doesn't want her daughter to get emotionally hurt.

      d. Rosaura doesn't have an appropriate dress.

_____ **10.** The line, "The magician turned around as if to look for spies" uses a

      a. simile.   b. metaphor.

11. The story is called "The Stolen Party." Who is the party stolen from and who does the stealing? Can the title have more than one meaning?

_____

_____

_____

_____

12. How did the ending make you feel? How does the ending reveal Heker's purpose and the story's theme?

_____

_____

_____

_____

13. What does the scene with the magician and the monkey add to the story? Is the monkey used symbolically?

_____

_____

_____

_____

14. List three points you highlighted, circled, or starred. Why did you consider these points important?

_____

_____

15. On a separate sheet, make a sketch of a key scene in the story, and under the sketch briefly explain why this scene is important. Be prepared to share your sketch with classmates and discuss why the scenes people picked are important.

Vocabulary

Use context clues to determine the meaning of each word by referring back to the paragraph where the word is used (the paragraph number is in parentheses). If you need help, consult a dictionary for the definition.

A. Put the words into the appropriate sentences below. Use each word once.

> **sneered** (1)   **boisterous** (19)   **shrugged** (26)   **instinctively** (31)   **infinitely** (73)

1. The _____ teens shouted and jumped throughout the entire concert; they came home tired, but happy.

2. The villain _____ at the audience as they hissed him off the stage.

3. This book is _____ more interesting than the last one I read; I stayed up until one o'clock to finish it.

4. When I asked my sister what she had done with the sweater she had borrowed, she simply _____ and went on reading. It was not a helpful reply.

5. Lexy _____ chased after the mouse when it ran across the floor. It is nice having a cat to take care of such problems.

B. Match each word to its antonym.

> **pompously** (11)   **impatient** (29)   **bony** (40)   **unmanly** (46)   **chattering** (52)

1. serene _____

2. plump _____

3. brave _____

4. quiet _____

5. modestly _____

The Short Story and You

1. Imagine what happens next in the story. Will Señora Ines put down her hand?

   _____

   _____

2. How does the story apply to different types of inequality you see around you?

   _____

   _____

3. Have you ever been treated unequally—in school, at work, or at a social event? How did it make you feel?

   _____

   _____

4. On a separate sheet, write a paragraph where you show what Rosaura and her mother discuss when they get home from the party. Use dialogue in your scene.

Take a Closer Look

Look at the photograph again. Do the children look like they are having a good time? How can you tell? List four elements that are making the party fun. What element could you take away that would "steal" the party from a child?

_____

_____

_____

_____

_____

Internet Activities

If needed, use a separate sheet of paper to fully record your responses. Include the Web address of any sites from which you gather information.

1. Do a search for the German term "bildungsroman." What does it mean? Explain how this term fits Heker's story. Search for films that could also belong in this genre. List three films you find. Have you seen any of these films?

_____

_____

_____

_____

2. Look up "monkey symbolism" or "monkey meanings." List three symbolic meanings about monkeys that you find. Also look up phrases that have the word monkey in them. Which of the meanings or phrases that you found would best fit the use of the monkey in this story?

_____

_____

_____

_____

_____

myreadinglab | Objectives Check

To check your progress in meeting chapter objectives, log in to www.myreadinglab.com, click on the Study Plan tab, and then on the Reading Skills tab. Choose Active Reading Strategies, Note Taking and Highlighting, Outlining and Summarizing, Graphics and Visuals, and Reading Textbooks from the list of subtopics. Read and view the resources in the Review Materials section, then complete the Practices and Tests in the Activities section. You can check your scores by clicking on the Gradebook tab.

CHAPTER 3

A Word about Words

To comprehend what you read you need to understand what the words mean, which makes vocabulary development an important part of a reading program. This text presents ten words per reading to increase your vocabulary. This chapter covers three ways to expand your vocabulary:

- Context Clues: When you read, you want to be aware of possible hints around an unknown word that can help you to understand the word. These hints are called context clues, and they come in five main types: synonym, antonym, example, definition, and general meaning. The Context Clue section provides activities to help you learn how to recognize and use these clues.

- Dictionary Use: Knowing how and when to use a dictionary can help you improve your vocabulary. The Dictionary Use section covers a variety of elements related to dictionaries, including dissecting the parts of a dictionary entry, ways to create flash cards, a reminder on the importance of multiple meanings for a word, and a discussion of denotations and connotations of words.

- Word Parts: Some words are made up of parts that have individual meanings. If you know the meaning of one or more of these parts, you can sometimes discover the meaning of an unknown word. The Word Parts section explains what word parts are and provides a list of prefixes, roots, and suffixes for you to learn as you work through the vocabulary exercises in the text.

Learning Objectives

- Recognize and use context clues.
- Dissect a dictionary entry.
- Create flash cards to learn new words.
- Appreciate that words can have multiple meanings.
- Realize the difference between denotations and connotations of words.
- Recognize word parts and use them to decode the meaning of unfamiliar words.

Expanding Your Vocabulary

Context Clues

The easiest way to boost your vocabulary is to read more. When reading look for context clues around a word you don't know. **Context** means the words surrounding a specific word. The context an unknown word is found in can give clues to the word's meaning. Context clues may come in a sentence before or after the unknown word or in the same sentence. Keep reading a passage when you encounter a word you don't know. The meaning may shortly become clear in the next few sentences or in the next paragraph. Context clues come in several forms. The following box explains five common types of context clues.

Types of Context Clues

Synonym—word that has a similar meaning to the unknown word

Antonym—word that means the opposite of the unknown word

Example—one illustration or a list of items that explains the unknown word

Definition—the writer provides the meaning of a word right after using the word (the definition may be given in parentheses, after a comma, in a footnote at the bottom of the page, or in a textbook, in a note in the margin)

General meaning—the meaning of the sentence or passage as a whole that clarifies the meaning of the unknown word

A context clue will not always be in the same sentence as the unknown word, but it can be. Use the context clues in each of the sentences below to match the word in bold to its definition. On the line after each sentence, write the type of context clue you found.

a. infrequently, irregularly   b. to speed up   c. uninviting

d. an external stimulus that promotes action   e. frighten

_____ 1. The clerk was able to **expedite** my passport application so that I could take a trip to Japan in the next two weeks. _____

_____ 2. Though the parking lots were busy, the textbooks huge, and I was without one friend, I didn't let the new experiences associated with college **intimidate** me. _____

_____ 3. The desert landscape was so **desolate** that I could not imagine spending the night in this bleak environment. _____

_____ 4. Unlike my brother who trains regularly, I tend to exercise **sporadically**. _____

_____ 5. Money is often the **incentive**, external stimulus, that motivates people to participate in demanding sporting events. _____

Now try finding clues in a larger context. In the following paragraph the four words in bold act as unfamiliar words. For each word there is a context clue to help you work out the meaning. Highlight or circle the context clues you find, and then read the explanation of the clues to see if you used the same methods to discover each word's meaning.

Example

After a tough day at work, the **incessant** noise from my son's room was giving me a headache. First, he played his music too loud, and when I admonished him about that, I was treated to the sounds of screeching cars from his favorite computer game. After I again scolded him for being too noisy, he made an effort to be quiet. With his birthday coming up, he realized it would be **prudent** on his part not to annoy me if he wanted any presents. I **advocated** for quiet reading time, but after ten minutes of reading, my son opposed that idea. The only solution he could see was going to a friend's house whose parents didn't have headaches.

Explanation

Incessant means "nonstop" and the music from the room and the sound effects from the computer game are examples of the constant noise. Admonished means "scolded," and scolded is used as a synonym in the sentence that follows the use of admonished. The definition of prudent as "wise" can be determined from the general meaning of the sentence where it would be wise of the son to be quiet if he wants any birthday presents. To understand what advocated means, one needs to notice the contrast between opposed and advocated. Knowing that opposed means "against," the contrast makes it clear that advocated means "in favor of" and that opposed is an antonym clue.

Find the context clues in the following paragraphs for the words in bold.

1. This paragraph uses synonym and antonym clues. Highlight or underline any synonyms or antonyms you find for the words in bold. Then, on the lines that follow the paragraph, write the synonym or a word that is opposite the antonym as your definition of the word.

At my great-aunt's **behest** I appeared at her house on Saturday morning. When she makes a command, everyone in the family obeys. I tried not to show my **angst** at being called before her. I summoned all of my courage and smiled when she walked into the living room. She said she wanted my gardening advice since I run a large nursery. I was **appalled** when she showed me a small garden filled with blue and green roses. The only aspect that delighted me was spying beautiful, natural tulips further away in the garden. I told her that I thought the flowers an interesting experiment, but that I much prefer their natural hues. I was sure she was going to **oust** me for my choice, but she did not eject me. Instead, she nodded and said, "I agree. Please join me for lunch."

Your Definition

1. behest _____

2. angst _____

3. appalled _____

4. oust _____

2. This paragraph uses example, definition, and general meaning clues. Highlight or underline any context clues you find. Then use the clues to write your own definitions on the lines next to the words that follow the paragraph. Identify the type of context clue you found for each word.

The office **conundrum** (problem) is what to do about Robert. He is a <u>produc-tive</u> employee, but he is also terribly **perverse**. If everyone else on the team wants to work on a project in the morning, he says he isn't available until the afternoon. If everyone agrees on a photograph to use in an ad campaign, he finds a problem with it. People now **spurn** working with him. The situation has become **rampant**. It isn't only colleagues on his floor, but those four floors above and below who aren't happy with him. Even people who telecommute and who have never met him in person don't want anything to do with him.

Your Definition and Type of Context Clue

1. conundrum _____

2. perverse _____

3. spurn _____

4. rampant _____

3.　　This paragraph uses all five types of context clues: synonym, antonym, example, definition, and general meaning. Highlight or underline any context clues you find. Then use the clues to write your own definitions on the lines next to the words that follow the paragraph. Identify the type of context clue you found for each word.

> Emma appeared to be an excellent student. Her professors thought she took **copious** notes. She was writing continuously during lectures, and her notebook was bursting with papers. From her many hours in the library, it was assumed that she had decided to **delve** even further into the subjects she was studying. Instead it was all a **façade**, a misleading appearance. Sometimes wisdom comes at a price, and Emma realized the **folly** of her inattention as her midterms were returned with poor grades. She vowed to **garner** more respect from her professors and from herself. To earn this respect, she started a study group for each of her classes, she took real notes instead of writing love letters, and she ditched the fashion magazines in the library for her textbooks.

Your Definition and Type of Context Clue

1. copious _____

2. delve _____

3. façade _____

4. folly _____

5. garner _____

Find the context clues in the following paragraphs for the words in bold. The paragraphs may contain any of the five types of context clues: synonym, antonym, example, definition, and general meaning. Highlight or underline any context clues

you find. Then use the clues to write your own definitions on the lines next to the words that follow the paragraph. Identify the type of context clue you found for each word.

1. We were enjoying a lovely meal on the restaurant's patio. It was wonderful to be eating **alfresco** now that the weather was warming up. Suddenly a jackhammer started across the street, which set off the alarms on at least three cars nearby. The **clamor** quickly disrupted the pleasant evening we had been enjoying. The **decorum** of the diners also disappeared. The rudeness of several diners was shocking to see. They yelled and even swore at the wait staff to do something. One waiter crossed the street to speak to the man with the jackhammer. I don't know what he said, but the man stopped his work. The restaurant managed to **placate** its diners with an offer of a free dessert. By the time we left, everyone seemed calm and likely to return.

    Your Definition and Type of Context Clue

    1. alfresco _____

    2. clamor _____

    3. decorum _____

    4. placate _____

2. The blue whale, the largest mammal on Earth, is an endangered animal. Blue whales are usually 80 to 100 feet long and weigh more than 100 tons. They eat about 8,000 pounds of **krill**[1] a day. Blue whales can be found in every ocean on the planet. Before heavy whaling began, the estimated population of blue whales was 350,000. About 99 percent of blue whales were killed during the whaling era. In 1966, the International Whaling Commission put a **moratorium** on hunting blue whales. Today estimates put the blue-whale population somewhere between 5,000 and 12,000. Blue whales, however, continue to face several **perils**. Increases in ocean noise levels could **impede** their ability to communicate using low-frequency signals, and global warming may disturb their migration patterns and alter their food supplies.

    _____
    [1] a shrimplike animal

    Your Definition and Type of Context Clue

    1. krill _____

    2. moratorium _____

    3. perils _____

    4. impede _____

Dictionary Use

Because there will not always be context clues to help you, at times you will need to refer to a dictionary for help. Below are suggestions of how to mark words when you are reading so that you don't have to stop and look up an unknown word as soon as you encounter it, which can make reading tiresome.

Methods of Marking Words

- Write the unfamiliar word and its page number on a piece of paper you keep in the book.

- Rip a sheet of paper into small pieces (or use sticky notes) and put the pieces between the pages where the words you don't know are located. If you have a pen, write the words on the slips of paper.

- Circle the words you don't know and flip through the book later to find them (use this method only if you own the book).

- Dog-ear the book (turn down the corner) on the page where the word you don't know is located (use this method only if you own the book).

- Repeat the word and page number to yourself a few times. Connect the page number to a significant date to help you remember it (use this method if you don't have a pen or paper handy).

When you finish reading, look up the words you marked in a dictionary. Write down the definition to help you remember it. The last two methods work best if you don't read many pages before looking up the words, or if there are just a few words you need to look up. If you come across a word you don't know and not understanding it keeps you from comprehending the passage, stop and look the word up right away.

Dictionary Entries

Becoming familiar with dictionary entries will make using a dictionary more pleasant. The words in a dictionary are arranged alphabetically. The words on a given page are signaled by **guide words** at the top of the page (see sample on page 78). If the word you are looking for comes alphabetically between these two words then your word is on that page. When using online dictionaries, you will simply type in the word you are looking for, so guide words will not be important, but the other features of an entry remain the same.

ACTIVITY 4

Use the sample guide words to decide on which page each of the six words would be found. Write the page number next to the entry word.

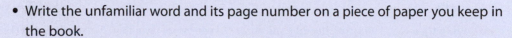

Page	Guide Words	Example: __60__ bingo
60	bin/birth	_____ 1. bite
61	birthday/blackboard	_____ 2. birch

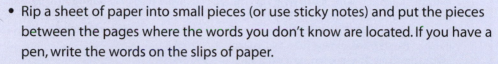

290	jam/ jazz	_____ 3. reminder
292	jewel/jog	_____ 4. jasmine
475	relative/remark	_____ 5. reliable
476	remarkable/renew	_____ 6. job

1436 → Guide words

wing tip • wintry

Entry →

wing tip n (ca. 1908) **1a** : the edge or outer margin of a bird's wing **b** usu **wingtip** : the outer end of an airplane wing **2** : a toe cap having a point that extends back toward the throat of the shoe and curving sides that extend toward the shank **3** : a shoe having a wing tip

¹wink \'wiŋk\ vb [ME, fr. OE wincian; akin to OHG winchan to stagger, wink and perh. to L vacillare to sway, Skt vañcati he goes crookedly] vi (bef. 12c) **1** : to shut one eye briefly as a signal or in teasing **2** : to close and open the eyelids quickly **3** : to avoid seeing or noting something — usu. used with at **4** : to gleam or flash intermittently: TWINKLE <her glasses ~ing in the sunlight — Harper Lee> **5 a** : to come to an end — usu. used with out **b** : to stop shining — usu. used with out **6** : to signal a message with a light ~ vt **1** : to cause to open and shut **2** : to affect or influence by or as if by blinking the eyes

²wink n (14c) **1** : a brief period of sleep : NAP <catching a ~> **2 a** : a hint or sign given by winking **b** : an act of winking **3** : the time of a wink: INSTANT <quick as a ~> **4** : a flicker of the eyelids: BLINK

wink·er \'wiŋ-kər\ n (1549) **1** : one that winks **2** : a horse's blinder

¹win·kle \'wiŋ-kəl\ n [by shortening] (1585) : ²PERIWINKLE

²winkle vi win·kled; win·kling \-k(ə-)liŋ\ [freq. of wink] (1791): TWINKLE

³winkle vt win·kled; win·kling \-k(ə-)liŋ\ [¹winkle; fr. the process of extracting a winkle from its shell] (1918) **1** chiefly Brit : to displace, remove, or evict from a position — usu. used with out **2** chiefly Brit : to obtain or draw out by effort — usu. used with out <no attempt to ~ out why they do it — Joan Bakewell>

win·ner\ 'wi-nər\ n (14c) : one that wins: as **a** : one that is successful esp. through praise-worthy ability and hard work **b** : a victor esp. in games and sports **c** : one that wins admiration **d** : a shot in a court game that is not returned and that scores for the player making it

win·ter·ize \'win-tə-,rīz\ vt -ized ; -iz·ing (1934) : to make ready for winter or winter use and esp. resistant or proof against winter weather <~ a car> — **win·ter·i·za·tion** \,win-tə-rə-'zā-shən\ n

win·ter—kill \'win-tər-,kil\ vt (ca. 1806) : to kill (as a plant) by exposure to winter conditions ~ vi : to die as a result of exposure to winter conditions — **winterkill** n

win·ter·ly \'win-tər-lē\ adj (1559) : of, relating to, or occurring in winter : WINTRY

winter melon n (ca. 1900) **1** : any of several muskmelons (as a casaba or honeydew melon) that are fruits of a cultivated vine (Cucumis melo indorus) **2** : a large white-fleshed melon that is the fruit of an Asian vine (Benincasa hispida) and is used esp. in Chinese cooking

winter quarters n pl but sing or pl in constr (1641) : a winter residence or station (as of a military unit or a circus)

winter savory n (1597) : a perennial European mint (Satureja montana) with leaves used for seasoning — compare SUMMER SAVORY

winter squash n (1775) : any of various hard-shelled squashes that belong to cultivars derived from several species (esp. Cucurbita maxima, C. moschata, and C. pepo) and that can be stored for several months

win·ter·tide \'win-tər-,tīd\ n (bef. 12c) : WINTERTIME

win·ter·time \-,tīm\n (14c) : the season of winter

win through vi (1644) : to survive difficulties and reach a desired or satisfactory end <win through to a better life beyond — B. F. Reilly>

win·tle \'wi-nᵊl,'win-tᵊl\ vi win·tled; win·tling \'win(t)-liŋ; 'wi-nᵊl-iŋ, 'win-tᵊl-\ [perh. fr. D dial. windtelen to reel] (1786) **1** Scot : STAGGER, REEL **2** Scot : WRIGGLE

win·try \'win-trē\ also **win·tery** \'win-t(ə-)rē\ adj win·tri·er; -est (bef. 12c) **1** : of, relating to, or characteristic of winter **2 a** : weathered by or as if by winter : AGED, HOARY **b** : CHEERLESS, CHILLING <a ~ greeting> — **win·tri·ness** \'win-trē-nəs\ n

Source: By permission, From *Merriam-Webster's Collegiate Dictionary*, Eleventh Edition © 2010 by Merriam-Webster, Incorporated (www.Merriam-Webster.com).

Dictionary entries generally contain the following information:

- **Pronunciation:** Symbols show how a word should be spoken, including how the word is divided into syllables and where the stress should be placed in a word. Every dictionary has a pronunciation method, and a pronunciation key or guide is usually found in the front pages, with a partial key at the bottom or top of each page. The differences in the pronunciation systems used by dictionaries are usually minimal.
- **Part of speech:** The part of speech is usually abbreviated, such as *n.* for noun, *v.* for verb, and *adj.* for adjective. A key to these abbreviations and others is usually found in the front of the dictionary.
- **Definition:** Usually the most common meaning is listed first followed by other meanings. Read each definition to see which one best fits the context of the word in what you are reading.
- **Example of the word in a sentence:** There may be a sentence, usually in italics, that follows each meaning to give you an idea of how the word is used.
- **Synonyms and antonyms:** *Synonyms* are words with similar meanings, and *antonyms* are words with opposite meanings. Reading the synonyms and antonyms can help you better understand how the word relates to other words, and a list of synonyms can help you when you are using the same word too often in what you are writing. You should also consider owning a **thesaurus**, a book that lists synonyms and antonyms.
- **Etymology:** The etymology is the history of a word. This section usually includes the language or languages the word came from, and may break the word into word parts. The etymology section may also include the year when the word was first coined or used in a specific way, such as having a scientific meaning. Words are created in many ways, though they often evolve from a foreign language, especially ancient Greek and Latin. Words can also come from a person's name, a place, or be made up. For example, when a man is called a *scrooge* because he is stingy, the word comes from the character Ebenezer Scrooge in *A Christmas Carol* by Charles Dickens. The tangerine gets its name from Tangier, Morocco, the port from which the fruit was first imported to Europe. And brunch (the meal that serves as both breakfast and lunch) was created by combining the *br* from breakfast with the *unch* from lunch. Learning the history of a word can sometimes help you remember its meaning.
- **Spelling of different forms of the word:** These other forms may include unusual plurals (for example, mouse and mice) and verb tenses, especially irregular forms (for example, go and went).

Look at the following entry to see each part identified.

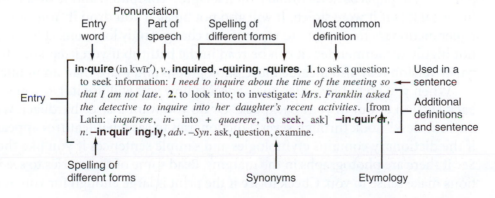

ACTIVITY 5

Practice identifying the parts of a dictionary entry by labeling the parts of the following entry.

① ② ③ ④ ⑤

af·fa·ble (af′ ə bəl), *adj.*, **af′fa·bil′i·ty**, *n.* **af′fa·bly**, *adv.* **1.** easy to speak to; approachable; friendly: *Gerry has several friends because he is so affable.* **⑥** **⑦** **2.** pleasant; gentle: *Rabbits are generally affable animals.* [from Latin *affābilis*, can be easily spoken to; from *affārī*, to speak to: *ad-* to + *fārī*, to **⑧** speak] *—Syn.* good-natured, agreeable, amiable.

⑨

1. _____   6. _____

2. _____   7. _____

3. _____   8. _____

4. _____   9. _____

5. _____

Online Dictionaries versus Paper Dictionaries

You may be unsure whether it is best to use an online dictionary or a paper version. The best choice is to have both available. Sometimes you will find an online dictionary more useful, while other times a paper version will best provide you with the information you need.

A major benefit of an online dictionary is that you can hear the pronunciation of a word. It can be very helpful to hear the word spoken if you are uncertain of the meaning of the pronunciation symbols or if the word seems quite foreign to you. Another benefit of some online dictionaries, such as dictionary.com, is that you get several dictionaries in one place. It can be helpful to compare definitions between dictionaries to find the meaning that is most clear to you. You can also check links to a thesaurus and word part definitions easily at online sites. Sometimes online dictionaries give fuller etymologies than paperback versions do. You can also subscribe to a word-of-the-day feature at some online dictionary sites to get an e-mail with the definition of a word delivered to your inbox each day to further increase your vocabulary. Possible online sites to consider include dictionary.com and Merriam-Webster's site at m-w.com.

The major benefit of a paper dictionary is that it works even if the power goes out or a power source isn't readily available. Another benefit is that it is still easier to transport a small paperback dictionary than a laptop computer, and it would not be such a financial loss if it were stolen. It will also not break if you drop it. You can easily carry a paper dictionary from room to room if you change study locations at home and, though not highly recommended, it can be read in the bathtub if you keep your fingers dry. A paper version may also include more photographs and maps than an online dictionary.

When you go to buy a dictionary, decide how you will use it. Do you want a paperback version to put in your backpack? Or do you want a large hardback version to put on your desk? Look through several dictionaries to see what features appeal to you. See if the dictionary contains etymologies and sample sentences if you like those features. See if there are photographs in the margins. Read some of the entries to see if the definitions make sense to you. Check to see if the print is large enough for you to read easily.

Also note that several disciplines have specialized dictionaries with meanings that apply to those fields, such as law or medicine, and you may need to get one of these at some point in your college career. There are also bilingual dictionaries, such as French/English or Spanish/English, that can be helpful for school or travel. Take time in picking out your dictionary because a good dictionary will be a friend for years to come. A few dictionaries to consider are *Merriam-Webster's Collegiate Dictionary*, *The American Heritage Dictionary*, *The Random House College Dictionary,* and *The Oxford Dictionary.*

In general, when you are reading, try to use context clues to discover the meaning of a word, but if you are still in doubt, don't hesitate to refer to a dictionary, online or paper, for the exact definition. And remember that dictionaries contain more than definitions and are an essential reference source for every student.

Flash Cards

When you encounter a word that you really want to remember the meaning of, it is helpful to write down the meaning of the word. You can do this in the margins of your textbook, in your notes, or, even better, by making flash cards. Just the process of making the flash cards will help you remember new words. This technique is especially valuable to use when you are learning vocabulary for a class. You will want to know the meanings of these words for tests, to use in papers you will write for the class, and to be able to apply them in class discussions. Index cards work well as flash cards. Which of the elements you use below on your card will depend on the word and your preferred learning methods. Try them all and see what works best for you.

- **Write the word on the front of the card.** You may also want to write the pronunciation of the word on the front so you know how to say the word.
- **On the back of the card put the definition.** Use a definition that makes sense to you, and keep the definition fairly simple.
- **Include the part of speech.** Use an abbreviation for the part of speech, such as *v.* for verb. Having the part of speech will help when you write your own sentence using the word.
- **Put the word in a sentence.** Use a sentence from the reading material where you encountered the word. Seeing the word in context can help you remember how the word is used. It also helps to create your own sentence that uses the word. When writing your own sentence, make it personal. Include yourself, people you know, or your town in your sentence to relate the word to your life.
- **Draw the word** if you are a visual learner. Your drawing doesn't have to be fancy. It is just a way to jog your memory.
- **Use a mnemonic device.** A mnemonic device is a method to help your memory, such as a formula, rhyme, or clue. For example, "In 1492, Columbus sailed the ocean blue" is a rhyme used to remember when an event took place. You can remember the difference in spellings for desert and dessert by noting that dessert is spelled "ss" and that you would like a <u>s</u>econd (with an "s") helping of dessert.
- **Circle any word parts** you find in a word, and write the meaning of the word part next to it. For example, a benefit is something that promotes good.

good ←

Do whatever it takes to make the cards meaningful for you. Then make the time to study your cards a little every day. Also enlist a friend to help you study the cards. Have the person hold up each card while you give the definition and use the word in a

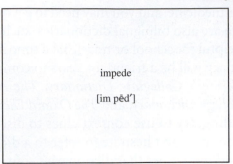

impede

[im pēd']

v. to block; to hinder; to slow or delay

I was warned that the fog could impede my drive, and it did slow me by two hours.

sentence. Don't quit until you are confident that you know the meaning of each word. Making flash cards can be a fun and easy way to learn new vocabulary.

Multiple Meanings

Many words have more than one meaning. This text uses the meaning that applies to how the word is used in the reading, but when you see the same word used in a way that does not fit the meaning you know, use context clues or check a dictionary to see if it has another meaning. For some words one meaning is used more often than others, but for other words two or three of their meanings are used quite often. For example, a club is "a heavy stick, especially one used as a weapon," "a group of people who meet periodically to share an interest in the same topic," and "a playing card suit designated by a black trefoil." All three meanings for club are frequently used. However, among the meanings for *exchange* as a noun, most people would know "giving of one thing and receiving another in its place" and "a short conversation," but the meaning of "a center where telephone connections are made" is rarely heard anymore. Even a short and seemingly simple word may have many meanings. *Merriam-Webster's Collegiate Dictionary* lists 24 meanings for the word *so*. As a reader, your job is to be aware of and prepared for the challenges and surprises that multiple meanings offer.

ACTIVITY 6

Pick the number of the definition that best fits the use of the word *cross* in each sentence. Make sure to indicate whether it is the noun, verb, or adjective definition.

Cross: *n.* 1. Any of a range of symbolic or decorative figures or structures in the form of a cross. 2. A symbol of several pre-Christian religions composed of two crossed lines. 3. Any trial or frustration. 4. A combination of the traits of two things. 5. *Biology.* A plant or animal produced by crossbreeding. *v.* 1. To pass from one side to the other. 2. To pass through or over; to intersect. 3. To put a line across. 4. To lay across or over. 5. To encounter in passing. 6. *Informal.* To oppose or interfere with. 7. *Biology.* To crossbreed. *adj.* 1. Passing crosswise; intersecting. 2. Contrary or opposing. 3. Irritated; annoyed. 4. Crossbred; hybrid.

1. After not seeing each other for five years, Vanessa and I crossed paths twice last week: at the county fair and at the shopping mall. _____

2. A mule is a cross between a male ass and a female horse._____

3. It isn't supposed to be good for one's legs to cross them._____

4. The cross on the hill has been there for one hundred years. The earliest settlers put it there after they survived their first winter in the valley._____

5. I am cross with Ryan because he forgot to pick me up at the train station and I had to call a taxi._____

Denotations and Connotations

It is important to realize that words have two kinds of meanings because careful writers use both kinds. A **denotation** is "the explicit or direct meaning of a word." This is the kind of definition you would find in the dictionary. A **connotation** is "the suggestive or associative meaning of a word beyond its literal definition." This is the emotional response a person has to a word. A mnemonic device for remembering the difference between the two is that denotation begins with a "d," and it is the dictionary or direct meaning, both beginning with a "d."

As a careful reader, you want to make sure you understand a writer's ideas by recognizing how words are used. When you write, you also want to make sure you are aware of the connotations of a word, so you can clearly express your ideas. Some connotations are personal reactions. For example, *elderly* means "rather old; past middle age." But the connotation of elderly tends to change with one's age. For a teenager, a person in his or her thirties could be elderly; for a 30-year-old, it becomes someone over 50; and for a 60-year-old, elderly may mean someone in his or her eighties. Other connotations have broader emotional responses. If you wanted to describe a thin person you could use the words *slim* or *bony*. What do you picture for each word? Talk to your classmates about their images. Are they similar?

Some words have positive connotations that most people feel good about (*forceful*) and other words have negative connotations that turn people off (*bossy*), though they may be describing the same trait in a person: The babysitter was forceful when she told the children it was eight o'clock and time for bed. The babysitter was bossy when she told the children it was eight o'clock and time for bed. Not all words have strong connotations. Most people don't get too excited when they read the word *desk*. But other words can bring out strong feelings. Do you see a person as being economical or stingy when you read the word *thrifty*? As you learn new words, think about their denotations and connotations and how those differences in meanings apply to the writer's intentions.

For each word below, put down whether your reaction to the word is positive, negative, or neutral. Once you have made your choices, compare your list with those of a few of your classmates. Were your reactions the same or different for most of the words? What do you think influenced your choices for each word?

1. dog _____

2. prank _____

3. eager _____

4. absolute _____

5. spinach _____

6. blond _____

7. fiery _____

8. plump _____

9. studying _____

10. rainy _____

11. desert _____

12. chocolate _____

Do you think the photograph of the desert influenced your choice in any way?

Word Parts

Some words are made up of parts that have individual meanings. If you know the meaning of one or more of these parts, you may be able to figure out the meaning of an unknown word. For example, you know what a bicycle is. Now someone tells you about a new invention called a tricycle. You know that *tri* means "three." You can, therefore, infer that a tricycle has three wheels. There are hundreds of word parts in existence. Most word parts come from ancient Greek and Latin. Word parts come in three forms:

prefix: a word part added to the beginning of a word that changes the meaning of the root

root: a word's basic part with its essential meaning

suffix: a word part added to the end of a word; indicates the part of speech

Sometimes it is easy to see the connection between a word part and a word's meaning. For example, "cis" means "to cut." Scissors are used for cutting, and the word contains "cis" within it. For other words, however, it isn't always clear how the word part reflects the meaning. In these cases, the word may have changed meaning over time so that the original word part doesn't convey the same meaning, or the connection is still there but the word's etymology needs to be reviewed to clearly see the connection. For example, genuine means "real or true." It comes from the Latin *genuinus*, which means "natural or native." The root is *gignere*, which means "bring into being, birth." It probably still isn't clear how birth comes to mean real. Digging further into the word's etymology, the word may come from the root *genu-*, which means "knee." An ancient custom had a father place a baby on his knee to demonstrate that he believed the child was his, or, in other words, his true child or genuine. Now the connection with the word part is clear, but it would not be obvious without some research. For these reasons, knowning the meaning of a word part won't always be helpful, but as a whole, it is good to learn a few common word parts to make understanding new words easier.

Prefixes and roots are the most helpful to learn of the three forms, and they will be focused on in the Word Part sections in each reading. Below are the word parts that you will be learning throughout this text. You can always refer back to these pages if you need to review the meaning of a word part used in any of the Vocabulary lessons.

Prefixes

Word part	Meaning	Sample word with definition
anti-	against	antiwar: against war
bene-	good	beneficial: for the good
bi-	two	bicycle: a vehicle with two wheels
bio-	life	biology: the study of life
col-, com-, con-	with, together	collaborate: work with others; combine: put together; confide: share a secret with
de-	down, from, away,	depart: to go away
dis-	not, opposite, apart, away from	disagree: not feel the same way
epi-	upon	epidermis: upon the skin, outer layer of skin
equ-	equal	equidistant: equal distance from
e-, ex-	out, former	exhale: breathe out; ex-wife: former wife
il-, im-, in-, ir-	not	illiterate: not able to read; impossible: not doable; invisible: not observable; irresponsible: not dependable
im-, in-	in, into, on	immerse: to get into; inhale: breathe in
inter-	among, between	international: between nations
mal-	bad	malfunction: bad performance
mono-	one	monarchy: rule by one person
pan-	all, everywhere	panorama: a wide view over all
para-	almost, beyond, beside	paraphrase: almost like the original statement
pre-	before	prefix: attached before the root word
sub-	under, below, nearly	submarine: ship that travels underwater
sym-, syn-	with, together	sympathize: feel together; synonym: sharing a meaning with another word
trans-	across	transport: carry across
un-	not	unfair: not just

Roots

Word part	Meaning	Sample word with definition
-apt-, -ept-	skill, ability	adapt: ability to change as needed; adept: skilled
-ced-, -ceed-, -cess-	go, yield	concede: to yield; proceed: go forward; access: able to go in or toward

(continued)

Roots (*continued*)

Word part	Meaning	Sample word with definition
-chron-	time	chronological: in time order
-cis-	cut	scissors: item used to cut paper or other material
-clar-	clear	clarity: clearness
-cred-	believe, trust	credible: believable
-dem-	people	democracy: rule by the people
-dic-, -dict-	to say, to tell, to use words	diction: a speaker's or writer's use of words; predict: to tell before
-fac-, -fic-	make, do	factory: a place that makes things; efficient: do well
-grad-, -gress-	step, go	gradual: step by step; progress: go forward
-graph-	write	autograph: write one's own name
-lect-	to select, to choose	elect: to choose someone by voting
-lev-	lift, light, rise	elevator: conveyance used to lift one in a building
-mis-, -mit-	send	mission: job one is sent on; transmit: to send across
-mort-	death	mortuary: where the dead are taken before burial
-opt-	best	optimist: one who looks at the best view
-pas-, -pat-, -path-	feeling, disease	passion: a strong feeling; pathology: study of diseases
-pen-	hang, weigh, pay	suspend: to hang down
-phil-	love	philanthropy: love of people
-pon-, -pos-	to put, to place	proponent: to put forward an idea; deposit: to put in
-spec-	see, look	inspect: look into
-tract-	pull, drag	extract: to pull out
-trib-	give	contribute: to give along with others
-ven-	come, move toward	convene: come together
-vi-	life	vivid: filled with life, bright
-vid-, -vis-	see	video: images one can see; visible: able to see
-vers-, -vert-	turn	reverse: turn back; avert: to turn away
-voc-, -vok-	voice, call	vocal: use one's voice; revoke: call back

Suffixes

Word part (with part of speech in parentheses)	Meaning	Sample word with definition
-able, -ible (*adj.*)	capable of, is, can be	comfortable: capable of being at ease; possible: can be done
-al (*adj.*)	of or relating to	natural: relating to nature

-ate (*v.*)	to make	liberate: to make free
-cide (*n.*)	killing	homicide: killing of a person
-er, -or (*n.*)	one who, person who	teacher: one who teaches; actor: person who acts
-ic (*adj.*)	relating to	dramatic: relating to drama
-ish (*adj.*)	near, relating or similar to	reddish: similar to red
-ism (*n.*)	action, practice, theory	patriotism: the practice of loving one's country
-ist (*n.*)	a person who	manicurist: a person who does hands and nails
-ive (*adj.*)	tending or inclined to	positive: inclined to think good thoughts
-ize (*v.*)	to make	standardize: to make the same
-ology (*n.*)	study or science of	biology: study of life
-phobia (*n.*)	fear of	claustrophobia: fear of small spaces
-y (*adj.*)	being, having	sunny: being filled with sun

Several styles of word part exercises follow each reading. Below are activities using two of the types to give you some initial practice in using a few of the word parts above.

ACTIVITY 8

Fill in the missing word part from the list below, and highlight or circle the meaning of the word part found in each question.

> de   con   chron   dict   phobia

1. My friend understands what it means to keep information _____ fidential. She would never share anything private I tell her with anyone else.

2. I like it when my history book uses _____ ological order to describe an event. I find it easier to understand what happened when the time frame for each action is clearly presented.

3. Cara didn't want to see the new penguin exhibit at the zoo because she suffers from ornitho _____. Her fear of birds comes from an incident in her childhood when she was bitten by a goose.

4. Our water sources are being _____ pleted. The drought has taken away more than half of the water that had been stored in our reservoirs.

5. To tell how to correctly use a word, it helps to refer to a _____ ionary.

ACTIVITY 9

Finish the sentences with the meaning of each word part. The word part is underlined to help you make the connection.

| study of | feelings | out | come | a person who |

1. I tried to <u>e</u>vade the trash can rolling toward my car, but I could not get _____out_____ of the way quick enough.

2. I expressed my _____ of sym<u>path</u>y for Tara's failing her driver's test again by sending her a funny card to cheer her up.

3. I am excited about traveling to Argentina. I know it is going to be an ad<u>ven</u>ture _____ true to see the country where my great-grandparents were born.

4. A column<u>ist</u> is _____ regularly writes an article for a newspaper or magazine.

5. I am interested in taking a zo<u>ology</u> class. I think the _____ animals is a fascinating subject.

A Strong Vocabulary

The more you read, the easier it will be to find context clues (most of the time you won't even realize you are using them), and the bigger your vocabulary will grow, which will make reading more enjoyable. Work through the vocabulary exercises after the readings to develop your context-clue hunting skills and to decide when you need to use a dictionary. Also pay attention to word parts as you encounter them, and use them to help you decipher unfamiliar words. Learning new vocabulary can be fun, and having a well-developed vocabulary will lead to better reading skills for all the reading situations you will face in life.

myreadinglab PEARSON **Objectives Check**

To check your progress in meeting chapter objectives, log in to www.myreadinglab.com, click on the Study Plan tab, and then on the Reading Skills tab. Choose Vocabulary from the list of subtopics. Read and view the resources in the Review Materials section, then complete the Practices and Tests in the Activities section. You can check your scores by clicking on the Gradebook tab.

CHAPTER 4

What could make an everyday drink special?

Everyday Life

Finding the Special in the Ordinary

Skill: Main Ideas

Have you ever stopped to think about your daily activities and what makes them special? Can drinking coffee, going to school, or playing video games be topics worth reading or writing about? Examining areas that we tend to take for granted can help us better appreciate those aspects of our lives. Learning more about an item or an event often allows us to gain respect for or further interest in the subject.

Looking for what is special in our everyday lives is similar to looking for the main idea. You need to pay attention to the details to appreciate the bigger picture. This chapter focuses on how to determine the writer's point about the subject: the main idea. You will learn how to find the topic of a reading, how to locate topic sentences, how to use them to piece together the main idea, and how to use a thesis statement or an implied main idea to show that you understand the point the writer wants to convey. While reading the following four articles or essays, textbook excerpt, and short story, think about how everyday items and events can have special meaning if we take the time to look and how understanding the main idea of a reading is the first step in appreciating a piece of writing.

- Find the topic of a reading.
- Locate topic sentences.
- Use topic sentences to piece together the main idea.
- Use a thesis statement or an implied main idea to show that you understand the writer's point.

Main Ideas

The **main idea** is the writer's point about a topic. It is the message the writer wants to convey to his or her readers. To understand a reading, it is essential to establish the main idea. In order to find the main idea, you need to be able to recognize the topic of the reading and topic sentences.

The Topic

Determine the topic of the reading. The **topic** is what the reading is about in general. For instance, the topic of a reading could be college, coffee, or childhood.

Example

Read the following paragraph and decide what the paragraph is generally about.
Test anxiety is a major problem for some people, but there are strategies that can help them deal with their fears. First, getting a good night's sleep and eating a healthy meal before a test are important. It also helps shortly before a test to do some form of relaxing exercise, such as taking a walk or stretching. Visualizing a peaceful situation (for example, lounging on the beach) before entering the testing environment can put people at ease. Finally, it is vital to think positively about the outcome of the test and release any negative thoughts. By following a few simple procedures, most people can free themselves from test anxiety.

The topic is ___test anxiety___. The paragraph explains ways to control test anxiety.

Find the topic for the following paragraphs.

1. I don't know which I like more: city or country life. I enjoy the hustle and bustle of the city. I like being able to go to the theater and try new restaurants. There seems to be something new happening every weekend in a big city. On the other hand, country life provides a sense of quiet and a time to commune with nature. I enjoy going for a walk and seeing cows, horses, and sheep in the pastures. I like knowing most of the people in a small town and stopping to talk to them when I go shopping. I grew up in a small town and had a fun time there, but I was still excited about moving to a big

city. Now that I live in a large city, I love it, but I also miss the charms of the country. Maybe someday I can live part-time in both environments.

The topic is <u>City life vs. Country life.</u>

2. Managing emotions does not mean suppressing them, any more than it means giving free rein to every feeling and impulse. As Goleman (1995) put it, "The goal is balance, not emotional suppression: every feeling has its value and significance. A life without passion would be a dull wasteland of neutrality, cut off and isolated from the richness of life itself" (p. 56). Thus, to manage emotions is to express them in an appropriate manner and not let them get out of control. For example, if not tempered with reason, uncontrolled anger can lead to rage and violence. People high in emotional intelligence have learned how to regulate their moods and not let anger, boredom, or depression ruin their day (or their lives). You manage your emotions when you do something to cheer yourself up, sooth your own hurts, reassure yourself, or otherwise temper an inappropriate or out-of-control emotion.

—from Wood, Wood, and Boyd, *Mastering the World of Psychology*, p. 203

The topic is <u>manageng emotions</u>

3. *The Incredible Hulk* movie of 2008 did an excellent job of presenting the Hulk's story. What made this film so good were the special effects, the humor, and the acting. Often portrayals of the Hulk make him look like a huge, silly green man. This movie did a great job of getting the Hulk's imposing size right without making him look ridiculous. The movie was also effective in showing Bruce Banner's transformation in a frightening way. The movie handled humor well with cameo appearances by former Hulk Lou Ferrigno and Hulk co-creator Stan Lee. There was also a nice tribute to the deceased Bill Bixby, another former Hulk. The acting was superb by all involved in the film. Edward Norton was convincing as Bruce Banner searching to rid himself of his Hulk personality, and his later acceptance of what he had to do. Tim Roth's portrayal of Emil Blonsky, the soldier who willingly doses himself with gamma radiation, is so energetic that the viewer truly feels his desire for strength and power.

The topic is <u>the incediable halk movie</u>

Topic Sentences

Establish the point of each paragraph, using topic sentences if provided, to uncover the main idea. In one essay, the writer might want to get the point across that college demands are easier to deal with if you organize your life at the beginning of the semester. Another writer might also deal with the topic of college, but have a different point to convey, such as college is especially stressful for many students today due to the increased pressures of working part-time and family commitments. To determine the writer's main idea read each paragraph and decide what point the writer is making in that paragraph.

Sometimes there is a **topic sentence** in a paragraph that explains the main idea of the paragraph. The topic sentence can be anywhere in a paragraph, but it is often the first or second sentence. Sometimes there are two topic sentences in a paragraph. The writer may start with a topic sentence and add another topic sentence at the end of the paragraph to clarify or emphasize the main idea of the paragraph. If there isn't a topic sentence, use the details in the paragraph to decide what point the paragraph is making, and express that point in your own words.

Example

Read the paragraph below, and find the topic sentence.

What are you going to do this weekend?[1] For many people their weekend activities tend to be too predictable.[2] There are several ways to add variety to your weekends.[3] Many cities have a Web site that lists current events and attractions.[4] Type in the name of your city and see what you find.[5] You may discover a museum that you have never been to; see what it is like.[6] You may find a map with a guided walk in a part of town you have never explored.[7] If there is an annual event you have never attended, give it a try.[8] You can also refer to your local newspaper.[9] Many newspapers have a "What's happening" section on Thursdays or Fridays telling about weekend events.[10] Also ask friends about something fun they have done in your area that you may never have thought of.[11] It is never too late to discover a new place or experience.[12]

Topic sentence(s): _*sentence 3*_ . The paragraph suggests several ways to find new things to do and what some new activities might be.

Identify the topic sentence or sentences in each paragraph below.

1. The ancients realized that they could not avoid the inevitable.[1] They made plans for how their wealth and property would be disposed.[2] You, too, cannot avoid the inevitable.[3] Face it![4] At some time, you will leave this earth.[5] Now is the time for you to determine and state legally how you want your money to be divided among your heirs.[6] Your estate can go to or be divided between your spouse, children (both biological and adopted), grandchildren, or even great-grandchildren.[7] You can leave all or a part to a friend, a niece, a nephew, or to the girl at the restaurant that smiles at you each morning when you come in for a cup of coffee and a roll.[8] You can also remember charities you supported in life and would like to continue supporting in death.[9]

    —from Konowalow, *Planning Your Future: Keys to Financial Freedom*, p. 110

    Topic sentence(s): _Sentence 6_

2. Spring is my favorite time of year.[1] The trees start to bloom in a beautiful show of pinks, whites, and yellows.[2] The air is fresh with the smell of newly mown grass.[3] The days significantly begin to grow longer and sunnier.[4] And though it might seem silly, I still get pleasure from coloring eggs and hiding them for my kids.[5] I also enjoy it when the kids hide the eggs for me and give me "hot and cold" clues.[6] After the long, cold days of winter, spring makes me feel young.[7]

Topic sentence(s): _Sentence 1_

3. The human olfactory system is capable of sensing and distinguishing 10,000 different odors.[1] But there are large individual differences in sensitivity to smells.[2] For example, perfumers and whiskey blenders can distinguish subtle variations in odors that are indistinguishable to the average person.[3] Women are generally more sensitive to odors than men are, and they are more sensitive still during ovulation.[4] Young people are more sensitive to odors than older people, and nonsmokers are more sensitive than smokers (Matlin and Foley, 1997).[5]

—from Wood, Wood, and Boyd, *Mastering the World of Psychology*, p. 73

Topic sentence(s): _Sentence 2_

4. The wells, or *cenotes,* at Chichen-Itza were important for the Mayans, and they continue to be so for today's anthropologists.[1] The wells made life at Chichen-Itza possible for the Maya.[2] The name *chichen* shows the importance of the wells.[3] *Chi* meant "mouths" in Mayan, and *chen* meant "wells."[4] The wells provided the source of water for a diverse and sophisticated society.[5] The *cenotes* also hold clues to the religious rituals of the Maya.[6] Several bodies have been found in the wells.[7] Human sacrifice was a part of Mayan religious practices.[8] Other items discovered in the *cenotes* include jewelry and dolls.[9] The Maya had many gods, and the sacrifices of young women and objects were probably done to control the anger of a rain god or pay respect to the god of maize.[10] The wells at Chichen-Itza kept the Maya alive, and they keep the culture of the Maya alive for modern anthropologists.[11]

Topic sentence(s): _Sentens 1+11_

ACTIVITY 3

Identify the topic sentence in the paragraphs below, or if the point is implied, put the main idea of the paragraph into your own words.

1. Do you treat others better than you treat yourself?[1] We often make time to take care of our kids, spouses, or other family members; do favors for friends; or help colleagues at work.[2] It is certainly noble to help others, but we also have to allow time for the activities that are important to keeping us healthy and happy.[3] For example, Marjorie wanted to get in shape by running three times a week after work; however, she agreed to take on another project that led to staying late at the office several nights a week.[4] Frank volunteered to help his brother move, but he hadn't realized that meant spending the whole weekend packing his brother's large collection of fishing magazines and wrapping his sister-in-law's miniature figurine collection piece by piece.[5] The romantic Sunday dinner he had arranged to have with his wife, who had been out of town for a week, disappeared with his generosity.[6] Sometimes one has to learn to say "no."[7]

Topic sentence: _____

_____

2.   I was $5,000 in debt.[1] I didn't know when I could reasonably expect to pay off the three credit cards I used regularly.[2] I was making car payments, and my rent just went up.[3] And the worst part was that I still headed to the mall every weekend.[4] Then my hours at work were cut 20 percent a week.[5] I didn't know what to do until a friend referred me to a class on money management at the local college.[6] We had lessons on how to be aware of our spending habits, how to cut expenses, and how to use credit wisely.[7] By the end of the fourth week of classes, I felt better about being able to control my money and my spending.[8]

Topic sentence: _____*money management*_____

_____

Thesis Statements and Implied Main Ideas

Find a thesis statement or express an implied main idea in your own words. The main idea of a work can be stated or implied. If the main idea is stated, you can look for a **thesis statement**, a sentence (or two) that clearly states the writer's position. This sentence can be anywhere in an essay. It is often found in the first or second paragraph, but it can come in a middle paragraph or in the final paragraph. You can express a stated main idea in a paper or in your notes by putting the thesis statement in quotation marks and quoting it.

Sample Thesis Statements

The following are thesis statements (or stated main ideas) that would fit in essays related to a few of the paragraphs above.

- Every season has its benefits and drawbacks, but spring especially appeals to me.
- One of the notable centers of Mayan culture was Chichen-Itza located on the Yucatan Peninsula.
- Learning to control one's money is an important life skill.

Writers, however, do not always include a thesis statement in an essay or textbook chapter. A stated main idea (or theme) is rarely found in fiction. If there is no stated main idea, then it is an **implied main idea**. An implied main idea is conveyed indirectly or suggested. You can figure out an implied main idea by taking the point of each paragraph and putting them together to reach a conclusion as to the main idea. You will need to put an implied main idea into your own words to express it in a paper, a summary, or your notes. If you reasoned correctly, the lack of a thesis statement will not hinder your ability to express the main idea.

You will have the opportunity to search for thesis statements and implied main ideas in the following readings, and questions related to finding stated or implied main ideas are included in the exercises after the readings.

Main Idea Checklist

✓ Determine the topic of the reading.

✓ Establish the point of each paragraph, using topic sentences if provided, to uncover the main idea.

✓ Find a thesis statement or express an implied main idea in your own words.

Get Time on Your Side

by Jennifer Nichols

Before You Read

1. Do you consider yourself good at time management?
2. Survey the bold headings and turn them into questions. Write two of your questions below.

   _____

   _____

   _____

3. What are two advantages to being organized and planning ahead?
4. Look at the photo and cartoon. What message(s) do they convey about human efficiency?

Jennifer Nichols is a freelance writer and a frequent contributor to *Careers and Colleges*, a magazine aimed at students about to enter college. Among the subjects she has covered for the magazine are applying to colleges, getting good grades, and developing a quality resume. The following article appeared in the March/April 2004 issue of *Careers and Colleges*.

Vocabulary Preview

Look for these words in the reading. Exercises to reinforce the learning of new vocabulary using these words follow the reading. The paragraph number where the word appears is in parentheses.

whirlwind (1)	**proverbial** (1)
prioritize (2)	**academic** (3)
rowdy (10)	**implementing** (12)
precedence (17)	**seminar** (19)
jot (22)	**mantra** (31)

The article begins on the next page.

Get Time On Your Side

1 College can be a whirlwind of deadlines and dates. But with some time management skills you don't have to scramble like the proverbial chicken with its head cut off.

Getting Started

2 Experts say that good time management is all about prioritizing. But that can be tough when you're trying to prioritize everything from classes to activities to socializing to sleep.

3 The first step is figuring out what's important to you. Dr. Edward O'Keefe, professor of psychology at Marist College in Poughkeepsie, New York, and author of *Self Management for College Students: The ABC Approach*, suggests listing your goals for college. Don't limit your goals to academic ones.

4 "You should use college to develop the rest of yourself, in addition to your academic self," says O'Keefe.

5 Seeing your goals on paper will help you determine what you feel is worth spending time on. If you want to develop your musical talents, for example, you may decide to play in the school orchestra. If you want to polish your writing skills, you may join the campus newspaper staff.

6 Next, figure out how you work best. College is all about independence—it's up to you and only you to decide when, where, and how you study. Ask yourself these questions:

7 **Do I work best with a full or empty schedule?** "My highest GPAs come when I've been directing a play, and my lowest GPAs are when I've found myself bored," says Jon Adler, a theater major from Bates College in Lewiston, Maine. "But my friend on the football team consistently does poorer during the football season than in the off-season."

8 **Am I a morning or evening person?** "The tendency is to say it's good to take an eight o'clock class," says Southampton's Alice Hynn,[1] "But some kids have a really tough time in the morning."

9 Others are like Leah McConaughey, a biology major at Bowdoin College. "I know that I get up early and can't stay up late at night," she says, "so trying to force myself to stay awake and study late into the evening is a waste of time."

10 **Can I tune out distractions easily?** The answer will tell you whether you'll be able to study in a rowdy dorm, or whether you'll have to schedule time to hit the library.

11 It's also a good idea to take a look at your "Achilles' heel"—a quality that may keep you from managing your time properly.

12 "Some students are unassertive," explains O'Keefe, "so they're going to have trouble implementing a time schedule unless they think of ways to keep people from occupying their time. Others lose time because when they're emotionally upset, they can't get anything done."

Mapping It Out

13 Once you have a good idea of what you want out of college—and how you're best equipped to get it—you can begin putting a schedule into play. Start by getting a calendar that lets you see an entire semester at once.

[1]Director of new student programs.

14 "You need to be able to look ahead and say, 'This week isn't bad, but in two weeks I'm going to have to do this, and I better start that paper because I have three papers due the next week,'" says Elizabeth Barnhart, director of the Baldwin Center for Learning and Teaching at Bowdoin College in Brunswick, Maine.

15 As you receive a syllabus for each class, transfer important dates—due dates for term papers, final exam and midterm dates, reading assignments, etc.—to the calendar. Presto—your entire semester is laid out before your very eyes!

16 "That way," says Kristin Kramer, a journalism major from Lehigh University in Bethlehem, Pennsylvania, "when you have two things due at the same time, you can't say, 'Oh, I didn't realize that.' You have no excuse."

17 Once you have your class requirements scheduled, you can work daily tasks around them. Use your goal list to determine what should take precedence in your schedule.

18 "I want to be a doctor, so my science classes are going to take priority," says Carrie Alme, an economics and chemistry major from Mount Holyoke College in South Hadley, Massachusetts. "Riding is important to me, so I take time in the morning to do that. You just go down the chain that way."

19 And don't forget about your social life. "All work and no play makes for an unbalanced student lifestyle," says Meigan Kelly, co-coordinator of the freshman seminar at Temple University in Philadelphia. "Schedule time for

COME QUICK — I'VE NOWHERE TO PUT MY YEARLY PLANNER!

fun and relaxation just like you'd schedule a class."

Keeping on Schedule

20 How can you make time management more habit-forming? Use these guidelines:

21 **Keep track of your time.** Flynn has students at Southampton College keep a week-long log of how they spend their time. "Very often they find they have much more free time than they thought," she says.

22 **Write stuff down.** You can go high tech (a laptop or handheld organizer) or low tech (day planner or notebook). But have something handy at all times to write notes to yourself or jot down to-do lists.

23 **Balance your class load.** Kelly says that scheduling all your classes on two or three days rather than throughout the week can turn ugly. "When you have tests or things due in the classes you have crammed together, it makes it difficult."

24 **Make use of daytime hours.** "College freshmen are in the old habit of waiting until nighttime to do their work," says Flynn. Instead of vegging in your room or hanging out in the student lounge, use that hour between classes to hit the books.

25 **Take a break.** Make sure your schedule includes short breaks between study sessions. Jennifer Adams, a history and design major from Mount Holyoke, likes to reward herself when she finishes a big project. "Going for a walk around the lake, drinking some hot cocoa, renting a video, going out with friends—it's very relaxing for me before I jump into something else."

26 **Talk to your professors.** As a freshman, McConaughey remembers being intimidated by her professors. But eventually, she realized they were human—and, for the most part, more than willing to help her if she got into time management jams.

27 **Get credit for work you do outside of class.** Adams took on the task of maintaining her school newspaper's Web site. She was able to use that work for her final project in a journalism class.

28 **Listen and learn.** "Put your notes on tape or tape lectures," says Marist's O'Keefe.

"Carry them with you and whenever there's dead time pop the tape in and listen to your notes."

29 And perhaps the most important time management advice of all: Don't sweat the small stuff. Things like laundry, cleaning your room, and calling your friends back home can fall through the cracks of even the best time manager's schedule, and that's OK.

30 "The only person who sees my laundry is me," says Adams. "It needs to get done, but is the world going to stop if it doesn't? Probably not."

Beware the Time Bandit Procrastination!

31 "I do my best work at the last minute." That's the procrastinator's mantra—but is it really true? Not usually, says Marist's Edward O'Keefe.

32 He suggests comparing a paper you wrote at the last minute with one you wrote over a period of time. If you can honestly say the first paper is better, then procrastination may be your bag. But if not, you may want to rethink the "last minute" strategy.

33 Here are some ways to help you get off the procrastination highway:

34 **Figure out what makes you procrastinate.** Do you have a hard time making decisions? Do you manage your time poorly? Are you not a good listener? Pinpoint the reason behind the procrastination.

35 **Learn to break tasks into manageable parts.** Many procrastinators fail to see that they don't have to do everything at once, says Meigan Kelly. "They don't understand that you could just do research one night, write an introduction one night, write the next section one night, and so on."

36 **Try doing the first draft of a paper in advance.** That'll give you extra time to edit and fine-tune the paper—and you might just learn to appreciate that time.

37 **Change your study environment.** Often, procrastinators will purposely distract themselves by trying to study in a room with a TV or other people, says Kelly. "If they change their environment, that can help them get the work done."

✳✳✳

38 The real time management experts? Students who are up to their ears in activities! C&C dug up some student go-getters and asked them to share their best time management tips.

39 **Who:** Jon Adler, Bates College, Lewiston, ME

Activities: Acts in and directs college theater productions

Advice: "Social support is important. Having people to vent to will alleviate stress and enable you to be more effective when you are working."

40 **Who:** Kristin Kramer, Lehigh University, Bethlehem, PA

Activities: Internship, lifestyles editor of the campus paper, part-time job

Advice: "Set aside study time at the same time each week. If you go to the library at the same time every week, it becomes a habit."

41 **Who:** Kerri Durand, Miami University of Ohio, Oxford, OH

Activities Delta Gamma sorority, Miami Marketing Enterprises, Golden Key National Honor Society

Advice: "I leave a section in my planner for things that can be put off. For example, getting my dad a sweatshirt. I have to do it, but it isn't going to stress me out if I don't get it done."

42 **Who:** Amanda Borsky, American University, Washington, DC

Activities: Part-time job, campus radio show

Advice: "If I'm working late at night, there's a certain point where I just shut down and I'm exhausted, so I'll go to bed and get up early."

43 **Who:** Leah McConaughey, Bowdoin College, Brunswick, ME

Activities: Habitat for Humanity, community center volunteer, part-time job

Advice: "I have a list of some things I can do in a short amount of time. During the day, you have little one-hour blocks of time that you want to fill."

Getting the Message

____ **1.** What is the topic of the article?

    a. working well with others   c. making plans

    b. time management   d. getting things done quickly

____ **2.** The topic sentence in paragraph 3 is

    a. sentence 1.   c. sentence 3.

    b. sentence 2.

____ **3.** The main idea of the article is that

    a. planning is a difficult process.

    b. being efficient is easy.

    c. time management skills are overrated.

    d. time management skills can help one cope with college demands.

____ **4.** Which type of supporting detail does Nichols mainly use?

    a. personal examples   c. statistics

    b. testimony   d. hypothetical examples

____ **5.** Which of the following is not a supporting detail used in the reading?

    a. Include short breaks between study sessions.

    b. Put your notes on tape or tape lectures.

    c. Make use of daytime hours.

    d. Read your notes every evening.

____ **6.** The sentence "When you have tests or things due in the classes you have crammed together, it makes it difficult" (par. 23) is

    a. a fact.   b. an opinion.

____ **7.** The material in the article is overall presented in _____ order.

    a. problem and solution

    b. chronological

    c. most to least important

    d. least to most important

____ **8.** Paragraphs 20–30 use the _____ pattern of organization.

    a. definition   c. process

    b. example   d. narrative

____ **9.** The writer's purpose is to _____ time management skills.

    a. inform students about

    b. persuade students to use

    c. entertain students about ways other students use

____ **10.** By having a section devoted to procrastination, one could infer that doing work at the last minute is

    a. not typical among college students.

    b. only a problem for college students.

    c. a problem for many students.

    d. easy to overcome.

11. Put the main idea of the section Beware the Time Bandit Procrastination into your own words.

_____

_____

_____

12. Is the tone of the article formal or informal? List three words or phrases (with the paragraph number) that illustrate the tone.

_____

_____

_____

13. Are the samples of student advice in paragraphs 39–43 effective support details? Explain why or why not. Imagine you were interviewed for the article and give one of your own pieces of advice on time management.

_____

_____

_____

14. List two questions or comments you wrote in the margins as you read the article.

_____

_____

_____

15. Create a Venn diagram showing the similarities and the differences between an efficient person and an inefficient person.

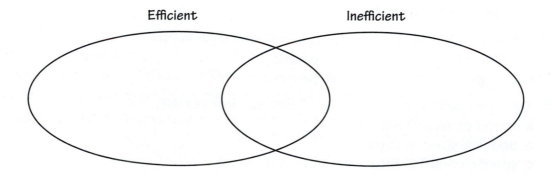

Efficient   Inefficient

Vocabulary

Use context clues to determine the meaning of each word by referring back to the paragraph where the word is used (the paragraph number is in parentheses). If you need help, consult a dictionary for the definition.

A. Put a *T* if the underlined vocabulary word is used correctly and an *F* if it is used incorrectly.

_____ 1. Yesterday was filled with a <u>whirlwind</u> (1) of activity: I sat outside and read a good book for six hours.

_____ 2. The <u>proverbial</u> (1) silver lining has not shown itself yet. I don't see how my car breaking down can have a good side to it.

_____ 3. My summer reading list is filled with <u>academic</u> (3) materials, such as *People*, Superman comics, and romance novels.

_____ 4. To improve my grades, studying will take <u>precedence</u> (17) over partying this semester.

_____ 5. I am taking a <u>seminar</u> (19) on financial planning offered by the college this summer. The class will help me learn how to better balance a budget.

B. Match the vocabulary word to its example.

> **prioritize** (2) **rowdy** (10) **implementing** (12) **jot** (22) **mantra** (31)

1. Alexander and his friends were being noisy and unruly, so his mother told them to play outside while she made an important phone call. _____

2. Colleen lives by the phrase "better late than never," which is why I received my birthday gift in August although my birthday is in March. _____

3. When I asked Sumiko what she was doing this weekend, she said, "First, I will finish my essay for English, because it is the most important thing I have to do, and if I have time, I will see the new action movie." _____

4. I was running late, so I quickly wrote the address on a napkin as I headed out the door.
_____

5. The restaurant has started using a menu that shows the calories of every item. _____

C. Word parts: Circle the meaning of the underlined word part found in each question. One of the words contains two word parts. Return to pages 85–87 if you need to review the meaning of a word part.

1. My son is very music<u>al</u> (5). Anything related to singing or instruments comes easily to him.

2. I am reading a book that was written in China hundreds of years ago. Our ability to <u>trans</u>fer (15) knowledge across time and space still amazes me.

3. Alicia is studying journal<u>ism</u> (16) because the practice of writing interests her.

4. Nathan is a true procrastinat<u>or</u> (31); he is the type of person who puts something off until minutes before it needs to be done.

5. I won't let anything <u>dis</u>tract (37) me from doing my homework. Even when my roommate invites me to join him in making a huge ice cream sundae, he will not drag me away from the work I need to do.

The Article and You

1. List three goals you have for yourself. Did you follow the advice given in paragraph 3 about setting goals?

_____

_____

2. Answer one of the three questions posed in paragraphs 7–10. Give a personal example that shows why your choice fits you.

_____

_____

3. Which of the tips under Keeping on Schedule do you use? Which one would you most recommend to a friend? Which one will you start using that you hadn't considered before? Give an example of how you will use one of the tips this month.

_____

_____

4. On a separate sheet of paper, write a paragraph where you explain whether you are a procrastinator, a semi-planner, or a master planner. Use examples from your work, school, or personal life that illustrate how you belong in the category.

Take a Closer Look

Look at the photo and cartoon again. Can you identify with the woman or the man? When you consider yourself and people you know, do you think most people have a good grasp of time management and organization?

_____

_____

Internet Activities

If needed, use a separate sheet of paper to fully record your responses. Include the Web address of any sites from which you gather information.

1. Search for "time management efficiency" or "time efficiency tips." List three tips you find that are not contained in the article. How helpful do you consider these tips?

_____

_____

2. Go to dartmouth.edu/~acskills/success/time. Pick two of the items under Time Management Resources to explore (e.g., take a planning quiz, watch a video, download a weekly planner). Once you have completed two activities, write a summary of what you learned.

The Blessed Bean: There's Nothing on Earth like Coffee

by Slim Randles

Slim Randles is a columnist for *New Mexico Magazine*. He has had an eventful life as a reporter, editor, and outdoorsman. Among his accomplishments are driving a team of sled dogs in the first Iditarod Race in Alaska, serving as a hunting guide in Alaska and New Mexico, and roping calves at rodeos. The following article originally appeared in the September 2005 edition of *New Mexico Magazine*.

Before You Read

1. What are your feelings about coffee?
2. What message does the word *blessed* in the title send about the writer's attitude toward coffee?
3. Survey the first four paragraphs. What impression do you get about the tone of the article?
4. Look at the photo. What comment does the photograph make about coffee's place in today's world?

Vocabulary Preview

Look for these words in the reading. Exercises to reinforce the learning of new vocabulary using these words follow the reading. The paragraph number where the word appears is in parentheses.

hyperactive (1)	kiosks (5)	essence (8)	industrialist (9)	inviolate (13)
Scylla (14)	Charybdis (14)	fount (14)	marrow (16)	blitzkrieg (19)

1 As a recyled cowboy, it gripes me to have to realize that for much of my happiness I am indebted to hyperactive sheep.

2 According to legend, sheep who were grazing in what is now Ethiopia started munching red berries—about A.D. 1000—and started frisking about and having fun.

3 The sheepherder, named Kaldi, chewed some of these berries, grinned, and said, "Man, I just can't live without my coffee."

4 Which just goes to show that some things never change.

5 Coffee, of course, is one of the world's three basic food groups, the other two being barbecue potato chips and corn dogs. Coffee has become so important in our daily lives that the entire Pacific Northwest has come down with a gang addiction. On a recent trip to Oregon, I noticed that every two blocks in all the bigger towns there were drive up coffee kiosks where you are able to pay $4 for a cup of coffee that tastes like it was filtered through shredded tires and whose name is unpronounceable.

6 And about the time the breakfast coffee rush wore down (shortly after 2 p.m.) a distinctly Pacific Northwest ritual began, known as "the afternoon perk."

7 Here came the long lines of cars again, with hands grasping $5 bills reaching out the car windows and shaking with the early stages of withdrawal.

8   Aah, the bean, the blessed bean. Oh bean, thou art craved in the deepest fibers of our being, thou infiltratest our cellular essence with the sunshine of morning and brusheth away the cobwebs of gloom.

9   Back when I was guiding hunters, I had one German industrialist who couldn't stand the way we made coffee. One morning in the tent, ol' Wilhelm said, "You Americans know nothing about coffee . . . get out of my vay!"

10   Wilhelm then filled a pot with water, threw in what appeared to be an equal amount of coffee and fended me off with a three-tined fork until this mess had boiled for about 10 minutes. I watched carefully, and my notes tell me that German coffee is done when the white speckles melt off the enamelware pot.

11   "Dis," pronounced Wilhelm, waving his arms as his eyes flew open, "is COFFEE! Vun cup, you are good for a veek!"

12   It was strong, all right. We hunted 75 hours straight and had a footrace back to the coffee pot when we finished.

13   On our ranches we have many different rules. Some ranches don't allow photography, some welcome fishermen, some shun outsiders who want to hunt. But all of them have one, inviolate rule: The coffee must go on. There is somewhere a pot of coffee in the house, and if it is empty, it is filled again immediately whether there is anyone there to drink it or not.

14   Friend or foe, process server or godfather, Scylla or Charybdis, it matters not. All are welcome at the caffeinated fount of New Mexico hospitality. You wouldn't even shoot a guy for dumping your daughter without giving him a cup of coffee first.

15   Coffee was even given a papal blessing back in 1600, you know. There were a bunch of Christians (obviously on decaf) who were petitioning Pope Clement VIII to ban coffee for being the devil's drink. He didn't want to do that without trying it first, being a fair-minded kinda guy, so he had some cardinal whip up a batch and he sucked it down. He gave the drink his blessing, said it was an official Christian beverage, had a mug made with "Clem" on it and hung it over the sink.

16   There is nothing on earth like coffee. It gets into the very marrow of our bones and makes us live long and happy and energetic lives.

17   Decaf, you say? (Decaf should be made legal grounds for divorce.)

18   Tea? (Point to the globe and show me what's left of the British Empire. 'Nuf said.)

19   Of course, you can take coffee ingestion to a ridiculous degree. Does the term "blitzkrieg" paint a picture? But for most of us, we take it black, we take it with cream and sugar, we take it any way we can get it, but we take it.

20   It's kept some people moving and writing columns years after they were declared literarily brain dead.

21   Long live nervous Ethiopian sheep. Please pass the sugar.

Getting the Message

_____ **1.** The topic of the article is
   a. sheep in Ethiopia.
   b. cowboy life.
   c. coffee drinkers in Oregon.
   d. coffee.

_____ **2.** The topic sentence in paragraph 13 is
   a. sentence 1.
   b. sentence 2.
   c. sentence 3.
   d. sentence 4.

_____ **3.** Which sentence best expresses the main idea of the article?
   a. Coffee is an addictive beverage.
   b. Cowboys love coffee.
   c. Coffee is a wonderful drink.
   d. Coffee makes people jumpy.

_____ **4.** Randles notes that _____ has a strong addiction to coffee.
   a. the Northeast
   b. the Pacific Northwest
   c. the South
   d. the Midwest

_____ **5.** Pope Clement
   a. hated the taste of coffee.
   b. said his coffee needed more sugar.
   c. decided he preferred cocoa to coffee.
   d. enjoyed his coffee.

_____ **6.** The line "There is nothing on earth like coffee" (par. 16) is
   a. a fact.
   b. an opinion.

_____ **7.** How is the information in paragraphs 9–12 presented?
   a. chronologically
   b. least to most important
   c. most to least important
   d. problem and solutions

_____ **8.** The article is organized as a _____.
   a. narrative
   b. definition
   c. process
   d. series of examples

_____ **9.** Part of Randles' purpose is to entertain his readers.

        a. true

        b. false

_____ **10.** It can be inferred from paragraph 14 that

        a. people in New Mexico don't have prejudices.

        b. violence is common in New Mexico.

        c. a lot of people in New Mexico have financial problems.

        d. in New Mexico it would be considered rude not to offer coffee to someone.

11. Is the main idea stated or implied? If stated, where is the thesis statement? If implied, put the main idea in your own words.

_____

12. What can be inferred from the lines "Tea? (Point to the globe and show me what's left of the British Empire. 'Nuf said.)" (par.18)?

_____

_____

_____

13. List three supporting details Randles uses to develop his point.

_____

_____

_____

_____

14. List two words or sentences you highlighted or underlined as you annotated the article. Why did you pick these points?

_____

_____

15. Paraphrase the line "Here came the long lines of cars again, with hands grasping $5 bills reaching out the car windows and shaking with the early stages of withdrawal" (par. 7).

_____

_____

Vocabulary

Use context clues to determine the meaning by looking back at the paragraph where the word is used (the paragraph number is in parentheses). If you need help, consult a dictionary for the definition.

A. Match the word to its synonym.

source	core	restless	stands	firm

1. hyperactive (1) _____
2. kiosks (5) _____
3. essence (8) _____
4. inviolate (13) _____
5. fount (14) _____

B. Match the word to its definition.

industrialist (9)	Scylla (14)	Charybdis (14)	marrow (16)	blitzkrieg (19)

1. in Greek mythology a whirlpool off the coast of Sicily _____
2. a rapid military attack or any quick, intense effort; in German, "lightning war" _____
3. a person who owns or manages companies or factories _____
4. the center or essential part _____
5. a rock off the coast of Italy; in mythology a sea monster who ate sailors and lived in a cave opposite Charybdis _____

C. Word parts: Fill in the missing word part from the list, and highlight or circle the meaning of the word part found in each question. One word uses two word parts. Return to pages 85–87 if you need to review the meaning of a word part.

ive	un	in	graph	dis	able

1. The hyperact_____ child was inclined to spend hours jumping on the furniture when he should have been studying.
2. The company's name cannot be correctly said by most people. It is so _____ pronounce_____ because it has ten consonants and only one vowel.
3. I _____tinctly told her not to wear the yellow dress to the party. Apart from anything else I might have said, I made that point particularly clear.
4. Photo_____y is a way to write with pictures. A good photo can really tell a story.
5. Her order not to be disturbed while on vacation was _____violate. I was not able to communicate with her by phone or computer.

The Article and You

1. Give three examples of humor Randles uses in his article. Do you think they are effective? Explain why you do or do not find the article amusing.

   _____

   _____

2. If you are a coffee drinker, which elements in the article do you most relate to? If you don't like coffee, describe someone you know who fits some of the traits Randles mentions.

   _____

   _____

3. Name two beverages and two foods you would choose to praise.

   _____

   _____

4. On a separate sheet of paper, write a paragraph in which you praise one of the beverages or foods you picked for question 3.

Take a Closer Look

Look at the photo again. Has your reaction toward the man changed since you read the article? How does the photo relate to one of the ideas about coffee expressed in the article?

   _____

   _____

Internet Activities

If needed, use a separate sheet of paper to fully record your responses. Include the Web address of any sites from which you gather information.

1. Look up "coffee history." Is there more to the story than Randles relates? Write a summary (approximately 150 words) on the history of coffee.

   _____

2. Randles tells how the German makes coffee. Search for "coffee around the world" or "coffee culture." Find recipes or customs from three different countries or regions. Use your findings to make a chart on differences in coffee preferences.

   _____

   _____

   _____

Professor Delves into Odd Culture of Freshmen

by Michelle Roberts

Before You Read

1. What do you remember about your first year of college? If you are currently experiencing your first year, what are some new experiences you have faced?

2. What do you think the word *odd* means in the article's title? Do you recall anything odd about freshman life?

3. How do you think a professor might explore the experience of being a freshman?

4. Look at the photo. Does it connect to any of your college experiences?

Michelle Roberts is an Associated Press writer. She has covered a variety of topics from polygamists in Texas to rare bird migrations. The Associated Press (AP) is "the largest and oldest news organization in the world"; it has 243 news bureaus in 97 countries. It provides news, photographs, and audio and visual materials to thousands of newspaper, radio, and television outlets. In the following article, Roberts reports on an experiment a professor undertook at Northern Arizona University located in Flagstaff, Arizona, which has a student population of 20,000. Notice that most of the paragraphs are quite short. Newspaper articles often have short paragraphs to make them easier to read when presented in narrow columns. If this reading was an essay in a magazine or book, many of the paragraphs could have been combined. The article was originally published in August 2005.

Vocabulary Preview

Look for these words in the reading. Exercises to reinforce the learning of new vocabulary using these words follow the reading. The paragraph number where the word appears is in parentheses.

baffled (1)   **undergraduates** (1)

anthropologists (2)   **empathized** (3)

chaotic (3)   **pseudonym** (4)

sabbatical (5)   **travails** (7)

hectic (13)   **anti-materialism** (17)

Professor Delves into Odd Culture of Freshmen

By MICHELLE ROBERTS
Associated Press writer

1 PHOENIX—As a professor at Northern Arizona University, Cathy Small was baffled by undergraduates. They seemed less engaged, less likely to do assigned reading and more likely to ask questions like, "Do you want it double-spaced?"

2 So she decided to study them as anthropologists research any foreign culture—she lived among them.

3 After moving into a dorm, eating cafeteria food and struggling with a five-course schedule, the 50-something Small said she empathized with students who struggle to balance chaotic class and work schedules.

4 "I'm trying to get really to what student culture is doing and tailor my teaching," said Small, who wrote a book on her research under the pseudonym Rebekah Nathan called *My Freshman Year: What a Professor Learned by Becoming a Student.*

5 Small took a sabbatical and spent the 2002–2003 school year conducting her research. With approval from the university's research board, she used her high school transcript to get admitted and moved into a dorm—though she did forgo the roommate experience by getting a single room.

6 She told students what she was doing if they asked, but found that most of them didn't, perhaps assuming she was just one of those who return to school at an older age.

7 Small spent the first semester taking classes outside her field of expertise, trying to immerse herself in student life. She didn't go to her Flagstaff home and didn't contact regular friends, trying to experience the loneliness and other travails of freshman life.

8 During her second semester, she did more formal interviews and focused on the research, which she published without identifying students or the university, although it eventually was outed by the media.

9 Small said she found that students downplayed publicly the effort they put into assigned reading or papers, but when interviewed, many said they were interested in their course work.

10 Her surveys also found that only about a third of what students were talking and thinking about outside of class was based on their course work.

11 That finding has led Small to change her course work to better connect to the real world and to skip reading assignments that don't have a direct purpose.

12 Part of the trick to college life, she learned from good students, was being able to quickly decipher what work needed to be done and what could be skipped. Those management skills helped students balance classes, part-time work and involvement in volunteer or professional groups, Small said.

13 She found some of the course work tough and had to seek tutoring for a class far outside her field of study. "It was a hectic life," she said.

14 Small also said she found current undergraduates faced more pressure to pick a major that readily translated into a job that could pay off student loans.

15 Travis Shumake, student body president and a senior at NAU's School of Hotel and Restaurant Management, said he sees that all the time—students choosing his program because it provides the "fastest results at the highest income."

16 Small said her generation wasn't as career-oriented in college.

17 "It was an era of anti-materialism. It was kind of nerdy then to talk about careers," she said. "Now, different things are nerdy."

Getting the Message

_C_ **1.** The topic of the article is

    a. college classes.

    b. dorm life.

    c. a professor's experiment.

    d. student lack of interest in their education.

_D_ **2.** The main idea of paragraphs 14–17 is that

    a. students today are busy with part-time work, classes, and volunteering.

    b. students don't show much interest in their course work.

    c. hotel management is an excellent field to get into.

    d. today's students are more career-oriented than when Small first went to college.

_C_ **3.** What is the main idea of the article?

    a. One can attend college at any age.

    b. Students don't care about their classes.

    c. Cathy Small understood her students better after experiencing their lives.

    d. Students should pick majors that will bring them big pay checks.

_A_ **4.** One of the reasons Small undertook her research was so that she could

    a. adapt her teaching to the interests and needs of her students.

    b. live in a dorm.

    c. take classes she had always been interested in.

    d. find a boyfriend.

_C_ **5.** When she was _____, Cathy Small returned to college.

    a. 36

    b. in her mid-40s

    c. 50-something

    d. well over 60

_B_ **6.** Small found that the courses she took were

    a. all too easy.   c. boring.

    b. not always easy.   d. humorous.

_A_ **7.** The sentence "Small took a sabbatical and spent the 2002–2003 school year conducting her research" is

    a. a fact.   b. an opinion.

_C_ **8.** The relationship between paragraphs one and two is one of

    a. comparison/contrast.

    b. narrative.

    c. cause and effect.

    d. process.

_A_ **9.** What does the word _but_ in the sixth paragraph signal?

    a. cause and effect   c. comparison

    b. contrast   d. time

_D_ **10.** It can be inferred from the article that Small

    a. has mostly lazy students each semester.

    b. is interested in changing careers.

    c. was unaffected by her experience.

    (d.) gained respect for the challenges her students faced while in college.

11. What are the main ideas of paragraphs 7 and 8?

She wanted to experience the lonelyness of college freshmun life and the actually go out and interview people.

12. What are three observations Small makes during her time as a freshman?

most students go for careers that held most financial support insted of whathey like,

13. What statistic is used in the article? Do you find it surprising? Why or why not?

_____

_____

_____

14. List three points you annotated in the article and explain how you marked them (e.g., underlined, circled, starred). Why did you mark these items?

_____

_____

_____

15. Jot a few ideas below, and then use a separate sheet of paper to write a 50- to 100-word summary of the article.

_____

_____

Vocabulary

Use context clues to determine the meaning by looking back at the paragraph where the word is used (the paragraph number is in parentheses). If you need help, consult a dictionary for the definition.

A. Match the word to its synonym.

problems	puzzled	alias	busy	understood

1. baffled (1) _____
2. empathized (3) _____
3. chaotic (3) _____
4. pseudonym (4) _____
5. travails (7) _____

B. Match the word to its definition.

undergraduates (1)	anthropologists (2)	sabbatical (5)	hectic (13)	anti-materialism (17)

1. a year of leave given to professors for research, rest, or travel _____
2. people who study the social behaviors and physical development of humans

   _____
3. busy; confused; wild _____
4. against the theory that possessions and physical comfort are the chief concerns in life

   _____
5. college students who haven't yet been given degrees _____

C. Word parts: Match each word to its definition, and highlight or circle the meaning of the word part found in the definition. The word part is underlined to help you make the connection. Return to pages 85–87 if you need to review the meaning of a word part.

anthropolog<u>ist</u> (2)	em<u>path</u>ize (3)	chaot<u>ic</u> (3)	<u>im</u>merse (7)	<u>anti</u>-materialism (17)

1. dive into _____
2. to identify with the feelings of another person _____
3. a person who studies people _____
4. against the practice of highly valuing things _____
5. relating to disorder _____

The Article and You

1. Which of the findings that Small makes apply to your college experiences?

_____

_____

2. If you had the opportunity to be an anthropologist, what group would you like to study? Consider a variety of groups such as sports teams, musicians, or people in other countries. Explain your choice.

_____

_____

3. What is your major? Do you consider your major career-oriented? Explain why or why not. How did you pick your major? If you haven't decided on a major yet, what are three of your possible choices, and are any of them career-oriented?

_____

_____

4. On a separate sheet of paper, write a paragraph where you imagine yourself as a professor returning to college to observe the students. Use your college and classes as examples as you become the anthropologist. Describe what you see students doing and talking about.

Take a Closer Look

Look at the photo again. What aspects of college life does it remind you of? Was your reaction positive, negative, or neutral? What do you think prompted your reaction?

_____

_____

Internet Activities

If needed, use a separate sheet of paper to fully record your responses. Include the Web address of any sites from which you gather information.

1. Look up "dealing with college pressures." What are three pressures facing students today? List three suggestions on how to deal with any of these pressures.

_____

_____

_____

_____

_____

2. Look up "popular college majors." List four currently popular majors. Would you consider them to be career-oriented? Explain why or why not.

_____

_____

_____

Behind Every Grad . . .

by Thomas L. Friedman

Before You Read

1. What saying is Friedman playing with in the title? What is the meaning of the saying?
2. What do you remember about graduation ceremonies you have attended?
3. Who was "behind" you when you graduated from high school? Was there more than one person?
4. Look at the photo and graph. What is your initial impression of the photograph and the information presented in the graph?

Vocabulary Preview

Look for these words in the reading. Exercises to reinforce the learning of new vocabulary using these words follow the reading. The paragraph number where the word appears is in parentheses.

commencement (1) **honorary** (2) **profound** (2) **lush** (3) **compensated** (7)

mentor (9) **advocacy** (9) **colleagues** (11) **recognition** (12) **obsolete** (13)

Thomas L. Friedman is the foreign-affairs columnist for the *New York Times*. He has been writing for the paper for over twenty-five years. He has won three Pulitzer Prizes, including one for his book *The Lexus and the Olive Tree*, published in 1999, which examines the effects of globalization on today's world. Among his other books are the bestseller *The World Is Flat*, published in 2005, and *Hot, Flat, and Crowded*, published in 2008. He is a graduate of Brandeis University with a degree in Mediterranean studies, and he has a master's degree from Oxford in modern Middle East studies. The following article appeared in the June 10, 2005, edition of the *New York Times*.

1 # You don't expect to
learn much at a graduation ceremony—especially if you're the commencement speaker. But I learned about a truly important program at the Williams College graduation last Sunday.

2 Every year, in addition to granting honorary degrees, Williams also honors four high school teachers. But not just any high school teachers. Williams asks each of the 500 or so members of its senior class to nominate a high school teacher who had a profound impact on their lives. Then each year a committee goes through the roughly 50 student nominations, does its own research with the high schools involved and chooses the four most inspiring teachers.

3 Each of the four teachers is given $2,000, plus a $1,000 donation to his or her high school. The winners and their families are then flown to Williams, located in the lush Berkshires, and honored as part of the graduation weekend.

4 On the day before last Sunday's graduation, all four of the high school teachers, and the students who nominated them, sat on stage at a campuswide event, and the dean of the college talked about how and why each high school teacher had influenced the Williams student, reading from the students' nominating letters. Later, the four teachers were introduced at a dinner along with the honorary degree recipients.

5 "Every time we do this, one of the [high school] teachers says to me, 'This is one of the great weekends of my life,'" said Williams's president, Morton Owen Schapiro. "But it is great for us, too. . . .

6   "When you are at a place like Williams and you are able to benefit from these wonderful kids, sometimes you take it for granted. You think we produce these kids. But as faculty members, we should always be reminded that we stand on the shoulders of great high school teachers, we get great material to work with: well educated, well trained, with a thirst for learning.

7   "So we have been doing our little part to recognize that. . . . We take these teachers, who are not well compensated and often underappreciated, and give them a great weekend."

8   If you think these awards are not important for the teachers receiving them, then you don't know anything about teachers.

9   I hurried to get my cap and gown off so I could interview Myra Loris, an international relations teacher at Highland Park High School, north of Chicago, who specializes in preparing kids to take part in the Model U.N. program. She was nominated by Alice Brown, a Williams senior who said in her nominating letter that Ms. Loris was a "very important teacher, role model and mentor. . . . Myra has inspired many students, like me, to pursue careers in law, international relations and political advocacy."

10   When she got the call from Williams saying she had won, Ms. Loris recalled, "I just kept saying, 'Wow.'" A teacher for 23 years, now nearing retirement, she added, "I just found it very affirming in a Zenlike way," an acknowledgement "that my days have value, my life has had some worth. Public school teachers don't get that very often," especially with No

Child Left Behind restrictions, which now require teachers to teach to the tests, and push out the window "all those things that really spark kids' imaginations"—like art and music.

11   Ms. Loris added, "A lot of my young colleagues were really excited and pleased for me, and everyone wants to hear when I get back what happened—and that is really important, because we are not getting people rushing into education. We send 90 percent of our kids on to college, but if you ask how many of them think of being teachers, you will get six kids. . . .

"There are great teachers in our high school, outstanding teachers, and they don't get enough recognition. A lot of kids would not be in college without them."

"To love to learn is to learn to learn."

    We are heading into an age in which jobs are likely to be invented and made obsolete faster and faster. The chances of today's college kids working in the same job for the same company their whole careers is about zero. In such an age, the greatest survival skill you can have is the ability to learn how to learn. The best way to learn how to learn is to love to learn, and the best way to love to learn is to have great teachers who inspire.

14   And the best way to ensure that we have teachers who inspire their students is if we recognize and reward those who clearly have done so.

15   Imagine if every college in America had a program like Williams's, and every spring, across the land, thousands of great teachers were acknowledged by the students they inspired? "No Great Teachers Left Behind." How about it?

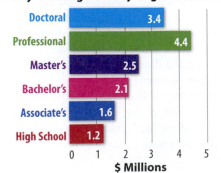

Expected Total Earnings For Forty Working Years by Degree Attained

Degree	$ Millions
Doctoral	3.4
Professional	4.4
Master's	2.5
Bachelor's	2.1
Associate's	1.6
High School	1.2

$ Millions

(A professional degree includes those obtained by lawyers, doctors, dentists, and veterinarians.)
Source: Information adapted from the U.S. Census Bureau.

Getting the Message

____ **1.** The topic of the article is

    a. graduation ceremonies.

    b. great teachers.

    c. a program that honors high school teachers.

    d. the problems teachers face today.

____ **2.** What is the main idea of the article?

    a. Graduation ceremonies should have more input from students.

    b. Great teachers should be recognized for the inspirational work they do.

    c. Most young people don't want to go into teaching because it doesn't pay well.

    d. There are too many restrictions in education today.

____ **3.** Friedman was at Williams College

    a. to accept an honorary degree.

    b. because he is president of the college.

    c. to give a speech.

    d. to see his daughter graduate.

____ **4.** For being one of the teachers that wins the nomination, the teacher

    a. receives $2,000, plus $1,000 for his or her high school.

    b. is given $1,000 for a favorite charity.

    c. is flown to Williams College to be honored at a ceremony.

    d. gets both a and c.

____ **5.** Myra Loris's reaction to the recognition can best be described as

    a. pleased.   c. upset.

    b. bored.   d. annoyed.

____ **6.** What types of supporting details does Friedman use?

    a. testimony and statistics

    b. facts and historical examples

    c. statistics and hypothetical examples

    d. reasons, facts, and testimony

____ **7.** Is the statement "There are great teachers in our high school, outstanding teachers, and they don't get enough recognition" a fact or opinion?

    a. fact   b. opinion

____ **8.** The transition word *so* that begins paragraph 7 shows _____ in relation to paragraph 6.

    a. comparison

    b. cause and effect

    c. contrast

    d. example

____ **9.** Friedman's purpose is to

    a. persuade more students to become teachers.

    b. inform people about the graduation ceremony at Williams College.

    c. persuade society to appreciate teachers more.

    d. entertain people with stories of what happened on graduation weekend.

____**10.** From the statements Loris makes in paragraphs 11 and 12, it can be inferred that she feels students aren't going into teaching because

    a. the pay isn't good.

    b. schools are too violent.

    c. teachers aren't appreciated enough.

    d. most students aren't smart enough to teach.

11. What is the main idea of paragraph 6? Is there a topic sentence?

_____

_____

12. What is the main idea of paragraph 13? Is there a topic sentence?

_____

_____

13. Why do you think Friedman ends the article with a question? How effective do you find his concluding paragraph?

_____

_____

_____

14. Provide a question you wrote in the margins as you annotated the reading. Was your question answered by the end of the reading?

_____

_____

15. Finish the informal outline of the article.

Thesis: _____

1. Friedman explains _____
   (par. 1–4)

2. The college president explains _____ (par. 5–7)

3. Friedman interviews _____
   _____ (par. 8–12)

4. Friedman develops _____ (par. 13–15)

Vocabulary

Use context clues to determine the meaning by looking back at the paragraph where the word is used (the paragraph number is in parentheses). If you need help, consult a dictionary for the definition.

A. Complete the sentences with the appropriate word. Use each word once.

> **commencement** (1)   **honorary** (2)   **profound** (2)   **mentor** (9)   **colleagues** (11)

1. Though I did not earn it, I was proud to receive the _____ degree to recognize the work I have done in developing the college's arts program.

2. I enjoyed the speaker at my _____ ceremony. Listening to his inspirational speech was a great way to finish my college education.

3. I am so grateful to my _____. In the last few months, she has helped me deal with several difficulties as I learn my new job.

4. I found Tina's statements about the college's problems quite _____; her insight is sure to help us deal with our challenges.

5. My _____ and I go to lunch together three times a week. The four of us have found that the more we learn about each other the better we work together at the office.

B. Match the word to its antonym.

> **opposition**   **current**   **dry**   **unpaid**   **ungratefulness**

1. lush (3) _____
2. compensated (7) _____
3. advocacy (9) _____
4. recognition (12) _____
5. obsolete (13) _____

C. Word parts: Fill in the missing meaning for the underlined word part. Return to pages 85–87 if you need to review the meaning of a word part.

> **step**   **good**   **voice**   **come**   **pay**

1. The e<u>ven</u>t is going to be huge; people are expected to _____ from all over the country.

2. The new park will <u>bene</u>fit everyone in the community. It is a _____ use for the land abandoned by the factory.

3. I will be highly com<u>pens</u>ated for my work at the youth camp. The _____ is good, and I am sure I will have wonderful experiences teaching the kids.

4. <u>Grad</u>uation is finally here. I could not have made it without my counselor helping me every _____ of the way.

5. The _____ of the average citizen needs to be heard, which is why I like the ad<u>voc</u>acy section in our local newspaper that lets people write about topics that are important to them.

The Article and You

1. Would you support a college graduation that honors high school teachers at your college? Explain why or why not. What would be the benefits and drawbacks of such a program and ceremony?

_____

_____

_____

2. Do you feel that your high school education prepared you for college? What were two of the strengths and weaknesses in the classes and programs at your high school?

_____

_____

3. If you could nominate one of your high school teachers to be honored at a graduation ceremony, which one would it be? Why?

_____

_____

4. On a separate sheet of paper, write a paragraph in which you agree or disagree with Friedman's statement that "In such an age, the greatest survival skill you can have is the ability to learn how to learn" (par. 13).

Take a Closer Look

Look at the photo and graph again. What mood does the photograph capture? Does the information about potential earnings surprise you? Does the photograph or information in the graph inspire you to finish getting your degree or to get an advanced degree?

_____

_____

Internet Activities

If needed, use a separate sheet of paper to fully record your responses. Include the Web address of any sites from which you gather information.

1. Look up "No Child Left Behind." What is the No Child Left Behind Act? Summarize two conflicting views about the act.

_____

2. Do a search on "graduation ceremonies" or "graduation ceremony traditions." What are three traditional elements found at a graduation ceremony? Give an example of an aspect that you found to be special or different at a ceremony (maybe something another country does).

_____

_____

Socialization into Gender

from *Essentials of Sociology: A Down-to-Earth Approach*

by James M. Henslin

Before You Read

1. Survey the headings. Which group do you think played the strongest role in determining your gender behavior?
2. What thoughts come to your mind when you hear the term *gender roles*?
3. Note the words in bold. How does Henslin define these words?
4. Look at the photos. How do they reflect gender roles?

Vocabulary Preview

Look for these words in the reading. Exercises to reinforce the learning of new vocabulary using these words follow the reading. The paragraph number where the word appears is in parentheses.

embedded (3)	**covertly** (4)	**touted** (14)	**stereotypes** (13)	**privileges** (16)
subordinate (17)	**domain** (20)	**protagonist** (20)	**predicament** (21)	**voluptuous** (21)

James M. Henslin was born in Minnesota, attended colleges in California and Indiana, and earned his master's and doctorate degrees in sociology from Washington University in St. Louis, Missouri. He is Professor Emeritus of Sociology from Southern Illinois University, Edwardsville. He fell in love with sociology in his teens. He enjoys looking at people and how they interact with each other. In his own words, "Sociology pries open the doors of society so you can see what goes on behind them." The following excerpt is taken from the sixth edition of his textbook *Essentials of Sociology: A Down-to-Earth Approach*.

1 # To channel our

behavior, society also uses **gender socialization**. By expecting different attitudes and behaviors from us *because* we are male or female, the human group nudges boys and girls in separate directions in life. This foundation of contrasting attitudes and behaviors is so thorough that as adults, most of us act, think, and even feel according to our culture's guidelines of what is appropriate for our sex.

2 How do we learn gender messages? The significance of gender in social life is emphasized throughout this book. For now, though, let's consider the influence of just the family and the mass media.

Gender Messages in the Family

3 Our parents are the first significant others who teach us our part in this symbolic division of the world. Their own gender orientations have become so firmly embedded that they do most of this teaching without even being aware of what they are doing. This is illustrated by a classic study done by psychologists Susan Goldberg and Michael Lewis (1969), whose results have been confirmed by other researchers (Fagot et al. 1985; Connors 1996).

4 *Goldberg and Lewis asked mothers to bring their 6-month-old infants into their laboratory, supposedly to observe the infants' development. Covertly, however, these*

researchers also observed the mothers. They found that the mothers kept their daughters closer to them. They also touched their daughters more and spoke to them more frequently than they did to their sons.

5   By the time the children were 13 months old, the girls stayed closer to their mothers during play, and they returned to their mothers sooner and more often than the boys did. When Goldberg and Lewis set up a barrier to separate the children from their mothers, who were holding toys, the girls were more likely to cry and motion for help; the boys were more likely to try to climb over the barrier. Goldberg and Lewis concluded that in our society mothers subconsciously reward their daughters for being passive and dependent, their sons for being active and independent.

6   These lessons continue throughout childhood. On the basis of their sex, children are given different kinds of toys. Parents let their preschool sons roam farther from home than their preschool daughters, and they subtly encourage the boys to participate in more rough-and-tumble play—even to get dirtier and to be more defiant (Gilman 1911/1971; Henslin 2003).

7   Such experiences in socialization lie at the heart of the sociological explanation of male-female differences. We should note, however, that some sociologists consider biology to be a cause of these differences. For example, were the infants in the Goldberg-Lewis study demonstrating built-in biological predispositions, with the mothers merely reinforcing—not causing—those differences? We shall return to this controversial issue in Chapter 10.

Gender Messages from Peers

8   Sociologists stress how this sorting process that begins in the family is reinforced as the child is exposed to other aspects of society. Of those other influences, one of the most powerful is the peer group, individuals of roughly the same age who are linked by common interests. Examples of peer groups are friends, classmates, and "the kids in the neighborhood." Consider how girls and boys teach one another what it means to be a female or a male in U.S. society.

9   Let's eavesdrop on a conversation between two eighth-grade girls studied by sociologist Donna Eder (2003). You can see how these girls are reinforcing gender images of appearance and behavior:

Cindy: The only thing that makes her look anything is all the makeup . . .

Penny: She had a picture, and she's standing like this. (Poses with one hand on her hip and one by her head.)

Cindy: Her face is probably this skinny, but it looks that big 'cause of all the makeup she has on it.

Penny: She's ugly, ugly, ugly.

10   Boys, of course, do the same thing. When sociologist Melissa Milkie (1994) studied junior high school boys, she found that much of their talk centered on movies and TV programs. Of the many images they saw, the boys would single out sex and violence. They would amuse one another by repeating lines, acting out parts, and joking and laughing at what they had seen.

11   If you know boys in their early teens, you've probably seen behavior like this. You may have been amused or even have shaken your head in disapproval. As a sociologist, however, Milkie peered beneath the surface. She concluded that the boys were using media images to discover who they are as males. They had gotten the message: To be a "real" male is to be obsessed with sex and violence. Not to joke and laugh about murder and promiscuous sex would have marked a boy as a "weenie," a label to be avoided at all costs.

Gender Messages in the Mass Media

12   Sociologists stress how this sorting process that begins in the family is reinforced as the child is exposed to other aspects of society. Especially important are the mass media, forms of communication that are directed to large audiences. Let's look at how images on television and movies and in video games reinforce society's expectations of gender.

13   **Television and Movies** Television and movies reinforce stereotypes of the sexes. In movies and on prime-time television, male characters outnumber female characters. Male characters on television are also more likely to be portrayed in higher-status positions (Vande Berg and Streckfuss 1992). Viewers get the message, for the more television people watch, the more they tend to have restrictive ideas about women's role in society (Signorielli 1989, 1990).

14   The times, though, they are a-changin'. Stereotype-breaking characters, such as the evil-fighting females on television who help to make the world right, are bound to produce changed ideas of the sexes. The path-breaking program *Xena, Warrior Princess,* a television series imported from New Zealand, portrayed Xena as super dominant. The powers of the teenager *Buffy, the Vampire Slayer,* were also remarkable. On *Alias,* Sydney Bristow exhibits extraordinary strength. In cartoons, Kim Possible divides her time between cheerleading practice and saving the world from evil, while, also with tongue in cheek, the Powerpuff Girls are touted as "the most elite kindergarten crime-fighting force ever assembled."

15   **Video Games** Many youths spend countless hours playing video games in arcades and at home. Even college students, especially men, relieve stress by escaping into video games (Jones 2003). Although sociologists have begun to study how the sexes are portrayed in these games, how the games affect their players' ideas of gender is unknown (Dietz 2000; Sellers 2000). Because these games are on the cutting edge of society, they sometimes also reflect cutting-edge changes in sex roles.

In Sum

16   All of us are born into a society in which "male" and "female" are significant symbols. Sorted into separate groups from childhood, girls and boys learn sharply different ideas of what to expect of themselves and of one another. These images begin in the family and later are reinforced by other social institutions. Each of us learns the meaning that our society associates with the sexes. These images become integrated into our views of the world, forming a picture of "how" males and females "are," and forcing an interpretation of the world in terms of gender. Because gender serves as a primary basis for **social inequality**—giving privileges and obligations to one group of people while denying them to another—gender images are especially important to understand.

Mass Media in Social Life

17   The mass media reflect women's changing role in society. Portrayals of women as passive, as subordinate, or as mere background objects remain, but a new image has broken through. Although this new image exaggerates changes, it does illustrate a fundamental change in social relations. As is mentioned in the text, Xena, the Warrior Princess, is an outstanding example of this change.

18   Although it is unusual to call video games a form of the mass media, like books and magazines they are made available to a mass audience. And with digital advances, they have crossed the line from what is traditionally thought of as games to something that more closely resembles interactive movies.

19   Sociologically, what is significant is that the *content* of video games socializes their users. As they play, gamers are exposed not only to action but also to ideas and images. The gender images of video games communicate powerful messages, just as they do in other forms of the mass media.

20   Lara Croft, an adventure-seeking archeologist and star of *Tomb Raider* and its many sequels, is the essence of the new gender image. Lara is smart, strong, and able to utterly vanquish foes. With both guns blazing, she is the cowboy of the twenty-first century, the term *cowboy* being purposefully chosen, as Lara breaks stereotypical gender roles and assumes what previously was the domain of men. She was the first female protagonist in a field of muscle-rippling, gun-toting macho caricatures (Taylor 1999).

21   Yet the old remains powerfully encapsulated in the new. As the photo makes evident, Lara is a fantasy girl for young men of the digital generation. No matter her foe, no matter her predicament, Lara oozes sex. Her form-fitting outfits, which flatter her voluptuous physique, reflect the mental images of the men who fashioned this digital character.

The mass media not only reflect gender stereotypes but also they play a role in changing them. Sometimes they do both simultaneously. The images of Xena, Warrior Princess, and of Lara Croft not only reflect women's changing role in society, but also, by exaggerating the change, they mold new stereotypes.

Lara has caught young men's fancy to such an extent that they have bombarded corporate headquarters with questions about her personal life. Lara is the star of two movies and a comic book. There is even a Lara Croft candy bar.

For Your Consideration

22   A sociologist who reviewed this text said, "It seems that for women to be defined as equal, we have to become symbolic males—warriors with breasts." Why is gender change mostly one-way—females adopting traditional male characteristics? To see why men get to keep their gender roles, these two questions should help: Who is moving into the traditional territory of the other? Do people prefer to imitate power or powerlessness?

23   Finally, consider just how far stereotypes have actually been left behind. The ultimate goal of the video game, after foes are vanquished, is to see Lara in a nightie.

Getting the Message

___ **1.** The topic of this selection is
   a. the differences between boys and girls.
   b. family and peer influences on children.
   c. television's role in society.
   d. children and gender issues.

___ **2.** Which is the topic sentence in paragraph 13?
   a. sentence 1
   b. sentence 2
   c. sentence 3
   d. sentence 4

___ **3.** Which is the topic sentence in paragraph 20?
   a. sentence 1
   b. sentence 2
   c. sentence 3
   d. sentence 4

___ **4.** Which sentence best expresses the main idea of the Mass Media in Social Life section?
   a. Women are now seen as the equals of men thanks to video games.
   b. Video games don't really have much of an influence on society.
   c. The mass media is beginning to show changes in women's roles in society.
   d. Lara Croft illustrates that the main role of women is to be sexy.

___ **5.** When parents teach gender behavior they
   a. have a very good reason for doing so.
   b. often do so without being aware of their actions.
   c. use a specific handbook.
   d. need to take classes on proper male and female behavior.

___ **6.** The excerpt mentions _____ as female characters that are helping to break stereotypes about women.
   a. Buffy the Vampire Slayer and Marge Simpson
   b. Catwoman and the Powerpuff Girls
   c. Kim Possible and Princess Leia
   d. Xena and Buffy

___ **7.** The Lara Croft character breaks stereotypical roles because she is
   a. fluent in four languages and a good cook.
   b. funny, brave, and sexy.
   c. strong, intelligent, and can beat up bad guys.
   d. knows how to use a gun, looks good in shorts, and doesn't back down.

___ **8.** The statement "In movies and on prime-time television, male characters outnumber female characters" (par. 13) is
   a. a fact.
   b. an opinion.

_____ **9.** Paragraphs 9 and 10 use the _____ organizational pattern to show what girls and boys talk about.

   a. cause and effect
   b. comparison and contrast
   c. definition
   d. narrative

_____ **10.** The word *Yet* in paragraph 21 of Mass Media in Social Life signals _____.

   a. comparison   c. time
   b. contrast   d. addition

11. What is the main idea of the Socialization into Gender excerpt? Is it implied or stated?

_____

_____

_____

_____

12. What does the In Sum section of the reading do?

_____

_____

13. Why does Henslin start with the family and then move to peer groups and the mass media to organize the section?

_____

_____

_____

14. From your notes in the margins, write down the question you would most like to discuss with the class.

_____

_____

15. Make an informal outline below of paragraphs 3–15 of the excerpt.

   Thesis: _____

   1. _____ par. 3–7

   2. _____ par. 8–11

   3. _____ par. 12–15

Vocabulary

Use context clues to determine the meaning by looking back at the paragraph where the word is used (the paragraph number is in parentheses). If you need help, consult a dictionary for the definition.

A. Match the word to its synonym.

publicized	rooted	secretly	area	lower

1. embedded (3) _____
2. covertly (4) _____
3. touted (14) _____
4. subordinate (17) _____
5. domain (20) _____

B. Match the word to its definition.

stereotypes (13)	privileges (16)	protagonist (20)	predicament (21)	voluptuous (21)

1. full and pleasing in shape _____
2. advantages or rights _____
3. a difficult situation _____
4. set images or opinions _____
5. a leading figure _____

C. Word parts: Make words from the reading by using the definitions and adding the following prefixes or suffixes to the appropriate words below. Return to pages 85–87 if you need to review the meaning of a word part.

dis	pre	sub	ist	ive

1. below the conscious mind   ___consciously
2. not supportive   ___approval
3. inclined to feel submissive   pass___
4. a person who studies the mind   psycholog___
5. having a tendency beforehand   ___disposition

The Textbook and You

1. What gender messages do you recall getting from your family, peers, or the media? Do any of them fit those mentioned in the reading?

_____

_____

2. Pick a movie you like or television show you regularly watch. List three gender images that are portrayed in the program.

_____

_____

_____

3. Considering the same show as in question 2, are the images stereotypical or breaking some of the traditional images of men and women? Give two examples from the show to support your view.

_____

_____

_____

4. On a separate sheet of paper, write a paragraph in which you describe an experience that taught you about gender roles or revealed the importance of gender roles to you. The experience could involve family, friends, or the media and be from your childhood or a more recent event.

Take a Closer Look

Look at the photos again. What does the photograph of the children demonstrate about gender roles and the main points about socialization presented in the reading? Do you think children today are still being led toward traditional gender occupations or are most jobs now seen as gender neutral? How does the Lara Croft photo demonstrate traditional and changing gender roles?

_____

_____

_____

Internet Activities

If needed, use a separate sheet of paper to fully record your responses. Include the Web address of any sites from which you gather information.

1. Look up one of the five television shows presented under the Gender Messages in the Mass Media section. Read about the show, and look at any photographs on the site. Summarize how women are presented in this show.

_____

_____

2. Look up "peer groups." Find a site that tells more about peer group influences. Make an outline of the main points you find.

Thank You, M'am

Before You Read

1. What connotations do you have for the word *M'am*?

2. Read the first three sentences. Have you ever been robbed or know someone who has been? What was your or your acquaintance's reaction?

3. Write your own question that you think the reading may address: _____
   _____
   _____

4. Look at the photo. What would you do to get a pair of shoes you really wanted?

Langston Hughes (1902–1967) was a versatile and prolific writer. He published numerous poems, essays, magazine articles, plays, and short stories, plus two novels and three autobiographies. He was born in Joplin, Missouri, but primarily lived in the Harlem area of New York City. He was influential in the Harlem Renaissance, a movement that celebrated African-American culture and creativity. The movement flourished in the 1920s and 1930s and was expressed through the works of musicians, artists, dancers, and writers. Hughes' early death was due to cancer. His house in Harlem was given status as a landmark in 1981. The following story was originally published in 1958.

Vocabulary Preview

Look for these words in the reading. Exercises to reinforce the learning of new vocabulary using these words follow the reading. The paragraph number where the word appears is in parentheses.

snatch (1)	frail (16)	half nelson (22)	kitchenette (22)	roomers (22)
suede (31)	daybed (35)	latching (44)	barren (46)	stoop (46)

1   **She was** a large woman with a large purse that had everything in it but a hammer and nails. It had a long strap, and she carried it slung across her shoulder. It was about eleven o'clock at night, dark, and she was walking alone, when a boy ran up behind her and tried to snatch her purse. The strap broke with the sudden single tug the boy gave it from behind. But the boy's weight and the weight of the purse combined caused him to lose his balance. Instead of taking off full blast as he had hoped, the boy fell on his back on the sidewalk and his legs flew up. The large woman simply turned around and kicked him right square in his blue-jeaned sitter. Then she reached down, picked the boy up by his shirtfront, and shook him until his teeth rattled.

2   After that the woman said, "Pick up my pocketbook, boy, and give it here."

3   She still held him tightly. But she bent down enough to permit him to stoop and pick up her purse. Then she said, "Now ain't you ashamed of yourself?"

4   Firmly gripped by his shirtfront, the boy said, "Yes'm."

5   The woman said, "What did you want to do it for?"

Langston Hughes: Thank You, M'am   **131**

Copyright © 2011 Pearson Education, Inc.

6   The boy said, "I didn't aim to."

7   She said, "You a lie!"

8   By that time two or three people passed, stopped, turned to look, and some stood watching.

9   "If I turn you loose, will you run?" asked the woman.

10   "Yes'm," said the boy.

11   "Then I won't turn you loose," said the woman. She did not release him.

12   "Lady, I'm sorry," whispered the boy.

13   "Um-hum! Your face is dirty. I got a great mind to wash your face for you. Ain't you got nobody home to tell you to wash your face"?

14   "No'm," said the boy.

15   "Then it will get washed this evening," said the large woman, starting up the street, dragging the frightened boy behind her.

16   He looked as if he were fourteen or fifteen, frail and willow-wild, in tennis shoes and blue jeans.

17   The woman said, "You ought to be my son. I would teach you right from wrong. Least I can do right now is to wash your face. Are you hungry?"

18   "No'm," said the being-dragged boy. "I just want you to turn me loose."

19   "Was I bothering *you* when I turned that corner?" asked the woman.

20   "No'm."

21   "But you put yourself in contact with *me*," said the woman. "If you think that that contact is not going to last awhile, you got another thought coming. When I get through with you, sir, you are going to remember Mrs. Luella Bates Washington Jones."

22   Sweat popped out on the boy's face and he began to struggle. Mrs. Jones stopped, jerked him around in front of her, put a half nelson about his neck, and continued to drag him up the street. When she got to her door, she dragged the boy inside, down a hall, and into a large kitchenette-furnished room at the rear of the house. She switched on the light and left the door open. The boy could hear other roomers laughing and talking in the large house. Some of their doors were open, too, so he knew he and the woman were not alone. The woman still had him by the neck in the middle of her room.

23   She said, "What is your name?"

24   "Roger," answered the boy.

25   "Then, Roger, you go to that sink and wash your face," said the woman, whereupon she turned him loose—at last. Roger looked at the door—looked at the woman—looked at the door—*and went to the sink.*

26   "Let the water run until it gets warm," she said. "Here's a clean towel."

27   "You gonna take me to jail?" asked the boy, bending over the sink.

28   "Not with that face, I would not take you nowhere," said the woman. "Here I am trying to get home to cook me a bite to eat, and you snatch my pocketbook! Maybe you ain't been to your supper either, late as it be. Have you?"

29   "There's nobody home at my house," said the boy.

30   "Then we'll eat," said the woman. "I believe you're hungry—or been hungry—to try to snatch my pocketbook!"

31   "I want a pair of blue suede shoes," said the boy.

32   "Well, you didn't have to snatch *my* pocketbook to get some suede shoes," said Mrs. Luella Bates Washington Jones. "You could've asked me."

33   "M'am?"

34   The water dripping from his face, the boy looked at her. There was a long pause. A very long pause. After he had dried his face and not knowing what else to do, dried it again, the boy turned around, wondering what next. The door was open. He could make a dash for it down the hall. He could run, run, run, *run*!

35   The woman was sitting on the daybed. After a while she said, "I were young once and I wanted things I could not get."

36   There was another long pause. The boy's mouth opened. Then he frowned, not knowing he frowned.

37   The woman said, "Um-hum! You thought I was going to say *but,* didn't you? You thought I was going to say, *but I didn't snatch people's pocketbooks.* Well, I wasn't going to say that." Pause. Silence. "I have done things, too, which I would not tell you, son—neither tell God, if He didn't already know. Everybody's got something in common. So you set down while I fix us something to eat. You might run that comb through your hair so you will look presentable."

38   In another corner of the room behind a screen was a gas plate and an icebox. Mrs. Jones got up and went behind the screen. The woman did not watch the boy to see if he was going to run now, nor did she watch her purse, which she left behind her on the daybed. But the boy took care to sit on the far side of the room, away from the purse, where he thought she could easily see him out of the corner of her eye if she wanted to. He did not trust the woman *not* to trust him. And he did not want to be mistrusted now.

39   "Do you need somebody to go to the store," asked the boy, "maybe to get some milk or something?"

40   "Don't believe I do," said the woman, "unless you just want sweet milk yourself. I was going to make cocoa out of this canned milk I got here."

41   "That will be fine," said the boy.

42   She heated some lima beans and ham she had in the icebox, made the cocoa, and set the table. The woman did not ask the boy anything about where he lived, or his folks, or anything else that would embarrass him. Instead, as they ate, she told him about her job in a hotel beauty shop that stayed open late, what the work was like, and how all kinds of women came in and out, blondes, redheads, and Spanish. Then she cut him a half of her ten-cent cake.

43   "Eat some more, son," she said.

44   When they were finished eating, she got up and said, "Now here, take this ten dollars and buy yourself some blue suede shoes. And next time, do not make the mistake of latching onto *my* pocketbook *nor nobody else's*—because shoes got by devilish ways will burn your feet. I got to get my rest now. But from here on in, son, I hope you will behave yourself."

45   She led him down the hall to the front door and opened it. "Good night! Behave yourself, boy!" she said, looking out into the street as he went down the steps.

46   The boy wanted to say something other than, "Thank you, m'am," to Mrs. Luella Bates Washington Jones, but although his lips moved, he couldn't even say that as he turned at the foot of the barren stoop and looked up at the large woman in the door. Then she shut the door.

Getting the Message

_____ **1.** What is the topic of the story?

    a. a failed robbery

    b. a boy's meeting with a special woman

    c. ways to earn money

    d. self-defense

_____ **2.** The dialogue in paragraphs 2–21 shows that the

    a. woman is frightened.

    b. boy is a professional thief.

    c. woman is strong-minded and the boy is afraid.

    d. woman and boy have met before.

_____ **3.** The story's theme is best expressed as

    a. don't try to steal from people who are bigger than you.

    b. a good meal can make a kid happy.

    c. kids will do anything to fit in.

    d. kindness can change a person's behavior.

_____ **4.** How old is Roger?

    a. 20

    b. 9 or 10

    c. 14 or 15

    d. The story doesn't say.

_____ **5.** Roger says he tried to rob the woman because he

    a. wanted a pair of blue suede shoes.

    b. needed money for his sick mother.

    c. was trying to get into a gang.

    d. was starving.

_____ **6.** The line "I believe you're hungry—or been hungry—to try to snatch my pocketbook" (par. 30) is

    a. a fact.

    b. an opinion.

_____ **7.** What pattern of organization does the story use?

    a. process

    b. narrative

    c. classification

    d. comparison and contrast

_____ **8.** _After_, used in paragraph 35, is a _____ transition word.

    a. comparison

    b. contrast

    c. cause and effect

    d. time

_____ **9.** The writer's main purpose is to

     a. inform people about youth violence.

     b. persuade his readers that how we treat people can influence their actions.

     c. entertain his readers with a funny story.

_____**10.** It can be inferred from Roger's "M'am?" after Mrs. Jones says Roger could have asked her for the money (par. 33) that he

     a. didn't hear what she said.

     b. is surprised to hear that she would have given him the money.

     c. is excited to think that she will give him the money.

     d. hasn't given up the idea of stealing the money.

11. Why does Hughes give the woman four names: Luella Bates Washington Jones?

_____

_____

12. What can be inferred about Roger's home life? Give examples of two sentences that led you to your conclusion.

_____

_____

_____

_____

13. Why does Roger not want to be mistrusted by paragraph 38? Does Mrs. Jones trust Roger at this point?

_____

_____

_____

_____

_____

14. List three lines of dialogue that you found especially revealing as you annotated the story.

_____

_____

15. On a separate sheet of paper, make a sketch of a scene you find especially significant in the story. Share your drawing with the class. Did most people pick the same scene? Discuss how the chosen scenes are important to the main idea of the story.

Vocabulary

Use context clues to determine the meaning by looking back at the paragraph where the word is used (the paragraph number is in parentheses). If you need help, consult a dictionary for the definition.

A. Complete each sentence with the appropriate word. Use each word once.

> **frail** (16)　　**half nelson** (22)　　**roomers** (22)　　**latching** (44)　　**barren** (46)

1. Once the wrestler got his opponent in a _____, the match ended quickly.
2. The desert was hot and _____; we couldn't find a place to escape the sun.
3. The boring man kept _____ on to me throughout the conference.
4. Mother was quite _____ after barely eating during her four weeks in the hospital.
5. Of the four _____ in the house, two always pay their rent on time.

B. Write a definition for each word, and then write your own sentence correctly using each word. Be prepared to share your definitions and sentences with the class.

1. snatch (1) _____
2. kitchenette (22) _____
3. suede (31) _____
4. daybed (35) _____
5. stoop (46) _____

C. Word parts: Fill in the missing word part using the word parts from the list below. Return to pages 85–87 if you need to review the meaning of a word part.

> **able**　　　　**er**　　　　**ish**　　　　**mit**　　　　**y**

1. The only time the camp would per_____ us to send a message home was if we were ill.
2. I don't consider being dirt_____ to be fun, so I didn't join the kids in playing in the mud.
3. A person who rents a room in a boarding house is considered to be a room_____.
4. I knew I was capable of making my room present_____ if I cleaned a little each day.
5. Lila's devil_____ nature did not make her popular. Having qualities similar to the devil's do not make one admired by most people.

The Short Story and You

1. In paragraph 21 the woman says, "When I get through with you, sir, you are going to remember Mrs. Luella Bates Washington Jones." If you were Roger, would you remember her? Explain why or why not.

   _____

   _____

2. Why can't Roger get any words out when he leaves Mrs. Jones's place? What would you have said if you were Roger?

_____

_____

3. If you were Mrs. Jones how would you have treated Roger? Explain why you would behave this way.

_____

_____

4. On a separate sheet, write a paragraph where you tell about a time when someone treated you kindly and how you reacted to the experience.

Take a Closer Look

Look at the photo again. Do you have a different reaction to the shoes now that you have read the story? Is there an item you have wanted so much you considered devious ways to get it? Do people put too much emphasis on material goods?

_____

_____

Internet Activities

If needed, use a separate sheet of paper to fully record your responses. Include the Web address of any sites from which you gather information.

1. Look up the terms "blue suede shoes", "ice box", and "sweet milk." In what time periods were these terms popular? If you were to set the story in a contemporary setting, what words might you replace these with? What other words in the story might you update?

2. Look up the Harlem Renaissance. Explain how "Thank You, M'am" relates to the goals of the movement.

PEARSON myreadinglab **Objectives Check**

To check your progress in meeting chapter objectives, log in to www.myreadinglab.com, click on the Study Plan tab, and then on the Reading Skills tab. Choose Main Idea from the list of subtopics. Read and view the resources in the Review Materials section, then complete the Practices and Tests in the Activities section. You can check your scores by clicking on the Gradebook tab.

CHAPTER 5

Why would a flag be in the news?

In the News

Lasting Issues That Spark Debate

Skill: Supporting Details

There are some issues that spark controversy for years, even centuries. Elements of the debate may change over the years and the issue may fade away for a time to be brought back by a current event. The legalization of drugs, especially marijuana, has been a concern for years, and the matter has been treated differently by various nations. Guns have been an important subject in America as evidenced by the Second Amendment's right to bear arms, but over two hundred years later what that amendment exactly means is still quite controversial. The Pledge of Allegiance has seen recent debate due to court decisions. And concerns over prejudice and equality have been with us for ages. Looking at these issues again reminds us how times have changed and what changes humans still need to consider.

Issues that are in the news usually have several sides to them, and those who take a side use various points to develop and support their ideas. These points are called supporting details. Supporting details are the evidence a writer gives to make a point. This chapter covers finding major and minor supporting details, recognizing different types of support, distinguishing a fact from an opinion, and evaluating the writer's use of supporting details. By analyzing the following four essays or articles, textbook excerpt, and short story you will become familiar with the importance of supporting details in developing a writer's main idea.

- Find major and minor supporting details.
- Recognize different types of supporting details.
- Distinguish a fact from an opinion.
- Evaluate the writer's use of supporting details.

Supporting Details

Supporting details are the proof a writer uses to make his or her point. Supporting details are also sometimes called evidence, especially in argumentative papers. By recognizing and analyzing the support a writer uses, you can find the writer's main idea and determine how convincing the writer's point is.

Major and Minor Supporting Details

Look for major and minor supporting details. The major supporting details are the larger points that the writer makes to defend the main idea. The topic sentence of a paragraph is often a major supporting detail. The minor supporting details in a paragraph work to prove the major supporting detail.

Example

Procrastination can be a student's biggest obstacle in college, but the problem can be managed. Many students are so intimidated by what appears to be an overwhelming assignment, such as a research paper, that they put off starting it until the week or even day before it is due, which usually leads to a poor paper and a poor grade. To avoid procrastinating, break a large job into smaller parts. Tackle the hardest parts first so that the later steps will be easy to accomplish. Also reward yourself for small accomplishments along the way to keep up your motivation.

Major supporting detail: _Procrastination can be a student's biggest obstacle in college, but the problem can be managed._

Minor supporting detail #1: _Break a large job into smaller parts._

Minor supporting detail #2: _Tackle the hardest parts first, so that the later steps will be easy to accomplish._

Minor supporting detail #3: _Reward yourself for small accomplishments along the way._

ACTIVITY 1

Identify the major supporting detail in the paragraph below, and list the minor supporting details.

How many times have you heard of a woman who is repeatedly beaten by her partner and wondered, "Why doesn't she just leave him?" There are many reasons why some women find it difficult to break their ties with their abusers. Many women, particularly those with small children, are financially dependent on their partners. Others fear retaliation against themselves or their children. Some hope the situation will change with time (it rarely does), and others stay because cultural or religious beliefs forbid divorce. Finally, some women still love the abusive partner and are concerned about what will happen to him if they leave.

—Donatelle, *Access to Health*, 10th ed., p. 116

Major supporting detail: _____

_____

Minor supporting detail #1: _____

Minor supporting detail #2: _____

Minor supporting detail #3: _____

Minor supporting detail #4: _____

_____

Minor supporting detail #5: _____

_____

Types of Supporting Details

Be able to identify the four main types of supporting details: examples, statistics, testimony, and reasons. A writer may use just one type or all four depending on the writer's subject matter and purpose. For example, an essay about a person's vacation may be filled solely with personal examples, whereas a report on the efficiency of the Roman army would likely use several public examples, facts, and possibly statistics.

Example

An example is an observation the writer provides. An example may be one or two sentences long, or it may be an extended one that lasts for several sentences, paragraphs, or an entire essay. Examples come in four forms: personal, public, hypothetical, and fact.

- **Personal examples** come from experiences the writer or someone the writer knows has had. (When I visited Niagara Falls, I wasn't expecting to be that impressed, but I ended up taking two hundred photos of the powerful falls.)
- **Public examples** come from books, newspapers, television shows, movies, or other forms of media that the writer has read, researched, or seen. The example may come from historical materials or current events. (The 1953 thriller *Niagara*, staring Marilyn Monroe and Joseph Cotton, brilliantly captures the magnificence of the falls in several scenes.)
- **Hypothetical examples** come from the writer's imagination, but they represent situations that could possibly happen. Hypothetical examples are sometimes introduced by the words *imagine* or *if*. (Imagine donning a blue poncho and stepping onto the *Maid of the Mist*. This remarkable boat cruise allows you to feel the splash and hear the roar of the falls up close.)
- **Facts** are pieces of information regarded as true or real, and they can be verified through research. Writers usually find their facts by doing research. (The first person to successfully go over Niagara Falls in a barrel was a schoolteacher, Annie Taylor, in 1901.)

Statistic

A statistic is a numerical comparison, which a writer usually finds through research or by conducting his or her own survey. (The continent of North America has 8 percent of the world's population, which is light compared to Asia which has about 60 percent.)

Testimony

Testimony is the opinion or statement of an expert on a subject, often given in his or her own words through the use of quotations. A writer can find testimony to use through research or by interviewing people. (Stephen Konowalow writes in *Planning Your Future: Keys to Financial Freedom*, "The best financial investment that you can make, at any age, is a college education, even though there are stories about people making 'big' money without a degree" (52).)

Reason

A reason is a sensible explanation that answers the question "Why?" (I don't want to go to the horror movie because I had nightmares the last time I saw one.)

At times you may be uncertain as to which type of evidence a detail is. You might wonder if an example is hypothetical or a public example. If it is important for your studies or to understand the reading, you can do some research to see if it is a public example. It isn't, however, essential to always put every detail into a specific category. Overall, you want to be aware of the different types of supporting details and to recognize their main characteristics so that you can evaluate the effectiveness of the details in relation to the main idea. Read the example below to see how various types of supporting details can be used in a paragraph.

Example

The paragraph below contains all four types of supporting details. Some types of details are used more than once.

The college needs to build an addition to the library.[1] When the college opened in 1955, there were 5,000 students enrolled and the library was 50,000 square feet.[2] With the current population at 30,000 students, a 75,000 square foot library isn't meeting student needs.[3] Students are often forced to sit on the floor to study because there are not enough desks or tables.[4] With only two checkout stations, it can take over an hour to get one's books.[5] Last week my friends and I tried to hold a study session, but the three study-group rooms were booked for every hour for the next three weeks.[6] Marion Post, the head librarian, reports, "There are often lines of students waiting to use the computers.[7] We've had to turn students away from the library several times this semester because there was no place for them to sit."[8] The college's population has grown 55% since the last renovation of the library in 1977.[9] It is apparent to anyone who has recently been in the library that the space is no longer capable of serving the needs of today's students.[10]

Major supporting detail: _sentence 1—The college needs to build an addition to the library._

Minor supporting details:

Example: _sentence 2 (fact), sentence 6 (personal)_

Statistic: _sentence 9_

Testimony: _sentences 7 and 8_

Reason: _sentence 3 (with facts included), sentence 4, sentence 5_

ACTIVITY 2

For the following paragraphs, write the major supporting detail, and list the minor supporting details by sentence and type: example (personal, public, hypothetical, or fact), statistic, testimony, or reason.

1. The exact reason for dreams is still a mystery, but the study of dreams can have benefits.[1] The renowned psychologist Sigmund Freud felt that dreams were the "royal road to the unconscious."[2] He felt that dreams were one's conscious mind trying to censor ideas it didn't want to face, so the images in dreams are often confusing and can have multiple meanings.[3] I have been interested in dream therapy because I have had very vivid dreams since I was a child.[4] I learned that vivid dreams take place during REM sleep when there is intense brain activity.[5] During a normal night, about 20 to 25 percent of one's sleep is REM sleep.[6] To get help interpreting a recurring dream I have been having, I recently went to see a psychologist.[7] I kept dreaming that I was shaving off Abraham Lincoln's beard.[8] I came to realize that my dream was a creative

response to a difficult situation I had been avoiding. [9] Lincoln represented both money and my husband, who also has a beard. [10] By shaving off the beard, I finally saw that the only way to deal with the debt I had been secretly accumulating was to quit hiding and tell my husband about it. [11]

Major supporting detail: _____

_____

Minor supporting details: _____

_____

2. Imagine it is your birthday. [1] You open a present and get a black shirt. [2] You already own 10 black shirts. [3] What you really want is to expand your wardrobe to green, blue, and even yellow shirts. [4] Would you have preferred getting a gift card so you could buy what you really wanted? [5] A recent survey shows that 22 percent of people don't like to give gift cards because they seem too impersonal. [6] On the other hand, 42 percent of people say they like getting gift cards so they can buy items they prefer. [7] Gift cards have their drawbacks, but for many occasions they are the most thoughtful gift because they allow people to get what they really want and need. [8]

Major supporting detail: _____

_____

_____

Minor supporting details: _____

_____

Fact or Opinion

While you are examining the supporting details in a reading you will want to be able to tell the difference between a fact and an opinion. Recognizing a fact from an opinion can help you decide whether the statement is appropriate for the writer's point and how trustworthy it may be. Opinions have their place in writing, for example when a critic is reviewing a movie or a restaurant. Your job is to decide whether a fact or an opinion is the proper type of supporting detail for each writing circumstance. A **fact**, as mentioned above, is information that can be verified through research. An **opinion** is a view or feeling a person has about something that cannot be supported by objective measures. It is a fact that Mount Kilimanjaro in Tanzania is the highest mountain in Africa at 19,340 feet (5,895 meters). It is an opinion that Tanzania has the loveliest scenery of any African country. A statement can contain a fact and an opinion though the overall message of the statement usually fits in one category more than the other.

Consider the following statement, "The 1906 earthquake in San Francisco was the worst natural disaster in American history." The statement contains the fact that San Francisco experienced an earthquake in 1906. The statement also contains the opinion that it was "the worst natural disaster." Someone else may argue that Hurricane Katrina in 2005 or the Galveston Hurricane of 1900 were worse. Overall, the statement expresses an opinion because viewpoints can differ on the assertion, especially considering whether one defines "worst" in terms of deaths, injuries, or dollars. Being able to recognize statements as facts or opinions will allow you to make an informed judgment on how well the writer has supported the main idea.

Determine if a statement is a fact by asking yourself whether you can find reliable information to verify the statement. Can you confirm the statement in a book, on a trustworthy Web site, or from a knowledgeable person on the topic? If you can, then the statement is a fact.

Determine if a statement is an opinion by asking yourself whether another view or side to the statement is possible. For example, examine the statement "Pie is the greatest dessert." Can you imagine someone liking cake, ice cream, or pudding better than pie? If you can, then the statement is an opinion.

Identify whether the following statements are facts or opinions. If you believe the statement is a fact, indicate where you could find reliable information to verify the statement. If you believe the statement is an opinion, give an example of another view or side.

1. Paris is the world's most exciting city.

    _____

2. U.S. President William McKinley was assassinated in 1901.

    _____

    _____

3. The Republic of Liberia is a country in Africa.

    _____

4. *Star Wars* is the best science-fiction movie ever.

    _____

    _____

5. Hank Aaron, one of the greatest baseball players ever, hit 755 home runs during his career.

    _____

    _____

6. Cell phone use should be banned in all restaurants.

    _____

    _____

ACTIVITY 4

Identify a few more facts or opinions by again asking yourself whether you can verify the information or think of another viewpoint. Put an *F* for fact or *O* for opinion on the line after the statement.

1. Brad Pitt starred in *The Curious Case of Benjamin Button*. ___

2. Lemonade is the best drink on a hot day. ___

3. Blue whales are the largest mammals on earth. ___

4. Estimates on the number dead from the Galveston Hurricane of 1900 range from 6,000 to 12,000. ___

5. Americans like large model cars and trucks because they believe bigger is better. ___

6. Though I don't like blue, research has shown it to have a calming effect on people. ___

7. Estimates put about 1,600 pandas left in the wild. ___

8. The Grand Canyon on average is one mile deep and nine miles wide, and it runs for 280 miles, making it the most spectacular natural wonder in the world. ___

Evaluating Supporting Details

Once you recognize the supporting details as major or minor, by type, and whether they are facts or opinions, you will want to evaluate the effectiveness of the details. The reader has four main goals in relation to understanding and using supporting details.

Decide if the types of supporting details used are effective for the writer's purpose. When a writer uses supporting details, ask yourself if the example, statistic, testimony, or reason is the best type of evidence the writer could have picked. For example, if Karl is explaining something that happened to him, then personal examples would be appropriate. However, if Karl is examining an event that happened hundreds of years before he was born, then personal examples would be out of place and historical public examples would likely be better choices.

Determine if there are enough details to make or prove the writer's point. Sometimes a writer only needs one or two supporting details to prove a point, while at other times these would be too few to convince most readers. In the example above about the library, the writer uses five different supporting details to show why a new library is needed. If the writer had only given the personal example of not being able to use a study-group room, there would not have been enough details to convince most people that the library is too small.

Determine if a supporting detail is relevant to the point being made. Each type of supporting detail should work to support the writer's main idea. Look to see if the writer gets off topic and introduces a detail that isn't important to the writer's main idea. These irrelevant points may show an inattentive writer, or they may be used on purpose to mislead the reader. In the example above about gift cards, if the writer had taken a few sentences to describe the shape of the present or explain what the wrapping paper looked like, those sentences would have been irrelevant and added nothing to the point of the paragraph.

Establish if a supporting detail is accurate or credible. You may need to do research to establish if a fact or statistic is accurate, or you may immediately recognize that the writer has not done much research. If the writer claims that France is in Asia, you can immediately begin to question the writer's details. When a writer is inaccurate about one or two points, you can begin to question whether any of the writer's points can be believed. When a writer uses testimony, see if he or she gives the credentials of the person. If the writer explains how this person is an expert on the subject (has a degree in the discipline, has written a book on the topic, has personally been involved in the experience), then the person can be considered a trustworthy source or credible. And just because someone is famous does not mean that the person knows anything about the subject being covered.

Example

While you read the paragraph below decide how effective the details are.

I was nervous when my girlfriend decided to go to college in New York City. She was going to be on the opposite side of the country from our hometown of San Francisco. She said we would see each other regularly, talk on the phone often, and e-mail each other daily. After a month, she sent an e-mail saying she'd gone to a concert with her friend Jordan. Who was this Jordan? How could she cheat on me with him? I jumped in my car minutes after reading the e-mail. I drove out of San Francisco at nine in the morning, and I was in New Your by three that afternoon. I would have arrived sooner, but I stopped in Kentucky to see the replica of the log cabin where Lincoln was born. Lincoln is my favorite president. I won a Halloween contest dressed as Lincoln when I was in seventh grade. When I got to New York, I discovered that Greta's new friend Jordan was a woman. I felt like such a fool for being so jealous. Since that experience, I have learned to trust my girlfriend and not act so rashly.

1. Are the supporting details effective for the writer's purpose? _A personal example is effective for this paragraph, and it clearly shows how rashly the writer acted._

2. Are there enough details to make or prove the writer's point? _One extended example for a paragraph is adequate support. For an essay, a paragraph that shows how the writer has not acted rashly recently would add support to his concluding statement._

3. Are all the supporting details relevant to the point being made? _Not all of the details are relevant. The information on visiting the log cabin in Kentucky and the writer's admiration of Lincoln add nothing to the main point of the paragraph._

4. Are all the supporting details accurate or credible? _It immediately seems that the writer is not being accurate in stating that it only took six hours to drive across the country (about 3,000 miles). This misinformation casts a doubt on whether the event happened at all._

ACTIVITY 5

Evaluate the use of supporting details in the following paragraphs.

A. The local real estate market is not doing well, but it could be worse. Foreclosures in Las Vegas for 2008 tripled from those in 2007 according to the company Foreclosures.com. Lenders took back 31,416 homes in 2008 compared to 11,509 in 2007. My friend Bob states, "There are a lot of homes for sale in my neighborhood." It could, however, be worse. We could be in California or Florida. We can only hope for improved sales in the years to come.

1. Are the supporting details effective for the writer's purpose? _____

_____

_____

2. Are there enough details to make or prove the writer's point? _____

_____

_____

3. Are all the supporting details relevant to the point being made? _____

_____

4. Are all the supporting details accurate or credible? _____

_____

_____

_____

B. It is easy to make blueberry pancakes. Check that you have the following ingredients on hand, and in about 20 minutes you can be sitting down to a delicious breakfast. Combine 1¼ cups flour, 2½ teaspoons baking powder, 3 tablespoons granulated sugar, ¾ teaspoons salt in a large bowl. In another bowl combine 1 beaten egg, some milk, 3 tablespoons of melted shortening or oil, and ½ cup of washed blueberries. Michigan produces the most blueberries in the United States. Add this mixture to the flour mixture, and stir until the flour is just moistened. Pour about ¼ cup of batter per pancake on a greased, hot griddle or use a skillet. Cook until the pancakes are golden brown on each side. This recipe makes about 12 pancakes.

1. Are the supporting details effective for the writer's purpose? _____

_____

_____

2. Are there enough details to make or prove the writer's point? _____

_____

3. Are all the supporting details relevant to the point being made? _____

_____

4. Are all the supporting details accurate or credible? _____

_____

_____

_____

Supporting Details

✔ Look for major and minor supporting details.

✔ Be able to identify the four main types of supporting details: examples, statistics, testimony, and reasons. Remember that examples can be personal, public, hypothetical, and facts.

✔ Determine if a statement is a fact by asking yourself whether you can find reliable information to verify the statement.

✔ Determine if a statement is an opinion by asking yourself whether another view or side to the statement is possible.

✔ Decide if the types of supporting details used are effective for the writer's purpose.

✔ Determine if there are enough details to make or prove the writer's point.

✔ Determine if a supporting detail is relevant to the point being made.

✔ Establish if a supporting detail is accurate or credible.

We Need to Get Smart about Marijuana

by Rick Steves

Before You Read

1. What do you think it means to "get smart" about marijuana?
2. Should marijuana be legalized?
3. Why do you think people decide to use marijuana?
4. Look at the photo. Where do you think these cans are being sold?

Rick Steves writes travel books and articles and hosts travel shows on public television and national public radio. Steves made his first trip to Europe in 1969, and he now spends about 120 days a year in Europe. He has written more than thirty guidebooks on European travel. He earned degrees in business administration and European history from the University of Washington. The following article was first published on March 26, 2008, on the editorial page of the *Seattle-Post Intelligencer* with Steves as a "Guest Columnist."

Vocabulary Preview

Look for these words in the reading. Exercises to reinforce the learning of new vocabulary using these words follow the reading. The paragraph number where the word appears is in parentheses.

persistent (2) **pragmatic** (2) **liberal** (4) **quaint** (4) **ambience** (4)

insulate (5) **consumption** (6) **deterrent** (9) **precious** (9) **counterproductive** (12)

1   As a parent helping two children navigate their teen years, and as a travel writer who has seen firsthand how Europe deals with its drug problem, I've thought a lot about U.S. drug policy—particularly our criminalization of marijuana.

2   Europe, like the U.S., is dealing with a persistent drug-abuse problem. But unlike us, Europe, which treats drug abuse primarily as a public health issue rather than a criminal issue, measures the success of its drug policy in terms of pragmatic harm reduction.

3   Europeans seek a cure that isn't more costly than the problem. While the U.S. spends its tax dollars on police, courts and prisons, Europe fights drug abuse by funding doctors, counselors and clinics. European Union policymakers estimate that for each euro invested in drug education and counseling, they save 15 euros in police and health costs. Similar estimates have been made for U.S. health-based approaches by the Rand Corp. and others.

4   While Europeans are as firmly opposed to hard drugs as we are, the difference in how they approach marijuana is striking. Take the Netherlands, with its famously liberal marijuana laws. On my last trip to Amsterdam, I visited a "coffee shop"—a cafe that openly and legally sells marijuana to people over 18. I sat and observed the very local, almost quaint scene: Neighbors were chatting. An older couple (who apparently didn't enjoy the trendy ambience) parked their bikes and dropped in for a baggie to go. An underage customer was shooed away. Then a police

officer showed up—but only to post a warning about the latest danger from chemical drugs on the streets.

5   Some concerned U.S. parents are comforted by the illusion of control created by our complete prohibition of marijuana. But the policy seems to be backfiring: Their kids say it's easier to buy marijuana than tobacco or alcohol. (You don't get carded when you buy something illegally.) Meanwhile, Dutch parents say their approach not only protects their younger children, but also helps insulate teens over 18 from street pushers trying to get them hooked on more addictive (and profitable) hard drugs.

6   After a decade of regulating marijuana, Dutch anti-drug abuse professionals agree there has been no significant increase in pot smoking among young people, and that overall cannabis use has increased only slightly. European and U.S. government statistics show per-capita consumption of marijuana for most of Europe (including the Netherlands) is about half that of the U.S., despite the criminal consequences facing American pot smokers.

7   When it comes to marijuana, European leaders understand that a society must choose: Tolerate alternative lifestyles or build more prisons. They've made their choice. We're still building more prisons.

8   According to *Forbes* magazine, 25 million Americans currently use marijuana (federal statistics indicate that one in three Americans has used marijuana at some point), which makes it a $113 billion untaxed industry in our country. The FBI reports that about 40 percent of the roughly 1.8 million annual drug arrests in the U.S. are for marijuana—the majority (89 percent) for simple possession.

9   Rather than act as a deterrent, criminalization of marijuana drains precious resources, clogs our legal system and distracts law enforcement attention from more pressing safety concerns.

10   But things are changing. For example, in Seattle, Initiative 75, which makes adult marijuana use the lowest law enforcement priority for local cops, was recently reviewed after four years in action. The results clearly show that during that period marijuana use didn't measurably increase, and street crime associated with drugs actually went down.

11   More and more U.S. parents, lawyers, police, judges and even travel writers feel it's time for a change. Obviously, like Europeans, we don't want anyone to harm themselves or others by misusing marijuana. We simply believe that regulating and taxing what many consider a harmless vice is smarter than outlawing it.

12   Like my European friends, I believe we can adopt a pragmatic policy toward marijuana, with a focus on harm reduction and public health, rather than tough-talking but counterproductive criminalization. The time has come to have an honest discussion about our marijuana laws and their effectiveness. We need to find a policy that is neither "hard on drugs" nor "soft on drugs"—but smart on drugs.

Getting the Message

_____ **1.** The topic of the article is
  a. marijuana. c. drug abuse.
  b. drug use in the Netherlands. d. how Americans use marijuana.

_____ **2.** Which sentence best expresses the main idea of the article?
  a. The Netherlands has a fair drug policy.
  b. Marijuana is a safe drug.
  c. America needs to reconsider its policies on marijuana use.
  d. The United States spends too much money fighting drug use.

_____ **3.** Steves uses the following types of support details:
  a. testimony and statistics.
  b. reasons and hypothetical examples.
  c. personal examples and testimony.
  d. statistics and examples.

_____ **4.** Which of the following sources does Steves use as support?
  a. the Rand Corporation, _Forbes_ magazine, and the FBI
  b. the European Union, the CIA, and judges
  c. the Dutch government, parents, drug users
  d. police officers, lawyers, and the FDA

_____ **5.** Paragraph _____ uses an extended example.
  a. 3 c. 6
  b. 4 d. 11

_____ **6.** The sentence "The time has come to have an honest discussion about our marijuana laws and their effectiveness" (par. 12) states
  a. a fact. b. an opinion.

_____ **7.** How is the article organized in paragraphs 2–7?
  a. process c. narrative
  b. classification d. comparison and contrast

_____ **8.** The transition words _like_ and _unlike_ in paragraph 2 show
  a. time. c. comparison and contrast.
  b. cause and effect. d. importance.

_____ **9.** Steves' purpose is to _____.
  a. inform b. persuade c. entertain

_____ **10.** "According to _Forbes_ magazine, 25 million Americans currently use marijuana . . . which makes it a $113 billion untaxed industry in our country" (par. 8). It can be inferred from this sentence that
  a. most Americans enjoy lighting up when they get home from work.
  b. marijuana use is harmful to American businesses.
  c. legalizing marijuana could make money for the government.
  d. companies want to legalize marijuana.

11. List two of the major supporting details found in the article.

_____

_____

_____

_____

_____

12. What are two of Steves' supporting details that you found most convincing? Briefly explain why.

_____

_____

13. Overall Steves presents the information in his article as a problem and solution. Identify the problem and the possible solutions Steves suggests.

_____

_____

_____

_____

14. List two of the questions or comments you wrote in the margins that you would like to discuss with the class.

_____

_____

15. Paraphrase the following sentence: "Some concerned U.S. parents are comforted by the illusion of control created by our complete prohibition of marijuana" (par. 5).

_____

_____

_____

Vocabulary

Use context clues to determine the meaning of each word by referring back to the paragraph where the word is used (the paragraph number is in parentheses). If you need help, consult a dictionary for the definition.

A. Match the word to its synonym.

persistent (2)	pragmatic (2)	liberal (4)	quaint (4)	precious (9)

1. valuable _____
2. charming _____
3. continuing _____
4. practical _____
5. open-minded _____

B. Match the word to its definition.

ambience (4)	insulate (5)	consumption (6)	deterrent (9)	counterproductive (12)

1. to place in an isolated condition; to separate _____
2. the act of using; intake _____
3. tending to obstruct rather than help one's purpose _____
4. the mood or atmosphere of a setting _____
5. something that prevents _____

C. Word parts: Fill in the missing word part from the list, and highlight or underline the meaning of the word part found in each question. One word is formed from two word parts. Return to pages 85–87 if you need to review the meaning of a word part.

il	anti	dis	ate	tract

1. The desire to insul_____ our children from harm cannot always be accomplished. We want to make their environments safe, but many children will still face scraped knees and broken bones as they grow.

2. The man was not allowed to run a bar in his house. He _____legally did so for three months before the police discovered what he was doing.

3. The woman tried to _____ her child from the display in the toy store window by pointing out other shops nearby. She was finally able to pull him away when she got him to notice the ice cream shop.

4. The college has a strong _____-drug policy. The administration and most students agree that they are against the use of any type of drug that is not prescribed by a doctor.

The Article and You

1. Do you think marijuana should be legalized in the United States as it is in the Netherlands? Explain why you feel this way.

   _____

   _____

2. How popular would a Netherland-style "coffee shop" be in your area?

   _____

   _____

3. List two benefits and two negatives to making marijuana use legal. Use information from the article and your own experiences.

   _____

   _____

   _____

4. On a separate sheet of paper, write a paragraph where you present an imaginary scene at a "coffee shop" that legally sells marijuana in your community. Who would come in? What would they buy? Use dialogue between the staff and customers to make the scene vivid.

Take a Closer Look

Look at the photo again. Did you immediately recognize what was for sale in the cans when you first looked at the photo? What is the significance of the colors on the cans? Do you think you will see these cans for sale in the United States in the next 10 years?

_____

_____

_____

Internet Activities

If needed, use a separate sheet of paper to fully record your responses. Include the Web address of any sites from which you gather information.

1. Look up "marijuana history." Write a summary of your findings showing how marijuana has been used by different cultures over the years.

   _____

   _____

2. Search for "marijuana use worldwide." Make a bar graph that lists the per-capita use for the United States and five other countries.

   _____

Have Gun, Will Show It

by Nicholas Riccardi

Before You Read

1. Look at the title of the article. What do you think "will show it" means?

2. What connotations do you have for the word *gun*?

3. Survey the first five paragraphs. Write a question you think the reading might address:

   _____

   _____

   _____

4. Look at the cartoon. What does it point out about guns in America today?

Nicholas Riccardi is a staff writer for the *Los Angeles Times*. His articles have appeared in newspapers across the country. Among the subjects he has covered are illegal immigration, militia groups, and the "balloon boy" from Colorado. The following article appeared in the June 7, 2008, issue of the *Times*.

Vocabulary Preview

Look for these words in the reading. Exercises to reinforce the learning of new vocabulary using these words follow the reading. The paragraph number where the word appears is in parentheses.

wary (6)	**flaunt (7)**
fledgling (9)	**novelty (15)**
gait (21)	**proximity (27)**
severe (32)	**spate (38)**
gangly (41)	**berate (46)**

The article begins on the next page.

Have gun, will show it

Owners wear their weapons openly to prove that normal folks carry arms too—even if other people shoot strange looks at them.

By NICHOLAS RICCARDI
Times Staff Writer

1   PROVO, UTAH — For years, Kevin Jensen carried a pistol everywhere he went, tucked in a shoulder holster beneath his clothes.

2   In hot weather the holster was almost unbearable. Pressed against Jensen's skin, the firearm was heavy and uncomfortable. Hiding the weapon made him feel like a criminal.

3   Then one evening he stumbled across a site that urged gun owners to do something revolutionary: Carry your gun openly for the world to see as you go about your business.

4   In most states there's no law against that.

5   Jensen thought about it and decided to give it a try. A couple of days later, his gun was visible, hanging from a black holster strapped around his hip as he walked into a Costco. His heart raced as he ordered a Polish dog at the counter. No one called the police. No one stopped him.

6   Now Jensen carries his Glock 23 openly into his bank, restaurants and shopping centers. He wore the gun to a Ron Paul rally. He and his wife, Clachelle, drop off their 5-year-old daughter at elementary school with pistols hanging from their hip holsters, and have never received a complaint or a wary look.

7   Jensen said he tries not to flaunt his gun. "We don't want to show up and say, 'Hey, we're here, we're armed, get used to it,'" he said.

8   But he and others who publicly display their guns have a common purpose.

9   The Jensens are part of a fledgling movement to make a firearm as common an accessory as an iPod. Called "open carry" by its supporters, the movement has attracted grandparents, graduate students and lifelong gun enthusiasts like the Jensens.

10   "What we're trying to say is, 'Hey, we're normal people who carry guns,'" said Travis Deveraux, 36, of West Valley, a Salt Lake City suburb. Deveraux works for a credit card company and sometimes walks around town wearing a cowboy hat and packing a pistol in plain sight. "We want the public to understand it's not just cops who can carry guns."

11   Police acknowledge the practice is legal, but some say it makes their lives tougher.

12   Police Chief John Greiner recalled that last year in Ogden, Utah, a man was openly carrying a shotgun on the street. When officers pulled up to ask him about the gun, he started firing. Police killed the man.

13   Greiner tells the story as a lesson for gun owners. "We've changed over the last 200 years from the days of the wild, wild West," Greiner said. "Most people don't openly carry. . . . If [people] truly want to open carry, they ought to expect they'll be challenged more until people become comfortable with it."

14   Jensen and others argue that police shouldn't judge the gun, but rather the actions of the person carrying it. Jensen, 28, isn't opposed to attention, however. It's part of the reason he brought his gun out in the open.

15   "At first, [open carry] was a little novelty," he said. "Then I realized the chances of me educating someone are bigger than ever using it [the gun] in self-defense. If it's in my pants or under my shirt I'm probably not going to do anything with it."

16   As Clachelle pushed the shopping cart holding their two young children during a recent trip to Costco, her husband admired the new holster wrapped around her waist. "I like the look of that low-rise gun belt," he said.

17   The Jensens' pistols were snapped into holsters attached to black belts that hug their waists. Guns are a fact of life in their household. Their 5-year-old daughter, Sierra, has a child-sized .22 rifle she handles only in her parents' presence.

18   Clachelle is the daughter of a Central California police chief and began shooting when she was about Sierra's age. She would take her parents' gun when she went out and hide it in her purse because the firearm made her feel safer.

19   "I love 'em," Clachelle said. "I wouldn't ever be without them."

20   Kevin Jensen's first encounter with guns came when he was 11: His grandfather died and left him a 16-gauge shotgun. The gun stayed locked away but

fascinated Jensen through his teen years. He convinced his older brother to take him shooting in the countryside near their home in a small town south of Salt Lake City.

21 "I immediately fell in love with it," said Jensen, a lean man with close-cropped hair and a precise gait that is a reminder of his five years in the Army Reserve. "I like things that go boom."

22 Jensen kept as many as 10 guns in the couple's 1930s-style bungalow in Santaquin, 21 miles southwest of Provo. In January 2005, he decided to get a permit to carry a concealed weapon, mainly for self-defense.

23 "I'm not going to hide in the corner of a school and mall and wait for the shooting to stop," he said.

24 When Jensen bought a Glock and the dealer threw in an external hip holster, he began researching the idea of carrying the gun in public and came upon OpenCarry.org.

25 Its website, run by two Virginia gun enthusiasts, claims 4,000 members nationwide. It summarizes the varying laws in each state that permit or forbid the practice. People everywhere have the right to prohibit weapons from their property, and firearms are often banned in government buildings such as courthouses.

26 According to an analysis by Legal Community Against Violence, a gun control group in San Francisco that tracks gun laws, at least eight states largely ban the practice, including Iowa and New Jersey. Those that allow it have different restrictions.

27 Utah has no law prohibiting anyone from carrying a gun in public, as long as it is two steps from firing—for example, the weapon may have a loaded clip but must be uncocked, with no bullets in the chamber. Those who obtain a concealed-weapons permit in Utah don't have that restriction. Also, youths under 18 can carry a gun openly with parental approval and a supervising adult in close proximity.

28 Most of the time people don't notice Jensen's gun. That's not uncommon, said John Pierce, a law student and computer consultant in Virginia who is a co-founder of OpenCarry.org.

"You have it easy. When I went to school we never had a day off for metal detector maintenance."

29   "People are carrying pagers, BlackBerrys, cellphones," Pierce said. "They see a black lump on your belt and their eyes slide off."

30   Sometimes the reactions are comical. Bill White, a 24-year-old graduate student in ancient languages at the University of Colorado at Boulder, wears his Colt pistol out in the open when he goes to his local Starbucks. Earlier this month a tourist from California spotted him and snapped a photo on his cellphone.

31   "He said it would prove he was in the Wild West," White recalled.

32   But there are times when the response is more severe. Deveraux has been stopped several times by police, most memorably in December when he was walking around his neighborhood.

33   An officer pulled up and pointed his gun at Deveraux, warning he would shoot to kill. In the end, eight officers arrived, cuffed Deveraux and took his gun before Deveraux convinced them they had no legal reason to detain him.

34   Deveraux saw the incident as not giving ground on his rights. "I'm proud that happened," he said.

35   Cases like this are talked about during regular gatherings of those who favor open carry. At a Sweet Tomatoes restaurant in the Salt Lake City suburb of Sandy, more than 40 civilians with guns strapped to their hips took over a corner of the restaurant, eating pasta and boisterously sharing stories.

36   Hassles with law enforcement were a badge of honor for some.

37   Travis White, 19, who has ear and chin piercings, congratulated Brandon Trask, 21, on carrying openly for the first time that night. "Just wait until you get confronted by a cop," White said. "It'll make you feel brave."

38   Having pistols strapped around their waists made Shel Anderson, 67, and his wife, Kaye, 63, feel more secure. Longtime recreational shooters, they began to carry their pistols openly after a spate of home-invasion robberies in their neighborhood. The firearms can serve as a warning to predators, they said.

39   "I decided I want to have as much of an advantage as I can have in this day and age," said Kaye Anderson, a retired schoolteacher.

40   Nearby, Scott Thompson picked over the remains of a salad, his Springfield Armory XD-35 sitting snugly in his hip holster.

41   The gangly graphics designer grew up in a home without guns and didn't think of owning one until he started dating a woman—now his wife—who lived in a rough neighborhood. One night last year, a youth had his head beaten in with a pipe outside her bedroom window. The next day, Thompson got a concealed-weapons permit.

42   Thompson found out about open carry last month while reading gun sites. He's become a convert. He likes the statement it makes.

43   Glancing around the restaurant, as armed families like the Jensens dined with men in cowboy hats and professionals like himself, Thompson smiled.

44   "I love this," he said. "I want people to be aware that crazy people are not the only ones with guns. Normal people carry them."

45   The Jensens' daughter, Sierra, and newborn son, Tyler, began to get restless, so the couple bundled up the children and pulled the manager of the restaurant aside to thank her for hosting them.

46   A patron appeared at Jensen's side and began to berate him. "What you guys are doing here is completely unacceptable," he said. "There are children here."

47   Jensen said that everyone in the restaurant had a legal right to carry. The man didn't back down and the Jensens left.

48   Days later, Jensen was still thinking about the reaction and the man's belief that guns are unsafe.

49   "People can feel that way and it doesn't bother me," he said. "If they have irrational fears, that's fine."

Getting the Message

_____ **1.** The topic of the article is
    a. kids and guns.
    b. violence in America.
    c. carrying guns.
    d. the freedom to own a gun in the United States.

_____ **2.** The main idea of the article is that
    a. more people are deciding to openly carry firearms.
    b. carrying guns in a restaurant is not a good idea.
    c. America needs to reexamine its gun-control laws.
    d. guns can be dangerous in the hands of young people.

_____ **3.** Which sentence expresses the major supporting detail in paragraph 6?
    a. sentence 1
    b. sentence 2
    c. sentence 3

_____ **4.** Which of the following are minor supporting details?
    a. Clachelle, the daughter of a Central California police chief, began shooting when she was about Sierra's age.
    b. Called _open carry_ by its supporters, the movement has attracted grandparents, graduate students, and lifelong gun enthusiasts like the Jensens.
    c. Nearby, Scott Thompson picked over the remains of a salad while his Springfield Armory XD-35 sat snugly in his hip holster.
    d. a and c

_____ **5.** In paragraphs 20 and 21 _____ are used as supporting details.
    a. an example and testimony
    b. facts and statistics
    c. reasons and testimony
    d. personal examples and facts

_____ **6.** Among the people Riccardi uses testimony from are _____ .
    a. a graphics designer and lawyers
    b. a senator and several moms
    c. members of an anti-gun group
    d. a police chief and a former schoolteacher

_____ **7.** The sentence "'Just wait until you get confronted by a cop,' White said. 'It'll make you feel brave'" (par. 37) is
    a. a fact.
    b. an opinion.

_____ **8.** In what order is the information presented?
    a. most to least important
    b. problem and solution
    c. chronological
    d. least to most important

_____ **9.** The purpose of the article is to
    a. inform people about a movement to openly carry guns in the United States.
    b. entertain people with stories about people who own guns.
    c. persuade people that America needs tougher gun-control laws.

_____ **10.** In can be inferred from the line "They see a black lump on your belt and their eyes slide off" (par. 29) that people

    a. are keen observers of each other.

    b. are used to seeing guns on people's hips.

    c. don't always pay careful attention to what they see.

    d. are afraid to look at a person who is carrying a gun.

11. Give an example of one fact and one opinion expressed in the article.

_____

_____

_____

_____

12. List three of the reasons people in the article give for carrying guns.

_____

_____

_____

13. Does the writer have enough supporting details to convince you that this movement is growing? Have you seen anyone openly carry a gun in your area?

_____

_____

_____

14. Give examples of three areas you annotated. Indicate the paragraph number, how you annotated it (e.g., underlined, circled, starred), and why you did so.

_____

_____

_____

15. On a separate sheet of paper, summarize the article in approximately 200 words.

Vocabulary

Use context clues to determine the meaning of each word by referring back to the paragraph where the word is used (the paragraph number is in parentheses). If you need help, consult a dictionary for the definition.

A. Finish the sentences with the appropriate words below. Use each word once.

flaunt (7)	fledgling (9)	novelty (15)	proximity (27)	gangly (41)

1. The _____ of my house to the park makes it the perfect place for the team to head after our soccer games.

2. Athough our team is filled with _____ players, some having only played for three weeks, we beat the best team in the league.

3. The _____ teenager nearly tripped over the desks as he entered the classroom. His writing, however, proved to be much more graceful than his form.

4. Pedro doesn't like to _____ his wealth by owning luxury cars or a huge house, but his sister is just the opposite. She likes to show off her money by wearing designer clothes and expensive jewelry.

5. The _____ of eating in restaurants every night wore out during the third week of the Longs' vacation.

B. Match the word to its synonym.

wave	bearing	suspicious	scold	harsh

1. wary (6) _____
2. gait (21) _____
3. severe (32) _____
4. spate (38) _____
5. berate (46) _____

C. Word parts: Circle the meaning of the underlined word part found within each question. Return to pages 85–87 if you need to review the meaning of a word part.

1. The scratches on my car were <u>vis</u>ible (5) from several feet away. I could see them as I walked up to the car in the parking lot.

2. Andrea lives in a <u>sub</u>urb (10) south of Portland. It is nearly in the city, but not quite.

3. I can handle internal problems at the meeting, but <u>ex</u>ternal (24) problems like the weather are out of my control.

4. My cousin considered mystery stories "fluff," but I was able to con<u>vert</u> (42) her into a fan after she read two of my favorite books. I was shocked that I was able to turn her on to mysteries so quickly.

5. It might be <u>ir</u>rational (49), but I am not going to have an ivy plant in my house. I believe it will bring bad luck.

The Article and You

1. Given the shootings that have occurred on college campuses and in work places during the past few years, would you feel more comfortable openly carrying a gun for protection? Explain why or why not.

   _____

   _____

2. Imagine that you are given 10 minutes with your state senator to discuss your views on gun control. List three things you would say. Refer to the article for possible topics to discuss.

   _____

   _____

3. Were you surprised by the comments about Jensen's daughter in paragraph 17? At what age, if any, do you think children should be allowed to handle firearms? Explain your choice.

   _____

   _____

4. On a separate sheet of paper, write a paragraph in which you address Jensen's comment in the final paragraph: "If they have irrational fears, that's fine." Who do you think has more irrational fears, those who do or do not carry guns?

Take a Closer Look

Look at the cartoon again. How is the cartoon related to guns? Think of three situations involving guns that have been in the news during the last 10 years. Do you think these situations have made a lasting impact on American society? Talk to people who are older and younger than yourself about their experiences associated with guns and gun use. Are most of your experiences similar or different?

   _____

Internet Activities

If needed, use a separate sheet of paper to fully record your responses. Include the Web address of any sites from which you gather information.

1. Look up OpenCarry.org (par. 24). What is the goal of this organization? Search for the laws in your state about openly carrying guns. Write a summary of what you learn.

   _____

2. Look up the Legal Community Against Violence (lcav.org) mentioned in paragraph 26. What is the goal of this organization? Search for your state on the site. Write a summary of what you learn, especially regarding "open carrying/exposed firearms." Compare or contrast this information with what you found on the OpenCarry.org site in question 1.

   _____

Under Whom?

Editorial from the *Los Angeles Times*

Before You Read

1. Read the first paragraph. Do you have an opinion about the "under God" addition?
2. Did you realize "under God" had been added to the pledge in 1954?
3. Do you know all the words to the Pledge of Allegiance?
4. Look at the photo. What is your initial response to the scene?

Vocabulary Preview

Look for these words in the reading. Exercises to reinforce the learning of new vocabulary using these words follow the reading. The paragraph number where the word appears is in parentheses.

anthem (2) **archaic** (2) **atheists** (3) **agnostics** (3) **animists** (3)
cogent (5) **monotheistic** (6) **ostensibly** (8) **nemesis** (8) **deification** (9)

The *Los Angeles Times* is the major newspaper for the city of Los Angeles in California. Los Angeles is the second largest city in the United States, with a population of almost four million. This article is an editorial, meaning it states a particular position on an issue, unlike most news stories which are supposed to be impartial. The editorial was written by the editorial board of the *Los Angeles Times*, which consists of various editors on the paper. It appeared in the September 18, 2005, edition of the paper.

1   **Even back** in 1953, the year before Congress added the words "under God" to the Pledge of Allegiance, most Americans probably thought the pledge was fine as it was.

2   For the 62 years the pledge survived without God, it served as a communal recitation that bound together all the people who felt obligation to and affection for this nation. Because our national anthem, with its archaic poetry and octave-and-a-half range, is all but unsingable for most people, the pledge was the bit of civic unity we all shared, words we all knew and could murmur in something approaching unison and harmony.

3   Unlike lawmakers who injected God in 1954 as a McCarthyite sneer at godless communism, many people now recognize that atheists, agnostics, animists and Buddhists—none of whom believe in an all-encompassing God—can be wonderful citizens. For all the renewed interest in religion in this country, it's unlikely today's Congress would add "under God."

4   Once in, though, taking the words out ends up looking like an attack on religious belief, which in our view is probably reason enough, as a matter of policy, to let it be. But courts don't have the luxury of deciding what's in the best interest of society; they have to decide specific legal disputes before them, and a federal judge in Sacramento on Wednesday ruled that the wording is unconstitutional, as the U.S. 9th Circuit Court of Appeals did three years ago.

5   Even judges who back the divine wording sometimes provide cogent arguments for why it should be omitted. Last month, a Virginia appeals court upheld a state law requiring the daily recitation of the pledge in public schools. "Undoubtedly, the pledge contains a religious phrase, and it is demeaning to persons of any faith to assert that the words 'under God' contain no religious significance," Judge Karen Williams wrote. However, she decided that the pledge is a patriotic activity, not a religious one.

6   Religion ought to be a private matter and should play no role in a daily, government-sanctioned ritual. Children aren't required to say the words, but what Williams rightly calls a "religious phrase" is chanted each day in their presence, and they and their parents have no choice. It's unlikely, though, that anyone has ever been converted to a monotheistic religion simply from listening to repetitions of the phrase.

7   The book *The Knickerbocker Tradition,* a collection of papers on American history published in 1974, describes a "widespread revulsion against institutional and established religion" among the first patriots. "The notion of separation of church and state," the book says, ". . . was a practical device making it possible for people of diverse beliefs and unbeliefs to carry on their political affairs together."

8   Religion tends to hijack civic culture during times of fear and stress. Even the ostensibly godless Josef Stalin, our initial Cold War nemesis, embraced religion during the Nazi invasion of communist Russia. The currency engraving "In God We Trust" is an artifact of the Civil War, and "under God" is a reminder of the height of the Cold War. Little wonder that Congress in these fearful times will not seriously consider removing words that should never have been added to what was a perfectly good pledge—and that the Supreme Court is unlikely to uphold the latest ruling.

9   The colonists, though, had the right idea for carrying forward government in a truly patriotic way—"for all," as the pledge ends. The pledge doesn't need deification. Its best and highest use is to bind us together as common citizens, regardless of faith, with a common commitment to this nation.

Getting the Message

____ **1.** What is the topic of the editorial?

    a. the United States flag   c. the Pledge of Allegiance

    b. religion   d. the Cold War

____ **2.** The topic sentence in paragraph 5 can be found in

    a. sentence 1.   c. sentence 3.

    b. sentence 2.   d. sentence 4.

____ **3.** The main idea can be found in

    a. paragraph 1.   c. paragraph 7.

    b. paragraph 5.   d. paragraph 9.

____ **4.** What kind of support is used in the editorial?

    a. examples   c. statistics

    b. testimony   d. a and b

____ **5.** "In God We Trust" was first engraved on American money during

    a. the Revolutionary War.   c. WWI.

    b. the Civil War.   d. the Cold War.

____ **6.** The sentence "Religion ought to be a private matter and should play no role in a daily, government-sanctioned ritual" (par. 6) is _____.

    a. a fact

    b. an opinion

____ **7.** How is paragraph 8 organized?

    a. narrative   c. examples

    b. definition   d. comparison and contrast

____ **8.** The transition word *Unlike* in paragraph 3 shows

    a. addition.   c. time.

    b. contrast.   d. cause and effect.

____ **9.** The tone of the editorial is _____.

    a. formal

    b. informal

____ **10.** "For the 62 years the pledge survived without God, it served as a communal recitation that bound together all the people who felt obligation to and affection for this nation" (par. 2). It can be inferred from this line and other information in the first paragraphs that the pledge was

    a. written in the early 1900s.

    b. written by an atheist.

    c. written in 1892.

    d. not popular with most people.

11. What is the main idea of paragraph 8? Either write the topic sentence or put the main idea in your own words if it is implied.

_____

_____

_____

12. List three of the major supporting points and the paragraph number where each is located. Use the topic sentence of the paragraph or put the point in your own words.

_____

_____

_____

13. List two types of support used in the editorial and give the paragraph number where each is found. Overall, do you feel there are enough details to make the editors' point?

_____

_____

_____

14. List two questions you wrote in the margins of the editorial. Explain why one of these questions is important to you.

_____

_____

_____

15. Paraphrase the line "Because our national anthem, with its archaic poetry and octave-and-a-half range, is all but unsingable for most people, the pledge was the bit of civic unity we all shared, words we all knew and could murmur in something approaching unison and harmony" (par. 2).

_____

_____

_____

Vocabulary

Use context clues to determine the meaning of each word by referring back to the paragraph where the word is used (the paragraph number is in parentheses). If you need help, consult a dictionary for the definition.

A. Match the word to its definition.

> those who don't believe in a god or higher power   convincing or forceful   outdated or old
>
> belief in one god or higher power   those who believe that natural objects have souls

1. archaic (2) _____

2. atheists (3) _____

3. animists (3) _____

4. cogent (5) _____

5. monotheistic (6) _____

B. Write a definition for each word, and then write your own sentence correctly using each word. Be prepared to share your definitions and sentences with the class.

1. anthem (2) _____

_____

2. agnostics (3) _____

_____

3. ostensibly (8) _____

_____

4. nemesis (8) _____

_____

5. deification (9) _____

_____

C. Word parts: Use the words to help you match the word part to its meaning. Return to pages 85–87 if you need to review the meaning of a word part.

_____ 1. -ist: atheist, animist, colonist   a. with, together

_____ 2. -un: unsingable, unconstitutional, undoubtedly   b. action, practice, theory

_____ 3. col-, com-, con-: collection, communism, converted   c. a person who

_____ 4. -ism: communism, patriotism, Buddhism   d. not

The Editorial and You

1. How important is the Pledge of Allegiance to you? When was the last time you said the Pledge of Allegiance?

2. Do you think the pledge serves to bring Americans together as stated in paragraph 2? Have you felt more connected to people when you have said the pledge with them?

_____

_____

_____

3. Do you agree that "The pledge doesn't need deification" (par. 9)? Explain your opinion.

_____

_____

_____

4. On a separate sheet of paper, write a paragraph on whether you think the Pledge of Allegiance should still be recited in elementary schools.

Take a Closer Look

Look at the photo again. After having read the editorial, does the photo strike you differently? Do the children look unified? Does the photo bring back any memories about your saying the pledge as a child?

_____

_____

_____

Internet Activities

If needed, use a separate sheet of paper to fully record your responses. Include the Web address of any sites from which you gather information.

1. In paragraph 3 the editors note that "God" was added "in 1954 as a McCarthyite sneer at godless communism. . . ." Look up "Joseph McCarthy." Examine two or three sites, and write a summary of who he was and what his role was in fighting communism in the 1950s.

_____

_____

2. Look up "Pledge of Allegiance." When was the pledge written and by whom? Write a roughly 150-word summary of other information you find on the history of the pledge. What is the current status of the debate on whether to take out "under God"?

_____

_____

_____

Complexion

by Richard Rodriguez

from *Hunger of Memory: The Education of Richard Rodriguez*

Before You Read

1. What does the word "complexion" make you think of?
2. What did your parents tell you about racial differences when you were growing up?
3. Who most influenced you when you were growing up?
4. Look at the photo. What is your immediate reaction to the people?

Vocabulary Preview

Look for these words in the reading. Exercises to reinforce the learning of new vocabulary using these words follow the reading. The paragraph number where the word appears is in parentheses.

surname (1) **mournfully** (1) **elixir** (4)

disparagingly (4) **imbued** (7) **menial** (8)

oppressive (11) **hauteur** (17)

dapper (19) **haggard** (19)

Richard Rodriguez grew up in California in the late 1940s and 1950s. He is a journalist and has been published in numerous periodicals including the *Wall Street Journal*, the *Los Angeles Times*, and *Time* magazine. He has written several books, including *Hunger of Memory: The Education of Richard Rodriguez*, an autobiography about Rodriguez's experiences growing up. The book was first published in 1982. "Complexion" is an excerpt from this book.

1 # Regarding my family, I see faces that do not
closely resemble my own. Like some other Mexican families, my family suggests Mexico's confused colonial past. Gathered around a table, we appear to be from separate continents. My father's face recalls faces I have seen in France. His complexion is white—he does not tan; he does not burn. Over the years, his dark wavy hair has grayed handsomely. But with time his face has sagged to a perpetual sigh. My mother, whose surname is inexplicably Irish—Moran—has an olive complexion. People have frequently wondered if, perhaps, she is Italian or Portuguese. And, in fact, she looks as though she could be from southern Europe. My mother's face has not aged as quickly as the rest of her body; it remains smooth and glowing—a cool tan— which her gray hair cleanly accentuates. My older brother has inherited her good looks. When he was a boy people would tell him that he looked like Mario Lanza, and hearing it he would smile with dimpled assurance. He would come home from high school with girl friends who seemed to me glamorous (because they were) blonds. And during those years I envied him his skin that burned red and peeled like the skin of the *gringos.* His complexion never darkened like mine. My youngest sister is exotically pale, almost ashen. She is delicately featured, Near Eastern, people have said. Only my older sister has a complexion as dark as mine, though her facial features are much less harshly defined than my own. To many people meeting her, she seems (they say) Polynesian. I am the only one in the family whose face is severely cut to the line of ancient Indian

ancestors. My face is mournfully long, in the classical Indian manner; my profile suggests one of those beak-nosed Mayan sculptures—the eaglelike face upturned, open-mouthed, against the deserted, primitive sky.

2   "We are Mexicans," my mother and father would say, and taught their four children to say whenever we (often) were asked about our ancestry. My mother and father scorned those "white" Mexican-Americans who tried to pass themselves off as Spanish. My parents would never have thought of denying their ancestry. I never denied it: My ancestry is Mexican, I told strangers mechanically. But I never forgot that only my older sister's complexion was as dark as mine.

3   My older sister never spoke to me about her complexion when she was a girl. But I guessed that she found her dark skin a burden. I knew that she suffered for being a "nigger." As she came home from grammar school, little boys came up behind her and pushed her down to the sidewalk. In high school, she struggled in the adolescent competition for boyfriends in a world of football games and proms, a world where her looks were plainly uncommon. In college, she was afraid and scornful when dark-skinned foreign students from countries like Turkey and India found her attractive. She revealed her fear of dark skin to me only in adulthood when, regarding her own three children, she quietly admitted relief that they were all light.

4   That is the kind of remark women in my family have often made before. As a boy, I'd stay in the kitchen (never seeming to attract any notice), listening while my aunts spoke of their pleasure at having light children. (The men, some of whom were dark-skinned from years of working out of doors, would be in another part of the house.) It was the woman's spoken concern: the fear of having a dark-skinned son or daughter. Remedies were exchanged. One aunt prescribed to her sisters the elixir of large doses of castor oil during the last weeks of pregnancy. (The remedy risked an abortion.) Children born dark grew up to have their faces treated regularly with a mixture of egg white and lemon juice concentrate. (In my case, the solution never would take.) One Mexican-American friend of my mother's, who regarded it a special blessing that she had a measure of English blood, spoke disparagingly of her husband, a construction worker, for being so dark. "He doesn't take care of himself," she complained. But the remark, I noticed, annoyed my mother, who sat tracing an invisible design with her finger on the tablecloth.

5   There was affection too and a kind of humor about these matters. With daring tenderness, one of my uncles would refer to his wife as *mi negra*. An aunt regularly called her dark child *mi feito* (my little ugly one), her smile only partially hidden as she bent down to dig her mouth under his ticklish chin. And at times relatives spoke scornfully of pale, white skin. A *gringo's* skin resembled *masa*—baker's dough—someone remarked. Everyone laughed. Voices chuckled over the fact that the *gringos* spent so many hours in summer sunning themselves. ("They need to get sun because they look like *los muertos*.")

6   I heard the laughing but remembered what the women had said, with unsmiling voices, concerning dark skin. Nothing I heard outside the house, regarding my skin, was so impressive to me.

7   In public I occasionally heard racial slurs. Complete strangers would yell out at me. A teenager drove past, shouting, "Hey, Greaser! Hey, Pancho!" Over his shoulder I saw the giggling face of his girl friend. A boy pedaled by and announced matter-of-factly, "I pee

on dirty Mexicans." Such remarks would be said so casually that I wouldn't quickly realize that they were being addressed to me. When I did, I would be paralyzed with embarrassment, unable to return the insult. (Those times I happened to be with white grammar school friends, *they* shouted back. Imbued with the mysterious kindness of children, my friends would never ask later why I hadn't yelled out in my own defense.)

8   In all, there could not have been more than a dozen incidents of name-calling. That there were so few suggests that I was not a primary victim of racial abuse. But that, even today, I can clearly remember particular incidents is proof of their impact. Because of such incidents, I listened when my parents remarked that Mexicans were often mistreated in California border towns. And in Texas. I listened carefully when I heard that two of my cousins had been refused admittance to an "all-white" swimming pool. And that an uncle had been told by some man to go back to Africa. I followed the progress of the southern black civil rights movement, which was gaining prominent notice in Sacramento's afternoon newspaper. But what most intrigued me was the connection between dark skin and poverty. Because I heard my mother speak so often about the relegation of dark people to menial labor, I considered the great victims of racism to be those who were poor and forced to do menial work. People like the farmworkers whose skin was dark from the sun.

9   After meeting a black grammar school friend of my sister's, I remember thinking that she wasn't really "black." What interested me was the fact that she wasn't poor. (Her well-dressed parents would come by after work to pick her up in a shiny green Oldsmobile.) By contrast, the garbage men who appeared every Friday morning seemed to me unmistakably black. (I didn't bother to ask my parents why Sacramento garbage men always were black. I thought I knew.) One morning I was in the backyard when a man opened the gate. He was an ugly, square-faced black man with popping red eyes, a pail slung over his shoulder. As he approached, I stood up. And in a voice that seemed to me very weak, I piped, "Hi." But the man paid me no heed. He strode past to the can by the garage. In a single broad movement, he overturned its contents into his larger pail. Our can came crashing down as he turned and left me watching, in awe.

10   "*Pobres negros*," my mother remarked when she'd notice a headline in the paper about a civil rights demonstration in the South. "How the *gringos* mistreat them." In the same tone of voice she'd tell me about the mistreatment her brother endured years before. (After my grandfather's death, my grandmother had come to America with her son and five daughters.) "My sisters, we were still all just teenagers. And since *mi pápa* was dead, my brother had to be the head of the family. He had to support us, to find work. But what skills did he have! Twenty years old. *Pobre*. He was tall, like your grandfather. And strong. He did construction work. 'Construction!' The *gringos* kept him digging all day, doing the dirtiest jobs. And they would pay him next to nothing. Sometimes they promised him one salary and paid him less when he finished. But what could he do? Report them? We weren't citizens then. He didn't even know English. And he was dark. What chances could he have? As soon as we sisters got older, he went right back to Mexico. He hated this country. He looked so tired when he left. Already with a hunchback. Still in his twenties. But old-looking. No life for him here. *Pobre*."

11   Dark skin was for my mother the most important symbol of a life of oppressive labor and poverty. But both my parents recognized other symbols as well.

12   My father noticed the feel of every hand he shook. (He'd smile sometimes—marvel more than scorn—remembering a man he'd met who had soft, uncalloused hands.)

13   My mother would grab a towel in the kitchen and rub my oily face sore when I came in from playing outside "Clean the *graza* off of your face!" *(Greaser!)*

14   Symbols: When my older sister, then in high school, asked my mother if she could do light housework in the afternoons for a rich lady we knew, my mother was frightened by the idea. For several weeks she troubled over it before granting conditional permission: "Just remember, you're not a maid. I don't want you wearing a uniform." My father echoed the same warning. Walking with him past a hotel, I watched as he stared at a doorman dressed like a Beefeater. "How can anyone let himself be dressed up like that? Like a clown. Don't you ever get a job where you have to put on a uniform." In summertime neighbors would ask me if I wanted to earn extra money by mowing their lawns. Again and again my mother worried: "Why did they ask *you?* Can't you find anything better?" Inevitably, she'd relent. She knew I needed the money. But I was instructed to work after dinner. ("When the sun's not so hot.") Even then, I'd have to wear a hat. *Un sombrero de* baseball.

15   *(Sombrero.* Watching gray cowboy movies, I'd brood over the meaning of the broad-rimmed hat—that troubling symbol—which comically distinguished a Mexican cowboy from real cowboys.)

16   From my father came no warnings concerning the sun. His fear was of dark factory jobs. He remembered too well his first jobs when he came to this country, not intending to stay, just to earn money enough to sail on to Australia. (In Mexico he had heard too many stories of discrimination in *los Estados Unidos.* So it was Australia, that distant island-continent, that loomed in his imagination as his "America.") The work my father found in San Francisco was work for the unskilled. A factory job. Then a cannery job. (He'd remember the noise and the heat.) Then a job at a warehouse.

(He'd remember the dark stench of old urine.) At one place there were fistfights; at another a supervisor who hated Chinese and Mexicans. Nowhere a union.

17   His memory of himself in those years is held by those jobs. Never making money enough for passage to Australia; slowly giving up the plan of returning to school to resume his third-grade education—to become an engineer. My memory of him in those years, however, is lifted from photographs in the family album which show him on his honeymoon with my mother—the woman who had convinced him to stay in America. I have studied their photographs often, seeking to find in those figures some clear resemblance to the man and the woman I've known as my parents. But the youthful faces in the photos remain, behind dark glasses, shadowy figures anticipating my mother and father.

18   They are pictured on the grounds of the Coronado Hotel near San Diego, standing in the pale light of a winter afternoon. She is wearing slacks. Her hair falls seductively over one side of her face. He appears wearing a double-breasted suit, an unneeded raincoat draped over his arm. Another shows them standing together, solemnly staring ahead. Their shoulders barely are touching. There is to their pose an aristocratic formality, an elegant Latin hauteur.

19   The man in those pictures is the same man who was fascinated by Italian grand opera. I have never known just what my father saw in the spectacle, but he has told me that he would take my mother to the Opera House every Friday night—if he had money enough for orchestra seats. ("Why go to sit in the balcony?") On Sundays he'd don Italian silk scarves and a camel's hair coat to take his new wife to the polo matches in Golden Gate Park. But one weekend my father stopped going to the opera and polo matches. He would blame the change in his life on one job—a warehouse job, working for a large corporation which today advertises its products with the smiling faces of children. "They made me an old man before my time," he'd say to me many years later. Afterward, jobs got easier and cleaner. Eventually, in middle age, he got a job making false teeth. But his youth was spent at the warehouse. "Everything changed," his wife remembers. The dapper young man in the old photographs yielded to the man I saw after dinner: haggard, asleep on the sofa. During "The Ed Sullivan Show" on Sunday nights, when Roberta Peters or Licia Albanese would appear on the tiny blue screen, his head would jerk up, alert. He'd sit forward while the notes of Puccini sounded before him. ("Un bel di.")

20   By the time they had a family, my parents no longer dressed in very fine clothes. Those symbols of great wealth and the reality of their lives too noisily clashed. No longer did they try to fit themselves, like paper-doll figures, behind trappings so foreign to their actual lives. My father no longer wore silk scarves or expensive wool suits. He sold his tuxedo to a secondhand store for five dollars. My mother sold her rabbit fur coat to the wife of a Spanish radio station disc jockey. ("It looks better on you than it does on me," she kept telling the lady until the sale was completed.) I was six years old at the time, but I recall watching the transaction with complete understanding. The woman I knew as my mother was already physically unlike the woman in her honeymoon photos. My mother's hair was short. Her shoulders were thick from carrying children. Her fingers were swollen red, toughened by housecleaning. Already my

mother would admit to foreseeing herself in her own mother, a woman grown old, bald and bowlegged, after a hard lifetime of working.

21   In their manner, both my parents continued to respect the symbols of what they considered to be upper-class life. Very early, they taught me the *propria* way of eating *como los ricos*. And I was carefully taught elaborate formulas of polite greeting and parting. The dark little boy would be invited by classmates to the rich houses on Forty-fourth and Forty-fifth streets. "How do you do?" or "I am very pleased to meet you," I would say, bowing slightly to the amused mothers of classmates. "Thank you very much for the dinner; it was very delicious."

22   I made an impression. I intended to make an impression, to be invited back. (I soon realized that the trick was to get the mother or father to notice me.) From those early days began my association with rich people, my fascination with their secret. My mother worried. She warned me not to come home expecting to have the things my friends possessed. But she needn't have said anything. When I went to the big houses, I remembered that I was, at best, a visitor to the world I saw there. For that reason, I was an especially watchful guest. I was my parents' child. Things most middle-class children wouldn't trouble to notice, I studied. Remembered to see: the starched black and white uniform worn by the maid who opened the door; the Mexican gardeners—their complexions as dark as my own. (One gardener's face, glassed by sweat, looked up to see me going inside.)

23   "Take Richard upstairs and show him your electric train," the mother said. But it was really the vast polished dining room table I'd come to appraise. Those nights when I was invited to stay for dinner, I'd notice that my friend's mother rang a small silver bell to tell the black woman when to bring in the food. The father, at his end of the table, ate while wearing his tie. When I was not required to speak, I'd skate the icy cut of crystal with my eye; my gaze would follow the golden threads etched onto the rim of china. With my mother's eyes I'd see my hostess's manicured nails and judge them to be marks of her leisure. Later, when my schoolmate's father would bid me goodnight, I would feel his soft fingers and palm when we shook hands. And turning to leave, I'd see my dark self, lit by chandelier light, in a tall hallway mirror.

Getting the Message

___ **1.** The topic of the selection is

  a. life in California.
  b. the influence of race.
  c. how to get along with the rich.
  d. horrible jobs.

___ **2.** What is the main idea of the reading?

  a. One's race defines who a person is.
  b. The wealthy can be kind if you are polite.
  c. Race and economic status are often interlinked.
  d. One can overcome any obstacle by working hard.

___ **3.** The major supporting detail in paragraph 16 is found in

  a. sentence 1.
  b. sentence 2.
  c. sentence 6.
  d. sentence 9.

___ **4.** Rodriguez mainly uses _____ to make his point.

  a. statistics
  b. facts
  c. personal examples
  d. testimony

___ **5.** Rodriguez states that members of his family could be thought of having these backgrounds based on their complexions:

  a. French, Portuguese, Nigerian, and Swedish.
  b. Italian, Cambodian, German, and Mexican.
  c. Portuguese, Polynesian, Polish, and Puerto Rican.
  d. Italian, Near Eastern, Polynesian, and Mayan.

___ **6.** Which are some of the symbols Rodriguez's parents saw as representing "a life of oppressive labor and poverty" (par. 11)?

  a. a job in a factory
  b. wearing a uniform
  c. dark skin
  d. all of the above

___ **7.** When Rodriguez's father sees a hotel doorman dressed in his uniform, he says, "How can anyone let himself be dressed up like that? Like a clown" (par. 14). His comment is

  a. a fact.
  b. an opinion.

___ **8.** Paragraph 3 is ordered using the _____ method.

  a. chronological
  b. problem and solution
  c. least to most important
  d. most to least important

___ **9.** "Because of such incidents, I listened when my parents remarked that Mexicans were often mistreated in California border towns" (par. 8). The word *because* shows

  a. cause and effect.
  b. comparison and contrast.
  c. time.
  d. example.

___ **10.** It can be inferred from the transformation of Rodriguez's parents (par. 18–20) that

  a. having kids makes one age quickly.
  b. parents only dress up for photographs.
  c. his parents didn't really care for opera or polo.
  d. hard work and little money can quickly age people.

11. List three of the minor supporting points in paragraph 19 that help to show the change in Rodriguez's father.

_____

_____

_____

_____

12. How is the information in the final paragraph relevant to the main idea?

_____

_____

_____

_____

13. What do the words in Spanish contribute to the selection?

_____

_____

_____

14. List two connections you made between either yourself, world events, or other media and the reading as you annotated the excerpt.

_____

_____

_____

15. Complete the outline by giving the paragraph numbers or summarizing what the given paragraphs are about.

    I. Rodriguez describes his Mexican heritage and the differing faces in his family. par. _____

    II. He shares his boyhood memories of family and public remarks he hears regarding skin color and race. par. _____

    III. _____ par. 9

    IV. Rodriguez presents his mother's story about her family's past. par. _____

    V. _____ par. 11–16

    VI. _____

       _____ par. 17–20

    VII. _____ par. 21–23

Vocabulary

Use context clues to determine the meaning of each word by referring back to the paragraph where the word is used (the paragraph number is in parentheses). If you need help, consult a dictionary for the definition.

A. Put a *T* for true if the underlined vocabulary word is used correctly in the sentence or an *F* for false if the vocabulary word is misused.

____ 1. The woman decided to change her <u>surname</u> (1) after she got married.

____ 2. I drank the <u>elixir</u> (4) the doctor gave me and felt better within an hour.

____ 3. I <u>imbued</u> (7) my cat with shampoo this weekend, and now he smells wonderful.

____ 4. I wouldn't want to be president of the United States; it is such a <u>menial</u> (8) job.

____ 5. The <u>hauteur</u> (17) of the supermodel didn't impress me. Even if one is rich and beautiful, it doesn't mean one has to be arrogant.

B. Match the vocabulary word to the example.

> **mournfully** (1)   **disparagingly** (4)   **oppressive** (11)   **dapper** (19)   **haggard** (19)

1. one's appearance after running a marathon _____

2. the way people would act at a funeral _____

3. a man's look when he wants to impress a woman _____

4. a parent's reaction to a teenager after she gets a tattoo without permission _____

5. the atmosphere at a job where one is forced to work ten hours straight in a hot and stuffy room _____

C. Word parts: Pick the best definition for each underlined word using your knowledge of word parts. Circle the word part in each of the underlined words. Return to pages 85–87 if you need to review the meaning of a word part.

a. filled, put into

b. the practice of believing that one's ethnic background is superior to others'

c. pulled toward

d. judgmentally, not positively

e. a step toward a goal

____ 1. I was <u>attracted</u> (4) to the house by the beautiful hanging pots out front.

____ 2. She <u>disparagingly</u> (4) said that my outfit looked like I had been dressed by a clown.

____ 3. People <u>imbued</u> (7) the painting with meanings the artist said he never intended.

____ 4. I am making good <u>progress</u> (8) toward completing my degree. I only have four classes left to take.

____ 5. Her <u>racism</u> (8) was not attractive. I did not like the comments she made about people from Asian countries.

The Essay and You

1. Do you think there is a connection between skin color or race and one's economic status? Give examples from your experiences or the news to support your view.

    _____

    _____

2. Rodriguez's parents had various ways of recognizing the rich and poor. Pick two of their symbols (par. 11–21) and explain whether you agree or disagree with their feelings about the symbol.

    _____

    _____

3. Pick two qualities that you associate with the rich or poor, and explain why you make these connections.

    _____

    _____

4. On a separate sheet of paper, write a paragraph where you explore the views on race and poverty that you established as a child or that you have today, or compare and contrast your beliefs from the two periods.

Take a Closer Look

Look at the photo again. Is your reaction to the people in the photograph different now that you've read the selection?

_____

Internet Activities

If needed, use a separate sheet of paper to fully record your responses. Include the Web address of any sites from which you gather information.

1. Look up "prejudice." List three types of prejudice that come up in your search. Pick one type and summarize the material from a Web site on the topic including what the prejudice is and who it is aimed at.

    _____

    _____

2. Find a Web site that deals with ways to combat prejudice. List four suggestions the site gives. Do the suggestions seem helpful?

    _____

    _____

Identity in Contemporary America

by Jacqueline Jones, Peter H. Wood, Thomas Borstelmann, Elaine Tyler May, and Vicki L. Ruiz

from *Created Equal*

Before You Read

1. Survey the headings and change them into questions. What issues do you think will be covered in this excerpt?

2. What do you think of when you hear the word *identity*?

3. List five words that you would use to describe your identity.

4. Look at the charts and the photo. Are you surprised by any of the information in the charts? What is your reaction to the passports?

Jacqueline Jones teaches at Brandeis University, Peter H. Wood at Duke University, Thomas Borstelmann at the University of Nebraska, Elaine Tyler May at the University of Minnesota, and Vicki L. Ruiz at the University of California, Irvine. Two of the goals these writers had in developing the textbook *Created Equal: A Social and Political History of the United States* were "to connect" students to the past and to provide "an inclusive view of the past" that shows the diversity of America's history and its people.

Vocabulary Preview

Look for these words in the reading. Exercises to reinforce the learning of new vocabulary using these words follow the reading. The paragraph number where the word appears is in parentheses.

myriad (3)	**absurdities** (4)	**sovereignty** (9)	**aspirations** (10)	**predecessors** (10)
wrenching (11)	**regimes** (11)	**ambivalence** (12)	**disdain** (12)	**vibrant** (13)

1   The 2000 U.S. Census revealed a society in the midst of change. Americans have long been known as a particularly restless and mobile people, and one out of five changed residences every year. The post-1965 wave of immigrants continued to rise (and foreign adoptions rose dramatically), bringing in millions of new Americans of Asian heritage. Latino Americans surpassed African Americans as the nation's largest minority. This latest surge in immigration boosted the number of Roman Catholics and Buddhists as American society remained by far the most openly religious—still primarily Protestant—of the industrialized nations. Geographically, Americans lived farther south and west than earlier generations.

2   Americans were older than they used to be: life expectancy rose to 77 from 45 years in 1900. More than half lived in suburbs. Average household size dropped by 50 percent over the twentieth century, as only one in four consisted of a married couple with children. Whereas in 1900 just 6 percent of married women worked outside the home, 61 percent did so by 2000, including 64 percent of those with children under age six. The "family wage" that so many men earned in the mid-twentieth century was disappearing, helping bring in its wake changes in gender roles as women became crucial breadwinners as well as homemakers and child-raisers.

Negotiating Multiple Identities

3   Americans derived their sense of identity from myriad sources, including nationality, work, socioeconomic status, religion, race, ethnicity, family, gender, religion, and sexual orientation. Since the struggles for equality that emerged dramatically in the 1960s, individual identities and group identities have often been in tension. The achievement of legal equality and the outlawing of explicit discrimination did not immediately change deeply embedded patterns of exclusionary behavior. The policy of affirmative action had developed as a preference in hiring or admission for members of an underrepresented group who were roughly comparable to others in qualifications. It aimed to balance some of the effects of existing but little-noticed habits of "affirmative action" for white Americans and men, as when colleges used lower admission standards for children of alumni or when powerful white men tended to hire other white men. Opponents of affirmative action called it "reverse discrimination" and argued that race and sex should no longer be criteria for success in a colorblind society that promoted individual achievement. By 2000, these opponents had succeeded in eliminating affirmative action from the admission process of the large state university systems of Texas and California. Supporters of the policy observed that employers and others were certainly not colorblind yet, so that a group remedy, such as affirmative action, remained essential for the advancement of more than a token few from groups that had faced discrimination in the past.

4   Ideas about racial identity remained at the heart of the controversy over affirmative action. Those who used the term *race* to group people according to skin color and other visible features, such as eye shape, commonly assumed that race had an important biological meaning as a way of distinguishing one human population from another. However, biologists noted that the genetic differences between races are miniscule compared with differences between individuals of the same race. They suggested that categorizing people by skin color made as much sense as organizing library books by the size and color of their covers rather than their internal contents. The mapping of the entire human genome by 2001 further clarified the biological insignificance of race. Indeed, the racial category "white" had changed over time to encompass such formerly excluded groups as Irish Americans and Jewish Americans. Despite its lack of scientific basis, the use of race as a primary marker of identity long served to preserve a higher status for Americans of European heritage. One could be mostly white yet still be "black," thanks to the one-drop tradition regarding African heritage (that any observable percentage of African "blood" defined a person as black). Thus, a white woman could have a black child in the United States, for example, but a black woman could not have a white child. The U.S. government's decision in the 2000 census to allow citizens to identify themselves as belonging to more than one racial group reflected the complications and occasional absurdities of racial categorization.

Social Change and Abiding Discrimination

5   One of the most striking changes in American society over the past five decades has been the desegregation of public life. Latinos and Asians became much more numerous in the United States, and African Americans emerged from the enforced separation of Jim Crow into greater prominence. Roughly one-third of blacks were middle-class, and thousands won election to local, state, and national political offices. Black Americans became central in the nation's cultural life in music, literature, theater, and sports. By 2001, even a new president from the Republican party—known since 1964 for its lack of support from black voters—appointed two African Americans to run the nation's foreign relations: Secretary of State Colin Powell and National Security Advisor Condoleezza Rice. Workplaces were racially integrated to an extent that would have been hard to imagine in 1950, and interracial marriages rose steeply in the final decades of the twentieth century.

6   The lives of women in the United States also changed dramatically during the last half of the twentieth century. Most worked outside the home, from jobs in the service and manufacturing sectors to careers in the professions and politics. In 2000, women made up one-third of the students in the nation's medical schools and one-half in law schools. Their presence in leading political positions ranged from local

Percent of Men and Women in Various Jobs in the United States

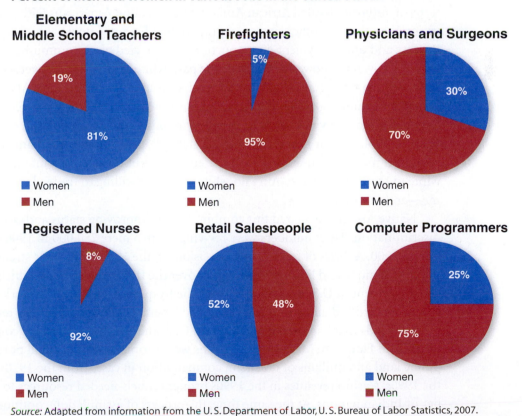

Source: Adapted from information from the U. S. Department of Labor, U. S. Bureau of Labor Statistics, 2007.

officials to more than a dozen U.S. senators, two U.S. Supreme Court justices, a U.S. attorney general, and a U.S. secretary of state. The passage of Title IX in 1972, prohibiting gender discrimination in school programs that received federal money, created a tidal wave of social change for American girls. In 1971, one in 27 girls played high school sports; by 1998, the ratio was one in three. Sports programs and teams for girls comparable to those for boys nourished a new generation of American women for whom athletic competition and achievement were the norm rather than the exception.

7   Anti-homosexual attitudes persisted as one of the nation's fiercest prejudices but nonetheless declined in mainstream American society during the 1980s and 1990s. Gay men and lesbians became more open and prominent in such public venues as television and politics, helping millions of other Americans shed some of the homophobia they had unknowingly learned during childhood.

8   These improvements for the majority of Americans who were not heterosexual white men jostled against abiding forms of discrimination and inequality. Violence and the threat of violence against homosexuals, people of color, and particularly women (primarily domestic violence at the hands of husbands and lovers) remained very real, but most prejudices found more subtle avenues of expression. Working women continued to average less than three-quarters the wages of working men. Many employers, police officers, store owners, bank loan officers, and others in positions of authority treated African Americans and Latino Americans with greater suspicion than they did other citizens, a practice that became known as racial profiling. Poverty and unemployment disproportionately affected black communities and families. Given the powerful legacy of the past, white individuals on average possessed ten times more real wealth (much of it inherited) than their African American counterparts. Residential neighborhoods and public schools remained largely segregated by race, and the deeply symbolic Confederate flag still occupied a place of public honor in several southern states. Popular black comedian Chris Rock reminded mostly white audiences of the enduring but unstated advantage of being white in the United States: "Ain't no white man here willing to trade places with me—and I'm rich!"

9   Native Americans shared this combination of improving status and continuing discrimination. Their numbers were reviving, from a mere 250,000 in 1900 to 2 million in 2000. A series of federal court decisions in the 1970s and 1980s strengthened Indians' "unique and limited" sovereignty over the tribal reservations, which constituted 2 percent of U.S. land. Starting with the Iroquois of upstate New York in 1970, several eastern Indian nations sued state and federal governments for the return of parts of lands that had been illegally seized from them in the past, or for compensation. From Florida to Maine, these nations won a combination of small portions of public land and millions of dollars in compensation in cases from the 1970s through the 1990s. Casino revenues in the 1990s brought much-needed resources to a number of Indian nations. At the same time, the process of assimilation continued as a

majority of Indians lived in urban areas and were married to non-Indians. Reservations suffered from severe unemployment rates and remained some of the poorest communities in the country, dependent on federal assistance for food and other basic necessities. Anti-Indian sentiments continued to surface in states as diverse as Montana, Wisconsin, Arizona, and New York.

Still an Immigrant Society

10   Economic opportunity and individual liberty still lured millions of people from other nations to the United States at the start of the new millennium. Some 800,000 now came legally each year, and another 300,000 entered without official papers. For the first time since the 1930s, one in ten Americans had been born abroad; in New York City the ratio was one in four. Fifteen percent came from Europe, 26 percent arrived from Asia, and 51 percent moved north from Latin America and the Caribbean. Like Italy in 1900, Mexico in 2000 became the most important single source of new Americans. The demographic transition of California in 2000 from a white majority to a more diverse ethnic and racial mix like that of Hawaii symbolized the nation's turn to the South and West, even as the aspirations and work habits of the newcomers remained very much the same as those of their European predecessors.

11   Only the hardiest and most motivated people made the difficult, emotionally wrenching, and often dangerous move to the United States. Many fled political persecution in countries such as Guatemala, Haiti, Vietnam, and Cuba. In contrast to the left-leaning and often socialist attitudes of immigrants in 1900, political refugees in 2000 were sometimes fierce anticommunists who helped pressure the U.S. government to take an even harder line toward regimes in Havana and Hanoi. Most immigrants came to stay, but some worked to save money and return home to their families, carrying with them not only money, but also bits of American culture.

Other people flowed outward too, as American students and tourists traveled all over the globe. Some Americans worked abroad, usually for U.S.-based multinationals such as oil companies, to earn better wages and then return home. Others served in the military, worked for aid agencies and church groups, or joined in the resurgence of the Peace Corps.

12 Despite increasing contacts overseas, Americans responded to the wave of new-comers with an ambivalence common in previous periods of high immigration. Many in the working class feared competition from highly motivated laborers accustomed to much lower wages. Many elites worried whether cultural diversity might weaken national unity. Conservative political leaders promoted new restrictions and stronger border patrols. Some members of Congress ridiculed the idea of there being value in traveling abroad by boasting that they did not even have passports. In 1998, the Republican House majority leader, Dick Armey of Texas, announced: "I've been to Europe once; I don't have to go again." Such disdain for other cultures among some American political leaders dismayed U.S. allies overseas.

13 Most Americans got used to having more immigrants around. Americans cheered for the one in four major league baseball players who were born in Latin America or had parents from there, and they became accustomed to the high number of Asian Americans in college classrooms. They also cheered for baseball players from Japan and heard more Spanish on college walkways. Many churches worked to help new arrivals adjust to life in the United States. Nearly all-white Iowa even began an immigrant recruitment drive to sustain a vibrant state economy that lacked sufficient workers. Above all, American employers depended on immigrant workers to keep the nation's powerful economy afloat—to pick its fruits and vegetables, tend its young children, and work in its factories.

Getting the Message

_____ **1.** What is the topic of this selection?

    a. America's problems   c. America's greatness

    b. America today   d. jobs in the United States

_____ **2.** The topic sentence in paragraph 8 can be found in

    a. sentence 1.   c. sentence 4.

    b. sentence 2.   d. sentence 6.

_____ **3.** The main idea of this excerpt is that America today

    a. is very similar to America 100 years ago.

    b. needs to no longer be concerned about immigration.

    c. continues to experience changes in several areas.

    d. is a perfect country.

_____ **4.** Paragraph 2 uses several _____ as supporting details.

    a. pieces of testimony   c. statistics

    b. reasons   d. examples

_____ **5.** In the section Social Change and Abiding Discrimination which of the following groups are discussed?

    a. Irish-Americans and Samoans

    b. Native Americans and homosexuals

    c. African-Americans and women

    d. b and c

_____ **6.** In 2000, _____ became the biggest source for immigrants to the United States.

    a. Vietnam   c. Guatemala

    b. Mexico   d. Italy

_____ **7.** The sentence "Average household size dropped by 50 percent over the twentieth century, as only one in four consisted of a married couple with children" (par. 2) is

    a. a fact.   b. an opinion.

_____ **8.** How are paragraphs 5–9 organized?

    a. cause and effect   c. comparison and contrast

    b. process   d. definition

_____ **9.** The purpose of this excerpt is to _____.

    a. inform   c. entertain

    b. persuade

_____ **10.** It can be inferred from the sentence "Nearly all-white Iowa even began an immigrant recruitment drive to sustain a vibrant state economy that lacked sufficient workers" (par.13) that

    a. Iowans were tired of not having a diverse minority population.

    b. immigrants were excited about going to Iowa.

    c. financial concerns are a reason places welcome immigrants.

    d. immigrants to Iowa would fit in perfectly.

11. List three of the changes in America from 1900 to 2000 mentioned in paragraph 2. Which one surprises you the most? Explain why.

_____

_____

_____

12. Give an example of a testimony, reason, statistic, and fact used in the Still an Immigrant Society section.

_____

_____

_____

_____

13. For paragraphs 5 through 9, give the number of the sentence that contains the topic sentence.

_____

_____

14. In the section Negotiating Multiple Identities, what points did you highlight and what method(s) did you use to highlight them?

_____

_____

15. Pick two of the groups mentioned in the Social Change and Abiding Discrimination section and make a Venn diagram that shows what characteristics the two groups share and how they are different.

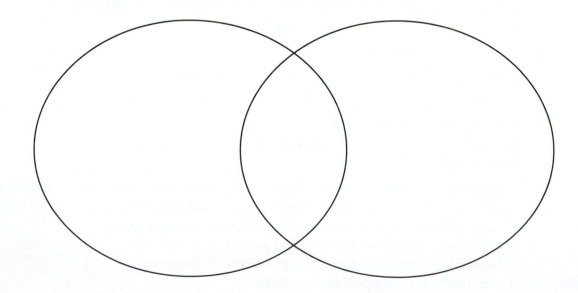

Vocabulary

Use context clues to determine the meaning of each word by referring back to the paragraph where the word is used (the paragraph number is in parentheses). If you need help, consult a dictionary for the definition.

A. Match the vocabulary word to its antonym.

> **myriad** (3)   **sovereignty** (9)   **ambivalence** (12)   **disdain** (12)   **vibrant** (13)

1. confidence _____
2. respect _____
3. few _____
4. dull _____
5. subjugation _____

B. Complete each sentence with the appropriate word. Use each word once.

> **absurdities** (4)   **aspirations** (10)   **predecessors** (10)   **wrenching** (11)   **regimes** (11)

1. My _____ did an excellent job of moving the company forward; I plan to continue where they left off.

2. The _____ of life are things we must all learn how to laugh at when we can't do anything about them.

3. The country has suffered in the last ten years from several oppressive _____. Today's election marks a turning point for the people and the government.

4. My _____ of being a singer were dashed when I stood in front of an audience and couldn't open my mouth.

5. I found the movie heart _____. The poor dog had to endure so many hardships as he traveled 2,000 miles to be reunited with the boy who had missed him so much.

C. Word parts: Provide the meanings for the word parts below, and follow the directions to find other words in the reading that use the same word parts. Return to pages 85–87 if you need to review the meaning of a word part.

1. anti-homosexual (7): against people who are attracted to those of their same gender. Look in paragraphs 9 and 11 for two other anti- words.

   anti- means _____   _____

2. reviving (9): bringing back to life. Look in paragraph 13 for another -vi- word.

   -vi- means _____   _____

3. explicit (3): out in the open, plain. Look in paragraph 3 for two other ex- or e- words.

   e- and ex- mean _____   _____

4. immigrants (1): people who come into a country. Look in paragraphs 8 and 12 for another im- or in- word.

   im- and in- mean _____   _____

The Textbook and You

1. Do you agree with some members of Congress who have "ridiculed the idea of there being value in traveling abroad by boasting that they did not even have passports" (par. 12)? What value do you think there could be in traveling overseas?

   _____

   _____

2. How do you feel about immigration? What benefits do you see? What problems?

   _____

   _____

   _____

3. Which of the points about identity did you most relate to? Explain why.

   _____

   _____

4. On a separate sheet of paper, write a paragraph where you explore where you get your sense of identity. Look at the beginning of paragraph 3 for possible sources.

Take a Closer Look

Look at the pie charts again. Do you think these are the types of work that people could obtain "their sense of identity from" (par. 3)? Do they show changes in gender roles (par. 2)? What do you find most interesting about the charts? Look at the photo again. Do you have a passport? How does having or not having a passport reflect a person's identity?

_____

_____

_____

Internet Activities

If needed, use a separate sheet of paper to fully record your responses. Include the Web address of any sites from which you gather information.

1. Look up "affirmative action." Find opposing views on the subject and make a chart that contrasts 3–4 points on each side. Evaluate how impartial you think the sites you visited are.

   _____

2. Pick one of the groups mentioned in the Social Change and Abiding Discrimination section and one of the issues associated with the group and investigate whether the disadvantages have improved, such as women and wages or African-Americans and poverty. Write a summary on what you find.

Harrison Bergeron

Before You Read

1. What idea about the reading does the title "Harrison Bergeron" give?

2. Survey the first paragraph. Does having everyone equal sound like a good idea?

3. Write a question that you think might apply to the short story.

4. Look at the photo. What are three or four words that come into your mind when you regard the ballet dancers?

Vocabulary Preview

Look for these words in the reading. Exercises to reinforce the learning of new vocabulary using these words follow the reading. The paragraph number where the word appears is in parentheses.

vigilance (1)	**clammy** (2)	**impediment** (37)	**calibrated** (43)	**symmetry** (45)
consternation (49)	**cowered** (53)	**synchronizing** (68)	**capered** (73)	**gamboled** (73)

Kurt Vonnegut (1922–2007) was one of America's foremost writers of novels, short stories, and essays. Among his well-known works are *Slaughterhouse-Five*, *Breakfast of Champions*, *Cat's Cradle*, and *Jailbird*. He served in World War II, and while a prisoner of war, he lived through the bombing of Dresden in 1945, which practically destroyed the city. He used this experience in writing *Slaughterhouse-Five*. His works combine several genres but often involve elements of science fiction. The following story was originally published in the *Magazine of Fantasy and Science Fiction* in October 1961.

1 **The year** was 2081, and everybody was finally equal. They weren't only equal before God and the law. They were equal every which way. Nobody was smarter than anybody else. Nobody was better looking than anybody else. Nobody was stronger or quicker than anybody else. All this equality was due to the 211th, 212th, and 213th Amendments to the Constitution, and to the unceasing vigilance of agents of the United States Handicapper General.

2 Some things about living still weren't quite right, though. April, for instance, still drove people crazy by not being springtime. And it was in that clammy month that the H-G men took George and Hazel Bergeron's fourteen-year-old son, Harrison, away.

3 It was tragic, all right, but George and Hazel couldn't think about it very hard.

Hazel had a perfectly average intelligence, which meant she couldn't think about anything except in short bursts. And George, while his intelligence was way above normal, had a little mental handicap radio in his ear. He was required by law to wear it at all times. It was tuned to a government transmitter. Every twenty seconds or so, the transmitter would send out some sharp noise to keep people like George from taking unfair advantage of their brains.

4 George and Hazel were watching television. There were tears on Hazel's cheeks, but she'd forgotten for the moment what they were about.

5 On the television screen were ballerinas.

6 A buzzer sounded in George's head. His thoughts fled in panic, like bandits from a burglar alarm.

7 "That was a real pretty dance, that dance they just did," said Hazel.

"Harrison Bergeron" from *Welcome to the Monkey House* by Kurt Vonnegut, Jr. Copyright © 1961 by Kurt Vonnegut, Jr. Used by permission of Dell Publishing, a division of Random House, Inc. For on-line information about other Random House, Inc. books and authors, see the Internet web site at http://www.randomhouse.com.

Copyright © 2011 Pearson Education, Inc.

Kurt Vonnegut: Harrison Bergeron **191**

8   "Huh?" said George.

9   "That dance—it was nice," said Hazel.

10   "Yup," said George. He tried to think a little about the ballerinas. They weren't really very good—no better than anybody else would have been, anyway. They were burdened with sashweights and bags of birdshot, and their faces were masked, so that no one, seeing a free and graceful gesture or pretty face, would feel like something the cat drug in. George was toying with the vague notion that maybe dancers shouldn't be handicapped. But he didn't get very far with it before another noise in his ear radio scattered his thoughts.

11   George winced. So did two of the eight ballerinas.

12   Hazel saw him wince. Having no mental handicap herself, she had to ask George what the latest sound had been.

13   "Sounded like somebody hitting a milk bottle with a ball peen hammer," said George.

14   "I'd think it would be real interesting, hearing all the different sounds," said Hazel, a little envious. "All the things they think up."

15   "Um," said George.

16   "Only, if I was a Handicapper General, you know what I would do?" said Hazel. Hazel, as a matter of fact, bore a strong resemblance to the Handicapper General, a woman named Diana Moon Glampers. "If I was Diana Moon Glampers," said Hazel, "I'd have chimes on Sunday—just chimes. Kind of in honor of religion."

17   "I could think, if it was just chimes," said George.

18   "Well—maybe make 'em real loud," said Hazel. "I think I'd make a good Handicapper General."

19   "Good as anybody else," said George.

20   "Who knows better'n I do what normal is?" Hazel said.

21   "Right," said George. He began to think glimmeringly about his abnormal son who was now in jail, about Harrison, but a twenty-one gun salute in his head stopped that.

22   "Boy!" said Hazel, "that was a doozy, wasn't it?"

23   It was such a doozy that George was white and trembling, and tears stood on the rims of his red eyes. Two of the eight

ballerinas had collapsed to the studio floor and were holding their temples.

24   "All of a sudden you look so tired," said Hazel. "Why don't you stretch out on the sofa, so's you can rest your handicap bag on the pillows, honeybunch." She was referring to the forty-seven pounds of birdshot in a canvas bag, which was padlocked around George's neck. "Go on and rest the bag for a while," she said. "I don't care if you're not equal to me for a while."

25   George weighed the bag with his hands. "I don't mind it," he said. I don't notice it anymore. It's part of me."

26   "You've been so tired lately—kind of wore out," said Hazel. "If there was just some way we could make a little hole in the bottom of the bag and just take out a few of them lead balls. Just a few."

27   "Two years in prison and two thousand dollars fine for every ball I took out," said George. "I don't call that a bargain."

28   "If you could just take out a few when you came home from work," said Hazel. "I mean—you don't compete with anybody around here. You just set around."

29   "If I tried to get away with it," said George, "then other people'd get away with it—and pretty soon we'd be right back to the dark ages again, with everybody competing against everybody else. You wouldn't like that, would you?"

30   "I'd hate it," said Hazel.

31   "There you are," said George. "The minute people start cheating on laws, what do you think happens to society?"

32   If Hazel hadn't been able to come up with an answer to this question, George couldn't have supplied one. A siren was going off in his head.

33   "Reckon it'd fall all apart," said Hazel.

34   "What would?" said George blankly.

35   "Society," said Hazel uncertainly. "Wasn't that what you just said?"

36   "Who knows?" said George.

37   The television program was suddenly interrupted for a news bulletin. It wasn't clear at first as to what the bulletin was about, since the announcer, like all announcers, had a serious speech impediment. For about half a minute, and in a state of high excitement, the announcer tried to say, "Ladies and gentlemen—"

38   He finally gave up, handed the bulletin to a ballerina to read.

39   "That's all right—" Hazel said of the announcer, "he tried. That's the big thing. He tried to do the best he could with what God gave him. He should get a nice raise for trying so hard."

40   "Ladies and gentlemen—" said the ballerina, reading the bulletin. She must have been extraordinarily beautiful, because the mask she wore was hideous. And it was easy to see that she was the strongest and most graceful of all the dancers, for her handicap bags were as big as those worn by two-hundred-pound men.

41   And she had to apologize at once for her voice, which was a very unfair voice for a woman to use. Her voice was a warm, luminous, timeless melody. "Excuse me—" she said, and she began again, making her voice absolutely uncompetitive.

42   "Harrison Bergeron, age fourteen," she said in a grackle squawk, "has just escaped from jail, where he was held on suspicion of plotting to overthrow the government. He is a genius and an athlete, is under-handicapped, and should be regarded as extremely dangerous."

43   A police photograph of Harrison Bergeron was flashed on the screen—upside down, then sideways, upside down again, then right side up. The picture showed the full length of Harrison against a background calibrated in feet and inches. He was exactly seven feet tall.

44   The rest of Harrison's appearance was Halloween and hardware. Nobody had ever borne heavier handicaps. He had outgrown hindrances faster than the H-G men could think them up. Instead of a little ear radio for a mental handicap, he wore a tremendous pair of earphones, and spectacles with thick wavy lenses. The spectacles were to make him not only half blind, but to give him whanging headaches besides.

45   Scrap metal was hung all over him. Ordinarily, there was a certain symmetry, a military neatness to the handicaps issued to strong people, but Harrison looked like a walking junkyard. In the race of life, Harrison carried three hundred pounds.

46   And to offset his good looks, the H-G men required that he wear at all times a red rubber ball for a nose, keep his eyebrows shaved off, and cover his even white teeth with black caps at snaggle-tooth random.

47   "If you see this boy," said the ballerina, "do not—I repeat, do not—try to reason with him."

48   There was a shriek of a door being torn from its hinges.

49   Screams and barking cries of consternation came from the television set. The photograph of Harrison Bergeron on the screen jumped again and again, as though dancing to the tune of an earthquake.

50   George Bergeron correctly identified the earthquake, and well he might have—for many was the time his own home had danced to the same crashing tune. "My God—" said George, "that must be Harrison!"

51   The realization was blasted from his mind instantly by the sound of an automobile collision in his head.

52   When George could open his eyes again, the photograph of Harrison was gone. A living, breathing Harrison filled the screen.

53   Clanking, clownish, and huge, Harrison stood in the center of the studio. The knob of the uprooted studio door was still in his hand. Ballerinas, technicians, musicians, and announcers cowered on their knees before him, expecting to die.

54   "I am the Emperor!" cried Harrison. "Do you hear? I am the emperor! Everybody must do what I say at once!" He stamped his foot and the studio shook.

55   "Even as I stand here—" he bellowed, "crippled, hobbled, sickened—I am a greater ruler than any man who ever lived! Now watch me become what I *can* become!"

56   Harrison tore the straps of his handicap harness like wet tissue paper, tore straps guaranteed to support five thousand pounds.

57   Harrison's scrap-iron handicaps crashed to the floor.

58   Harrison thrust his thumbs under the bar of the padlock that secured his head harness. The bar snapped like celery. Harrison smashed his headphones and spectacles against the wall.

59   He flung away his rubber-ball nose, revealed a man that would have awed Thor, the god of Thunder.

60   "I shall now select my Empress!" he said, looking down on the cowering people. "Let the first woman who dares rise to her feet claim her mate and her throne!"

61   A moment passed, and then a ballerina arose, swaying like a willow.

62   Harrison plucked the mental handicap from her ear, snapped off her physical handicaps with marvelous delicacy. Last of all, he removed her mask.

63   She was blindingly beautiful!

64   "Now—" said Harrison, taking her hand, "shall we show the people the meaning of the word dance? Music!" he commanded.

65   The musicians scrambled back into their chairs, and Harrison stripped them of their handicaps, too. "Play your best," he told them, "and I'll make you barons and dukes and earls."

66   The music began. It was normal at first—cheap, silly, false. But Harrison snatched two musicians from their chairs, waved them like batons as he sang the music he wanted played. He slammed them back into their chairs.

67   The music began again and was much improved.

68   Harrison and his Empress merely listened to the music for a while— listened gravely, as though synchronizing their heartbeats with it.

69   They shifted their weights to their toes.

70   Harrison placed his big hands on the girl's tiny waist, letting her sense the weightlessness that would soon be hers.

71   And then, in an explosion of joy and grace, into the air they sprang!

72   Not only were the laws of the land abandoned, but the law of gravity and the laws of motion as well.

73   They reeled, whirled, swiveled, flounced, capered, gamboled, and spun.

74   They leaped like deer on the moon.

75   The studio ceiling was thirty feet high, but each leap brought the dancers nearer to it.

76   It became their obvious intention to kiss the ceiling.

77   They kissed it.

78   And then, neutralizing gravity with love and pure will, they remained suspended in air inches below the ceiling, and they kissed each other for a long, long time.

79   It was then that Diana Moon Glampers, the Handicapper General, came into the studio with a double-barreled ten-gauge shotgun. She fired twice, and the Emperor and Empress were dead before they hit the floor.

80   Diana Moon Glampers loaded the gun again. She aimed at the musicians and told them they had ten seconds to get their handicaps back on.

81   It was then that the Bergerons' television tube burned out.

82   Hazel turned to comment about the blackout to George. But George had gone to the kitchen for a can of beer.

83   George came back in with the beer, paused while a handicap signal shook him. And then he sat down again. "You been crying?" he said to Hazel.

84   "Yup," she said.

85   "What about?" he said.

86   "I forget," she said. "Something real sad on television."

87   "What was it?" he said.

88   "It's all kind of mixed up in my mind," said Hazel.

89   "Forget sad things," said George.

90   "I always do," said Hazel.

91   "That's my girl," said George. He winced. There was the sound of a riveting gun in his head.

92   "Gee—I could tell that one was a doozy," said Hazel.

93   "You can say that again," said George.

94   "Gee—I could tell that one was a doozy."

Getting the Message

____ **1.** The story is about _____.
    a. an equal society in the future.
    b. an unusual ballet demonstration.
    c. a husband and wife.
    d. a perfect society.

____ **2.** Diana Moon Glampers is the _____.
    a. president   c. Handicapper General
    b. lead ballerina   d. television announcer

____ **3.** George wears a radio in his ear because he
    a. has a hearing problem.
    b. has above normal intelligence.
    c. is learning a second language with it.
    d. is addicted to listening to sporting events.

____ **4.** Why won't George take any of the lead balls out of his handicap bag?
    a. He likes the heaviness of it.
    b. He doesn't want to pay a fine or go to jail.
    c. He feels if he starts to break the laws others will too.
    d. b and c

____ **5.** Some of Harrison's handicaps include
    a. glasses with wavy lenses.
    b. wearing six hundred pounds of scrap metal.
    c. a red rubber ball on his a nose and shaved-off eyebrows.
    d. a and c.

____ **6.** The story uses a _____ pattern of organization.
    a. comparison and contrast   c. definition
    b. narrative   d. classification

____ **7.** Vonnegut likely had which two purposes for writing this story?
    a. to entertain and persuade   c. to persuade and inform
    b. to inform and entertain

____ **8.** What tone is revealed in the line "Hazel had a perfectly average intelligence, which meant she couldn't think about anything except in short bursts" (par. 3)?
    a. serious   c. excited
    b. mocking   d. sad

____ **9.** From the end of story it can be inferred that
    a. Hazel and George aren't happily married.
    b. Harrison didn't like his parents.
    c. Hazel and George are going to start a revolution.
    d. Hazel and George don't remember what happened to their son.

_____ **10.** The sentence "His thoughts fled in panic, like bandits from a burglar alarm" (par. 6) is a

a. simile.   b. metaphor.

11. What does the dialogue between George and Hazel add to the story?

_____

_____

_____

_____

12. Give three examples of handicaps Vonnegut mentions that show how equality was enforced in the areas of intelligence, looks, strength and liveliness, as mentioned in paragraph 1, and give the paragraph number where you find the information.

_____

_____

_____

_____

13. List three similes or metaphors in the story with the paragraph number. Which one is your favorite? Why?

_____

_____

_____

_____

_____

14. List two of the questions you wrote in the margins of the story. Were your questions answered by the end of the story? Which question would you most like to discuss with the class?

_____

_____

_____

15. On a separate sheet of paper draw a sketch of Harrison Bergeron when he is fully handicapped. Look carefully at your sketch. How can the sketch help you to better understand the story and the constraints put on the people in this society?

_____

_____

_____

Vocabulary

Use context clues to determine the meaning of each word by referring back to the paragraph where the word is used (the paragraph number is in parentheses). If you need help, consult a dictionary for the definition.

A. Match the word to its synonym.

> **vigilance** (1) **impediment** (37) **symmetry** (45) **cowered** (53) **capered** (73)

1. evenness _____
2. danced _____
3. watchfulness _____
4. trembled _____
5. obstacle _____

B. Write a definition, and then write your own sentence correctly using each word. Be prepared to share your definitions and sentences with the class.

1. clammy (2) _____
2. calibrated (43) _____
3. consternation (49) _____
4. synchronizing (68) _____
5. gamboled (73) _____

C. Word parts: Finish the sentences with the meaning of each word part. The word part is underlined to help you make the connection. Use one meaning twice, and two words use two word parts. Return to pages 85–87 if you need to review the meaning of a word part.

> **across**   **together**   **time**   **look**   **send**

1. The <u>sym</u>metry of the building made it appealing; all of its features fit well _____.
2. The <u>synchron</u>izing of the music and the fireworks meant they had to start at the same _____, so they would progress _____ as planned.
3. The <u>trans</u>mi<u>tter</u> was used to _____ messages all _____ the country.
4. He cleaned his <u>spec</u>tacles so he could _____ out of them clearly.

The Short Story and You

1. List two of your strengths that would need to be handicapped if you lived in the 2081 of the story. Devise a handicap for one of these strengths and then describe your reaction to it.

_____

_____

2. Is competition always bad as George says, "and pretty soon we'd be right back to the dark ages again, with everybody competing against everybody else" (par. 29)? Give an example of a time in your life when competition was beneficial and a time when it wasn't so positive.

_____

_____

3. Reread paragraph 39. Do you agree with Hazel that "He should get a nice raise for trying so hard"? Should people be rewarded for "trying" at work, in school, or in sports? Or is it more important to meet or exceed a standard to get a reward? Explain your choice.

_____

_____

4. On a separate sheet of paper, write a paragraph that examines what kinds of activities or goods would no longer exist (or be worth experiencing if they do exist) in 2081 since everyone is equal, such as sporting events or gourmet meals.

Take a Closer Look

Look at the photo again. What handicaps would you give the ballet dancers if you were the Handicapper General? What would society lose if these ballet dancers were no longer allowed to jump as high or perform as usual?

_____

_____

Internet Activities

If needed, use a separate sheet of paper to fully record your responses. Include the Web address of any sites from which you gather information.

1. Look up "Kurt Vonnegut." List five books he wrote. Read a review of one of these books. Does it sound interesting to you? Explain why or why not.

_____

_____

2. Write your connotative response to the word *equality*. Then record the definitions from an online dictionary. Which meaning best fits the type of equality shown in the story?

_____

 **Objectives Check**

To check your progress in meeting chapter objectives, log in to www.myreadinglab.com, click on the Study Plan tab, and then on the Reading Skills tab. Choose Supporting Details from the list of subtopics. Read and view the resources in the Review Materials section, then complete the Practices and Tests in the Activities section. You can check your scores by clicking on the Gradebook tab.

CHAPTER 6

How would you describe your relationship with money?

Work and the Dollar

How They Influence Decisions

Skill: Organization

Almost daily we are faced with decisions involving money. Our decisions range from how to make money in rewarding jobs to how to spend our money wisely. Most people will spend at least 30 to 40 years of their life working. Work and money can determine how you feel about yourself, how you take care of yourself, and how you interact with others. Better understanding our attitudes and reactions toward work and the dollar can help us to improve our lives and our relationships with others.

Just as we need to be organized in our approaches to work and money, every reading has an organizational structure. Understanding how a reading is put together can help you to uncover the writer's main idea, to follow the writer's points, and to determine whether the writer has made a strong point. Organization involves three main areas: the order the information is presented in, the patterns used in paragraphs and for the reading as a whole, and the transition words and phrases that the writer uses to move from point to point. This chapter will present the details of each of these areas. As you read the four essays or articles, textbook excerpt, and short story, think about how work and money influence your life and consider the role organizational choices have in developing a reading.

- Recognize the order in which information is presented.
- Identify patterns of organization.
- Determine the function of transition words and phrases.

Organization

Organization is how something is put together. We all face organizational challenges. You may have asked yourself: How should I organize my binder to best keep track of my course work? How can I set up my closet to easily get dressed in the morning? A writer asks similar questions in crafting an essay, article, textbook, or short story. Follow the guidelines below to decide how a work is organized.

Methods of Ordering Information

Determine the order of the information presented. There are four common methods of presenting information: chronological (or time order), from the least to the most important point, from the most important to least important point, and a problem and its solution or solutions. The box below gives more details on each method.

Common Methods of Ordering Information

Chronological: This approach puts information in time order.

Least to most important point: This method starts with a point that isn't as important and builds up to the most important point. Readers tend to remember the last point they read, so by putting the most important point at the end of an essay, it is more likely to stick in the reader's mind.

Most to least important point: This strategy starts with the most important point and then gives other smaller points. This method is used either to grab the reader's attention or in places where readers may not read the whole piece, such as a newspaper, which readers tend to skim for information.

Problem and solution: This technique starts by presenting the problem and then offers one or more solutions to the problem.

Identify each method in the paragraphs below.

1. I can't wait for my vacation. I have always wanted to see San Diego. I want to relax on the beach, visit the world-famous zoo, and eat lots of delicious Mexican food in Old Town. I'm also thrilled that I'll get to visit with a friend who recently moved there. We haven't seen each other in 3 years, so I can't wait to get together again. Most

importantly, I am looking for this vacation to relieve the stress I've been under at work. My doctor says my blood pressure is getting into dangerous territory, so I need to take the time to unwind and enjoy myself.

The order: _____

2. If you want to successfully plan a child's birthday party there are four easy steps to follow. First, talk to your child about what kind of party he or she would like to have. Discuss some of your child's interests. If your son likes pirates, make that the theme of the party. If your daughter loves getting wet and the weather is right, have a water party. By involving your child in the planning process, the party will be more meaningful to him or her. Next discuss with your child how many kids to invite. The theme of the party may help dictate how many kids can come. Don't invite more children than can comfortably fit in your living room. Hard choices may need to be made, but, in the end, the party will be more fun if it isn't too crowded. Once you have the theme and guest list, start planning the games and food. Keep the games related to the theme, but make them simple and fun. Not every game needs to have a winner. For the food, again try to relate it to the theme, but keep in mind what your child likes to eat. Try to provide a variety of food, including some healthy choices of fruits and vegetables along with the cake and ice cream. Finally, plan the decorations, and have your child help in making some of them. By following this simple process you can have a fun and meaningful party for your child and for you.

The order: _____

3. The Frasers can no longer get into their garage. They have boxes stacked to the ceiling, tools and bikes lined up against the walls, and half-filled cans of paint in one corner. They used to be able to drive their car into the garage, but they haven't been able to do that for the last 2 years. They would love to be able to park the car in the garage again and to easily get at the items they need. What the Frasers need to do is start going through the boxes they have been storing in the garage. Every evening they need to pull out one box and go through it. If they don't need the items in the box, they can throw them away, recycle them, give them to a charity, or set them aside for a garage sale that they will have within one month. If the items are important, they need to store them in the house where they can be used or buy shelving for the garage so that they can easily see and use the items. Once the boxes have been cleared out, they need to decide which tools they need. Those tools can be organized on peg boards along a wall or placed in a stand. The bikes can be hung on hooks. The unused paint can be put on the shelves if there is still a need for them for touch-up jobs, or the cans should be properly disposed of if they are no longer useable.

The order: _____

4. The mayor has resigned from office effective this Friday. The major reason for the mayor's resignation is the recent revelation that he has been giving highly profitable city contracts to his friends and family for the last 2 years. Items that should have been open to competitive bids, such as the building of the new arts center, have gone to people close to the mayor through his decisions alone. Along with the contract problems, the mayor has been accused of charging the city for personal expenses, such as dry cleaning and yard care at his home. Additionally, there are rumors that he has been engaged in an extramarital affair with his secretary, though nothing has ever been proven.

The order: _____

Patterns of Organization

Look for common patterns of organization. There are seven common ways to organize material in a whole piece of writing or in individual paragraphs. These methods help writers to clearly present their information. The seven common types are cause and effect, classification, comparison and contrast, definition, example, narrative, and process. Writers also often use a combination method where several patterns are used throughout an essay in different paragraphs. The following box gives more details on each pattern.

Common Patterns of Organization

Cause and effect examines the reasons for and/or the results of an event. An essay can study the reasons for a war or what influences the war had on society, or it can do both.

Classification puts items into categories to understand the characteristics of each item. Scientific papers often use classification to show the traits of the items being studied, whether they are animals, rocks, or personality types.

Comparison and contrast looks at similarities and/or differences between items or subjects. This pattern can be used to show how the dream of something is different from the reality or how two people are similar and different in work and personal styles.

Definition tries to describe a term that may have more than one meaning or has an emotional association attached to it. Terms such as *love*, *patriotism*, and *art* are all ripe for a definition essay because not everyone agrees on what these words mean.

Example uses one extended instance or several shorter instances to prove a point. Example essays are a popular organizational pattern because most topics can be supported with examples.

Narrative tells a story and usually uses chronological order. This method is frequently used to tell about personal experiences and in fictional works, such as short stories.

Process tells how to do something or how something is done and usually uses chronological order. A recipe follows a process, as do directions on how to put something together.

ACTIVITY 2

Identify each pattern in the paragraphs below.

1. Sarah and Mark equally enjoy their college classes, but they have highly different objectives when it comes to getting a degree. Sarah's goal is to get a degree in a field that pays good money and to finish college as fast as possible. She is getting degrees in business and computer science as both subjects offer diverse job possibilities, and they have excellent prospects for continued growth. There are several high-paying positions in the worlds of finance and technology. Sarah is taking 21 units each fall and spring semester and another 9 units in the summer in order to graduate in 3 years instead of 4. On the other hand, Mark's goal is to explore several possible majors to find one that is personally rewarding. He is taking classes in philosophy, anthropology, and English to learn more about the world and its people. Unlike Sarah, he isn't especially concerned if his degree leads to a high-paying job. He wants a job that gives his life a purpose. Instead of Sarah's intense schedule, he takes two or three classes a semester and plans to be going to college for 8 to 10 years while he works part-time.

   Pattern of organization: _____

2. If you have boxes of stuff piled in your house and garage and you aren't inclined to have a yard sale, you have four options to deal with your belongings. Sort your posses-sions into the following categories: keep, throw away, recycle, and give away. If an item is useful, put it somewhere you can easily use it, or if it is decorative and you like it, find a place to attractively display it. If it is broken or worn out, throw it away. Recycle paper, or shred it for recycling if it contains personal information, such as old bank statements or tax forms. If you have glass, plastic, or metal items that you no longer want, take advantage of your community's recycling options for those types of items. If something is still useful but it no longer suits your needs, give it to a charity. Clothes that no longer fit and gifts that you were never fond of belong in this category. Taking the time to organize your belongings into these four categories will make it easier to decide what to do with each item and make your house a friendlier place.

   Pattern of organization: _____

3. It was the first week of June and the weather was beginning to warm up. Mary Jane knew this summer had to be different than last year's. She couldn't take another summer of flattering comments about her older sister: Doesn't Zoe swim beautifully? Let's hear Zoe play the piano after dinner. Zoe made that gorgeous dress she wore to the dance. No, this summer Mary Jane would be the center of attention. When the fam-ily headed up to their cabin in the woods the next week, Mary Jane was ready. On the

third night, family and friends gathered around the piano to hear Zoe play. Meanwhile, Mary Jane snuck off to the boat house. She had a large nail and a small hammer hidden under her jacket. Mary Jane chuckled to herself, "Soon Zoe won't be singing anymore."

Pattern of organization: _____

4. Applying for a scholarship through the college involves five easy steps. First come to the counseling office to pick up the list of scholarships the college offers. Read through the list and pick the scholarships you qualify for. We have scholarships based on a variety of factors including financial need, grade point average, musical abilities, and athletics. Next ask a counselor for the forms for each scholarship you would like to apply for. Fill out the forms with the needed information, which usually takes less than 30 minutes per form. Finally hand in the forms by the deadline, and you are set.

Pattern of organization: _____

5. As the saying goes, "I don't know much about art, but I know what I like." And that may be the most valid definition for art there is. A painting can influence people in so many different ways. One person may be intensely moved by it, another person may only pay it a moment's notice, and another person may be deeply offended by it. What makes a painting, sculpture, or photograph art is the individual's reaction to the piece. If the work gets a person to think or feel about it, then the work can be considered art. Because most pieces hanging in museums have caused a reaction in a fairly large number of people, they are generally considered to be art. When you see a large, completely black canvas in a museum and you think, "that's not art," remember that the person right behind you may find the canvas terribly fascinating.

Pattern of organization: _____

6. *Treasure Island* is an excellent book. I first read it at the age of 12 and again just a few months ago. I love the way the book starts with Jim Hawkins joining Squire Trelawney on a search for buried treasure. I was as excited as Jim to discover the buried treasure. Another reason the book is so good is Long John Silver. He is such an ambiguous character that he keeps the story interesting. For example, in one scene he is joking with Jim and telling sea stories, and a few hours later he downs a man with his crutch and stabs him with a knife. I dare say there is hardly a more colorful character in literature. What I also enjoyed about the book is how Jim grows up. For instance, he learns that honorable men can behave badly at times, and, through Silver, he also sees that bad men have their good sides. If you have never read the book or haven't picked it up since childhood, it is definitely time to join in the adventure.

Pattern of organization: _____

7. There were several reasons for the United States' entry into World War I. One reason was the sinking of the British ocean liner the *Lusitania* in May of 1915 by a German U-boat (submarine). On board the liner were 128 U.S. citizens as well as thousands of other passengers. Because the Germans were attacking passenger ships without issuing a warning that would give people time to evacuate the ships, as required by international law, Americans were angry. America's entry was also fueled by the Zimmerman telegram sent by the German ambassador offering help to Mexican revolutionaries to reclaim territory in Arizona, New Mexico, and Texas. As a result of the telegram being leaked to the press, many Americans now felt threatened by the war within their own country. Finally, due to the Russian Revolution in 1917, which overthrew a monarchy, President Wilson could declare that the United States was free to join Russia, France, and Britain in a war that would make the world "safe for democracy."

Pattern of organization: _____

ACTIVITY 3

Sometimes the topic sentence in a paragraph, or the thesis sentence of a whole essay, indicates which pattern of organization will be used. Read the following sentences and look for words that will help you identify the pattern of organization that would be used in a full paragraph or essay. Refer back to the box on page 202 if you need to review the characteristics of each pattern.

1. Packing for a vacation is easy to do if you follow five simple steps. _____

2. The two largest cities in the United States—New York City and Los Angeles—share some similarities, but their differences are more prevalent. _____

3. The main reasons for the college's financial troubles can be traced back to three decisions made in the two years previous to the crisis. _____

4. Pet owners fall into four categories. _____

5. What people see as "necessary" today misses many of the essential aspects of this term. _____

6. Three instances vividly illustrate why traveling with Vivian is not a fun experience.

_____

7. It was the fourth week of my freshman year in college when I learned the true value of friendship. _____

8. The budget cuts the college has been forced to make have impacted numerous programs and the results will be felt for several years. _____

Transition Words and Phrases

Identify transition words and phrases to help you verify the order of the information and patterns of organization. Transition words and phrases help a writer move from one point to another. They also help to show relationships between ideas. Transition words can come at the beginning of a sentence or in the middle of a sentence. They can connect ideas between sentences or within a sentence. By recognizing transition words, you can pick up on signals the writer is giving. If the writer uses the transition word *but*, you know a contrast is coming. If the writer uses the transitional phrase *to illustrate*, you have been given the signal that an example is going to be used. If the writer uses the word *later*, you become aware that a change in time has occurred. The following box lists some common transition words and phrases and explains what they show. Note that a few of the words fit in more than one category.

Common Transition Words and Phrases

Addition: also, and, another, further, furthermore, in addition, next, first, second, third, finally

Cause and Effect: because, since, due to, as a result, hence, so, then, thus, therefore, subsequently, consequently

Comparison: also, likewise, equally, similarly, in the same way

Contrast: but, yet, however, nevertheless, in contrast, instead, on the other hand, unlike, conversely

Example: for example, for instance, such as, to illustrate

Importance: first, second, third, next, least, of lesser concern, greatest, major, most important, most importantly

Time: after, before, first, next, then, meanwhile, later, eventually, soon, suddenly, when, while, during, now, finally

Return to the 7 paragraphs in Activity 2 and circle the transition words you find. Note how the transition words are used in each paragraph to help the writer organize his or her points.

Complete the following sentences by choosing from the transition words and phrases in the box above. Also, on the line after each sentence, identify the type of transition you used. You will use some categories more than once.

Example

I can only agree to go to the movie ____*after*____ I finish my homework. ____*time*____

1. _____, we must clean the storm grates in front of the house, or we could face flooding problems when the heavy rains begin this weekend. _____

2. I wanted to go to the movie, _____ I decided to stay home and study. _____

3. I forgot to bring my notebook to school this morning, _____ I forgot that I had a test in chemistry. _____

4. _____ I meet with my adviser, I want to decide what classes I'm interested in taking next semester. _____

5. I was late for the meeting _____ my car had a flat tire. _____

6. I'm not good in the kitchen; _____, last night I undercooked the pasta and this morning I burnt a piece of toast. _____

7. _____ poor planning, we had to cancel the fun run. _____

8. Lisa can't stand John, and _____ John dislikes Lisa's friend Dana. _____

9. The finance committee will adjourn for the summer on the fifth of June; _____, members will not answer any questions regarding the new budget until September. _____

10. _____ Gemma, I don't have a fear of heights; I would love to go skydiving with you. _____

Organization Checklist

✔ Determine the order of the information presented.

✔ Look for common patterns of organization.

✔ Identify transition words and phrases to help you verify the order of the information and patterns of organization.

Life Stages of Debt

by Sheyna Steiner

Before You Read

1. Survey the bold headings in the article. Where do you think you fit in the stages?

2. Are you currently in debt? Are you worried about ever being in debt?

3. What do you think are two reasons people go into debt?

4. Look at the photo and cartoon. How do you think they will relate to the topic of the article?

Vocabulary Preview

Look for these words in the reading. Exercises to reinforce the learning of new vocabulary using these words follow the reading. The paragraph number where the word appears is in parentheses.

mortgage (7)	**metropolitan** (32)
cushy (18)	**accumulate** (39)
precarious (37)	**superficial** (16)
pensions (49)	**perpetuate** (36)
norm (12)	**sedate** (48)

Sheyna Steiner is a reporter for Bankrate.com, an online site devoted to financial information. Steiner graduated from Sarah Lawrence College with a degree in creative writing. She worked as a writer's assistant in Los Angeles for awhile, and following various other jobs, she came to Bankrate.com as an editorial assistant. Steiner mainly works on the site's Financial Literacy series. Bankrate.com provides information on mortgages, auto loans, credit cards, taxes, insurance, retirement, and investments. The site includes calculators to figure out credit card payments, mortgage rates, and retirement needs among other topics. The following article was originally published in February 2008.

The article begins on the next page.

Source: Bankrate.com, N. Palm Beach, FL 2010

Life Stages of Debt

1   An indispensable tool in modern life, debt happens for many reasons.

2   As the economic struggle of the Depression and rationing of World War II fades from the collective consciousness, Americans feel more confident taking on debt and optimistic about their ability to pay it all back and start saving one day in the future.

3   Robert Manning, Ph.D., author of "Credit Card Nation," studied the financial practices of Americans across generations to discover what influences spending in specific age groups. The research professor and director of the Center for Consumer Financial Services at Rochester Institute of Technology also examined the different attitudes toward debt to find out why people owe so much more today than they did 40 years ago.

4   "You really can't overgeneralize," says Manning. "You have to look at people in particular life cycles to find out why they spent more on those particular items than did a previous generation."

5   Experts explain that debt starts from youth and continues on through life, often into those not-so-golden years.

College

6   "Borrowing to pay for college has become the primary way that most students pay for college," says Tamara Draut, director of the Economic Opportunity Program at Demos and author of "Strapped: Why America's 20- and 30-Somethings Can't Get Ahead."

7   Parents who are unable to save the staggering amount of money needed to fund an undergraduate degree for their kids have a few choices. They can go into debt by getting a PLUS loan or by taking out a second mortgage—or they can put the burden on their children.

8   "If you look at the way we used to do it, we had pressures on states to keep tuitions low and affordable for middle-income households, and for lower-income households we had grant aid that covered about three-fourths of the cost of going to college," says Draut.

9   "Now the majority of aid is debt-based aid and the grants cover about a third of the cost of school."

10   According to the College Board's "Trends in College Pricing 2007," average tuition costs for the 2007–2008 academic year are $23,712 at a private school and $6,185 for a public school. Add in room and board and the totals come to $32,307 and $13,589, respectively.

11   The borrowing doesn't stop there for college students. Undergraduates make easy targets for credit card companies that often give out swag for signing up for a card. Already susceptible to the slings and arrows of outrageously shallow peer assessments based on clothing and music preferences, kids can bump up against their credit limit pretty quickly.

12   "Young people are starting off graduation not only in debt, but it also shows that that competitive pressure that they experienced in high school is what they see as the norm when they go to college," says Manning.

13   "As we start to see the competitive consumption start at an earlier and earlier age, it's not surprising that it then continues in older age groups," he says.

Young singles

14   Getting established in the world costs money—lots of money. In a cruel twist, people starting careers fresh out of school often don't have a lot of it.

15   Some lucky people can fall back on their parents for help, but not everyone has that option or wants to take it.

16   "It's unfortunate but people have always judged others on superficial stuff. So you have to have nice clothes, a nice car, a nice apartment," says Lewis Mandell, professor of finance and managerial economics at the University of Buffalo.

17   "You have to be willing to spend money at bars just to socialize. I think this is considered the norm, it's not considered extravagant. But even normative behavior is expensive," Mandell says.

18   But college graduates can probably waltz into a cushy corporate job that offers ample pay for a worker bee living in the big city, right?

19   Not necessarily.

20   "Earnings have been really flat for young people with college degrees," says Draut.

21   "Incomes are not really keeping up with costs, but one particular difference is that you're talking about a starting salary and a lot of debt that has to be repaid," she says.

22   With tight budgets and soaring living expenses, young people end up on a tightrope between paydays and too often credit cards are their only safety net.

23   "There is not a lot of cushion left at the end of every month, which makes young

"This is a big day. Little Jimmy received his first credit card offer this morning."

people very vulnerable to amassing large amounts of credit card debt when the car breaks down or when they need to go to the dentist," says Draut.

24 But if college graduates are feeling bruised by harsh economic realities, those without college degrees feel it even more.

25 "The potential for a young worker without a college degree has plummeted within a generation," Draut says. "They make a lot less than they used to and all of the benefits that we used to think of coming with your first real job have disappeared."

Young families

26 For young people already struggling with living expenses and stagnating wages, adding a baby can stretch finances to the breaking point.

27 According to Draut, couples with children are twice as likely to file for bankruptcy.

28 "This is a time when you've got loans that have to be repaid. You have earnings that are starting lower and growing slower, and then you add a new baby into the mix—which has always been an added expense. It's nothing new for this generation," she says.

29 "What's new is that those student loans, those credit cards, don't go away overnight."

30 This life stage also ushers in new housing needs. Whereas a studio or one bedroom apartment may have been sufficient a couple of years earlier, with the addition of a spouse and a child, space becomes an issue—as does the school district in which the housing is located.

31 "You get married in the late 20s now in the states and you have a kid and then you want, of course, to live in a nice house in a neighborhood with a good school. The American way of life virtually compels most people to take on a lot of consumer debt and it doesn't really give you an opportunity to get rid of it," says Mandell.

32 Home values in good neighborhoods force many young families to confront difficult choices. The best jobs are located in metropolitan areas, but those areas don't come cheap, says Draut.

33 "A starter home market has disappeared for a lot of high-cost areas," she says.

Mature families

34 Typically, older families have reached a certain level of security. But Manning found that families currently in this age group spend more and save less than did previous generations.

35 "One of the most striking findings of my study was the elasticity of demand for people who have children—there's never a good reason to not indulge our children these days," says Manning. "Instead of saving money for their children to go to college, parents are spending that money while the kids are in high school."

36 Indulging the short-term whims of teenagers can further perpetuate the debt cycle, obligating children to take on loans for college as well as diverting money from retirement savings.

37 Debt in this stage can be particularly precarious, especially if savings are spare.

38 Many parents take on debt to fund children's education—for instance, by taking out a second mortgage—which puts them in the uncomfortable position of either entering retirement with more debt or using money that would otherwise be saved for retirement to service the debt.

39 If parents put off saving for retirement until the kids are out of the house and out of school, they may not have enough time to accumulate adequate funds.

40 "It just means that people aren't going to be able to retire, and that's fine for people who enjoy their work and are in good health. But for people

who aren't in such good health, that's one of the costs of debt that's going to really come back and bite them," says Mandell.

Empty nesters

41   In his study, "Living with Debt," Manning found that older people weren't necessarily shifting their spending into a lower gear.

42   "By the time we see older people, they are used to living on debt and don't want to cut back on their standard of living. So they're maintaining. While their savings rate may go up, they're spending more—maybe on helping their children. It was remarkable how many people in their 50s, 60s and 70s are helping a child or maybe a grandchild," says Manning.

43   With the kids out of the house and the accompanying pipeline into the wallet of mom and dad removed, empty nesters should be sitting pretty.

44   Using data from the 2001 Survey of Consumer Finances conducted by the Federal Reserve, Tansel Yilmazer, assistant professor in the Department of Consumer Sciences and Retailing at Purdue University, found that debt does decline with time.

45   "In general, the probability of carrying debt decreased with age," she says.

46   However, some experts believe that this could be changing, or shifting with the changing demographic. People are having children later in life and reaching the empty nest phase later as well. As acceptance of debt has increased, the older population is increasingly indebted.

47   "Some of them, of course, are maybe opting to work longer periods of time. That certainly is a trend that may be part of the changing life cycle

stages," says Mandell. But he adds that attitudes toward debt at this stage are also changing.

48   "Also I think that the thinking that '60 is the new 40' is really encouraging older people who might in previous generations have been a little bit more sedate in their lifestyles. Now you look on TV and see a 60-year-old doing helicopter skiing and sailing boats across the Atlantic single-handedly. So I think the notion of settling into an empty nest sedate lifestyle is going against the grain."

Seniors

49   Retirement is on shaky ground. No longer assured of pensions, today's retirees are easing into their golden years with less savings and more debt. If acceptance of debt and lack of savings are symptoms of the debt epidemic, this stage of life is where the ravages of the disease really flare up.

50   Throughout their lives, people are spending what they used to save, says Manning. "And so the real crisis is being deferred to retirement."

51   "We're seeing retirees leaving the workforce now with as much as $60,000 in unsecured debt," says David Jones, president of the Association of Independent Consumer Credit Counseling Agencies.

52   The cycle of debt has a domino effect. As today's young

people take on more debt for education, they will spend the money they should have been saving for their retirements to pay off that debt.

53   Today's retirees are also impacted by skyrocketing education costs.

54   A bigger percentage of retirees today still owe on their mortgages and that's not isolated from what's happening to young people around college. A lot of people are taking out second or third mortgages to help pay for college," says Draut.

55   "That's moved mortgage payments to the retirement years which used to be much more uncommon than it is today," says Draut.

56   For seniors in good health, that leaves only one option—work. Those that find themselves in debt and in poor health will struggle.

57   "There are going to be very bad endings for a lot of people," says Mandell.

58   He points out several forces conspiring against seniors, including expected cuts in Social Security and diminished pensions. "The one thing that may save them is that, with the shrinking labor force, if they are valuable to their employer, they might get the opportunity to work until they're 92," he says.

59   "This may not be what people had originally hoped for."

Getting the Message

____ 1. Where is the main idea of the article stated?

    a. paragraph 1   c. paragraph 5

    b. paragraph 2   d. paragraph 51

____ 2. The main idea of the Empty Nesters section is that

    a. people in their 60s today are more daring than past generations.

    b. older people remain in debt because they are not changing their spending patterns.

    c. older people continue to have debt because they are returning to college.

    d. empty nesters enjoy helping their children and grandchildren financially.

____ 3. Why do more students come out of college with debt today than past generations did?

    a. Parents aren't able to save enough for their children to attend college because tuition costs have gone up, so more students borrow money to go to college.

    b. Grant aid used to cover more of the cost of college than it does today.

    c. Credit card companies target college students to sign up for cards.

    d. All of the above.

____ 4. Two circumstances that can lead young families into debt are

    a. college costs and indulging children.

    b. having a baby and housing needs.

    c. buying new clothes and helping children.

    d. a more active lifestyle and getting a bigger house.

____ 5. The sentence "But Manning found that families in this age group spend more and save less than did previous generations" (par. 34) presents

    a. a fact.   b. an opinion.

____ 6. The article overall presents the information using _____ order.

    a. chronological   c. most to least important

    b. least to most important   d. problem and solution

____ 7. The article uses the _____ pattern of organization.

    a. comparison/contrast   c. narrative

    b. classification   d. definition

____ 8. In paragraph 15, what type of transition word is used?

    a. addition   c. comparison

    b. time   d. contrast

____ 9. Steiner's purpose is to

    a. convince people to spend less.

    b. get people to laugh at the situation of being in debt.

    c. share information on the increased debt of Americans.

____ 10. It can be inferred from the line "This may not be what people had originally hoped for" (par. 59) that Mandell

    a. thinks working until 92 is a great idea.

    b. sees most people as being in good financial shape in their later years.

    c. sees having debt in one's later years as a potential problem.

    d. isn't concerned that people may work into their 80s and 90s.

11. List two of the reasons given in paragraphs 14–25 as to why debt for young singles is more likely today.

_____

_____

_____

12. List three transition words found in paragraphs 46–48 and the type of transition each shows (e.g., time, contrast, addition).

_____

_____

13. The article gives several reasons why people are more in debt now than in the past. List two of the reasons that you think people have some control over and two that they have little control over. Give the paragraph number where you find each reason.

Some control over: _____

_____

_____

Little control over: _____

_____

14. Look at your annotations of the article. Which one of the questions or comments you wrote in the margins would you most like to discuss with the class?

_____

_____

15. Create a Venn diagram that compares the debt issues of those in the "College" and "Empty Nesters" categories. Show how each group accumulates debt differently and what areas they share.

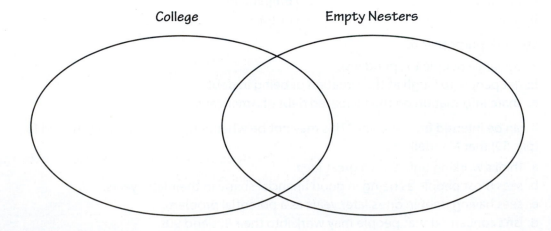

College   Empty Nesters

Vocabulary

Use context clues to determine the meaning by looking back at the paragraph where the word is used (the paragraph number is in parentheses). If you need help, consult a dictionary for the definition.

A. Match each vocabulary word below to its synonym.

> **norm** (12)   **superficial** (16)   **cushy** (18)   **perpetuate** (36)   **precarious** (37)

1. comfortable _____

2. insecure _____

3. standard _____

4. continue _____

5. outward _____

B. Complete each sentence using the correct vocabulary word. Use each word once.

> **mortgage** (7)   **metropolitan** (32)   **accumulate** (39)   **sedate** (48)   **pensions** (49)

1. I'm moving to a _____ area; I'm tired of living in the country.

2. The workers saw their _____ reduced after the company lost several big contracts and its stock fell. The loss of funds was especially going to hurt those close to retiring.

3. I am going to try to get a lower _____ rate. I am having a hard time making the monthly payments on my house.

4. It has been hard for me to adapt to a more _____ lifestyle since I broke my leg. I can't wait to get back to bike riding and rock climbing.

5. I can't believe all the junk I was able to _____ after living in this house for ten years. I need to have a yard sale before I move.

C. Word parts: Match each word to its appropriate definition. The word part is underlined to help you make the connection. Some of the words have more than one word part. Return to pages 85–87 if you need to review the meaning of a word part.

> **optimistic** (2)   **credit** (3)   **graduates** (18)   **expense** (28)   **epidemic** (49)

1. something one has to pay out _____

2. those who step beyond the walls of a college with a degree _____

3. relating to something that falls upon people, like a disease _____

4. relating to the feeling that the best will happen _____

5. trust given to a person by a bank or other financial institution through the lending of money

_____

The Article and You

1. List three of the circumstances that can lead to debt mentioned in the article that you think might most happen to you (for example, tuition expenses).

_____

_____

2. Reread paragraph 16. Do you judge people "on superficial stuff"? Do you feel judged, and does it influence what you buy?

_____

_____

3. Do you want to work until you are 92, as mentioned in paragraph 58? Explain why or why not. At what age do you hope to retire?

_____

_____

4. On a separate sheet of paper, write a paragraph where you imagine that you are $5,000 in debt. In the paragraph explain at least two things you can do to break the cycle of debt that owing this money could cause.

Take a Closer Look

Look at the photo again. After reading about the stages of debt, has your view of the shoppers changed? Visualize a pile of items you have bought in the last year. Are there things that you bought that you didn't need? Have you noticed a change in your shopping habits or those of people you know due to recent economic conditions?

What humorous technique does the cartoon use? Does the article reveal some truth to the statement the cartoon makes?

_____

_____

_____

Internet Activity

If needed, use a separate sheet of paper to fully record your responses. Include the Web address of any sites from which you gather information.

1. Go to bankrate.com. Try one of the calculators on the site. What did you learn from the calculator?

_____

_____

2. Look up "debt relief." How many sites are there? Pick one site that offers suggestions for dealing with debt. List five of the suggestions that you think will help you manage your money.

_____

_____

_____

_____

How to Buy Happiness: Choosing between Stuff and Experiences

by Cynthia G. Wagner

Before You Read

1. Consider the title and subtitle and think about which makes you happier: "stuff" or "experiences."
2. How do you think "stuff" makes people happy?
3. How do you think "experiences" make people happy?
4. Look at the photos. Which of the photographs most appeals to you?

Vocabulary Preview

Look for these words in the reading. Exercises to reinforce the learning of new vocabulary using these words follow the reading. The paragraph number where the word appears is in parentheses.

durable (1)   **tangible** (1)   **reinterpretation** (3)   **vividly** (3)   **fritz** (4)
component (5)   **pursue** (7)   **materialistic** (7)   **experiential** (7)   **trend** (8)

Cynthia G. Wagner is managing editor of *The Futurist*. She has covered a variety of topics for the magazine from meddling to climate change. *The Futurist* is published bimonthly by the World Future Society. The magazine contains articles on ideas related to the future. It is read by roughly 25,000 people worldwide. Articles by public figures such as Isaac Asimov, Al Gore, Margaret Mead, and Gene Roddenberry have appeared in the magazine since it began in 1967. Wagner is also editor of *Futurist Update*, a monthly newsletter e-mailed to World Future Society members. The article below appeared in the September/October 2007 issue of *The Futurist*.

1 **Durable goods** like high-definition plasma TVs last longer than a typical family vacation, so most economists (and retailers), would probably advise you to invest in some tangible thing rather than a trip to an amusement park to keep the family happy.

2 But a psychologist says: Not so fast!

3 The memories of experiences such as vacations last longer and can contribute more to happiness than can material possessions, says happiness researcher Leaf Van Boven of the University of Colorado at Boulder. He suggests that experiences are more open to positive reinterpretation years after the fact—your mental editing will help you forget how long you stood in line and remember more vividly your child's joy on the merry-go-round.

4   "The nice thing about memory is that we sort of forget about all those inconveniences," Van Boven explains. "We put this very favorable spin on experiences, and that's harder to do for material possessions, because they are what they are." And if the high-def TV goes on the fritz so you can't watch your home movies anyway, it's great to have memories to rely on.

5   Memory-making experiences have even more value than material possessions in their contribution to social relationships, Van Boven argues. Experiences have "social value, and we know that social relationships are a huge component of well-being and life satisfaction."

6   Experiences also help individuals achieve personal goals in ways that material goods usually cannot, such as challenging oneself to overcome fear by rock climbing, learning a new skill such as dancing, or cleansing one's soul by volunteering for a summer.

7   Material things are less likely to have this effect on people's lives, or even to be viewed this way, says Van Boven. He adds that people who pursue experiences rather than possessions are often more admired by others: "When you are known as being experiential, you become a more likeable person than when you are known as a materialistic person."

8   But it may be easier just to buy toys to make us happy, rather than planning a memorable and rewarding vacation, and the trend in the United States is toward fewer and shorter vacations.

9   "I think part of the reason is that it's very easy to believe that we are going to take a lot of vacations in the future, but for right now, we need to work hard to earn the money so that we can go take these vacations. We know this doesn't always happen," Van Boven concludes.

Getting the Message

____ **1.** The main idea of the article is that
   a. neither experiences nor stuff ever make people happy.
   b. possessions may make people happier than experiences do.
   c. experiences may make people happier than possessions do.
   d. people who find happiness from experiences are caring people.

____ **2.** What are the possible benefits of experiences?
   a. They help build strong social relationships.
   b. They allow people to achieve their goals.
   c. They are easy to organize.
   d. a and b.

____ **3.** Van Boven feels that social relationships help to make people happier and healthier.
   a. true   b. false

____ **4.** According to information in the article, why might a family look back on a rain-soaked camping trip as a positive experience?
   a. People actually enjoy trips that involve inconveniences.
   b. They had great pancakes on the last morning.
   c. People's memories tend to forget the bad parts of experiences.
   d. They were able to buy souvenirs at a gift shop that they can keep forever.

____ **5.** The article uses _____ to develop its points.
   a. testimony   c. facts
   b. statistics   d. personal examples

____ **6.** The statement "'When you are known as being experiential, you become a more likeable person than when you are known as a materialist person'" (par. 7) is
   a. a fact.   b. an opinion.

____ **7.** The article is mainly organized as a _____ piece.
   a. process
   b. comparison and contrast
   c. classification
   d. definition

____ **8.** Paragraph 2 begins with a _____ transition word.
   a. addition   c. comparison
   b. time   d. contrast

____ **9.** The writer's purpose is to
   a. persuade people to buy more stuff.
   b. convince people to take more vacations.
   c. explain how experiences can make people happier than owning things.
   d. make people laugh at how humans spend their money.

_____ **10.** It can be inferred from the first paragraph that

      a. some people think short-term events make people happier.

      b. some people believe that if something lasts longer it will make people happier.

      c. most people don't know how to measure happiness.

      d. everyone should own a plasma TV.

11. If experiences make people happier, why don't people seek out more experiences than stuff? Use both information in the article and your own ideas to answer the question.

_____

_____

_____

_____

12. Does the writer use enough examples to convince you that personal experiences allow people to achieve goals in ways that physical items cannot (par. 6)? Explain why or why not. What two experiences do you think could help you achieve personal goals?

_____

_____

_____

13. Using your inference skills, why do you think experiences could make people "more likeable" (par. 7)?

_____

_____

_____

_____

14. Compare your annotations of "Life Stages of Debt" with the ones for this article. Give an example of any similar observations you made. Do you think if people had more experiences than stuff, they would be less in debt?

_____

_____

_____

15. On another sheet of paper make a sketch of your bedroom which shows at least ten items you own. Does the sketch make you rethink your possessions or are you comfortable with what you own?

_____

_____

Vocabulary

Use context clues to determine the meaning of each word by referring back to the paragraph where the word is used (the paragraph number is in parentheses). If you need help, consult a dictionary for the definition.

A. Match the vocabulary word to its antonym.

> **durable** (1)   **tangible** (1)   **fritz** (4)   **pursue** (7)   **materialistic** (7)

1. avoid _____   4. generous _____
2. indefinite _____   5. mend _____
3. short-lived _____

B. Finish the paragraph by using the vocabulary words. Use each word once.

> **reinterpretation** (3)   **vividly** (3)   **component** (5)   **experiential** (7)   **trend** (8)

An interesting _____ in vacations involves trips where people participate in local jobs. This kind of vacation especially appeals to the _____ traveler. Not everyone will want to pick grapes in France or make a rug in Morocco. An important _____ in this type of travel is a willingness to give anything a try. A person could spend hours chasing animals, eat unusual food, or end the day covered in mud. Some travelers love this type of vacation because they see a country more _____. The intensity of their experiences makes them feel a part of the country. If this style of travel becomes more popular, there may need to be a _____ of what a vacation is.

C. Word parts: Fill in the missing word parts from the list below, and underline the meaning of each word part found in the question. The words use one, two, or three word parts and one word part is used twice. Return to pages 85–87 if you need to review the meaning of a word part.

> **con**   **com**   **trib**   **pon**   **vi**   **vid**   **ven**   **pos**   **in**

1. The plans have not come together due to several _____iences that have kept me from having time to work on the project.

2. When Erikson moved out, he was able to place all of his _____sessions in two suitcases. I was amazed.

3. I was able to see life so much more _____ly after I got glasses.

4. We put the furniture like this so that every _____ent of the room works well with each other.

5. If we all give together, we can _____ute more than one hundred hours of volunteering to the school this spring.

The Article and You

1. List four items you own that make you happy.

   _____

   _____

2. List four of your experiences that have made you happy.

_____

_____

3. Compare your lists. If you had to make a choice, did the stuff or experiences make you happier? Explain why you made your choice.

_____

_____

4. On a separate sheet, write a paragraph in which you analyze three of your friends. Explain whether these friends are more "experiential" or "materialistic." Do you admire one of these friends more that the other two? Does your attitude have anything to do with that person being more experiential as Van Boven suggests in paragraph 7?

Take a Closer Look

Look at the photos again. What opinion do you have about the people who own the living room? What is your opinion about the people doing an activity (skiing or going on vacation)? How do your opinions fit with the main idea of the article?

_____

_____

_____

Internet Activities

If needed, use a separate sheet of paper to fully record your responses. Include the Web address of any sites from which you gather information.

1. Look up the cost of two expensive items (over $400) that you would like to own, such as jewelry, furniture, sports equipment, and high-end electronics. Then look up the cost of a flight and a hotel night for a place you would like to visit. Record the price of each item. Would you rather spend your money on the stuff or the experience? Explain why.

_____

_____

2. Look up "Americans and vacations." How many paid vacation days do most Americans get a year? How does this compare to other countries? Are Americans using all of their vacation days? What are three popular vacation spots for Americans? Why do you think these places would appeal to so many Americans? Would you like to go to any of these places or have you been to any of them? If you have been, did the experience make you happy?

_____

_____

_____

_____

_____

For Love or Money: Workers Weigh Professional Passion with the Need to Make a Living

by Michelle Goodman

Before You Read

1. Are you more focused on getting a job that you will enjoy or one that pays well?
2. What jobs do you think people do for "love"?
3. What jobs do you think people do for the money?
4. Look at the photos. Why do you think people pick these careers?

Michelle Goodman has been a freelance writer for 18 years. Before breaking out on her own, she worked as a reporter, publicist, and editor. She writes a column for ABCNews.com and the blog *Nine to Thrive* for NWjobs.com. She has written two books about flexible, nontraditional jobs. Her writing has appeared in a variety of places including CNN.com, the *Seattle Times,* and PayScale.com. She earned her bachelor's degree in journalism from George Washington University. The following article appeared in a specialty publication of NWjobs.com on March 28, 2010.

Vocabulary Preview

Look for these words in the reading. Exercises to reinforce the learning of new vocabulary using these words follow the reading. The paragraph number where the word appears is in parentheses.

portfolio (1)	**lucrative** (1)	**protracted** (2)	**ensuring** (8)	**bliss** (11)
sector (12)	**repercussions** (12)	**ecstatic** (12)	**primary** (14)	**understatement** (15)

Financially

1 **speaking,** Chris Pesce had it all: the mortgage-free house, the savings, the investment portfolio. But like some who choose a lucrative career over one that feeds the soul, the copyright and trademark lawyer wasn't feeling the love for his work.

2 A decade into his "not very satisfying" career, he cried uncle. There was no protracted period of soul-searching, no sleepless nights pondering "What now?" Pesce already knew his next move.

3 "I had always imagined how much fun it would be to teach high school math," the 45-year-old Seattle resident says. "My best—and worst—high school teachers were math teachers, so I knew that a quality math teacher can make all the difference."

4 So back to school Pesce went, first to refresh his calculus at a local community college and

then to earn his master's degree in teaching. After several years working in the Seattle Public Schools system, he now teaches at a small private high school.

5 Pesce didn't just close his eyes, take a flying leap off that proverbial cliff and pray it would all work out. He did the necessary recon, visiting high schools and talking to teachers to learn more about the profession.

6 That's a smart move, says Alexandra Levit, author of "New Job, New You: A Guide to Reinventing Yourself in a Bright New Career."

7 "Many times, dream careers are not as glamorous as they sound," she says. "You want to get the reality check before investing substantial amounts of time, energy and money."

8 For Pesce, that also meant ensuring he could afford the nearly 50 percent pay cut—and that

his wife, who works as a physical therapist, was on board with it. Fortunately, the answers were yes and yes.

9   A decade after making his career 180, Pesce is still feeling the love for his work.

10   "When a student turns things around because you show faith in them, or when they come back years later to thank you, that makes the job completely worthwhile," he says.

11   Of course, not everyone finds his or her professional bliss. And some who find it can't afford to follow it.

12   Take "Charlotte," a communications professional in the technology sector who didn't want her real name used for fear of repercussions at work. After a layoff last year, Charlotte found herself unemployed for six months. Because she had never been too ecstatic about the work she did, part of her was relieved.

13   One week of introspection led to another. Before she knew it, Charlotte had accepted a job

she felt passionate about with a social-service agency. There was only one problem: the nearly 50 percent pay cut.

14   "I was scared I was going to lose my home," says Charlotte, who's the primary breadwinner in her household. "I was worried I wasn't going to be able to put any more money into retirement. I felt like I was stuck."

15   Several months of financial stress later, Charlotte found a high-tech job and snatched it up. To say it was a relief would be an understatement.

16   "This gives me breathing room," she says. "I can start putting money in my savings account again." She also can afford some of the pricier pursuits that feed her soul outside the office, such as art and exercise classes.

17   As long as you have enough time after work for friends, family and hobbies, Levit says, "this is actually a terrific approach. There's no rule that says that you have to feel 100 percent passionate about your day job."

But what about Charlotte's dream of working in the social-service sector?

"Maybe someday I will go back," she says. "But I don't trust the economy yet. I'm too afraid to take a low-paying job when a high-paying job is right there.

20   "In the meantime, I'm trying to stimulate the economy as much as I can."

"Passion vs. paycheck is a tough balancing act"

Getting the Message

_____ **1.** The topic of the article is _____.

    a. jobs

    b. teaching

    c. finding the right job

    d. stressful jobs

_____ **2.** What is the main idea of the article?

    a. Most people like their jobs.

    b. It doesn't matter what a job pays as long as you enjoy it.

    c. Having a job that pays well is more important than enjoying what you do.

    d. It can be difficult to find a job that is personally fulfilling and also pays well.

_____ **3.** Which type of supporting detail does Goodman use?

    a. statistics

    b. testimony

    c. personal examples

    d. a and c

_____ **4.** The article contains the following minor detail(s):

    a. Pesce teaches at a small private high school.

    b. It is smart to research a career one is interested in.

    c. Charlotte takes exercise classes.

    d. a and c

_____ **5.** The sentence "'As long as you have enough time after work for friends, family and hobbies, Levit says, 'this is actually a terrific approach'" (par. 17) is

    a. a fact.

    b. an opinion.

_____ **6.** The article mainly uses _____ order to present the information.

    a. chronological

    b. least to most important

    c. most to least important

    d. problem and solution

_____ **7.** The article as a whole uses which pattern of organization?

    a. comparison and contrast

    b. cause and effect

    c. narrative

    d. classification

_____ **8.** Paragraph 4 mainly uses _____ transition words.

    a. comparison

    b. time

    c. addition

    d. contrast

9. Goodman's purpose is to
   a. entertain people with stories about interesting jobs.
   b. persuade people to work more.
   c. inform people about the challenge of finding a job that fits all of a person's needs.
   d. persuade people to work at jobs they love.

10. It can be inferred from the last line in the article (par. 20) that Charlotte
   a. is going into debt.
   b. is putting most of her money in a savings account.
   c. has bought a lot of new clothes recently.
   d. is spending some of the money she is earning from her high-paying job.

11. Find at least one contrast word, cause and effect word, and time transition word in the article. Give the paragraph number where each is located.

_____

_____

_____

12. Is the tone of the article formal or informal? List three words or phrases (with paragraph numbers) that helped you reach your conclusion.

_____

_____

_____

13. Is Goodman using the false dilemma fallacy? Is there an alternative she doesn't mention?

_____

_____

14. What is a question or comment you wrote in the margins as you annotated the article that you would like to discuss with the class?

_____

_____

15. Paraphrase the line "Of course, not everyone finds his or her professional bliss" (par. 11).

_____

_____

Vocabulary

Use context clues to determine the meaning by looking back at the paragraph where the word is used (the paragraph number is in parentheses). If you need help, refer to a dictionary for the definition.

A. Match the word to its definition.

1. portfolio (1) ____   a. a part or area, especially of a nation's economy
2. ensure(ing) (8) ____   b. an expression in terms weaker than required
3. sector (12) ____   c. a list of assets a person owns
4. repercussion(s) (12) ____   d. an often indirect result of an action
5. understatement (15) ____   e. to make certain

B. Replace the underlined word in each sentence with its synonym from the list below.

> **lucrative** (1)   **protracted** (2)   **bliss** (11)   **ecstatic** (12)   **primary** (14)

1. Keri was <u>thrilled</u> to put on the polka-dot bridesmaid dress; she always considered dots fun to wear. _____

2. The company's last job was so <u>profitable</u> that every employee was given a trip to Hawaii as a bonus. _____

3. The <u>extended</u> negotiations were exhausting for both sides. _____

4. Dan's <u>main</u> goal for the weekend is to finish his history paper. _____

5. Javier finds <u>happiness</u> in tending his garden, while pleasure for his wife is reading a good book. _____

C. Word parts: Answer each question by supplying the meaning of the word part found in the underlined word. Return to pages 85–87 if you need to review the meaning of a word part.

> **drag**   **a person who**   **feel**   **study or science of**

1. What is <u>technology</u>? the _____ mechanical or industrial arts
2. What is a <u>therapist</u>? _____ aids in treating sick or injured patients
3. What happens when something is <u>protracted</u>? It can _____ on.
4. What happens when people are <u>passionate</u> about a subject? They _____ strongly about it.

The Article and You

1. What is a job that you have "always imagined how much fun it would be" (par. 3) or that you see as your "dream career" (par. 7)? What attracts you to this occupation?

   _____

   _____

2. Goodman quotes Levit as saying "'There's no rule that says that you have to feel 100 percent passionate about your day job.'" But what percentage do you think a person should love a job in order to have a fulfilling life? How did you reach this conclusion?

_____

_____

_____

3. What do you think of Charlotte's decision? What would you have done in her place?

_____

_____

_____

4. On a separate sheet of paper, write a paragraph where you describe a day in the life of a person who loves his or her job. You can use yourself, someone you know, or create a hypothetical person. Give the person a specific job and show what the person does at work, how he or she interacts with others, and what makes the job so rewarding.

Take a Closer Look

Look at the photos again. Do these look like jobs people do for love, for money, or for both reasons? Explain your choices.

_____

_____

Internet Activities

If needed, use a separate sheet of paper to fully record your responses. Include the Web address of any sites from which you gather information.

1. Do a search for the job you picked in question 1 of the Article and You section. Areas to investigate include what education or special training the job requires, what the working conditions are like, and what it pays. Write a summary about the information you find. Do you still have an interest in someday pursuing this career?

_____

_____

2. Paragraph 17 mentions having "time after work for friends, family and hobbies," which is important even when one loves a job. Look up "balancing work and personal life." Find a site that provides tips on how to maintain a balance among the various areas in a person's life. List three of the tips that you find most helpful.

_____

_____

_____

School Again

from *Dust Tracks on a Road*

by Zora Neale Hurston

Before You Read

1. Skim the dialogue in paragraphs 5–15. What do you think dialogue adds to a reading?

2. The selection shows how blacks were treated in the first part of the twentieth century. How do you think the treatment of African-Americans has changed since then?

3. Write a question that you think the reading might address: _____
_____

4. Look at the photo. What impressions do you get about the barbershop?

Vocabulary Preview

Look for these words in the reading. Exercises to reinforce the learning of new vocabulary using these words follow the reading. The paragraph number where the word appears is in parentheses.

belligerently (5)	loathsome (21)	ironic (20)
martyr (19)	crusader (10)	fiendish (21)
sanction (20)	melee (19)	
patronage (20)	militant (20)	

Zora Neale Hurston (1891–1960) was a woman of many accomplishments. She was a novelist, short story writer, anthropologist, and folklorist. She grew up in Eatonville, Florida. She was a leader in the Harlem Renaissance movement in the 1920s. In 1927 she received a bachelor's degree in anthropology from Barnard College. She studied voodoo rituals in Haiti in the 1930s. Her novel *Their Eyes Were Watching God* was made into a movie starring Halle Berry in 2005. This excerpt, which examines an incident that happened while she was a manicurist at a barbershop, is from her autobiography *Dust Tracks on a Road*, published in 1942.

1 **Mr. Robinson arranged** for me to come to work at three-thirty every afternoon and work until eight-thirty. In that way, I was able to support myself. Soon, most of the customers knew I was a student, and tipped me accordingly. I averaged twelve to fifteen dollars a week.

2 Mr. Robinson's 1410 G Street shop was frequented by bankers, Senators, Cabinet Members, Congressmen, and Gentlemen of the Press. The National Press Club was one block down the same street, the Treasury Building was one block up the street and the Capitol not far away. . . .

3 I learned things from holding the hands of men like that. The talk was of world affairs, national happenings, personalities, the latest quips from the cloak rooms of Congress and such things. I heard many things from the

White House and the Senate before they appeared in print. They probably were bursting to talk to somebody, and I was safe. If I told, nobody would have believed me anyway. Besides, I was much flattered by being told and warned not to repeat what I had heard. Sometimes a Senator, a banker, a newspaper correspondent attached to the White House would all be sitting around my table at one time. While I worked on one, the others waited, and they all talked. Sometimes they concentrated on teasing me. At other times they talked about what had happened, or what they reasoned was bound to happen. Intimate stories about personalities, their secret love affairs, cloak room retorts, and the like. Soon they took me for granted and would say, "Zora knows how to keep a secret. She's all right." Now, I know that my discretion really didn't matter. They were relieving their pent-up feelings where it could do no harm. . . .

4   An incident happened that made me realize how theories go by the board when a person's livelihood is threatened. A man, a Negro, came into the shop one afternoon and sat down in Banks's chair. Banks was the manager and had the first chair by the door. It was so surprising that for a minute Banks just looked at him and never said a word. Finally, he found his tongue and asked, "What do you want?"

5   "Hair-cut and shave," the man said belligerently.

6   "But you can't get no hair-cut and shave here. Mr. Robinson has a fine shop for Negroes on U Street near Fifteenth," Banks told him.

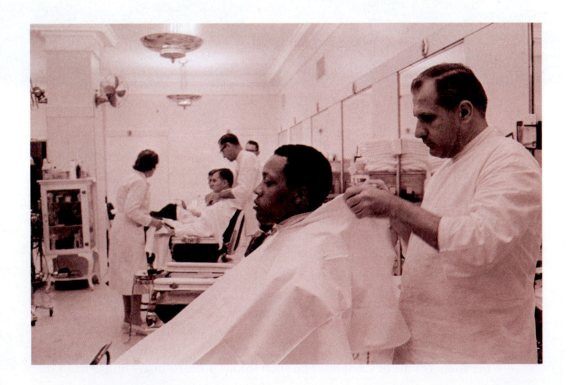

7   "I know it, but I want one here. The Constitution of the United States—"

8   But by that time, Banks had him by the arm. Not roughly, but he was helping him out of his chair, nevertheless.

9   "I don't know how to cut your hair," Banks objected. "I was trained on straight hair. Nobody in here knows how."

10 "Oh, don't hand me that stuff!" the crusader snarled. "Don't be such an Uncle Tom."

11 "Run on, fellow. You can't get waited on in here."

12 "I'll stay right here until I do. I know my rights. Things like this have got to be broken up. I'll get waited on all right, or sue the place."

13 "Go ahead and sue," Banks retorted. "Go on uptown, and get your hair cut, man. Don't be so hard headed for nothing."

14 "I'm getting waited on right here!"

15 "You're next, Mr. Powell," Banks said to a waiting customer. "Sorry mister, but you better go on uptown."

16 "But I have a right to be waited on wherever I please," the Negro said and started towards Updyke's chair which was being emptied. Updyke whirled his chair around so that he could not sit down and stepped in front of it. "Don't you touch *my* chair!" Updyke glared. "Go on about your business."

17 But instead of going, he made to get into the chair by force.

18 "Don't argue with him! Throw him out of here!" somebody in the back cried. And in a minute, barbers, customers all lathered and with hair half cut, and porters, were all helping to throw the Negro out.

19 The rush carried him way out into the middle of G Street and flung him down. He tried to lie there and be a martyr, but the roar of oncoming cars made him jump up and scurry off. We never heard any more about it. I did not participate in the melee, but I wanted him thrown out, too. My business was threatened.

20 It was only that night in bed that I analyzed the whole thing and realized that I was giving sanction to Jim Crow, which theoretically, I was supposed to resist. But here were ten Negro barbers, three porters and two manicurists all stirred up at the threat of our living through loss of patronage. Nobody thought it out at the moment. It was an instinctive thing. That was the first time it was called to my attention that self-interest rides over all sorts of lives. I have seen the same thing happen hundreds of times since, and now I understand it. One sees it breaking over racial, national, religious and class lines. Anglo-Saxon against Anglo-Saxon, Jew against Jew, Negro against Negro, and all sorts of combinations of the three against other combinations of the three. Off-hand, you might say that we fifteen Negroes should have felt the racial thing and served him. He was one of us. Perhaps it would have been a beautiful thing if Banks had turned to the shop crowded with customers and announced that this man was going to be served like everybody else even at the risk of losing their patronage with all of the other employees lined up in the center of the floor shouting, "So say we all!" It would have been a stirring gesture, and made the headlines for a day. Then we

could all have gone home to our unpaid rents and bills and things like that. I could leave school and begin my wanderings again. The "militant" Negro who would have been the cause of it all would have perched on the smuddled-up wreck of things and crowed. Nobody ever found out who or what he was. Perhaps he did what he did on the spur of the moment, not realizing that serving him would have ruined Mr. Robinson, another Negro who had got what he had the hard way. For not only would the G Street shop have been forced to close, but the F Street shop and all of his other six downtown shops. Wrecking George Robinson like that on a "race" angle would have been ironic tragedy. He always helped out any Negro who was trying to do anything progressive as far as he was able. He had no education himself, but he was for it. He would give any Howard University student a job in his shops if they could qualify, even if it was only a few hours a week.

21   So I do not know what was the ultimate right in this case. I do know how I felt at the time. There is always something fiendish and loathsome about a person who threatens to deprive you of your way of making a living. That is just human-like, I reckon.

Getting the Message

___ **1.** The main idea of the passage is that

    a. there should be separate barber shops for white and black customers.

    b. Hurston should have been supportive of the man who wanted a haircut and shave.

    c. people will react negatively to those who threaten their jobs, even if what the people are doing is not necessarily morally right.

    d. the man was wrong to try to get a haircut and shave at this barbershop.

___ **2.** The topic sentence in paragraph 20 can be found in sentence _____.

    a. 1   c. 5

    b. 2   d. 7

___ **3.** Hurston uses _____ as supporting details.

    a. personal examples

    b. statistics

    c. facts

    d. testimony

___ **4.** How many of the people in the barbershop wanted the man thrown out?

    a. only Banks and Updyke

    b. all of the barbers

    c. only the white customers

    d. everyone in the shop

___ **5.** What are Hurston's statements in paragraph 21?

    a. facts   b. opinions

___ **6.** The excerpt uses the _____ pattern of organization.

    a. definition   c. classification

    b. narrative   d. comparison and contrast

___ **7.** What technique is often found in the organizational pattern used in this selection?

    a. items are put in categories

    b. short paragraphs

    c. the most important point is presented last

    d. dialogue

___ **8.** Paragraphs 6–8 use _____ transition words.

    a. time   c. contrast

    b. addition   d. comparison

___ **9.** Hurston's purpose is to

    a. show that they did the right thing.

    b. consider why they didn't serve the man.

    c. relate a humorous incident.

    d. convince people to do the right thing even if it means possibly losing a job.

_____**10.** It can be inferred from the situation that what Banks says in paragraph 9

      a. truly reveals his limited skills.

      b. is a way to get the man to leave because the shop is too busy to serve him.

      c. is an excuse not to serve the man.

      d. is his way to get rid of a man who doesn't tip well.

11. Why do you think Hurston uses dialogue in this scene?

_____

_____

12. Why would it have been an "ironic tragedy" (par. 20) if the man had ruined Mr. Robinson's businesses?

_____

_____

_____

13. Is Hurston using the false dilemma (or black or white thinking) fallacy when she states that had the fifteen Negros banned together to support the man getting a haircut and shave "it would have been a stirring gesture, and made the headlines for a day. Then we could all have gone home to our unpaid rents and bills and things like that" (par. 20)? Could there have been a different result?

_____

_____

14. Look back at your annotations. List three items that you starred or used other markings to identify as important sections.

_____

_____

15. Paraphrase the line "There is always something fiendish and loathsome about a person who threatens to deprive you of your way of making a living" (par. 21).

_____

_____

Vocabulary

Use context clues to determine the meaning by looking back at the paragraph where the word is used (the paragraph number is in parentheses). If you need help, refer to a dictionary for the definition.

A. Put a *T* if the underlined vocabulary word is used correctly in the sentence and an *F* if it is not.

_____ 1. The angry man entered the room and <u>belligerently</u> (5) began ordering people about.

_____ 2. Nita was an active participant in the <u>melee</u> (19); she shook hands and smiled at people.

_____ 3. Thanks to the <u>patronage</u> (20) of the Chef's Club, we were able to award ten scholarships to students who can now pursue their love of cooking.

_____ 4. It is <u>ironic</u> (20) that Verda broke her favorite vase while putting flowers in it after it had survived a cross-country trip and an accident involving the moving van.

_____ 5. The <u>fiendish</u> (21) woman brought cookies and milk to share at the meeting.

B. Finish the sentences with the correct vocabulary word. Use each word once.

> **crusader** (10)   **martyr** (19)   **sanction** (20)   **militant** (20)   **loathsome** (21)

1. I'm not usually a _____ person, but I'm going to start a protest against Mr. Bothell's mowing of his lawn at five in the morning.

2. Max is a great _____ for preserving our local parks, but he really doesn't need to wear a cape to every city council meeting.

3. Lois was a true _____ in getting sick children needed health care. She spent hours campaigning at the state capitol, and her dedication cost her her marriage.

4. How could anyone be so _____ as to steal the money the kids made from their lemonade stand?

5. I don't usually _____ your staying out so late, but since you were helping to rescue people from the fire, it is all right this time.

C. Word parts: Highlight or circle the meaning of the underlined word part found in each question. Return to pages 85–87 if you need to review the meaning of a word part.

1. One who fights for something is a crusad<u>er</u>, and one who shops is a custom<u>er.</u>

2. Something relating to an ethnic group or race is rac<u>ial.</u>

3. If one is inclined to use one's natural feelings, one is instinct<u>ive.</u>

4. When one is inclined to take steps to accomplish something, one is pro<u>gress</u>ive.

5. Someone who has qualities similar to a wicked person is fiend<u>ish.</u>

The Essay and You

1. Imagine that one day at work the company announces that it will be outsourcing your job to another country. How would you react? How would the situation be similar to Hurston's experience?

_____

_____

2. In today's world, what would be a similar situation to what happens in the excerpt where people are not treated equally because they are different from the majority (or those in power) in some way?

_____

_____

3. Besides at work, list a situation you might be involved in where self-interest could take over instead of concern for a larger group you belong to, such as your gender or community. Also consider Hurston's categories: "racial, national, religious and class lines" (par. 20).

_____

_____

_____

_____

4. On a separate sheet of paper, write a paragraph where you pretend you were working at the barbershop on the day the man came in. Explain how you would have reacted to the incident.

Take a Closer Look

Look at the photo again. How does the photograph show a different scene from what happens in Hurston's situation? In what year do you think the photograph was taken?

_____

_____

_____

Internet Activities

If needed, use a separate sheet of paper to fully record your responses. Include the Web address of any sites from which you gather information.

1. Look up the terms *Uncle Tom* (par. 10) and *Jim Crow* (par. 20). Write brief definitions for each. Have you ever heard either term used?

_____

_____

_____

_____

2. Look up Howard University (par. 20). Write a summary of the information you find about the school.

Becoming Financially Independent

from *Planning Your Future: Keys to Financial Freedom*

Before You Read

1. Survey the bold headings. What do you think the chapter is going to be about?

2. At what age do you want to retire?

3. What do you see yourself doing during your retirement years?

4. Look at the photo and graph. What do they reveal about saving?

Vocabulary Preview

Look for these words in the reading. Exercises to reinforce the learning of new vocabulary using these words follow the reading. The paragraph number where the word appears is in parentheses.

expenditures (2) **factor** (4) **optimize** (4) **inflation** (6) **prognosis** (9)

formulate (12) **ensuing** (16) **octogenarian** (18) **acquaintance** (18) **compound** (21)

Stephan Konowalow teaches study skills at the College of Southern Nevada. He formerly taught sociology, as well as being a counselor and administrator, for 28 years at Delta College in Michigan. He has a doctorate degree from Wayne State University. He has written books on dealing with stress and money management. The following excerpt is from Chapter 2 of the textbook *Planning Your Future: Keys to Financial Freedom*. Note how the writer refers back to Chapter 1. Textbook writers sometimes ask readers to refer to past chapters or look for more information on a topic in later chapters.

1 **How would** you define financial independence? Do you have a dollar amount in mind? In Chapter 1, I suggested that to retire comfortably today you would need approximately $500,000 in a retirement fund. That may sound like a lot of money. But for some people, it may be only 10% of what they plan to have in their retirement fund. Can you imagine a retirement fund balance of $5,000,000 or $10,000,000? It is not impossible. It just takes planning. With planning, you can have all that you need and more.

Key to Financial Independence: Spend Less

2 The key to building financial independence sounds so simple: Spend less than you make. Yet, many people spend more than they make, and they do this on a regular basis. Are you living beyond your income? What did you learn about your expenditures when you completed the Brief Monthly Statement Worksheet (Exhibit 1.1)? Did you learn that you have too much credit card debt, that you have little to no cash, or that your paycheck doesn't meet your minimum monthly financial necessities?

3 To repeat the major theme of Chapter 1, *now* is the time to plan for your financial future. It does not matter how old you are—the important thing is that you begin *now* to put your finances in order. Using the agreement below, set down your retirement savings goals, as the first step in developing an investment plan.

y

z

w

"Becoming Financially Independent" (pp. 17–22) from *Planning Your Future: Keys to Financial Freedom* by Stephen Konowalow. Copyright © 2003 by Pearson Education, Inc. Reprinted by permission of Pearson Education, Inc., Boston, MA.

KEY: *Begin now to put money in your savings/investment fund first.* That's right—you now come first. All your other bills are paid *after* you have paid yourself. This means that you must spend less than you are currently spending to have enough income to cover all your expenses *and* your #1 priority—a payment to your retirement fund.

An Agreement of Understanding with Myself

My goal is to save the following amount of money each month: $_____.

By not wasting this money, I will have $_____ at the end of each month.

My goal is to save/invest $_____ per year for the next _____ years.

My nest egg goal is $ _____.

Signed by: _____   Date _____

4   It is up to you to honor your agreement and to achieve each of your stated goals. You and you alone are the single most important factor in your own success. Besides learning to pay yourself first the amount you have decided you need, learn why you need to save for retirement and how to optimize your investments.

5   Exercise: Using the lines below, write a paragraph summarizing three or more things that you learned from this section.

_____

_____

_____

_____

_____

The Need to Save for Retirement

6   How much money will you need in your retirement years? The goal is to have a nest egg of about $500,000, but with inflation, $1,000,000 or more would be preferable. Begin now, and you can easily set aside that amount over the next 30, 35, or 40 years. It does not matter whether you are from a wealthy family. Anyone can achieve wealth with consistent planning and regular monthly contributions to a retirement program.

7   Although it may be difficult for you to think about saving or investing money today, it is a necessity. Having income tomorrow requires putting away money now. Whether you want to admit it, you will not work forever. Wouldn't your retirement years be brighter if you were financially secure?

The Expectation: You Will Live 20 Years Beyond Retirement

8   Are you in good health, today?   ❏ Yes   ❏ No
     Do you expect to be in good health when you retire?   ❏ Yes   ❏ No

9   The prognosis is good for you—whether male or female—to live more than 20 years beyond retirement. Research into life expectancy shows that people retiring at 65 today can expect to live another 25 years or more. This means that if you have a fairly risk-free

lifestyle, take care of yourself, and have good genes, you could live to be 90, 100, or even older.

10   One study, the "Grandfather Economic Heath Care Report," found that men who were 65 years old in 2000 could expect to live another 16 years, to age 81; women could expect to live another 19 years, to age 84 (http://home.att.net/~mwhodges/healthcare. htm). Other reports show these numbers to be low, so it gets better.

11   A 65-year-old male has a 50% chance of living another 21 years and 50% of females 65 years of age can expect to live another 25 years. Of men and women aged 65 in 1940, only 7.4% had a life expectancy of 90, but by 1980, 24.4% of a similar population could expect to live to 90. If we project further, 50% of people who were 65 in 2000 have a life expectancy of about 90. Because the percentage of people projected to live beyond 90 keeps increasing, it would not be surprising if more than 50% of the men and women who reach 65 in 2040 lived beyond 90 years of age.

12   Today, the possibility for you to live 25, 30, or more years beyond your retirement is more a reality than ever before. The reality of longer life beyond retirement raises a question: Assuming you live 25 to 30 years after you stop working, how will you support yourself? If you are married, how will you ensure that your family has sufficient income to enjoy these years? Where will your money come from, if you can only expect a small amount from Social Security? The answer is *planning*. Now is the time to formulate a plan to make those years enjoyable. You must plan today to have money in retirement for tomorrow.

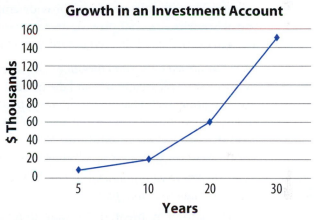

Growth in an Investment Account

With a yearly contribution of $1,200 at an 8% interest rate, compounded monthly.

13   Perhaps you don't believe that you will live to age 90 or even close to it. If interested, you can actually determine your life expectancy. Knowing this information will certainly motivate you more to plan for your retirement. To find out how close to 100 you can expect to live, bring up the life calculator site at the following URL: http://geography.miningco.com/cs/lifeex-pectancy/. Click on the Living to 100 Life Expectancy Calculator link and do the ex-ercise. You may be surprised at how much time you can expect after retirement.

14   Whatever the answer, you are likely to live beyond 65 years of age, and neither your employer nor the government can provide all the money you will need in your nonworking years. This is *your* responsibility.

15   The Department of Labor reports that the average male and female (married or unmar-ried, but without children) works approximately 37.5 years. The married female or a female with children works approximately 30 years. This means that you can expect to be retired for as long as you have worked, and possibly longer. When you make the decision to retire, you need to know how you will fund the next 30 and more years of your and your family's life. Again, you are responsible for the results.

16   Whether you are male or female, assume that you will work only until you are 65. In the ensuing years, how will you support yourself and, if relevant, your family? One tends to assume that children would be grown by then and be living on their own. This may not be an accurate assumption in today's world, however.

17   Around 30 years ago, a trend toward parenting at an older age became recognized. Since the 1970s, many more men and women have had children at older ages, even 40 and 50. It is, there-fore, more possible than it used to be that children will still be at home when their parents retire.

18   Moreover, health research reports that working tends to promote health and longer lives. As an octogenarian acquaintance related to me, "Work is what keeps me young and alive." The late George Burns, who died when he was over 100, showed that although the body may slow down, the mind becomes sharper with age. Retired men and women are active and busy. Research also demonstrates a strong relationship between living longer and having set aside a retirement fund.

19   Exercise: Using the lines below, write a paragraph summarizing three or more things you learned from this section.

_____

_____

_____

_____

Optimizing Your Investment: Taking Advantage of Time, Savings, and Compound Interest

20   The environment of money management is changing quickly. You will be at an advantage if you know how to be part of this change. Generally held expectations about work and retirement are gone—no longer true: One does not work at one job until retirement; employers no longer provide employees with a full retirement package; and Social Security does not provide an adequate income in retirement. Also, many people are retiring before 65 or even before they reach 62.

21   **KEY:** *Get started saving and investing early.* The earlier you start investing in your retirement, the more you will accumulate and the more comfortably you can expect to live in the future. Accumulating wealth has to do with the amount set aside for saving, the time for it to grow, and the rate of interest on your investment. Savings, time, and compound interest will have an immense effect upon your future wealth. Because time counts and keeps on counting, learn how to use time to your advantage by making now a solid financial plan for your future.

KEY: *The key to your financial success will be your willingness to start planning early and to follow through with that plan.*

22   Think for a moment. If you want to remember your daily schedule, you maintain a calendar—a plan. If you want to take a trip, you make a travel plan. If you want to run a business, you develop a business plan. In all areas of your life, planning is a major component of success.

23   Financial success and security result from continuous financial planning. Although it may sound extreme, financial planning must begin at birth and can only end with your death. **KEY:** *Financial planning is a lifelong commitment.* This is why you cannot wait to develop the skills needed to become financially independent and secure.

24   Exercise: Using the lines below, write a paragraph summarizing three or more things you learned from this section.

_____

_____

_____

_____

Getting the Message

_____ **1.** What is the main idea of the excerpt?

    a. People should wait until they are in their 50s to start retirement planning.

    b. Retirement planning needs to be started early in life.

    c. Social Security provides all the money a person needs during retirement.

    d. People don't need to worry much about retirement because they will probably die three to five years after retiring.

_____ **2.** The topic sentence in paragraph 1 can be found in sentence _____.

    a. 1   c. 6

    b. 3   d. 9

_____ **3.** Which of the following is a reason given in the chapter for needing to plan for retirement?

    a. People are living longer.

    b. People are having children later in life, and they may still be taking caring of their kids when they retire.

    c. Retired people are still active.

    d. All of the above.

_____ **4.** _____ can be found as supporting details in the chapter.

    a. Personal examples

    b. Testimony

    c. Statistics

    d. Historical public examples

_____ **5.** In relation to the point of paragraph 3, the word _____ has a special importance.

    a. financial

    b. investment

    c. now

    d. retirement

_____ **6.** The sentence "Accumulating wealth has to do with the amount set aside for saving, the time for it to grow, and the rate of interest on your investment" (par. 21) is

    a. a fact.

    b. an opinion.

_____ **7.** Konowalow presents the information in the chapter using _____ order.

    a. problem and solution

    b. least to most important

    c. most to least important

    d. chronological

_____ **8.** The chapter uses the _____ pattern of organization.

    a. narrative

    b. cause and effect

    c. comparison and contrast

    d. examples

____ **9.** Konowalow's purpose is to
   a. persuade people to start saving for retirement early.
   b. explain the benefits of saving.
   c. present an amusing account of the benefits of saving.
   d. convince people that saving isn't that important.

____ **10.** It can be inferred from Konowalow's extensive use of research in paragraphs 9–11 that
   a. he likes numbers.
   b. there are a lot of studies available about life expectancy.
   c. people are eating healthier.
   d. he wants to thoroughly convince his readers that they may live for at least 20 years after they retire.

11. Give the major supporting point for paragraph 6 and paragraph 22. Identify whether the point is stated or implied. What do the supporting points have in common?

_____

_____

_____

_____

12. What elements make this textbook excerpt interactive?

_____

_____

_____

13. What do the four "Key" statements have in common, and in which paragraphs can they be found?

_____

_____

14. List two questions you wrote in the margins of this selection.

_____

_____

15. On a separate sheet of paper, summarize in 50 words or less the section Key to Financial Independence: Spend Less.

Vocabulary

Use context clues to determine the meaning by looking back at the paragraph where the word is used (the paragraph number is in parentheses). If you need help, consult a dictionary for the definition.

A. Match the word to its synonym.

1. forecast _____
2. associate _____
3. prepare _____
4. expense _____
5. part _____

> expenditure(s) (2) **formulate** (12)
> **factor** (4) **acquaintance** (18)
> **prognosis** (9)

B. Write the definition and a sentence for each of the words below. Try to use context clues in your sentences that help to show what the vocabulary word means.

1. optimize (4) _____
2. inflation (6) _____
3. ensuing (16) _____
4. octogenarian (18) _____
5. compound (21) _____

C. Word parts: Fill in the missing word part or parts using the word parts from the list below. Return to pages 85–87 if you need to review the meaning of a word part.

com	ex	mit	opt	pen	trib	ate	ize

1. I have been paying out a lot of money lately. My _____ditures are more than I made last month.

2. I want to make the best use of my vacation time, so, to _____im _____ my experience, I am getting up at dawn and not going to bed until midnight.

3. I want to give my all to our group project. I want my con_____utions to be meaningful.

4. I will send Kate an e-mail to confirm my _____ment to the project. I am excited to work with people who want to built a park for the kids in our neighborhood.

5. When you make plans for a party, it helps to fully formul_____ your menu before you head to the grocery, so you don't have to make multiple trips.

The Textbook and You

1. Have you started a "savings/investment fund" as advised in paragraph 3 yet? Explain why or why not.

   _____

   _____

2. What one piece of advice from this chapter would you want to share with a friend?

   _____

   _____

3. Make a bar graph that shows a plan of how much money you have or will put yearly into an investment fund for each decade of your life up to your 60s. Put the decades 20s, 30s, 40s, and 50s along the bottom, and place the numbers $1,000, $2,000, $3,000, $4,000, and $5,000 or higher along the left side.

4. On a separate sheet of paper, write a paragraph that describes what you plan to be doing in your retirement years. Show whether you will you be "active and busy" (par. 18), and indicate whether you will be working (full- or part-time) into your 70s or 80s.

Take a Closer Look

Look at the photo again. Did you have a piggy bank as a child? Did it help you to save money? Look at the graph again. If a person begins investing at age 30, how much money will the person have at 60? What rate of interest is the graph based on? How much money does Konowalow recommend a person have at retirement? If the graph represents the person's only retirement funds, will this person have enough money to retire comfortably?

_____

_____

_____

_____

Internet Activities

If needed, use a separate sheet of paper to fully record your responses. Include the Web address of any sites from which you gather information.

1. Visit livingto100.com (mentioned in paragraph 13) and try the life calculator. How long can you expect to live? How useful do you consider the calculator?

_____

_____

2. Look up "retirement planning." Pick a site and look at the advice it gives. How much money does it indicate you need to retire? Does the amount seem realistic to you?

_____

_____

Hot Dog Grotto

by Katy Tallorin

Before You Read

1. What image does the title create?
2. Read the first three paragraphs. What words would you use to describe the story's tone so far?
3. Have you ever worked in a fast-food job or known someone who has?
4. Look at the photo. What situations do you connect with hot dogs?

Vocabulary Preview

Look for these words in the reading. Exercises to reinforce the learning of new vocabulary using these words follow the reading. The paragraph number where the word appears is in parentheses.

glossy (3)   morgue (3)   philosophy (4)   dweeb (5)   grotto (15)
dinero (15)   double-time (19)   glimmers (21)   epiphany (22)   wretched (22)

Katy Tallorin is a writer and teacher. She has written numerous short stories and is currently working on a series of young-adult novels. She has taught English and physical education in middle and high schools. She was born in California and now lives in Washington. The following story was written especially for *Reading Now*. It draws on her own youthful experience of working in fast food.

Once I had nothing/then I had much/But I often wonder, which was my crutch?

—The Distressed

1 "What's worse?" she asked me as she scooped sauerkraut into the extras tray next to the cash register. "Having no money, but totally having time, having freedom—or *having* money but you're screwed. I mean, you have money, but your job sucks, you're always tired, and you have no time to spend your money."

2 Another week (what is this number 20, maybe?) at Hot Dog Grotto—the suckiest fast food in sucky Chula Vista in the suckiest strip mall anywhere in the world. Outside it's black top on top of black top. Inside it's six tables with uneven legs semi-glued to the floor with years of spilled soda.

3 I'm looking at her, and I just see how beautiful she is. Her black hair is glossy and a little wild, and her visor just keeps it contained. She has a tiny nose and red lips, and I know she's, like, 16, and I'm half-loser and half-cool at 19, but she seems like an angel in this pork morgue.

4 It's close to 90 degrees in the shop, and I have to stop and concentrate just to consider her question. It takes me back to my first, and only, semester of college when I took Intro to Philosophy. Yeah, which is worse? Having money but no time to use it or having tons of time but no—

5 "Um, hey—bro?" a customer says looking at me in that Earth-to-dweeb way that purchasers of fast food have—superior because they're on the other side of the counter.

6 "Yeah, get me two of the two-dog Krauter specials."

7 He's young, maybe the same age as me, and there's a great-looking girl with him who acts like she'd rather be anywhere than here.

8   "Right," I say snapping back to this sweaty world and away from my 'which is worse' debate.

9   Cheryl chirps to the dude, "What drinks would you like with that?" and the guy is all smiles.

10   "Oh, hi," he says, and then he wipes his hand across his brow like he's freshening up for her. "A Coke and a Diet Coke. Thanks," he says with a wink.

11   I get no thanks as I hand over two baskets of food and collect his five dollars. Big spender, big date.

12   Cheryl turns around to wipe down the condensation on the soda machine and mutters, "Whatta jerk." I smile.

13   A small victory for he of the name-tag life.

14   When I started here, I mopped the floors and cleaned the toilets at night and took my classes during the day. I started doing some cooking during the night shift and cleaning the nasty roller-grill after closing. Then the owner asked me if I wanted more hours and more money. He made me the 10 a.m–6 p.m. manager. Now I make, like, fifty cents more per hour than when I cleaned the toilets.

15   But I have a bitchin' name tag: Richard, it says on top, and under my name MANAGER. I dumped my semester of philosophy and psychology and English, so I could get forty hours at Hot Dog Grotto and make some real dinero. With that name tag I'd start living the dream: make money, meet women, and move out.

16   Well, most of that did work out, but not precisely as I had imagined. My apartment is just a room I rent from an old dude above his garage. The women are usually under 12 or over 60. The money is there, but it's more like change and less like cash.

17   I realize I'm daydreaming again when Cheryl elbows me gently, and I see an entire Little League team come in. There's, like, 12 kids and 20 adults. I scramble to get their orders, and Cheryl is filling cups with root beer and topping off the ketchup and mustard at the extras station.

18   One dad wants extra onions, and we're really low. Cheryl hates doing the onions, so we have a standing deal that onion chopping is my thing.

19   Cheryl keeps putting orders together, while I turn to the back counter to double-time more onions. I'm on, like, onion number three when I really start crying. I stare at the cutting board and tell myself, let it be. I don't even know what that's supposed to mean.

20   My eyes are red as I refill the onion tray and load the dad up on extra onions. I see kids with their red baskets full of hot dogs drenched in ketchup, and I look at this one kid's chest where the team name is: The Saints.

21   The kids are all eating now, and Cheryl is right beside me. The light glimmers above her head like a halo as she wipes down the mustard squirter that was totaled by the ball team. She's smiling.

22   Today on Camino Blanco at 1:12 p.m., I was visited by saints, tested by an angel, and had an epiphany chopping onions. This is still the stickiest, greasiest crap hole, and I still don't know 'which is worse,' but for now this wretched minimum-wage sweat box is my classroom. Right now, this is it—it's all I have.

Getting the Message

_____ **1.** The theme of the story is that

    a. fast-food jobs are fun.

    b. work isn't always easy.

    c. if one is getting paid any job is rewarding.

    d. people can learn from situations they dislike.

_____ **2.** What are some of Cheryl's traits?

    a. She is 16 and has black hair.

    b. She really enjoys working at Hot Dog Grotto.

    c. She hates chopping onions.

    d. a and c

_____ **3.** The story uses the _____ pattern of organization.

    a. process   c. narrative

    b. classification   d. comparison and contrast

_____ **4.** The transition word _but_ in paragraph 16 shows _____.

    a. contrast   c. time

    b. cause and effect   d. examples

_____ **5.** One of Tallorin's purposes is to

    a. explain how a fast-food place is run.

    b. entertain people with funny events at a hot-dog place.

    c. persuade people to find ways to learn from any experience.

    d. persuade people to take minimum-wage jobs.

_____ **6.** The setting as described in paragraph 2 helps to create a _____ tone.

    a. happy   c. mysterious

    b. dissatisfied   d. angry

_____ **7.** The main conflict in the story is

    a. within Richard.

    b. between Richard and the "Big spender."

    c. between Richard and society.

    d. between Richard and nature.

_____ **8.** The writer's diction, such as the use of slang words (i.e. _dweeb_ and _dinero),_ helps to show that Richard is

    a. highly educated.   c. male.

    b. young.   d. from Europe.

_____ **9.** What can you infer about Richard from his decision to leave college?

    a. He had a definite plan for his future career.

    b. He really liked his classes.

    c. He hated his classes.

    d. He had immediate goals that didn't relate to his education.

_____**10.** The sentence "The light glimmers above her head like a halo as she wipes down the mustard squirter that was totaled by the ball team" (par. 21) uses a

a. simile.   b. metaphor.

11. Richard mentions having a "bitchin' name tag: Richard, it says on top, and under my name MANAGER" (par. 15). Do you think he is truly proud of being a manager? Explain why or why not.

_____

_____

_____

12. List three supporting details that reveal Richard's outlook toward his job.

_____

_____

_____

13. What is the climax of the story?

_____

_____

_____

14. List two passages that you highlighted as key scenes in the story.

_____

_____

15. Finish the informal outline of the story.

   1. Cheryl asks _____ par. 1

   2. Richard describes _____ par. 2

   3. Richard describes _____ par. 3

   4. Richard reflects on _____ par. 4

   5. Richard deals _____ par. 5–11

   6. Richard is _____ par. 12–13

   7. Richard _____ par. 14–16

   8. A Little League team _____ par. 17–18

   9. Richard _____

      _____ par. 19–21

  10. Richard realizes _____

      _____ par. 22

Vocabulary

Use context clues to determine the meaning by looking back at the paragraph where the word is used (the paragraph number is in parentheses). If you need help, refer to a dictionary for the definition.

A. Put a *T* if the underlined vocabulary word is used correctly in the sentence and an *F* if it is not.

_____ 1. I couldn't work in a <u>morgue</u> (3) surrounded by dead bodies all day.

_____ 2. While in Italy, June visited a lovely <u>grotto</u> (15); the water in the cave was a gorgeous blue.

_____ 3. If I <u>double-time</u> (19) my yard work, it will take me twice as long to complete it.

_____ 4. Ben Franklin caught <u>glimmers</u> (21) of his neighbor's candle as she moved through her house locking it for the night.

_____ 5. The party was <u>wretched</u> (22). I ate my favorite foods and danced all night.

B. Complete each sentence with the correct vocabulary word. Use each word once.

glossy (3)	philosophy (4)	dweeb (5)	dinero (15)	epiphany (22)

1. In my _____ class, we discuss what beauty, life, and death mean in various cultures.

2. When I ran out of _____, my date ran out on me.

3. One evening as I did the laundry and emptied the trash, I had an _____ : My kids could help with the household chores.

4. The magazine printed on _____ paper was shiny and attractive to readers.

5. When my friends and I gather to solve math problems on the weekend, my brother calls it a _____ convention.

C. Word parts: Fill in the missing meaning for the underlined word part. Return to pages 85–87 if you need to review the meaning of a word part.

being	cut	upon	see	love

1. My <u>phil</u>osophy toward life is to _____ every minute and every experience.

2. This is pre<u>cise</u>ly the report I wanted. You _____ long passages as I asked.

3. Reggie was swea<u>ty</u> after his run. _____ sticky isn't a feeling he enjoys.

4. Anita puts on a <u>vis</u>or so she can _____ clearly in the bright sun.

5. Carol had an <u>epi</u>phany _____ entering the concert hall: Music was her destiny.

The Short Story and You

1. Give your answer to Cheryl's question in paragraph 1. Is a happy medium possible?

_____

_____

2. Do you agree that customers tend to act "superior" (par. 5) to people who work at fast-food places? What are you basing your decision on: your experiences behind the counter, what you have seen other people do, or how you act when you order?

_____

_____

3. What do you see Richard doing in two months? Explain your reasoning. Does your choice relate to what he might have learned from the Grotto as his classroom (par. 22)?

_____

_____

4. On a separate sheet of paper, write a paragraph about a job you disliked (a paid or volunteer experience). Clearly explain what made the situation painful. Also explain whether you learned anything from the experience.

Take a Closer Look

Look at the photo again. Do you now see the hot dogs differently? How do you think Richard would respond to the photo? Do you have a visual in your mind for an experience you didn't enjoy?

_____

_____

Internet Activities

If needed, use a separate sheet of paper to fully record your responses. Include the Web address of any sites from which you gather information.

1. Go to careercast.com and click on the JobsRated tab. Read the articles on the 10 best and 10 worst jobs. List three jobs in each category. Do you agree with their placement? What qualities were used to rate these jobs?

_____

2. Look up "minimum wage jobs." List three jobs you find. Pick one of these jobs and explain why you think it should or should not be paid the minimum wage. Do you know the minimum wage for your state? If not, look it up at dol.gov/minwage/america.

_____

_____

myreadinglab ▌ Objectives Check

To check your progress in meeting chapter objectives, log in to www.myreadinglab.com, click on the Study Plan tab, and then on the Reading Skills tab. Choose Patterns of Organization and Pattern of Organization—Time Order from the list of subtopics. Read and view the resources in the Review Materials section, then complete the Practices and Tests in the Activities section. You can check your scores by clicking on the Gradebook tab.

CHAPTER 7

Do you take good care of all aspects of your health?

Health

Preserving the Mind and Body

Our health affects every facet of our lives. If we feel good, physically and mentally, we can accomplish almost anything. If we don't feel well, we may not even be able to get out of bed. Staying healthy concerns both our minds—memory, relationships, and attitudes—and our bodies—how we eat, sleep, exercise, and otherwise use our bodies. By learning how to take better care of our health, we learn how to take better care of all aspects of our lives.

As health plays a major role in our lives, so does purpose and tone in developing and understanding a reading. The purpose is why the writer composed the piece. If you can decipher what the writer's intention was in creating an essay, textbook, or story, then it is easier to find the main idea and understand other aspects of the reading. Related to purpose is tone. The tone is the writer's attitude toward the subject. Is the writer angry, excited, or objective? Being able to clarify the writer's tone will aid you in understanding the writer's purpose. This chapter focuses on the details of uncovering a writer's purpose and tone. As you read the four essays or articles, textbook excerpt, and short story, consider the importance of purpose and tone in understanding a reading and think about the health issues you face today and may need to face in the future.

Skills: Purpose and Tone

- Decipher the writer's purpose.
- Establish the writer's tone.
- Recognize irony and exaggeration.

Purpose and Tone

Purpose

The writer's **purpose** is why the writer wrote a piece. There are three major reasons people write: to inform, to persuade, and to entertain. A piece of writing can include two or even all three purposes, but one of the three usually stands out as the overall purpose. You likely encounter all three purposes in items you read weekly.

Decide on the writer's main purpose: to inform, to persuade, or to entertain.

To inform: If the writer is telling you something without showing a preference, then the purpose is likely to inform. If a writer looks at both sides of an issue equally, then the purpose is probably to inform. When writers want to inform, they may explain a concept, describe an event, or investigate a situation. Recipes and instructions (e.g., on how to play a game, sign up for classes, or build something) are common examples of writing to inform. Most newspaper articles and textbooks are written to inform.

To persuade: On the other hand, if the writer shows a preference for one side, then the purpose is probably to persuade. If the writer encourages you to do something, then the writer's goal is to persuade. Look for words like *should*, *must*, and *need to* to show persuasion: "You should vote for Grant Harrison for mayor if you want a safer city" or "You must wash your clothes with Smile Bright if you want to keep them looking their best." Also look for a prominent use of adjectives in persuasive writing. For example, a product might be described as "amazing" or a proposal as "disastrous." Persuasion can be seen in advertisements on television, in magazines, or on billboards. Persuasion is also a large part of the literature sent at election time. Any time a writer wants you to buy an item, go somewhere, or vote for someone or something then persuasion is involved.

To entertain: If you get some type of emotional enjoyment out of what you are reading—such as laughing, crying, or being scared—then the writer's purpose is likely to entertain. You may be entertained by laughing at the comic strips in the newspaper, being amazed by new inventions in a science-fiction story, crying over a failed relationship in a romance novel, or biting your nails while reading a horror story. The purpose for all of these types of readings is to entertain. Remember that a writer may also be trying to inform or persuade while entertaining the reader.

Read the paragraphs below to determine which of the three purposes each one shows. Put the paragraph number on the line next to the purpose it matches.

to inform ___3___   to persuade ___1___   to entertain _____

1. You won't want to miss the club's major event of the year: the Spring Banquet to be held Friday, March 27, at 7 p.m. at the swanky, newly remodeled Community Center. We are honored this year to have a local five-star Italian restaurant cater the event. Dinner starts with an outstanding Caesar salad, followed by mouth-watering lasagna and fabulous garlic bread, with a club favorite for dessert, spumoni. You will definitely want to be part of the election of club officers. This is the time you get to cast your vote for next year's leaders. We will also be treated to a video presentation of Jake's exciting trip down the Amazon. I've seen some of the footage, and it is amazing! Hurry and make your reservations with Margaret by the 24th at (619) 555–3265. You'll be sorry if you miss the must event of the year.

2. Planes are arriving, boats are docking, and traffic is backing up. Everyone's headed to town for the Spring Banquet to be held Friday, March 27, at 7 p.m. at the gorgeous Community Center. Emeril, Bobby Flay, Rachel Ray—no top-notch chef can beat the cuisine made by the chef from the local Italian restaurant who will be catering the event. When our chef was but a lad in Italy, people walked from villages hundreds of miles away to taste his lasagna. And the spumoni you'll experience for dessert is truly fit for a Roman god. Of course, the election of officers brings excitement to the night. We can expect well over a hundred people to run for the five open positions. Will your choice win? Finally, see Jake battle piranha in the Amazon River, dodge darts from blowguns shot by local tribes, and save the rain forest single-handedly in his fascinating video presentation. Our boy does it again! Call Margaret at (619) 555–3265 to make your reservations before Brad, Angelina, and George take all the seats!

3. The Spring Banquet will be Friday, March 27, at 7 p.m. in the Community Center. We will have a dinner catered by a local Italian restaurant: Caesar salad, lasagna, garlic bread, and spumoni. After dinner we will hold the election of club officers and see a video presentation of Jake's recent trip down the Amazon. Make reservations by the 24th with Margaret at (619) 555–3265.

Tone

Tone is the writer's attitude toward the subject. You need to determine if the writer is angry or pleased or expressing any other emotion on the topic. Sometimes writers are neutral or objective about a matter, especially when the purpose is to inform. It isn't often you read how to put a bike together and the instructions have anything other than an objective tone. Understanding the writer's tone will help you uncover the writer's purpose. You experience tone of voice all the time. When a person shouts or whispers, you react differently. Similarly, you respond differently to tone in a piece of writing. Try reading a passage aloud to help you determine its tone.

Establish the tone by noting the *diction*, choice of words, used by the writer.
For example, decide how angry the woman is by looking at the words she could choose in writing a letter to a company:

"I'm furious with your company for selling slippers that fall apart in a month!"
"I'm upset with your company for selling slippers that fall apart in a month."
"I'm disappointed with your company for selling slippers that fall apart in a month."

Whether the woman chooses to use *furious, upset,* or *disappointed* will show the company how mad she is about their product. Also pay attention to the writer's use of punctuation marks. An exclamation point can signal excitement, disgust, or anger.

Pay attention to two general tones: formal and informal. If the writer's tone is formal, it can distance the reader, which may mean that the writer's purpose is informative. Formal tones are usually found in instructions, legal documents, job applications, and in academic works such as term papers and essays. An informal tone usually tries to bring in the reader. Sometimes an informal tone is used to persuade readers by making them feel a part of a group that uses a specific product or votes a certain way. A writer's use of the pronouns *you, your, us,* and *we* often signify an informal tone. An informal tone is probably what you use when you send a letter or e-mail to a friend.

Determine the writer's intended audience. Writers usually change their tone and diction depending on whom they are writing for. A few categories to consider when thinking about who the writer's intended audience might be include age group, knowledge of the topic (e.g., beginners or experts), region, and intimacy. For example, in writing for children, writers usually use simpler words than they do when writing for adults. A writer might explain the following to adults with poison ivy: "Scratching the rash can exacerbate your predicament." While the writer would likely choose different words when addressing children: "Scratching the rash can make your problem worse." In writing for experts in a field, a writer may use terms that are particular to that area. For instance, a computer specialist might write the following sentence: "Software developers in our company are proficient in RPG, C+, and Java." If the same person was writing for a general audience, he or she would likely explain that RPG, C+, and Java are computer languages. When writing for a general audience, writers choose words that most people will be familiar with or give definitions for terms that are typically used in a certain field. Reporters for the local newspaper don't have to explain where major attractions are in the city, but if the same article was going to be published in a national magazine, a reporter would want to clarify points that only locals would know. When you are writing to a friend, your tone will likely be more intimate than the one you would use when sending out cover letters for a job. By looking at how the writer's diction may be influenced by the writer's intended audience, you can better come to understand the writer's tone and purpose.

Look for irony and exaggeration, two techniques that can show tone and purpose.

Irony involves either the use of words to state the opposite of their precise meaning or a clash between what is expected to happen and what really does. For example, if your friend says, "You must be thrilled about going to math today" and he knows you don't like math and that you have a big test, then you know he is being ironic since his use of *thrilled* clearly isn't what you would be feeling. The clash between expectations and reality can be seen anytime an event is envisioned as turning out wonderfully and it flops instead—the big dance, the playoffs, or a blind date. When the differences between expectation and reality don't happen to us, we often find them funny, which is why writers like to use irony for humorous effect, especially in literature. Sometimes with time, we can also see the humor in the ironic situations we personally encounter. By detecting irony, you can establish a writer's tone and decide if the irony is being used to entertain the reader or for another purpose such as to persuade.

Exaggeration means that the writer enlarges or overstates a situation to usually unbelievable proportions. If a writer wants to show how difficult a hike was in a humorous way, the mountain becomes twice as big, the sun beats down at 200 degrees, and the distance becomes a 100 miles. Exaggeration also makes action movies and stories entertaining as the protagonist jumps amazing distances, battles numerous enemies single-handily, or builds a weapon out of gum and a paperclip. The chase scenes in James Bond movies, for example, show how exaggeration lends itself to the fun of the film. When a writer uses exaggeration, decide if its purpose is to entertain or possibly to persuade. A couple of circumstances where a writer might exaggerate to persuade include describing a situation as being extraordinarily horrible so that people will vote for a change in a government policy or showing how overwhelmed the writer is in order to excite sympathy and hopefully recruit someone to help with whatever needs to be done. Carefully examine a writer's use of exaggeration to see how it fits in with the tone of the reading and the writer's purpose.

Label the writer's tone using one or two words. When you feel you can identify the writer's tone, label it with a word or two. In the example of the letter to the company above, the writer is obviously "irritated," no matter which of the three words she eventually chooses to use. By labeling the writer's tone, you can use that information to help establish the writer's purpose. If the tone is "objective," then likely the writer's purpose is to inform. If the writer's tone is "excited," the writer may be trying to persuade you to participate in an event or buy a product. In the previous example, the writer's irritated or angry tone probably indicates a purpose of trying to persuade the company to refund her money or send a replacement pair of slippers. In a longer work, such as a novel, the writer may have several tones throughout the work.

Selecting Tone Words

The list below presents words that describe various tones a writer might use. Refer back to this list when you need help in picking a word or two to label a writer's tone. This list is not exhaustive; you should choose any word that you think best fits the tone of a reading.

Tone Words

alarming, shocking	mean, hurtful
aggressive	mocking
angry, mad	nostalgic, sentimental
apologetic	objective, factual
arrogant, superior	optimistic, hopeful
calming	pessimistic, negative
complaining	proud
confident	questioning, analytical
cozy, warm	romantic, loving
bizarre, odd	rude, offensive
direct	sad, depressed
disapproving, condemning	scary, ominous
dramatic	serious
encouraging	silly, playful
excited, enthusiastic	subjective, opinionated
forceful	sympathetic, caring
formal, proper	thoughtful, reflective
friendly	uncertain, ambivalent
happy	urgent
humorous, funny	worried, concerned
informal, relaxed	zealous, passionate
ironic	

ACTIVITY 2

Think about the readings you have covered so far in this text or other materials you have recently read (or consider something you have written) to help you write six of your own tone words below.

_____ _____

_____ _____

_____ _____

ACTIVITY 3

Read the following journal entries from four travelers on the same day trip. Pay attention to each writer's diction to help you match the writer's tone to one of the choices below. Put the number of the paragraph on the line next to the matching tone.

complaining _____   ironic _____   objective _____   enthusiastic _____

1. Wow, what a day! The sun was shining brightly at 7:30 a.m. when we left, and we enjoyed a scenic 50-mile drive to the Flaubert Mansion. The mansion was magnificent. We toured 20 of the rooms, and each was spectacular. The guide gave us so many wonderful details about how the furniture was made. She also pointed out the varied color schemes in the rooms from dazzling pink to calming blue. Lunch at the Le Petite Café was great. Their world-famous onion soup was delicious; the best I have ever had. We were back by three. I couldn't believe how fast the day went by!

2. I was forced up at six to board the stupid bus by 7:30 a.m. We were hauled to another famous building—really just another example of the excesses of the rich. We had to trudge through 20 rooms hearing annoying details about what type of wood every piece of furniture was made of and noting the ridiculous colors each room was painted. Lunch at Le Petite Café was a disaster. My "world-famous" onion soup tasted like soggy cardboard. We finally made it back at three—what a relief!

3. Today we left at 7:30 a.m. to drive 50 miles to the Flaubert Mansion. It was built in the mid-1600s by the Duc de Dijon. The mansion has more than 100 rooms, and we toured 20 of them. The rooms are decorated with furniture from different time periods and painted in a diversity of colors. We ate lunch at the Le Petite Café. I had their world-famous soup à l'oignon (onion soup). We returned to the hotel at three.

4. When I awoke, I was so excited! For weeks I had pictured the day: driving through the pleasant countryside, appreciating the gorgeous interiors of the Flaubert Mansion, and sipping onion soup at the renowned Le Petite Café. Instead I became nauseous during the ride and ended up with a sore shoulder caused by a seatmate who slumped down and fell asleep on me. The mansion's supposedly superb handcrafted furniture looked more like well-worn couches and chairs I'd find at a thrift store. And the color combinations on the walls reminded me of the décor in my colorblind grandma's house. The cheese in my world-famous onion soup at Le Petite Café was barely melted, and yet the pieces of bread were blackened. It didn't really matter as I burnt the roof of my mouth on the first sip, so I couldn't taste anything well after that. Though the clock at the hotel showed that we were back at three, my body told me I'd been gone for weeks.

Purpose and Tone Checklist

✔ Decide on the writer's main purpose: to inform, to persuade, or to entertain.

✔ Establish the tone by noting the diction, choice of words, used by the writer.

✔ Pay attention to two general tones: formal and informal.

✔ Determine the writer's intended audience.

✔ Look for irony and exaggeration, two techniques that can show tone and purpose.

✔ Label the writer's tone using one or two words.

The Great Awakening

by Catherine Price

Before You Read

1. How much sleep do you usually get a night?
2. What do you consider the benefits of a good night's sleep?
3. Do you feel that you sleep well each night?
4. Look at the photo. How do you think the photo relates to the topic of the article?

Vocabulary Preview

Look for these words in the reading. Exercises to reinforce the learning of new vocabulary using these words follow the reading. The paragraph number where the word appears is in parentheses.

haymakers (1)	prone (1)	unassuming (1)
accredited (2)	quadrupled (2)	havoc (4)
crucial (4)	deprivation (5)	daunting (6)
elusive (6)		

Catherine Price is a free-lance writer. Among the publications her articles have appeared in are the *Los Angeles Times*, the *New York Times*, *Health Magazine*, *Popular Science*, and *Salon*. She is the founder and editor-in-chief of *Salt*, an online magazine filled with articles, blogs, and photos. The following article originally appeared in the magazine *Outside* in June 2008.

1 **Americans like to** brag that they can run on six hours of sleep. Funny, because anything less than eight turns me into the type of person who will throw haymakers in the grocery checkout line. It may sound spoiled to complain about oversleeping, but for a 29-year-old runner and biker like me, the notion of having to spend one-third of my life in bed seems criminally unfair. Early this year I began to worry that I might be prone to too much sleep, so in March I paid a visit to the California Center for Sleep Disorders, an unassuming clinic in a Fremont, California, strip mall. That night I found myself lying—very much awake—in a windowless room with 15 electrodes attached to my body, straps around my chest, and a plastic cannula (a tube to monitor breathing) up my nose.

2 It turns out that I'm one of many people willing to go to such extremes to learn about sleep. With so many of us shorting ourselves on rest—the National Sleep Foundation reports that some 50 million of us have chronic sleep problems, and the NSF's 2008 nationwide poll shows that, on average, we get six hours and 40 minutes of shut-eye nightly—the sleep-correction industry is booming. Americans shelled out more than $3 billion for 54 million sleeping-pill prescriptions in 2007, and the number of accredited sleep clinics like the one I visited has quadrupled since 1996. The upshot of all this attention? While researchers have yet to answer the Big One—the question of why we need sleep to begin with—we understand better than ever the effects of

inadequate rest. And the results go far beyond the familiar cycle of coffee in the morning and sleep aids (or Scotch) at night.

3   To wit: As little as 20 hours without sleep leaves you with the same impaired attention and slow reflexes of someone who is legally drunk. Chris Eatough, six-time winner of the World Solo 24 Hours of Adrenaline Championship mountain-bike race, says that during a day-long competition, his vision will occasionally stop. "I'll be flying down-hill with rocks and trees to dodge," he says, "and I'll get a snapshot of the trail that doesn't change for four or five seconds."

4   New research also suggests that insufficient rest wreaks havoc on your emotions and intelligence. Last October, Matthew Walker, a sleep researcher at the University of California, Berkeley, found that when he showed people unpleasant images, such as attacking sharks and vipers, sleep-deprived subjects had a 60 percent stronger emotional response than well-rested ones. Sleep also appears crucial to learning and memory: Walker recently found that we're about 40 percent less effective at forming new memories if we haven't had sufficient sleep beforehand. "It's not practice that makes perfect," he says. "It's practice with a night's sleep that seems to make perfect."

5   The list goes on: Research suggests that those who don't sleep enough have higher stress levels and an increased risk of heart attack. In 2004, researchers at the University of Chicago Medical Center found that sleep deprivation screws with the hormones tied to appetite and insulin resistance. Translation: Not sleeping can make you fat and put you at a higher risk of Type 2 diabetes.

6   Sounds daunting, especially since most of us don't get those elusive eight hours. (Think your Red Bull–charged system needs less? You're wrong. As you tire, your perception of what's normal changes, and you don't recognize that you're impaired.) But here's the good news: There are plenty of nonpharmaceutical methods for improving sleep—and you don't need to shove a tube up your nose to figure out what to do. (That might not help much. I slept horribly at the clinic, waking up 14 times per hour, above the normal rate of zero to five.) Set up your bedroom the right way, eat well, and exercise with the end of the day in mind and you can ditch that third cup of coffee. Your body knows how to sleep. Your job is learning how to get out of the way.

Getting the Message

____ 1. The main idea of the article is stated in paragraph _____.

   a. 1   c. 5
   b. 2   d. 6

____ 2. The central idea of paragraph 3 is that

   a. endurance events are dangerous.
   b. even a short amount of time without sleep can lead to serious problems.
   c. sleep deprivation is worse than being drunk.
   d. loss of sleep leads to bad eyesight.

____ 3. Which of the following are effects of sleep deprivation mentioned in the article?

   a. slower reflexes, impaired attention, and more frequent headaches
   b. an increased risk of heart attack, harder to form new memories, and sharper vision
   c. stronger emotional responses, harder to form new memories, and higher stress levels
   d. disturbs hormones connected with insulin resistance and leads to weight loss

____ 4. Two types of supporting details used in the article are

   a. personal and hypothetical examples.
   b. statistics and testimony.
   c. hypothetical examples and testimony.
   d. historical examples and statistics.

____ 5. Does the following sentence express a fact or an opinion?

   "Americans shelled out more than $3 billion for 54 million sleeping-pill prescriptions in 2007, and the number of accredited sleep clinics like the one I visited has quadrupled since 1996" (par. 2).

   a. fact
   b. opinion

____ 6. In what order is the information presented?

   a. problem and solution
   b. chronological
   c. most to least important
   d. least to most important

____ 7. The article uses a _____ pattern of organization.

   a. comparison and contrast
   b. narrative
   c. definition
   d. cause and effect

____ 8. Sentence _____ in paragraph 6 uses a contrast transition word.

   a. 1   c. 5
   b. 4   d. 8

_____ 9. Price's purpose is to
   a. persuade people that there are consequences for not getting enough sleep.
   b. get people to laugh at their sleep patterns.
   c. share information on sleeping.

_____ 10. It can be inferred from the line "And the results go far beyond the familiar cycle of coffee in the morning and sleep aids (or Scotch) at night" (par. 2) that
   a. the writer likes to drink Scotch.
   b. Scotch is the best drink to make people tired.
   c. some people use alcohol as a way to induce sleep.
   d. Scotch is cheaper than sleeping pills.

11. List three of the institutions or people that Price uses as support and give the paragraph number where the information is found. How credible to you think these sources are?

_____

_____

_____

_____

_____

_____

12. List three words that show whether the tone of the article is formal or informal.

_____

_____

_____

13. Give examples of two sentences that show Price's purpose for writing the article.

_____

_____

_____

_____

14. Look at your annotations of the article. Which one of the comments or questions that you wrote in the margins would you most like to discuss with the class?

_____

_____

15. On a separate sheet of paper, write a summary of the article in about 100 words.

Vocabulary

Use context clues to determine the meaning by looking back at the paragraph where the word is used (the paragraph number is in parentheses). If you need help, consult a dictionary for the definition.

A. Match each vocabulary word below to its synonym.

unassuming (1)	prone (1)	havoc (4)	daunting (6)	elusive (6)

1. slippery _____
2. frightening _____
3. tending _____
4. plain _____
5. disorder _____

B. Complete each sentence using the correct vocabulary word. Use each word once.

haymakers (2)	accredited (3)	quadrupled (3)	crucial (5)	deprivation (6)

1. My cousin considers it a _____ to be without room service at a hotel. On the other hand, I'm used to camping, so sleeping in a bed is a luxury for me.

2. It is _____ that I be on time to work my first day. I don't want my boss to get a bad impression of me.

3. I can't continue to throw _____ at people when I'm upset; I broke my friend's nose and hurt my hand the last time I was angry.

4. The college was _____ after a team came to review the policies, administration, and faculty, and they found that the college met the necessary requirements.

5. Our profits have _____ since we began staying open longer. I can't believe that we are earning four times as much by staying open until nine instead of six.

C. Word parts: Finish the sentences with the meaning of each underlined word part. Use each meaning once. Return to pages 85–87 if you need to review the meaning of a word part.

time	make	not	away	trust

1. Many people consider it a <u>de</u>privation to do without a television, but I don't feel that it has taken anything _____ from my life to have been without one for the past year.

2. She was so <u>un</u>assuming that I did _____ notice her sitting in the corner.

3. I have a <u>chron</u>ic problem with my knee. It has been hurting off and on for about six years, which is a long _____ to be in pain.

4. Now that the college is ac<u>cred</u>ited, I _____ that it meets the state's standards.

5. We have a sufficient amount of food to _____ a filling meal for the six of us.

The Article and You

1. What is the longest you have gone without sleep? Did you experience any of the harmful effects of sleep deprivation mentioned in the article? Describe the situation.

_____

_____

2. What techniques or substances have you used to stay awake or get to sleep? How well did they work? Have you used any of the ones mentioned in the article?

_____

_____

3. Rate the quality of your sleep on most nights, with 10 being excellent and 0 horrible. What elements contribute to your score?

_____

_____

_____

4. On a separate sheet of paper, write a paragraph that describes your sleeping habits. Include information on how many hours of sleep you usually get each night and what times you usually go to sleep and get up.

Take a Closer Look

Look at the photo again. After reading about the importance of sleep, how well do you think this person is sleeping? What idea is the photograph playing with?

_____

_____

_____

Internet Activities

If needed, use a separate sheet of paper to fully record your responses. Include the Web address of any sites from which you gather information.

1. Look up the California Center for Sleep Disorders mentioned in paragraph 1 or the National Sleep Foundation mentioned in paragraph 2. Summarize the advice either site offers on ways to get a good night's sleep.

_____

_____

_____

_____

2. Look up "sleep cycle." How many stages are there in the cycle? Write a summary of how the cycle works.

_____

_____

Sun Savvy: Myth or Reality?

by Tracy Davis

Tracy Davis is a science reporter for the *Ann Arbor News*. She has covered a variety of topics for the paper including hybrid cars, the swine flu, and the environment. Ann Arbor is located in the southeastern part of Michigan and is home to the University of Michigan. The following article was originally published in July 2007.

Before You Read

1. Do you work on getting a tan?
2. Survey the five myth statements. Are you aware of any of these beliefs?
3. Have you ever used a tanning bed?
4. Look at the photo and cartoon. Do the people in the photo look healthy? What is your reaction to the cartoon?

Vocabulary Preview

Look for these words in the reading. Exercises to reinforce the learning of new vocabulary using these words follow the reading. The paragraph number where the word appears is in parentheses.

burnished (3)	**pasty** (19)	**melanoma** (11)
impart (6)	**conventional** (4)	**carcinogen** (15)
malignant (11)	**dermatology** (8)	**alliteratively** (20)
pigment (13)		

The article begins on the next page.

"Sun Savvy: Myth or Reality? From Blistering to Bronze, the Truth about Tanning" by Tracy Davis from *The Ann Arbor* (Michigan) *News*. Copyright © 2007 by *The Ann Arbor News*. All rights reserved. Used with permission of *The Ann Arbor News*.

Sun Savvy: Myth or Reality?

From Blistering to Bronze, the Truth about Tanning

By TRACY DAVIS
The Ann Arbor (Mich.) News

1 It's the time of year when the tank tops and shorts come out and blindingly white skin begins to see the light.

2 It's also the time when many outdoorsy types and sun worshippers experience their first sunburn, intentional or not.

3 Although we all know skin in its natural, untanned state is most healthy, many of us think we look healthier, thinner—heck, even hotter—with a burnished glow suggestive of leisurely hours under the sun.

4 With that in mind, here's a look at the conventional wisdom and realities of the burn-peel-tan life.

5 **MYTH:** Sunless tanning, also known as fake-a-bake, is risk-free.

6 **REALITY:** It is true that using any of a variety of lotions, sprays, gels, creams and powders from the multi-million-dollar sunless-tanning industry can impart a sun-kissed glow without exposure to dangerous UV rays.

7 But some researchers worry that the fashion for a bronzed look, even a cosmetically induced one, may encourage many people to seek a tanned appearance at any cost.

8 According to a study published last year in the *Journal of the American Academy of Dermatology*, young women who used sunless tanners were more likely to have been sunburned and to have visited tanning parlors compared with those who were not interested in and did not use such bronzing lotions.

9 The study, conducted at Boston University School of Medicine, also reported that, although many self-tanning products do not contain sunscreen, a number of young women believe they offer sun protection.

10 **MYTH:** A blistering sunburn is painful, but no big deal.

11 **REALITY:** False. Just one blistering sunburn doubles the likelihood of developing malignant melanoma, a deadly skin cancer, according to the National Institutes of Health.

12 **MYTH:** People with dark skin won't sunburn, aren't at risk for skin cancer and don't need sunscreen.

13 **REALITY:** Yes, people who have more pigment in their skin are less likely to burn and are less at risk for skin cancer. But everyone needs sunscreen, said Michigan dermatologist Dr. A. Craig Cattell.

14 **MYTH:** Tanning beds are safer than the sun.

15 **REALITY:** Uh, like, no. The U.S. Department of Health and Human Services has declared UV radiation from the sun and artificial sources, such as tanning beds and sun lamps, as a known carcinogen.

16 And a 2005 Swedish study demonstrated that regular exposure to tanning beds significantly elevates a person's risk for developing melanoma. Research has found that tanning lamps emit UV rays that can be up to 15 times stronger than the sun, according to the American Academy of Dermatology.

17 **MYTH:** If spending a little time in the sun allows the skin to produce healthy vitamin D, then the more time, the better.

18 **REALITY:** Maximum production of vitamin D occurs after brief exposure to UV radiation. The exact amount of time depends on many factors including geographic location, time of day, time of year, and skin type. A fair-skinned person in Boston or New York can get adequate vitamin D production in two to five minutes at noon, according to the academy.

19 So how's a pasty body supposed to play it safe in the sun?

20 The American Cancer Society has this alliteratively pleasing advice: Slip, slop, slap.

21 As in, slip on a long-sleeved shirt, slop on sunscreen of SPF 15 or higher and slap on a hat. It's the old abstinence line, but it works, say the experts.

Getting the Message

____ **1.** The topic of the article is

    a. tanning lotions.

    b. tanning beds.

    c. tanning.

    d. getting enough vitamin D.

____ **2.** What is the main idea of the article?

    a. It is safer to use a tanning lotion than sit out in the sun.

    b. Tanning is dangerous.

    c. If one's skin is dark, it doesn't matter how much sun exposure one gets.

    d. Wearing a hat is good protection from the sun.

____ **3.** Davis uses _____ as supporting details in paragraph 18.

    a. personal examples

    b. facts

    c. reasons

    d. all of the above

____ **4.** When people go out in the sun, the American Cancer Society recommends that they

    a. slip, sleep, shade.

    b. flip, flop, flap.

    c. slip, slop, slap.

    d. put on sunscreen, wear a hat, and spend 20 minutes outside to get enough vitamin D.

____ **5.** The statement "Research has found that tanning lamps emit UV rays that can be up to 15 times stronger than the sun, according to the American Academy of Dermatology" (par. 16) expresses

    a. a fact.

    b. an opinion.

____ **6.** The article uses the _____ pattern of organization.

    a. definition

    b. narrative

    c. classification

    d. comparison and contrast

____ **7.** The transition word *although* that begins paragraph 3 shows _____.

    a. comparison

    b. cause and effect

    c. contrast

    d. an example

____ **8.** The writer's purpose is to

    a. present misconceptions about tanning.

    b. warn people about the dangers of tanning.

    c. amuse people with tidbits about tanning.

    d. a and b.

_____ **9.** Which of the following words or phrases show the informal tone of the article?

    a. heck, even hotter (par. 3)

    b. According to a study published last year in the _Journal of the American Academy of Dermatology_. . . . (par. 8)

    c. Uh, like, no. (par. 15)

    d. a and c

_____ **10.** From the myth versus reality format, what can be inferred about people's knowledge of tanning?

    a. Almost all people know about the various dangers of tanning.

    b. People realize sun exposure can be unsafe, but they don't know about the dangers of tanning bed.

    c. Misconceptions about various tanning strategies and dangers still exist.

    d. People don't care about the dangers associated with tanning.

11. What are two words you would use to describe the tone of the article?

_____

12. How do the last three paragraphs support Davis's purpose?

_____

_____

_____

_____

13. How effective do you think the myth or reality format is for this topic? Explain why you feel this way.

_____

_____

14. Look at your annotations of the article. Which one of the comments or questions that you wrote in the margins would you most like to discuss with the class? Was your question answered by the end of the reading?

_____

_____

15. Paraphrase the line "If spending a little time in the sun allows the skin to produce healthy vitamin D, then the more time, the better" (par. 17).

_____

_____

_____

Vocabulary

Use context clues to determine the meaning of each word by referring back to the paragraph where the word is used (the paragraph number is in parentheses). If you need help, consult a dictionary for the definition.

A. Match the word to its definition.

> **dermatology** (8)   **melanoma** (11)   **pigment** (13)   **carcinogen** (15)   **alliteratively** (20)

1. any cancer-producing substance _____

2. a serious, often deadly, type of skin cancer _____

3. the branch of science that deals with the skin and its diseases _____

4. using words in a manner where the same sounds or the same kinds of sounds are repeated at the beginning of words or in stressed syllables _____

5. a substance that causes a characteristic color in animal or plant tissue _____

B. Match the word to its antonym.

> **benign**   **alternative**   **dull**   **dark**   **conceal**

1. burnished (3) _____   4. malignant (11) _____
2. conventional (4) _____   5. pasty (19) _____
3. impart (6) _____

C. Word parts: Fill in the missing word part from the list, and highlight or circle the meaning of the word part found in each question. One word uses two word parts. Return to pages 85–87 if you need to review the meaning of a word part.

> **mal**   **con**   **ven**   **im**   **ology**

1. Because I had skin problems as a teen, I want to study dermat_____ in college.

2. The mole on my back turned out to be a bad one. The doctor discovered that it was _____ignant, and I had to have it removed.

3. When I want to get into a subject, I take a class because instructors have so much knowledge to _____part to their students.

4. I am sometimes suspicious of _____tional wisdom. It can be beneficial when people come together to agree on a subject, but after a few years those ideas can become outdated, and they may need to be revisited.

The Article and You

1. Did the article change any of your perceptions about tanning? Explain why or why not.

_____

_____

2. What do you do to protect yourself when you go out in the sun? Do you follow the American Cancer Society's advice? Or if you don't do anything, explain why.

_____

_____

3. What is a topic you would like to see explored in the "Myth or Reality" format? Why did you pick this topic? Why would it fit well in the "Myth or Reality" format?

_____

_____

4. On a separate sheet of paper, write a paragraph that explains two of the dangers of tanning that you learned about or learned more about from the article.

Take a Closer Look

Look at the photo again. Now that you have read the article, what do you see that the people are doing right and wrong to protect themselves from the sun?

Look at the cartoon again. How does the cartoon reveal, and poke fun at, the popularity of tanning?

_____

_____

_____

_____

_____

_____

Internet Activities

If needed, use a separate sheet of paper to fully record your responses. Include the Web address of any sites from which you gather information.

1. Go to the National Institutes of Health Web site and pick an article to read that offers advice about sun tanning. Write a summary of the information you find.

_____

_____

2. Visit the Indoor Tanning Association's Web site and read the FAQs on "Indoor Tanning." Summarize the information you find and include your evaluation on how reasonable the group's claims sound. How does the information contrast from what you found on the National Institutes of Health Web site?

_____

_____

Cross-Train Your Brain

by Kate Hanley

Before You Read

1. After you survey the headings, what do you think it means to "cross-train" your brain?
2. How good is your memory?
3. What do you do to keep your memory in shape?
4. Look at the photos. How do you think the activities the people are engaged in will relate to the reading?

Vocabulary Preview

Look for these words in the reading. Exercises to reinforce the learning of new vocabulary using these words follow the reading. The paragraph number where the word appears is in parentheses.

regimen (1)   adage (2)   nimbly (3)   cognitive (3)

salient (4)   acuity (5)   hailed (6)   antioxidant (6)

boon (7)   dementia (8)

Kate Hanley is a writer and yoga instructor. Her articles have appeared in various magazines including *Yoga Journal, Yoga Life, Delicious Living,* and *Health.* She is also the founder of MsMindbody.com. From this Web site, she writes a newsletter that each week explores "one simple thing" a person can do to live healthier. Hanley has interests in various methods of making people healthier including yoga, herbal medicines, and meditation. The following article originally appeared in the June 2007 issue of *Body + Soul.*

Reclaim your memory with diet, exercise, sleep—and brushing up on your Italian.

1   Sure, you sometimes forget where you parked. And every once in a while you blank on a particular word ("I know it starts with an 'a.'") But you're not worried. When your memory really starts to slip, you'll rely on tried-and-true mental calisthenics to kick that brain back into shape. Unfortunately, maintaining your memory takes more than a Sudoku or Scrabble habit. It requires a broader approach—the same diet, exercise, and self-care regimen that keeps you healthy overall. "When people combine memory-improving techniques with healthy lifestyle changes, they can see dramatic results in their memory function," explains Gary Small, M.D., director of the UCLA Memory and Aging Research Center and author of several books on memory, including *The Healthy Brain Kit.*

2   So what causes memory loss in the first place? "Over time, several things happen," notes Thomas Crook, Ph.D., former chairman of a National Institute of Mental Health task force and author of *The Memory Advantage.* "We lose brain cells, the connections between surviving brain cells become weaker, and the chemicals that send messages within the brain become less efficient." Here's the good news, though: While some basic forgetfulness ("Did I mail that letter?") is common, it doesn't necessarily signal Alzheimer's down the road. Plus, not all types of memory lessen with age. Procedural

memory, which governs physical skill, for example, generally stays consistent—proving the old adage "It's like riding a bike." And some higher-level brain functions, such as judgment and wisdom, grow stronger.

3   While nothing can make you recall information as nimbly as you could in your twenties (your prime memory years, says Small), we're not doomed to a steady cognitive downslide. The choices you make now to cross-train your brain can affect how it functions over time. So put down that crossword puzzle and learn about some surprising other ways you can boost brain health and enhance your memory.

Imprint the Info

4   You can't remember what you didn't hear in the first place. Often, what we call forgetfulness is actually the result of distraction, which prevents salient details from making a lasting impression in our brains. Whether you're meeting someone for the first time or learning how to use the phone system, says Crook, be sure you're really focused as you take in the new information. (That means no multitasking.)

Try This   Before you're faced with having to absorb information (like listening to the car salesperson explain all the buttons on your dashboard), jot down any other thoughts to get them out of the way. You'll better clear your mind for the influx of new material.

Hit the Hay

5   As fatigue rises, memory declines, says Crook, which makes getting enough sleep a no-brainer for greater mental acuity and recall. In fact, he says, if you need an alarm to wake you up, you may well be sleep deprived.

Try This   If you feel like you're not sleeping enough, go to bed half an hour earlier for a week and take note of how much sharper you feel.

Eat a Brain-Healthy Diet

6   As we age, our brain cells become less adept at warding off the effects of inflammation (one of the body's healing responses that, when overstimulated, is associated with many chronic diseases) and oxidation (the same process that causes a cut apple to turn brown). This contributes to impaired cognitive function. To stay sharp, says Andrew Weil, M.D., co-author of *The Healthy Brain Kit* and author of *Healthy Aging: A Lifelong Guide to Your Physical and Spiritual Well-Being,* eat foods and spices hailed for their anti-inflammatory and antioxidant properties, including oily fish (salmon, sardines, herring), fruits and vegetables, extra virgin olive oil, and turmeric. Also avoid saturated fats (in foods like full-fat dairy products and red meat), trans fats, and partially hydrogenated oils, as well as foods high in refined carbs and sugars. In a 2002 study, UCLA researchers found that rats fed a saturated-fat, refined-sugar diet experienced drops in their spatial memory after just two months.

Try This   Commit to eating one more serving of fish and healthy fats each week. Swap out two cans of soda for two cups of green tea (another powerful antioxidant) each day.

Get Moving

7   Exercise isn't just good for your body; it's a boon for your brain, too. Among many studies showing that exercise helps benefit memory, a 2001 study found that elderly women who walked more each week than their peers had a substantially lower risk of experiencing cognitive decline.

Try This   Crook recommends exercise that gets your heart pumping—biking, swimming, fast-paced walking—three to six times per week. Include resistance training exercises with weights three times per week.

Learn for the Sake of It

8   An open mind plus a willingness to learn make a winning combination, says Weil. Since the central nervous system is plastic in nature, it continues to change in response to shifting needs and stimuli. "The more you learn, the more connections you create in your brain," he says. "This results in a richer, denser neural network that will be slower to produce symptoms of dementia." (And it can't hurt on the memory front, either.)

9   The process of learning something new may feel frustrating, but it brings big rewards, Weil says. "It requires real effort to change what you're used to," he says. "But that mental challenge is what forces the pathways and connections in the brain to stay dynamic." One of the most effective brain workouts? Learn a foreign language. "You don't even have to master the language to reap the benefits," says Weil. Just engaging in the learning process will keep your memory in top shape.

Try This   Challenge yourself to begin learning something new. Teach yourself Excel or a graphics software program. Take a class at a local college on a topic that's just outside of your comfort zone (i.e., math if you're a literature person, philosophy if you're a science person). Give salsa-dancing a whirl. Take up Russian.

Take Time to Decompress

10   You may do your best thinking under pressure. But long-term stress negatively affects your memory. "Stress hormones have been shown to shrink memory centers in the brain," Small explains. On the other hand, doing activities that calm you—whether through a more formal practice like yoga and tai chi or something less structured

(weeding, long baths, listening to music)—improves your mental and physical health. In a 2004 study, kids who participated in yoga camp showed a 43 percent increase on spatial memory tests, as compared to no improvement in kids who took the tests after attending a fine arts camp or who didn't attend camp at all.

Try This Put stress reduction on the schedule. Start by signing up for a mind/body wellness class in your area.

Widen the Lens

11 One of the biggest challenges to overall cognitive functioning and memory, says clinical psychologist Les Fehmi, Ph.D., co-author of *The Open-Focus Brain,* is a cluttered mind, which makes it difficult to take in or access information. The solution? Change the way you pay attention to what's going on around you. The kind of focus you need to drive a car, for instance, can be draining to maintain. "When you open your focus to include the space around you," says Fehmi, "the brain engages more cells at a slower speed, which helps you maximize your attention and retention."

Try This Teach your brain to relax its focus. With your eyes closed, imagine the space surrounding you. "As you expand that awareness from the wall and ceiling to the horizon," says Fehmi, "the brain starts to slow down and can release the stress resulting from a vigilant focus—and heal itself."

Getting the Message

_____ 1. What is the topic of the article?

    a. getting in better shape   c. memory loss

    b. memory improvement   d. eating right and exercising more

_____ 2. The topic sentence in paragraph 9 can be found in

    a. sentence 1.   c. sentence 5.

    b. sentence 2.   d. sentences 1 and 7.

_____ 3. The main idea of the article is that

    a. memory loss is a natural process.

    b. eating more fish will improve your memory.

    c. improving one's memory is best done through a variety of activities.

    d. sleep and exercise are the two most important ways to improve one's memory.

_____ 4. Which years are one's "prime memory years"?

    a. the teens   c. the forties

    b. the twenties   d. the sixties

_____ 5. The sentence "Among the many studies showing that exercise helps benefit memory, a 2001 study found that elderly women who walked more each week than their peers had a substantially lower risk of experiencing cognitive decline" (par. 7) expresses

    a. a fact.   b. an opinion.

_____ 6. The article uses the following patterns of organization:

    a. process and definition.   c. cause and effect and classification.

    b. comparison/contrast and narrative.   d. examples and definition.

_____ 7. What types of transition words are used in paragraph 2?

    a. contrast, comparison, time   c. addition, contrast, example

    b. importance, contrast   d. cause and effect, comparison, addition

_____ 8. Hanley's main purpose is to entertain her readers.

    a. true   b. false

_____ 9. The tone of the article can be labeled as _____.

    a. angry   c. encouraging

    b. sad   d. romantic

_____ 10. It can be inferred from paragraph 6 that

    a. most people reading the article are vegetarians.

    b. soda is still a popular choice of beverage.

    c. red meat has several health benefits.

    d. all fish are safe to eat.

11. List two people Hanley uses as support. Do they seem like credible sources? Explain why or why not.

_____

_____

_____

_____

_____

_____

12. What do the headings add to the article?

_____

_____

_____

_____

13. What is the writer's purpose? Give examples of two sentences or passages that support your choice.

_____

_____

_____

_____

_____

14. List two points you annotated in the article. Why did you pick these points?

_____

_____

_____

15. On a separate sheet of paper, make a formal outline of the article.

Vocabulary

Use context clues to determine the meaning of each word by referring back to the paragraph where the word is used (the paragraph number is in parentheses). If you need help, consult a dictionary for the definition.

A. Circle the correct meaning of each word.

1. nimbly (3)   quickly   slowly
2. salient (4)   unimportant   important
3. acuity (5)   sharpness   dullness
4. boon (7)   a disaster   a benefit
5. dementia (8)   improved memory skills   a deterioration of mental abilities

B. Write a definition for each word, and then write your own sentence correctly using each word. Be prepared to share your definitions and sentences with the class.

1. regimen (1) _____

_____

2. adage (2) _____

_____

3. cognitive (3) _____

_____

4. hail(ed) (6) _____

_____

5. antioxidant (6) _____

_____

C. Word parts: Use the following words to help you match the word part to its meaning. Return to pages 85–87 if you need to review the meaning of a word part.

1. anti-: antioxidant, antisocial, antifreeze   ____   a. life
2. de-: dementia, deduct, decrease   ____   b. inclined to
3. -vi-: vigilant, vivid, viable   ____   c. against
4. -ive: cognitive, active, negative   ____   d. away

The Article and You

1. Which two of the methods to "enhance your memory" mentioned in the article do you most need to develop?

_____

_____

2. Think back on what you ate yesterday. List five items you ate. How close were you to eating brain-healthy food? Did you eat any of the foods listed in paragraph 6?

_____

_____

3. What are three subjects or activities you would like to explore to keep your mind alert as mentioned in paragraph 8?

_____

_____

4. On a separate sheet of paper, write a paragraph describing how you will incorporate memory cross-training into your life starting next week or how you already use at least three of the techniques mentioned in the reading.

Take a Closer Look

Look at the photos again. Has your reaction to the activities the people are engaged in changed since you read the article?

_____

_____

Internet Activities

If needed, use a separate sheet of paper to fully record your responses. Include the Web address of any sites from which you gather information.

1. Look up "stress reduction techniques" and find a site that lists various techniques. List four techniques, and then write a summary that gives more details about two of the techniques.

_____

_____

_____

2. Look up "brain foods." List five foods recommended for good brain health and what the benefits of each food are.

_____

_____

_____

How We Eat Reflects and Defines Our Personal and Cultural Identity

from *Eating Well for Optimum Health*

by Andrew Weil, M.D.

Andrew Weil, M.D., is a Clinical Professor of Medicine at the University of Arizona. He is also the director of the Program in Integrative Medicine at the same university and founded the Foundation for Integrative Medicine in Tucson, Arizona. Integrative medicine involves looking at the body, spirit, and mind in making health decisions. Weil received his undergraduate and medical degrees from Harvard University. In 2005, he was named one of the 100 most influential people in the world by *Time* magazine. He has written several best-selling books, including *Eight Weeks to Optimum Health, Spontaneous Healing,* and *Healthy Aging.* The following excerpt is from *Eating Well for Optimum Health: The Essential Guide to Food, Diet, and Nutrition* published in 2000.

Before You Read

1. Read the first paragraph. What foods do you eat that reflect your cultural, religious, or family heritage?

2. Are there any foods you won't eat?

3. Write your own question that you think the reading may address:

   _____

4. Look at the photos. Do you recognize these foods?

Vocabulary Preview

Look for these words in the reading. Exercises to reinforce the learning of new vocabulary using these words follow the reading. The paragraph number where the word appears is in parentheses.

secular (2)	**pagan** (2)	**equinox** (2)	**taboos** (4)	**penchant** (6)
staple (7)	**pine** (8)	**scarcity** (10)	**neophobia** (11)	**optimum** (13)

1　# On Thursday nights, people throughout
Sweden sit down to the same meal, beginning with a thick soup made from yellow split peas. They take pleasure and comfort both in the food and in the knowledge that they are joining their countrymen and women in a national ritual that transcends both space and time—their grandparents and great-grandparents ate this weekly meal as well. Eating particular foods thus helps define identity and membership in ethnic and national groups and in family.

2　Ritual meals featuring special foods help renew bonds between friends, family members, and communities on both sacred and secular feast days. Consider the Jewish Passover seder, where those in attendance ask and answer questions about the special items on the menu. "Why on this night do we eat only unleavened bread [*matzoh*] when on all other nights we eat either leavened or unleavened bread?" The answer reminds the diners of their distant ancestors who labored as slaves in Egypt and had to flee so quickly that they could not allow the dough for their bread to rise. A delicious spread *charoset,* made of finely chopped walnuts and apples, moistened with sweet wine, and often flavored with cinnamon, appears only at the seder. It symbolizes the mortar used by the enslaved Israelites to construct the Pharaoh's buildings. Participants eat some of it spread on matzoh with a topping of pungent horseradish—sometimes so pungent that it brings tears to the eyes. This combination, said to be the invention of Rabbi Hillel, a great Jewish sage who lived around the time of Jesus, is supposed to remind those who eat it of the inseparability of sweetness and bitterness, of joy and sorrow, in human life. Passover and Easter both evolved from older pagan festivals celebrating the return of light and life at the spring equinox. Hard-boiled eggs appear on tables at both holidays because eggs are symbols of fertility and renewal, as do spring greens as symbols of new growth.

3   Special foods are also prominent at secular celebrations of the new year in cultures around the world. If you are Japanese, this most important holiday of the year, when you would clean your house from top to bottom and visit, and be visited by, friends and relatives, would feature the preparation and eating of *mochi,* a sticky treat made from glutinous sweet rice, traditionally and laboriously prepared in company by soaking, steaming, and pounding it in huge mortars with wooden clubs. (Electric countertop *mochi* makers, a recent invention, have made the process effortless and taken away some of the power of the ritual.) In the American South, the special dish is often boiled black-eyed peas, supposed to bring good luck for the coming year.

4   Of course, identity defined and secured by food and eating habits has as much to do with forbidden and disliked foods as with those that are enjoyed and promoted. Orthodox Jews will not eat pork. Orthodox Hindus will not eat meat. Orthodox Muslims do not consume alcohol. Food taboos are common, sometimes elaborate,

and oftentimes genuine attempts to connect to, and respect, religious beliefs and traditions. On the other hand, some food taboos seem ridiculous. And the taboos of one group may strike another group as most peculiar, emphasizing the "otherness" of those who refuse to eat fish, fowl, garlic, or sugar, for example. And so identity is further strengthened by defining oneself and one's culture or social group as different through eating or not eating what other people eat.

5   Most readers of this book will shun insects as food, regarding peoples who eat them as very different, indeed. The relish with which Australian aborigines eat witchetty grubs, the fat larvae of cossid moths, is a sure sign of their differentness and primitiveness. But if we want to be accepted by other people on their territory, we may have to swallow our aversions. My friend Wade Davis, a fellow alumnus of ethnobotanical training at the Harvard Botanical Museum, has made a career of studying and writing about native peoples throughout the world. His success stems, in part, from a noteworthy ability to win the trust of others. He says, "It can be as simple as willingness to eat what's put in front of you. If you walk into an Indian village and say, 'I'm sorry, I don't eat grubs,' well, that's going to create a barrier."

6   Conversely, barriers may be reinforced when people from one culture move to foreign territory and consume foods their new neighbors shun. In the Western world dogs are not considered food, because people identify with them, value them as pets, and appreciate their qualities of intelligence, affection, and loyalty. But in some parts of Asia people like to eat dogs, some of which—young, black dogs, for example—are considered especially delicious and nourishing. When large numbers of immigrants from Southeast Asia came to the United States in the wake of the Vietnam War, this dietary difference created bitter friction. Residents of California did not react well to the new arrivals' penchant for nabbing and eating their pets, surely a sign of a "barbaric" culture.*

7   The power of food to define social and cultural identity may also depend on particular ingredients, combinations of ingredients, or preparations that provide instantly recognizable textures, flavors, and aromas. The steamed rice of Japan that sticks together, and has a subtle, earthy flavor is nothing like the steamed rice of India, whose grains are separate, drier, and more aromatic. *Poi*, the sour, pasty staple made from taro root, is a unique food of Hawaii and related cultures of Oceania. Lemongrass,

---

* Of course, the ultimate food taboo is against eating one's own kind. Many animals observe it, as do most humans. Authorities differ about the existence of human societies that practice cannibalism regularly rather than as isolated incidents, but it is clear that many societies have attributed the practice to others.

chile, mint, and garlic occur together only in the cuisines of Southeast Asia. Olive oil, tomatoes, garlic, and basil create a signature flavor of the cooking of southern Italy, while olive oil, lemon juice, garlic, mint, and cumin in combination announce the Middle Eastern origin of a dish, and tomato, peanuts, and chile are a characteristic flavor principle of West African cuisine.

8   Often, it is these culture-specific tastes, odors, and textures that people long for when they have left their native lands and that occasion such joy when people reconnect with them. The French pine for their excellent bread when they travel in other countries, Indians for their curries, Japanese for their rice. And often, when people have abandoned their traditional foods, whether by choice or by circumstance, they will seek them out again when they are sick, infirm, or otherwise in need. For example, I am told that it is common for Japanese who have long eaten Western diets to come back to meals of fish, rice, vegetables, and miso soup in their old age. Perhaps their digestive systems are better adapted to these dishes or perhaps the associations of the foods, their reinforcing of cultural identity, is comforting.

9   I present these ideas to point out another obstacle to motivating people to change their eating habits in order to improve health. There is a great deal of psychological, social, and cultural investment in what we eat, and unless this aspect of food is acknowledged, change will not be possible. Let me give a few examples of the problem. In India, a principal cooking fat is *ghee,* a form of clarified butter—that is, butter that has been heated and strained to remove milk solids. Ghee has a distinctive, nutty flavor appealing to both Indians and Westerners and is more stable than butter; it can be stored unrefrigerated. It is also pure butterfat, the most saturated of dietary fats, and a major contributor to atherosclerosis and coronary heart disease, rates of which are currently very high in India. But it won't do simply to tell Indians that ghee is unhealthy and that they should switch to olive oil. As a product of the cow, ghee is regarded as a blessing from the gods by Hindus, who use it in religious rites, among other things, to anoint sacred objects. How could such a holy substance be harmful to the body? Hindus ask. Besides, olive oil tastes funny to them, especially in curry.

10   Many Japanese do not care for the flavor of olive oil either, but their traditional diet is so low in both total fat and saturated fat that they need not worry on that score. Where they could do better is in consumption of the fiber in whole grains, since their staple, white rice, provides very little. Most Japanese resist eating brown rice, however, for several reasons. They have long regarded it as a food of the lower social classes, much as Europeans used to look down on whole-grain bread as peasant food. In addition, during World War II, when white rice was hard to get, many families ate brown rice as a scarcity food, so it has a further negative association for the older generation. Finally, many Japanese believe their intestinal tracts are shorter and more delicate than those of Westerners and hence less able to process "rough" foods like unpolished grains. It does not help that brown rice is a favorite food of hippies, followers of macrobiotics, and other—to them—dietary extremists.

11   Nor is it easy to persuade Americans to eat tofu or bean curd, a classic and beloved food of Japan, China, and Korea. Made from soy milk by a process analogous to making fresh farmer's cheese from cow's milk, tofu is a good protein source, with a far healthier fat than butterfat and a good measure of soy isoflavones, compounds that appear to offer significant protection to women against breast cancer and to men against prostate cancer. Some of the American resistance to tofu is simple neophobia, fear of novel foods, but besides that, in its more common forms, tofu has a very bland taste and a squishy texture that Americans find unappealing. Japanese love the delicate flavor and custardlike texture of freshly made tofu. They flock to famous, centuries-old tofu restaurants in Kyoto to eat blocks of it, steamed over hot water, with no flavoring other than a bit of soy sauce and fresh ginger. I have known many American housewives who have read of the health benefits of tofu, bought cartons of it in grocery stores, and attempted to serve it as is to their families with disastrous results. Kids put it directly into the "yuck" pile, and husbands wouldn't touch it.

12   There are ways around these obstacles if you recognize them. The suggestion can be made to Indians that ghee is terrific for rubbing on things, including the skin, but that it should be ingested in moderation, perhaps added in small quantities to healthier oils as a flavoring. Japanese can be encouraged to try forms of rice that are *somewhat* polished—light brown rice—or to eat mixtures of white and brown rice or to introduce brown rice into the diet gradually. As for tofu, it can be made into dishes that Americans like by disguising it with familiar flavors and textures. I've tasted a delicious nondairy chocolate cream pie made from tofu, for example, as well as a robust Italian-style pasta sauce made with ground, sautèed tofu instead of ground meat. Most Americans who were served these dishes would never suspect they were eating bean curd.

13   Eating well means, among other things, not rejecting or giving up the characteristics of cuisine that help define oneself or one's society but rather adapting them to conform to dietary principles that promote optimum health.

Getting the Message

_____ **1.** What is the topic of this selection?

    a. eating well   c. eating for good health

    b. food and culture   d. unusual food habits

_____ **2.** The topic sentence of paragraph 10 can be found in

    a. sentence 1.   c. sentence 4.

    b. sentence 3.   d. sentence 7.

_____ **3.** In which paragraph is the main idea stated?

    a. paragraph 1   c. paragraph 9

    b. paragraph 4   d. paragraph 13

_____ **4.** Weil mainly uses _____ to make his point.

    a. examples   c. statistics

    b. testimony   d. reasons

_____ **5.** The following can be considered major details in the reading:

    a. people in Sweden eat the same meal on Thursday nights and Australian aborigines eat witchetty grubs.

    b. most people in India and Japan do not like olive oil and many Americans don't like tofu.

    c. the foods people eat and the ones they consider taboo create bonds within a culture.

    d. the use of specific ingredients or combinations of ingredients in food create bonds in a culture and the French miss their bread when they travel abroad.

_____ **6.** The information in the essay is presented in _____ order.

    a. chronological   c. most to least important

    b. problem and solution   d. least to most important

_____ **7.** Weil's intended audience is most likely

    a. children in Japan.   c. adults in Western cultures.

    b. experts on Australian aborigines.   d. his friends in Arizona.

_____ **8.** The tone of the essay can be labeled as _____

    a. angry.   c. upset.

    b. excited.   d. objective.

_____ **9.** What can be inferred from the example about Sweden that begins the essay?

    a. Swedes love yellow split peas.

    b. It is cold in Sweden, so it is comforting to have soup once a week.

    c. Swedes have a deep admiration for traditions and national identity.

    d. Swedes don't have much imagination when it comes to meal planning.

_____ **10.** Which fallacy does Weil avoid using in paragraph 12 by suggesting compromises?

    a. hasty generalization   c. slippery slope

    b. appeal to emotion   d. false dilemma

11. State Weil's purpose in your own words. Then give an example of a sentence from the essay that helps to show this purpose.

_____

_____

_____

_____

12. Give two examples of different contrast words and addition words and give the paragraph number where the use occurs.

_____

_____

_____

13. List two foods Weil uses as examples to show that food rituals are important in various cultures. Suggest two foods that would be appropriate for a weekly meal in the United States similar to what Sweden has (par. 1). Do you think the U.S. would ever implement such a meal? Explain your reasoning.

_____

_____

_____

_____

14. List two questions or comments you wrote in the margins as you read the selection.

_____

_____

15. Finish the outline of the essay by filling in the missing paragraph numbers or writing the central idea for the given paragraphs.

Thesis: Food holds important cultural and social significance, which can keep people from making healthy food choices.

1. Food rituals are important in religious and secular settings. Par. _____

2. Food taboos help to create cultural identity. Par. _____

3. Specific ingredients or combinations of ingredients help people identify food with a culture and attach people of that culture to the food. Par. _____

4. _____ Par. 9–12

5. _____

   _____ Par. 13

Vocabulary

Use context clues to determine the meaning of each word by referring back to the paragraph where the word is used (the paragraph number is in parentheses). If you need help, consult a dictionary for the definition.

A. Put a *T* if the underlined vocabulary word is used correctly and an *F* if it is used incorrectly.

_____ 1. I like living the secular (2) life, which is why I joined a monastery.

_____ 2. I have a penchant (6) for red. Over half of the clothes in my closet are red.

_____ 3. Snails are a staple (7) that most Americans eat three to four times a week.

_____ 4. My neighbor suffers from neophobia (11). I took him a plate of tamales, but he said he couldn't eat them because he has a fear of trying new things.

_____ 5. I often eat French fries and hamburgers, and I watch six hours of television a day because I want to do the optimum (13) to make my life healthy.

B. Match the word to the correct example.

pagan (2)	equinox (2)	taboos (4)	pine (8)	scarcity (10)

1. This event occurs approximately on March 21 and September 23 each year. _____

2. The Romans had several gods including Jupiter, Juno, Apollo, and Venus. _____

3. This is usually considered the availability of water in the desert. _____

4. The child felt this way toward his parents the first few days at camp. _____

5. In the United States, these usually include discussing politics at parties, asking someone how much money he or she makes, and eating cats. _____

C. Word parts: Highlight or underline the meaning of the underlined word part contained in each question. Return to pages 85–87 if you need to review the meaning of a word part.

1. I like the spring and fall equinoxes because the equal hours of light and dark make the world feel balanced.

2. It dawned on me that my friend suffers from neophobia when she refused to try a new dish that I considered delicious. She then confessed that a fear of new things keeps her from having some great experiences, but she is just too afraid to make changes.

3. The guide told me that the best place to take a photo of the ruins is from the top of this hill. I hope it is the optimum spot because it was a steep climb up here.

4. The recipe called for clarified butter, so I had to gently heat the butter to make it clear.

5. I have such a strong aversion to spinach that I have to turn away from the table when my mother serves it to the rest of the family.

The Essay and You

1. How adventurous of an eater would you rate yourself on a 1–10 scale, with 10 being a "willingness to eat what's put in front of you," such as grubs (par. 5)? What is the most unusual food you have ever had?

_____

_____

2. If you moved oversees, what food do you think you would long for as Weil says people often do (par. 8)? Why is this food important to you?

_____

_____

3. Weil states that "There is a great deal of psychological, social, and cultural investment in what we eat . . . " (par. 9). Is there a food you eat that is unhealthy for you, but you eat it for one of these reasons? What is a way you can still eat the food, but in a healthier manner as Weil suggests for ghee and white rice in paragraph 12?

_____

_____

_____

4. On a separate sheet of paper, write a paragraph that describes a special meal you have had. Clearly indicate what made it so special, whether it was celebrating traditions, the food, the people you were with, the setting, or a combination of these elements.

Take a Closer Look

Look at the photos again. What is the connection between the two foods? Do you have a special food your family eats to celebrate a holiday? Bring in a photograph of the food and share your tradition with the rest of the class.

_____

_____

_____

Internet Activities

If needed, use a separate sheet of paper to fully record your responses. Include the Web address of any sites from which you gather information.

1. Pick one of the foods mentioned in the reading (such as taro, tofu, or witchetty grubs) and do a search for it. Summarize the information you find, including who eats it, when, where, and how it is eaten.

_____

_____

2. Look up "food taboos." Pick one food to research and make an outline of your findings. Include in your outline who does and who does not eat this food and why it is taboo to consume it.

_____

_____

_____

Healthy Relationships

from *Access to Health*

by Rebecca J. Donatelle

Before You Read

1. Survey the chapter. Note the headings, table, and bold words. Change the headings into questions. Write one of your questions below:

   _____

2. Use three words to describe your relationship with a family member. As you read, note whether these words relate to "healthy" family relationships.

3. How have you found or made friends throughout your life?

4. Look at the photo and table. What does the photo reveal about families? How does the table reflect your definition of family?

Rebecca J. Donatelle is a professor at Oregon State University in Corvallis, Oregon. She received her Ph.D. from the University of Oregon in Eugene. She teaches courses in the Department of Public Health. Among the courses she has taught are Stress and Health, Control of Chronic Diseases, and Violence and Public Health. One of her research areas is women's health. She has examined women who smoke during pregnancy and afterward, and she has looked into the factors that influence health behaviors in women who suffer chronic problems such as lower back pain. The following excerpt comes from the tenth edition of her textbook *Access to Health*.

Vocabulary Preview

Look for these words in the reading. Exercises to reinforce the learning of new vocabulary using these words follow the reading. The paragraph number where the word appears is in parentheses.

thrive (1)	**vitally** (2)	**culminate** (3)	**affirmation** (6)	**validated** (7)
introspection (8)	**constitute** (10)	**equity** (14)	**consensus** (15)	**revelation** (15)

1 **Humans are social** animals—we have a basic need to fit in to a human "pack," to feel loved and appreciated by others. We thrive in environments where we feel secure, needed, and respected, particularly if we are cared about by people who really matter to us. Although we can exist without these close interactions, our lives are enhanced and our days are more fulfilling when we can share our successes and failures with others. In fact, a study done by researchers at the Harvard School of Public Health shows that the ability to relate well with people throughout your life can have almost as much impact on your health as exercise and good nutrition.

2 All relationships involve a degree of risk. Only by taking these risks, however, can we grow and truly experience all that life has to offer. In this chapter, we examine healthy relationships and the communication skills necessary to create and maintain them. Why is communication so important? For one thing, the way we communicate influences whether or not we are accepted by others. For another, most of us sincerely want to express ourselves clearly and honestly in our relationships. Clear communication can help us bridge our differences, and it can also affect health. Expressing ourselves well and knowing how to understand what others are saying are both vitally important to communication. These abilities lay the

groundwork for healthy relationships, and satisfying relationships are significant factors in overall health.

Characterizing and Forming Intimate Relationships

3 **Does an intimate relationship have to be sexual?** Most people think of intimacy as two people having a loving, intense, often sexual, relationship in which there is a mutual desire for closeness, touching, and physical expression. However, in her book *The Dance of Intimacy*, Dr. Harriet Goldhor Lerner defines intimacy as "being who we are in a relationship and allowing the other person to be the same. An intimate relationship is one in which neither party silences or betrays the self and each party expresses strength and vulnerability, weakness and competence in a balanced way." Thus, intimacy is less a physical state than it is a state of the mind, heart, and essence of those who share it. It may culminate in a physical way, but it is much more complex than the act of sexual intercourse or sexual expression. In fact, intimacy is sometimes described as an attitude; one that defines the quality of how two people relate to one another and their level of emotional and spiritual connectedness to each other in the times between lovemaking, as well as during lovemaking.

4 Experts in the field of interpersonal relationships define **intimate relationships** in terms of four characteristics: *behavioral interdependence, need fulfillment, emotional atttachment*, and *emotional availability*. Each of these characteristics may be related to interactions with family, close friends, and romantic partners.

5 *Behavioral interdependence* refers to the mutual impact that people have on each other as their lives and daily activities intertwine. What one person does influences what the

---

intimate relationships
Relationships with family members, friends, and romantic partners, characterized by closeness and understanding.

---

other person wants to do and can do. Behavioral interdependence may become stronger over time to the point that each person would feel a great void if the other were gone.

6 Intimate relationships also fulfill psychological needs and so are a means of *need fulfillment*. Through relationships with others, we fulfill our needs for:

- *Intimacy,* someone with whom we can share our feelings freely
- *Social integration,* someone with whom we can share worries and concerns
- *Nurturance,* someone whom we can take care of and who will take care of us
- *Assistance,* someone to help us in times of need
- *Affirmation,* someone who will reassure us of our own worth and tell us that we matter

7 In rewarding, intimate relationships, partners and friends meet each other's needs. They disclose feelings, share confidences, and provide support and reassurance. Each person comes away feeling better for the interaction and validated by the other person.

8 In addition to behavioral interdependence and need fulfillment, intimate relationships involve strong bonds of

emotional attachment, or feelings of love and attachment. *Emotional availability,* the ability to give to and receive from others emotionally without fear of being hurt or rejected, is the fourth characteristic of intimate relationships. At times, all of us may limit our emotional availability—for example, after a painful breakup we may decide not to jump into another relationship immediately. Holding back can offer time for introspection and healing as well as considering the "lessons learned." However, because of intense trauma, some people find it difficult ever to be fully available emotionally. This limits their ability to experience and enjoy intimate relationships.

9   In the early years of life, families provide the most significant relationships. Gradually, the circle widens to include friends, coworkers, and acquaintances. Ultimately, most of us develop romantic relationships with a significant other. Each of these relationships plays a significant role in psychological, social, spiritual, and physical health.

Families: The Ties That Bind

10   A family is a recognizable group of people with roles, tasks, boundaries, and personalities whose central focus is to protect, care for, love, and socialize one another. Because the family is a dynamic institution that changes as society changes, the definition of family, and the individuals believed to constitute family membership, change over time as well. Who are members of today's families? Historically, most families have been made up of people related by blood, marriage, and long-term committed relationships or adoption. Yet today, many other groups of people are being recognized and functioning as family units (see Table 5.1). Although there is no "best" family type, we do know the key roles and tasks a healthy family nurtures and supports. Healthy

TABLE 5.1   Today's Changing Families

The United States is a melting pot of family types. The estimated percentages of school-aged children living in various family structures is listed below.

Family Structure	School-aged children living in identified family structure (%)
Nuclear family: husband and wife plus biological offspring	58
Stepparent family: one biological parent plus one stepparent	10
Blended family: parents plus children born to several families	5
Adoptive family: two parents	2
Single mother, never married	10
Single mother, divorced	10
Single father, divorced and never remarried	5

Source: Based on data from the U.S. Census Bureau, 2000.

families foster a sense of security and feelings of belonging that are central to growth and development. It is from our **family of origin,** the people present in our household during our first years of life, that we initially learn about feelings, problem solving, love, intimacy, and gender roles. We learn to negotiate relationships and have opportunities to communicate effectively, develop attitudes, beliefs, and values, and explore spiritual belief systems. It is not uncommon when we establish relationships outside of the family to rely on these initial experiences and skills modeled by our family of origin.

Establishing Friendships

11   *A Friend is one who knows you as you are, understands where you've been, accepts who you've become, and still gently invites you to grow.*

—Author Unknown

12   Good friends can make a boring day fun, a cold day warm, or a gut-wrenching worry disappear. They can make us feel that we matter and that we have the strength to get through just about anything. They can also make us angry, disappoint us, or seriously jolt our comfortable ideas about right and wrong.

13   Friendships are relationships between two or more people that involve mutual respect, trust, support, and intimacy that may or may not include sexual intimacy. Like our family, our friends should have identified roles and boundaries. Persons in friendships should communicate their understandings, needs, expectations, limitations, and affections.

14   Psychologists believe that people are attracted to and form relationships with people who give them positive reinforcement and that they dislike those who punish or overcriticize them. The basic idea is simple: you like people who like you. Another factor that affects the development of a friendship is a real or perceived similarity in attitudes, opinions, and background. In addition, true friends have a sense of equity in which they share confidences, contribute fairly and equally to maintaining the friendship, and consistently try to give as much as they get back from the interactions.

15   Psychologists Jeffrey Turner and Laurna Rubinson summarized the consensus among experts on characteristics that make a good friendship:

- *Enjoyment.* Although temporary states of anger, disappointment, or mutual annoyance may occur, friends enjoy each other's company most of the time.
- *Acceptance.* Friends accept each other as they are, without trying to change or make the other into a different person.
- *Mutual trust.* Each assumes that the other will act in his or her friend's best interest.
- *Respect.* Friends respect each other; each assumes that the other exercises good judgment in making life choices.
- *Mutual assistance.* Friends are inclined to assist and support one another. Specifically, they can count on each other in times of need, trouble, or personal distress.
- *Confiding.* Friends share experiences and feelings with each other that they don't share with other people.
- *Understanding.* Friends have a sense of what each person values. They are not puzzled or mystified by each other's actions.
- *Spontaneity.* Friends feel free to be themselves in the relationship, without being required to play a role or inhibit revelation of personal traits.

16   Take a few minutes to examine one of your current friendships. How many of these characteristics can you identify in that relationship?

---

family of origin
People present in the household during a child's first years of life—usually parents and siblings.

Getting the Message

____ **1.** What is the topic of this selection?

    a. being a good friend

    b. family groups

    c. meeting new friends

    d. relationships

____ **2.** The topic sentence in paragraph 3 can be found in

    a. sentence 1.

    b. sentence 2.

    c. sentence 5.

    d. sentence 7.

____ **3.** What is the main idea of the selection?

    a. Most people have healthy relationships with their family members and friends.

    b. Forming intimate relationships with others involves several characteristics.

    c. Intimate relationships are only formed through touch.

    d. Family and friends are people we can always trust.

____ **4.** The excerpt uses _____ as supporting details.

    a. examples and statistics

    b. facts and personal examples

    c. examples and testimony

    d. statistics and hypothetical examples

____ **5.** Which patterns of organization are used in the selection?

    a. definition, examples, classification

    b. examples, process, and contrast

    c. narrative and cause and effect

    d. comparison/contrast and classification

____ **6.** The transition word *thus* in paragraph 3 shows _____.

    a. comparison

    b. contrast

    c. cause and effect

    d. example

____ **7.** Donatelle's purpose is to

    a. inform.

    b. persuade.

    c. entertain.

    d. entertain and persuade.

____ **8.** The tone of this chapter can best be described as_____.

    a. angry

    b. cheerful

    c. objective

    d. sad

_____ **9.** From the information in paragraph 10, it can be inferred that

    a. most families are healthy families.

    b. most families have problems with communication.

    c. what happens to one as a child isn't that important to one's later life.

    d. what happens to one as a child can have a major impact on one's later life.

_____ **10.** It is fair to say that Donatelle uses the appeal to emotion fallacy in this section.

    a. true   b. false

11. Finish the sentence about the writer's purpose. Donatelle's purpose is to _____ her readers _____

_____

_____

12. What are important terms to learn in this selection? How do you know they are important?

_____

_____

_____

13. How do the bulleted items in paragraphs 6 and 15 help you to comprehend the writer's point?

_____

_____

_____

14. List three words or terms you highlighted or circled as important to learn in this selection.

_____

_____

_____

15. On a separate sheet of paper, write a summary (about 150 words) of the excerpt.

Vocabulary

Use context clues to determine the meaning of each word by referring back to the paragraph where the word is used (the paragraph number is in parentheses). If you need help, consult a dictionary for the definition.

A. Match the word to its synonym.

> fairness   end   agreement   confirmed   prosper

1. thrive (1) _____
2. culminate (3) _____
3. validated (7) _____
4. equity (14) _____
5. consensus (15) _____

B. Match the word to its definition.

> **vitally** (2)   **interdependence** (4)   **affirmation** (6)   **introspection** (8)   **revelation** (15)

1. self-examination _____
2. to a crucial degree _____
3. a discovery or disclosure _____
4. mutual reliance _____
5. confirmation of anything _____

C. Word parts: Pick the best definition for each underlined word. Highlight or circle any word parts you find to help you make the connections. Return to pages 85–87 if you need to review the meaning of a word part.

    a. look into one's feelings   d. relating to interactions between people

    b. the state of being equal   e. relating to life

    c. to make fit for the company of others

____ 1. It is <u>vital</u> that I see the doctor today. I have fallen down twice, and my vision is blurry.

____ 2. After some <u>introspection</u>, I decided the job offer was worth accepting.

____ 3. The part-time workers demanded <u>equity</u>, or they would go on strike.

____ 4. Learning manners at the dinner table is one way families <u>socialize</u> children.

____ 5. After taking a class in <u>interpersonal</u> communication, conversations with my girlfriend have been much more meaningful.

The Textbook and You

  1. How well do you feel your relationships are meeting the five needs mentioned in paragraph 6?

    _____

    _____

2. Pick one of the areas mentioned in paragraph 10 that a child sees modeled by his or her "family of origin" (such as problem solving, gender roles, or spiritual beliefs) and explain what you learned from your family.

_____

_____

_____

3. Use the information in paragraph 15 to answer the question in paragraph 16:"How many of these characteristics can you identify in that relationship?"

_____

_____

_____

4. On a separate sheet of paper, write a paragraph about a healthy relationship you have or have had at any point in your life. Use some of the information in the reading to support your thesis that the relationship is/was healthy.

Take a Closer Look

Look at the table and photo again. What does the table reveal about American society? Do you think the changes might have an impact on how families help children to grow? How does the photo reflect the roles of the "family of origin" mentioned in the reading?

_____

_____

_____

_____

Internet Activities

If needed, use a separate sheet of paper to fully record your responses. Include the Web address of any sites from which you gather information.

1. Look up "qualities of healthy families." Find a site that describes what makes a healthy family. List two pieces of advice given on the site.

_____

_____

2. Look up "strong friendships." Find a site that offers advice on building healthy friendships. Compare and contrast that information to the information in the reading using a Venn diagram.

_____

The Masque of the Red Death

by Edgar Allan Poe

Before You Read

1. What do you think the "Red Death" might be?

2. What tone does the title help to create?

3. Read the first paragraph. To what events or diseases can you connect the "Red Death"?

4. Look at the photo. What feeling or feelings do you get from the mask?

Vocabulary Preview

Look for these words in the reading. Exercises to reinforce the learning of new vocabulary using these words follow the reading. The paragraph number where the word appears is in parentheses.

pestilence (1)	**dissolution** (1)
sagacious (2)	**dominions** (2)
egress (2)	**disconcert** (5)
revel (6)	**wanton** (7)
writhed (7)	**impetuosity** (13)

Edgar Allan Poe (1809–1849) published numerous essays, magazine articles, poems, and short stories. After a turbulent youth and false starts at college, he settled into the life of a writer. He was the editor of the *Southern Literary Messenger* in 1835 and various other magazines in the 1840s. In 1845, his poem "The Raven" was an instant success, which helped to establish his name as a writer with the general public. After his wife died of tuberculosis in 1847, Poe supposedly took to drinking more heavily. He was found unconscious in the streets of Baltimore on October 7, 1849, and taken to a hospital. He died there of uncertain causes. Speculations include alcohol, drugs, heart disease, suicide, and tuberculosis. Poe is known for his horror and mystery stories, and he is considered by many as the inventor of the detective genre. The following story was originally published in 1842.

1 The "Red Death" had long devastated the country. No pestilence had ever been so fatal, or so hideous. Blood was its Avatar and its seal—the redness and the horror of blood. There were sharp pains, and sudden dizziness, and then profuse bleeding at the pores, with dissolution. The scarlet stains upon the body and especially upon the face of the victim, were the pest ban which shut him out from the aid and from the sympathy of his fellow-men. And the whole seizure, progress and termination of the disease, were the incidents of half an hour.

2 But the Prince Prospero was happy and dauntless and sagacious. When his dominions were half depopulated, he summoned to his presence a thousand hale and light-hearted friends from among the knights and dames of his court, and with these retired to the deep seclusion of one of his castellated abbeys. This was an extensive and magnificent structure, the creation of the prince's own

eccentric yet august taste. A strong and lofty wall girdled it in. This wall had gates of iron. The courtiers, having entered, brought furnaces and massy hammers and welded the bolts. They resolved to leave means neither of ingress or egress to the sudden impulses of despair or of frenzy from within. The abbey was amply provisioned. With such precautions the courtiers might bid defiance to contagion. The external world could take care of itself. In the meantime it was folly to grieve, or to think. The prince had provided all the appliances of pleasure. There were buffoons, there were improvisatori, there were ballet-dancers, there were musicians, there was Beauty, there was wine. All these and security were within. Without was the "Red Death."

3   It was toward the close of the fifth or sixth month of his seclusion, and while the pestilence raged most furiously abroad, that the Prince Prospero entertained his thousand friends at a masked ball of the most unusual magnificence.

4   It was a voluptuous scene, that masquerade. But first let me tell of the rooms in which it was held. There were seven—an imperial suite. In many palaces, however, such suites form a long and straight vista, while the folding doors slide back nearly to the walls on either hand, so that the view of the whole extent is scarcely impeded. Here the case was very different; as might have been expected from the duke's love of the *bizarre.* The apartments were so irregularly disposed that the vision embraced but little more than one at a time. There was a sharp turn at every twenty or thirty yards, and at each turn a novel effect. To the right and left, in the middle of each wall, a tall and narrow Gothic window looked out upon a closed corridor which pursued the windings of the suite. These windows were of stained glass whose color varied in accordance with the prevailing hue of the decorations of the chamber into which it opened. That at the eastern extremity was hung, for example, in blue—and vividly blue were its windows. The second chamber was purple in its ornaments and tapestries, and here the panes were purple. The third was green throughout, and so were the casements. The fourth was furnished and lighted with orange—the fifth with white—the sixth with violet. The seventh apartment was closely shrouded in black velvet tapestries that hung all over the ceiling and down the walls, falling in heavy folds upon a carpet of the same material and hue. But in this chamber only, the color of the windows failed to correspond with the decorations. The panes here were scarlet—a deep blood color. Now in no one of the seven apartments was there any lamp or candelabrum, amid the profusion of golden ornaments that lay scattered to and fro or depended from the roof. There was no light of any kind emanating from lamp or candle within the suite of chambers. But in the corridors that followed the suite, there stood, opposite to each window, a heavy tripod, bearing a brazier of fire that projected its rays through the

tinted glass and so glaringly illumined the room. And thus were produced a multitude of gaudy and fantastic appearances. But in the western or black chamber the effect of the fire-light that streamed upon the dark hangings through the blood-tinted panes, was ghastly in the extreme, and produced so wild a look upon the countenances of those who entered, that there were few of the company bold enough to set foot within its precincts at all.

5   It was in this apartment, also, that there stood against the western wall, a gigantic clock of ebony. Its pendulum swung to and fro with a dull, heavy, monotonous clang; and when the minute-hand made the circuit of the face, and the hour was to be stricken, there came from the brazen lungs of the clock a sound which was clear and loud and deep and exceedingly musical, but of so peculiar a note and emphasis that, at each lapse of an hour, the musicians of the orchestra were constrained to pause, momentarily, in their performance, to hearken to the sound; and thus the waltzers perforce ceased their evolutions; and there was a brief disconcert of the whole gay company; and, while the chimes of the clock yet rang, it was observed that the giddiest grew pale, and the more aged and sedate passed their hands over their brows as if in confused reverie or meditation. But when the echoes had fully ceased, a light laughter at once pervaded the assembly; the musicians looked at each other and smiled as if at their own nervousness and folly, and made whispering vows, each to the other, that the next chiming of the clock should produce in them no similar emotion; and then, after the lapse of sixty minutes, (which embrace three thousand and six hundred seconds of the Time that flies,) there came yet another chiming of the clock, and then were the same disconcert and tremulousness and meditation as before.

6   But, in spite of these things, it was a gay and magnificent revel. The tastes of the duke were peculiar. He had a fine eye for colors and effects. He disregarded the *decora* of mere fashion. His plans were bold and fiery, and his conceptions glowed with barbaric lustre. There are some who would have thought him mad. His followers felt that he was not. It was necessary to hear and see and touch him to be *sure* that he was not.

7   He had directed, in great part, the moveable embellishments of the seven chambers, upon occasion of this great *fête;* and it was his own guiding taste which had given character to the masqueraders. Be sure they were grotesque. There were much glare and glitter and piquancy and phantasm—much of what has been since seen in "Hernani." There were arabesque figures with unsuited limbs and appointments. There were delirious fancies such as the madman fashions. There was much of the beautiful, much of the wanton, much of the *bizarre,* something of the terrible, and not a little of that which might have excited disgust. To and fro in the seven chambers there stalked, in fact, a multitude of dreams. And these—the dreams—writhed in and about, taking hue from the rooms, and causing the wild music of the orchestra to seem as the echo of their steps. And, anon, there strikes the ebony clock which stands in the hall of the velvet. And then, for a moment, all is still, and all is silent save the voice of the clock. The dreams are stiff-frozen as they stand. But the echoes of the chime die away—they have endured but an instant— and a light, half-subdued laughter floats after them as they depart. And now again the music swells, and the dreams live, and writhe to and fro more merrily than ever, taking hue from the many-tinted windows through which stream the rays from the tripods. But

to the chamber which lies most westwardly of the seven, there are now none of the maskers who venture; for the night is waning away; and there flows a ruddier light through the blood-colored panes; and the blackness of the sable drapery appalls; and to him whose foot falls upon the sable carpet, there comes from the near clock of ebony a muffled peal more solemnly emphatic than any which reaches *their* ears who indulge in the more remote gaieties of the other apartments.

8   But these other apartments were densely crowded, and in them beat feverishly the heart of life. And the revel went whirlingly on, until at length there commenced the sounding of midnight upon the clock. And then the music ceased, as I have told; and the evolutions of the waltzers were quieted; and there was an uneasy cessation of all things as before. But now there were twelve strokes to be sounded by the bell of the clock; and thus it happened, perhaps, that more of thought crept, with more of time, into the meditations of the thoughtful among those who revelled. And thus, too, it happened, perhaps, that before the last echoes of the last chime had utterly sunk into silence; there were many individuals in the crowd who had found leisure to become aware of the presence of a masked figure which had arrested the attention of no single individual before. And the rumor of this new presence having spread itself whisperingly around, there arose at length from the whole company a buzz, or murmur, expressive of disapprobation and surprise—then, finally, of terror, of horror, and of disgust.

9   In an assembly of phantasms such as I have painted, it may well be supposed that no ordinary appearance could have excited such sensation. In truth the masquerade license of the night was nearly unlimited; but the figure in question had out-Heroded Herod, and gone beyond the bounds of even the prince's indefinite decorum. There are chords in the hearts of the most reckless which cannot be touched without emotion. Even with the utterly lost, to whom life and death are equally jests, there are matters of which no jest can be made. The whole company, indeed, seemed now deeply to feel that in the costume and bearing of the stranger neither wit nor propriety existed. The figure was tall and gaunt, and shrouded from head to foot in the habiliments of the grave. The mask which concealed the visage was made so nearly to resemble the countenance of a stiffened corpse that the closest scrutiny must have had difficulty in detecting the cheat. And yet all this might have been endured, if not approved, by the mad revellers around. But the mummer had gone so far as to assume the type of the Red Death. His vesture was dabbled in *blood*—and his broad brow, with all the features of the face, was besprinkled with the scarlet horror.

10   When the eyes of Prince Prospero fell upon this spectral image (which with a slow and solemn movement, as if more fully to sustain its *rôle,* stalked to and fro among the waltzers) he was seen to be convulsed, in the first moment with a strong shudder either of terror or distaste; but, in the next, his brow reddened with rage.

11   "Who dares?" he demanded hoarsely of the courtiers who stood near him—"who dares insult us with this blasphemous mockery? Seize him and unmask him—that we may know whom we have to hang at sunrise, from the battlements!"

12   It was in the eastern or blue chamber in which stood the Prince Prospero as he uttered these words. They rang throughout the seven rooms loudly and clearly—for the prince was a bold and robust man, and the music had become hushed at the waving of his hand.

13   It was in the blue room where stood the prince, with a group of pale courtiers by his side. At first, as he spoke, there was a slight rushing movement of this group in the direction of the intruder, who at the moment was also near at hand, and now, with deliberate and stately step, made closer approach to the speaker. But from a certain nameless awe with which the mad assumptions of the mummer had inspired the whole party, there were found none who put forth hand to seize him; so that, unimpeded, he passed within a yard of the prince's person; and, while the vast assembly, as if with one impulse, shrank from the centres of the rooms to the walls, he made his way uninterruptedly, but with the same solemn and measured step which had distinguished him from the first, through the blue chamber to the purple—through the purple to the green—through the green to the orange—through this again to the white—and even thence to the violet, ere a decided movement had been made to arrest him. It was then, however, that the Prince Prospero, maddening with rage and the shame of his own momentary cowardice, rushed hurriedly through the six chambers, while none followed him on account of a deadly terror that had seized upon all. He bore aloft a drawn dagger, and had approached, in rapid impetuosity, to within three or four feet of the retreating figure, when the latter, having attained the extremity of the velvet apartment, turned suddenly and confronted his pursuer. There was a sharp cry—and the dagger dropped gleaming upon the sable carpet, upon which, instantly afterwards, fell prostrate in death the Prince Prospero. Then, summoning the wild courage of despair, a throng of the revellers at once threw themselves into the black apartment, and, seizing the mummer, whose tall figure stood erect and motionless within the shadow of the ebony clock, gasped in unutterable horror at finding the grave-cerements and corpse-like mask which they handled with so violent a rudeness, untenanted by any tangible form.

14   And now was acknowledged the presence of the Red Death. He had come like a thief in the night. And one by one dropped the revellers in the blood-bedewed halls of their revel, and died each in the despairing posture of his fall. And the life of the ebony clock went out with that of the last of the gay. And the flames of the tripods expired. And Darkness and Decay and the Red Death held illimitable dominion over all.

Getting the Message

____ **1.** The theme of the story is that

    a. throwing a masquerade party can be fun.
    b. one can't hide from diseases or death.
    c. multicolored rooms add drama to a party.
    d. unhealthy behaviors can be fatal.

____ **2.** Which words best describe Prince Prospero?

    a. kind and fun
    b. angry and mean
    c. excitable and amusing
    d. bizarre and arrogant

____ **3.** During what time period does the story likely take place?

    a. near the end of the Roman Empire (300–400)
    b. the late Middle Ages (1300–1400)
    c. the Industrial Revolution (the 1800s)
    d. the Information Age (after 1990)

____ **4.** The story uses the _____ pattern of organization.

    a. narrative
    b. process
    c. classification
    d. comparison and contrast

____ **5.** Three of the paragraphs in the story begin with a _____ transition word.

    a. comparison
    b. example
    c. contrast
    d. time

____ **6.** Poe's purpose is to

    a. inform.
    b. persuade.
    c. entertain.
    d. entertain and persuade.

____ **7.** The word _____ would be appropriate to describe the tone of the story.

    a. cozy
    b. silly
    c. ominous
    d. wild

____ **8.** Which element of the story greatly aids in creating the tone?

    a. the dialogue
    b. the plot
    c. the setting
    d. the characters

9. It can be inferred from Prince Prospero's reaction to the masked figure that he is

    a. upset because the figure's costume is better than his.

    b. angry because the figure dared to dress like the Red Death.

    c. excited because the costume is so realistic.

    d. happy because someone attempted to look like the Red Death.

10. Which type of figurative language is used in the line "He had come like a thief in the night" (par. 14)?

    a. a simile

    b. a metaphor

11. Explain how the ebony clock is used as a symbol in the story?

_____

_____

_____

12. List four words or phrases that help to convey the tone of the story.

_____

_____

_____

_____

13. What type of conflict does the story show? How is this conflict different from what you would expect in real life?

_____

_____

_____

14. List four words, phrases, or characters you circled or otherwise highlighted in the story. Briefly explain why you thought these points important.

_____

_____

_____

15. On a separate sheet of paper, make a map of the seven rooms and label each room with the appropriate color. Refer to paragraph 4 to help you create the map. Does looking at your completed map help you to see what happens in the story more clearly? Compare your map to ones drawn by a couple of your classmates. Are they similar?

Vocabulary

Use context clues to determine the meaning of each word by referring back to the paragraph where the word is used (the paragraph number is in parentheses). If you need help, consult a dictionary for the definition.

A. Complete each sentence with the appropriate word. Use each word once.

pestilence (1)	dissolution (1)	sagacious (2)	dominions (2)	writhed (7)

1. My English professor is a _____ woman. She is wise not only in her subject matter but also to the ways of college students who try devious methods to complete assignments.
2. The _____ moved quickly, killing thousands before a cure could be found.
3. The prince's _____ were threatened when a rival prince assembled a massive army.
4. The man _____ in pain until the drugs the nurse gave him calmed his system.
5. The _____ of the club shocked customers who had been coming for 20 years.

B. Finish the reading by filling in the missing words from the list below.

egress (2)	disconcert (5)	revel (6)	wanton (7)	impetuosity (13)

I was invited to a party by a couple I just met. They said it was a _____ not to be missed. I decided to be spontaneous and go. At first it was fun but, after a few hours, I was amazed at the _____ behavior I saw. It is usually difficult to _____ me, but I found the lewd dancing, heavy drinking, and other activities disturbing. By midnight, I was looking about for any means of _____. I regretted my _____. In the future, I will not act so rashly.

C. Word parts: Finish the sentences with the meaning of each word part. Use one meaning twice. The word part is underlined to help you make the connection. Return to pages 85–87 if you need to review the meaning of a word part.

see	away	one	into	out

1. The pestilence is <u>de</u>populating (2) the country. It has already taken _____ half of the people in some cities.
2. This building is confusing. It is hard to find a means of <u>in</u>gress (2) when one wants to go _____ it, and even harder to find any way to <u>e</u>gress (2) once one wants to go _____.
3. A meeting can become <u>mono</u>tonous (5) if only _____ topic is discussed for hours.
4. I wanted to _____ what his <u>vis</u>age (9) looked like when he experienced the <u>vis</u>ta (4) from the balcony, and he discovered that he could _____ the ocean.

The Short Story and You

1. How would you have reacted if you were one of the friends Prince Prospero had invited to stay at the abbey?

_____

_____

2. Pretend you are at the masked ball walking through the seven rooms with a friend. Record two of the comments you make to your friend about the décor of the rooms.

_____

_____

3. Explain how the story relates to one of today's health issues and some people's reactions to it?

_____

_____

4. On a separate sheet of paper, write a paragraph in which you imagine yourself as one of the last revelers standing at the ball. Write your impressions of what you saw that night, including what you felt on seeing the "tall and gaunt" figure (par. 9) and about what happened to Prince Prospero.

Take a Closer Look

Look at the photo again. What does wearing a mask do to a person? Why do you think Poe set the story at a masked ball?

_____

_____

_____

Internet Activities

If needed, use a separate sheet of paper to fully record your responses. Include the Web address of any sites from which you gather information.

1. Look up "Hernani" (par. 7) or "out-Heroded Herod" (par. 9) and write a summary of your findings.

_____

_____

2. Go to the site for the Centers for Disease Control (CDC) and look at the "Diseases and Conditions" section. Pick a disease society has recently faced. What does the CDC recommend a person do to help prevent or cope with this disease?

_____

_____

_____

myreadinglab — Objectives Check

To check your progress in meeting chapter objectives, log in to www.myreadinglab.com, click on the Study Plan tab, and then on the Reading Skills tab. Choose Purpose and Tone from the list of subtopics. Read and view the resources in the Review Materials section, then complete the Practices and Tests in the Activities section. You can check your scores by clicking on the Gradebook tab.

CHAPTER 8

How do you use scientific and technological developments?

Science and Technology

Investigating New Realms

Skill: Making Inferences

Science and technology continue to play bigger roles in our lives each year. Science investigates new worlds whether they lie in the stars, in the seas, or in our brains. Technology touches us every day whether we use a computer, watch television, or grab a bite from the refrigerator. The ways we communicate with each other have especially been impacted by technological innovations. Our lives would be immensely different without the developments science and technology have brought to us. Where we've been, where we are, and where we may go are all fascinating aspects of science and technology.

Those involved in scientific and technological fields rely on inferences to help them develop their ideas. Making inferences involves thoroughly looking at the evidence in order to reach a conclusion. Careful readers use inference to decipher various elements in what they read. Writers, especially of fiction, do not always plainly state their ideas. Like Sherlock Holmes, the reader needs to deduce what is going on by using a variety of reading skills to look for the writer's true meaning. The reader is required to closely examine the supporting details, the organization, and tone to figure out what the writer means in a sentence, a paragraph, or the whole reading. Using inference lets you be the detective or the scientist seeking answers. This chapter focuses on the skills needed to make accurate inferences. As you read the four essays or articles, textbook excerpt, and short story, think about how science and technology impact your life and how through inference we can come to better understand the impact of these areas on our lives.

Making Inferences

Sometimes writers do not directly state what they mean, so you will need to make inferences to figure out the writer's real purpose. Making an **inference** means using evidence to come to a conclusion. You infer what happens when you take into account the circumstances surrounding an event and you use prior knowledge gathered from similar situations or what you have read. You make inferences all the time. If your roommate isn't home when you expect him to be, but you notice that his basketball isn't sitting in its usual corner (the evidence), you can infer that he is playing ball. You may even be able to take that inference further by using your prior knowledge to deduce that he is at the park on the corner where you two usually play. When you are reading a mystery and a character doesn't make it to dinner and two other characters have already been killed, you could infer that she has become the next victim. As you continue to read, you may discover that an initial inference is incorrect, but you can revise an inference with each new bit of evidence you collect.

Inference Clues

Look for evidence in the reading to support your reasoning. Look at the supporting details the writer uses to make your conclusions when a point is not directly stated.

Use your prior knowledge about a subject. There may be times when you read something that you have absolutely no knowledge about, but more often you can use common sense, information you have learned from other reading sources, or your personal experiences to help you make a deduction.

Look at the organization of a reading. If something in an essay or story seems unclear to you, consider how the writer put the reading together to help you make any inferences. For example, if an essay is using comparison and contrast, but one side has a lot more negatives mentioned than the other, then you may be able to infer a bias in the writer's position. If a short story is using time order and a character says something happened at a different time than was previously presented, you should become suspicious. Use inference to decide why the character made a statement that contradicts the other information provided.

Pay attention to the writer's tone and diction. You especially want to look for irony. If a writer states that Jennifer is a generous person, but then shows her paying less than her share at lunch and deciding to get her hair done instead of helping a friend, you can infer that the writer's statement about Jennifer is ironic. If you ignore a writer's use of irony, you may miss the point of the reading. Paying attention to the writer's diction can also help you make inferences on the writer's purpose and audience. If the writer is using words from a particular occupation (such as medical terms), then you can infer that the writer is not aiming his or her text at the general public, but for specialists in that field.

Read the following sentences and paragraphs, and make inferences using the above skills.

1. Honey, did we bring a map?

   What can be inferred about the situation? _____
   _____

2. Matt says, "I'm excited about going to Jim and Keri's for dinner. Who wouldn't love burnt meatloaf and watching 500 photos of their trip to Cleveland?"

   What can you infer about Matt's statement? _____
   _____

3. A woman is walking down the street calling, "Here, Mr. Snuggles! Snuggles? It's time to come home, Mr. Snuggles!"

   What is the woman doing? _____

4. You see Bill come to work carrying balloons and a large pink box. When you walk by the conference room, you notice he is setting out paper plates. Later you see him running in and out of people's offices with a card and pen in his hand.

   What is likely to happen that day? _____

5. The man was breathing hard as he answered the door. His face glistened with beads of sweat, and his hands shook.

   "We just have a few questions, Mr. Jackson. Your neighbor called and said she'd heard your wife scream. That was about twenty minutes ago. Can we speak with her?" the police officer inquired.

   His voice trembled as he replied, "She's gone to the grocery."

   What can be inferred about the situation? _____

Read the following paragraphs, and see what inferences you can make. The situations are open-ended to allow you to make more than one inference. Once you have made your inferences, compare answers with your classmates. Did you come up with similar possibilities? Be prepared to explain what evidence in the paragraph and what prior knowledge of your own you used to reach your conclusions.

Copyright © 2011 Pearson Education, Inc.

Making Inferences **311**

1. Angie's neighbor watched as a shiny black sportscar pulled up in front of Angie's house. Angie got out of the passenger's side. A man in his mid-30s to 40s exited the driver's side. He opened the trunk and set a small suitcase on the sidewalk. He gave Angie a hug and then drove off. Angie stood there smiling.

   What inferences can be made from this scene?

   _____

   _____

   _____

   _____

2. When Inspector Stevens arrived at the office, he began by talking with the manager, Mr. Stanley.

   "When Hal didn't show up for work on Monday or Tuesday, I got worried. I called his house about midday on Tuesday, but no one answered. I tried his cell phone too, but it went straight to voice mail. I left a message, but Hal never called back. I know his wife is out of town at a conference. Unfortunately, neither I nor anyone else in the office knows where it is being held. Hal is usually a very responsible guy."

   "Did anything strange happen on Friday?" Inspector Stevens inquired.

   "In the afternoon he mentioned having an upset stomach, but he and a couple colleagues had gone out for a spicy lunch. And just as he was leaving for the day, he told Allan that he was beginning to feel better."

   "I will have to talk to Allan. Anything else?"

   "He told me that he was really looking forward to reconnecting with his old school friend Casey over the weekend."

   What can be inferred about Hal's whereabouts from this scene?

   _____

   _____

   _____

   _____

   _____

3. Katy grabbed a cart and headed straight to the produce section. She tossed in a pineapple, a cantaloupe, a honeydew melon, and a bunch of bananas. She flung two cucumbers, a red onion, and a bag of baby carrots into the cart. She threw in three heads of red lettuce and six Roma tomatoes. She added five Fuji apples and a box of blueberries and made her way to the checkout line.

What can be inferred about Katy from her purchases?

_____

_____

_____

_____

_____

Bias

Watch for a writer's bias toward the topic. An area where your inference skills are especially needed is looking for bias in a reading. **Bias** is a preference or prejudice that can hinder one's objective decision making. We all have biases, which come from our upbringing and experiences. Biases can be developed from several causes, including our gender, economic position, ethnic backgrounds, religious and political beliefs, where we live or grew up, and even our hobbies and interests. For example, Anthony is an avid bicycle rider with a bias toward spending transportation funds for better bike lanes and separate pathways. He could let his hobby influence whom he would vote for in an election if one of the candidates favors bicycle riding as a sound transportation alternative. His bias toward bike riding, however, could get in the way of his judgment if he ignores other attributes of the candidate that may not be ones he approves of. It is helpful if we are aware of our biases and how they influence us. There are times, however, when a bias may be so ingrained that we are absolutely unaware of it. The same is true for writers. They may try to be objective and not bring personal prejudices into their writing, especially if the writer's purpose is to inform. However, when writers want to persuade their audience, they may consciously or subconsciously introduce their biases into their writing.

As an active reader, you need to search for biases a writer may include in a work. To look for bias, you need to use several reading skills. Examine the supporting details the writer uses to see if they are appropriate for the topic. Also stop and think about details the writer might have included but didn't and why the writer left them out. Study how the reading is organized. For example, if the writer uses the cause and effect pattern, are all relevant causes examined? Look at the writer's diction. Does the writer use words with positive connotations to support his or her side, while picking words with negative connotations to present the other side? By using your inference skills combined with the other reading skills, you can determine if a writer is being objective or showing a preference, and this knowledge is important in deciding whether the writer's main idea is convincing.

ACTIVITY 3

Use your inference skills to detect two types of bias the writer displays in the paragraph below. Pick from the following list of areas that can cause biases:

age	gender	religion	nationality	hobby	politics

When I was given a toy as a child, it lasted for years. In my family, we handed toy soldiers, stuffed animals, and baby dolls down from one child to the next. Today most toys rarely last a year. And it isn't that kids are harder on toys these days. The problem is that most toys are no longer made in the United States. Manufacturers in other parts of the world don't put the craftsmanship into items that American workers did. Today most factory owners just want to get things made fast and cheaply. They have even gone so far as to put children at risk by using dangerous chemicals in what they make. I'm glad I was a kid 50 years ago. Today's children don't know the joys of having safe and durable toys.

Biases: _____

Inference Checklist

✔ Look for evidence in the reading to support your reasoning.

✔ Use your prior knowledge about a subject.

✔ Look at the organization of a reading.

✔ Pay attention to the writer's tone and diction.

✔ Watch for a writer's bias toward the topic.

Kids Led the Way, But Texting's GR8 for All

by Kevin Simpson

Kevin Simpson is a reporter for the *Denver Post*. He has covered diverse issues from the Columbine shootings and economics to technology and health care. The *Denver Post* serves the areas around Denver, Colorado, and it is one of the largest newspapers in the United States. The following article was originally published in December 2007.

Before You Read

1. Survey the reading. Change the headings into questions. Write one of your questions below:

   _____

   _____

   _____

2. What types of technology do you use to stay in touch with family and friends?

3. At what age did you learn to use a computer or a cell phone? Was it difficult to learn to use either?

4. Look at the photo. What do you think text messaging means to these people?

Vocabulary Preview

Look for these words in the reading. Exercises to reinforce the learning of new vocabulary using these words follow the reading. The paragraph number where the word appears is in parentheses.

demographics (5)	**precise** (5)	**pandemic** (33)
banter (14)	**inept** (32)	**rudiments** (14)
abreast (5)	**hence** (14)	**podcast** (35)
utility (31)		

The article begins on the next page.

Kids Led the Way,
But Texting's GR8 for All

By KEVIN SIMPSON
The Denver Post

1 Bring up significant technological mileposts and 55-year-old Jan Scott thinks: electric typewriter.

2 But guided by her college-student son, Scott, who labels herself "techno-challenged," has bravely embraced another technology: the youth-dominated world of text messaging.

3 "It keeps me connected with him and what's going on in his life," the Littleton, Colo., mother says of her wireless link to 24-year-old Brandon. "And it's a fun way for him to teach me something. I taught him a lot over the years. It's time he pays back."

4 Statistics point emphatically to kids and young adults under 25 driving the tidal surge in text messaging—up fourfold in the past two years to almost 30 billion messages a month, according to the CTIA, a wireless industry trade group.

5 But growing evidence reveals that more mature demographics have been pulled—sometimes willingly, sometimes not—into the mix. They fumble with their cell phone keypads to connect with, and keep track of, their quick-thumbed kids; to stay abreast of their younger colleagues; and to enjoy quick, precise communication uncomplicated by any immediate human connection.

6 "Make no mistake, kids are the early adopters," said CTIA spokesman Joe Farren. "But everyone is doing it, and doing more and more of it."

7 Why now? Industry sources point to quadrupled U.S. wireless subscribership over the past decade—the number last month surpassed 250 million—that has saturated the nation with cell phones and their attendant text-messaging capabilities.

8 With almost any cell phone, users can tap out messages of up to 160 characters and send them, usually to other cell phones. Both parties incur a per-message charge, about 10 or 15 cents, unless they purchase a bulk plan.

Everyone into the pool

9 Although more succinct than e-mail, text messages free busy users from their computers—and the time-consuming pleasantries of direct phone contact.

10 The users of 8-year-old BlackBerry technology, whose addiction to the device spawned the nickname "CrackBerry," already know well the pleasures of wireless text communication. But now, almost everybody's in the game.

11 The uses for texting range from social interaction, a favorite among teens, to commercial transactions, to news and weather alerts, to voting for your favorite contestant on "American Idol"—the TV show some credit with giving the nation a primetime texting tutorial.

12 When it comes to sending texts every day, teens and young adults rule, according to Mark Donovan, a senior analyst at Seattle-based M:Metrics, which studies mobile and wireless industries. About 21 percent of all users text daily, compared with 42 percent of 13- to 17-year-olds and 47 percent of those ages 18–24.

13 "The value of it has got nothing to do with the technology," Donovan said, "but rather the ability to be connected to people you love."

14 Hence, parents and grandparents have begun to pick up at least the rudiments of text messaging. But they're less likely to engage in the idle banter that consumes 13-year-old girls and less likely to embrace the "predictive text" typing functions that fill in entire words with minimal keystrokes and allow thumbs to blaze across the keypads.

15 They don't seek out the technology as much as adapt to its utility.

16 That definitely was the case for Jan Scott, who realized the usefulness of text messaging for communicating with a son while he took classes at the University of Colorado Denver.

17 They could coordinate schedules. He could let her know if he was staying late. She could arrange to pick him up at the light-rail station.

18 But first, Mom had to master the basics.

19 "She was hesitant," recalled Brandon. "She couldn't figure it out on her own, so I had to show her. She's teaching you your whole life, and it's suddenly turned around. But she came around pretty quick."

Staying connected

20 The process of young people instructing their parents can be gratifying for both—and the actual messaging can smooth relationships during a critical time, said Michal Ann Strahilevitz, a marketing professor at Golden Gate University in San Francisco with a background in social psychology.

21 "It enables them to communicate during a period of growing, where children are wanting independence and parents are wanting to stay in touch," she said. "Text messaging is sort of a compromise."

22 It also can be a connecting point. That's precisely what technology expert and radio host Ken Colburn impresses on his audiences.

23 The Arizona-based president of Data Doctors Computer Services advises parents looking for a way to connect with their kids to surprise them some day, perhaps while they're at school, with a simple text message: "I love you. What would you like for dinner?"

24 "Using that technology to start bridging the gap is very relevant," he said, "because it's ever present in everything we do. Everyone has a cell phone. I've had a lot of parents say they were able to actually talk about things in text messages that they couldn't have talked about in person—or at least opened the door to a conversation."

25 Terry Whitney got pulled into texting by a friend. But later, work demands sealed the deal.

26 One day, the 45-year-old legislative director for the Colorado state Senate Majority Office found himself staring at a text message sent to his cell phone by a buddy. He didn't respond. He didn't know how.

27 "Oh, dude, it's easy," his friend explained in person a couple of days later.

28 "He took my phone and pointed to what I needed to do," recalls Whitney. "And boom! It's like riding a bike. With a lot of my guy friends, it's almost preferable to making a phone call. It's the way guys talk. It's very rudimentary—yes, no. There's not the need to be emotive or hear someone's voice."

Conquering phobias

29 When he started working at the Capitol in 2005, texting became a necessity—especially on the floor of the House or Senate, where he couldn't make phone calls. Eventually, his boss required everyone in the office to carry a plan that allowed unlimited texting.

30 "Probably not a day goes by that I don't text at least a couple of times," Whitney said. "During the legislative session, it could be 20 a day."

31 Aside from the obvious utility, or the connection potential between parent and child, text messaging can touch on some deeper sociological turf.

32 As adults grow older, says one expert, their communications habits become driven, in part, by a desire that their children or colleagues not view them as hopelessly, technologically inept.

33 "The aging process now is almost a pandemic of phobias," said Tom Donohue, a professor of mass communication at Virginia Commonwealth University who has studied the social impact of media since the 1970s. "So it's a kind of a badge that says, 'I'm staying current and young.'"

34 Consider Eons.com, a social-networking site geared toward baby boomers age 50 and older.

A recent survey of 2,000 members found that 41 percent send and receive text messages on their cell phones, and 38 percent have sent one in the past 30 days.

35   Then there's Grandparents .com, launched by 62-year-old chief executive Jerry Shereshewsky, whose site tackles technology issues such as how to produce a podcast for a long-distance bedtime story.

36   He points to the growing over-45 demographic on such hip sites as Facebook (25 percent), Classmates.com (37 percent) and MySpace (27 percent) as further evidence that older adults are tackling technology in ways their parents never could.

37   "It's not quite all about 20-year-olds," he says. "With our grandparent user base, it's another way to be in contact with their grandchildren, speaking in their language. It makes them very contemporary."

Getting the Message

____ **1.** The topic of the article is

    a. recent inventions.   c. text messaging.

    b. child and adult relationships.   d. changes in communication.

____ **2.** What is the main idea of the article?

    a. People in their 60s are more likely to learn how to use new technologies than past generations.

    b. Text messaging is becoming common for people of all ages because it has many benefits.

    c. Text messaging is best left to young people who can type quickly.

    d. Text messaging is a fad.

____ **3.** Among the types of supporting details Simpson uses are

    a. personal examples, testimony, and facts.

    b. hypothetical examples, testimony, and reasons.

    c. public examples, testimony, and statistics.

    d. statistics and examples.

____ **4.** The article reports that a recent survey shows that _____ percent of adults over 50 send or receive cell phone text messages.

    a. 21   c. 41

    b. 38   d. 62

____ **5.** In what order is the information presented?

    a. chronological   c. most to least important

    b. least to most important   d. problem and solution

____ **6.** Overall the article uses the _____ pattern of organization.

    a. comparison and contrast   c. process

    b. narrative   d. cause and effect

____ **7.** The transition word *hence* (par. 14) shows

    a. cause and effect.   c. comparison.

    b. time.   d. contrast.

____ **8.** Simpson's purpose is to

    a. inform people about the growing use of text messaging by people of all ages.

    b. entertain people with stories of how kids and adults use text messaging.

    c. persuade more people to start text messaging.

____ **9.** The tone of the article can be labeled as _____.

    a. proud   c. objective

    b. ironic   d. excited

____ **10.** What can be inferred from paragraph 28?

    a. Men love to talk on the phone.

    b. Men don't like showing their emotions.

    c. Men like text messaging because they can fully express themselves.

    d. Text messaging is hard to do.

11. Give two examples of sentences that show the motives that drive older people to use text messaging. Give the paragraph number where you find each sentence.

_____

_____

_____

_____

_____

12. Give an example of a sentence that states a fact and of one that expresses an opinion.

_____

_____

_____

_____

13. What can be inferred from the comment, "I've had a lot of parents say they were able to actually talk about things in text messages that they couldn't have talked about in person—or at least opened the door to a conversation" (par. 24)?

_____

_____

_____

_____

14. Look at your annotations of the article. Which one of the questions or comments you wrote in the margins would you most like to discuss with the class?

_____

_____

15. Create a Venn diagram that compares how teens and young adults use text messaging versus older adults.

Teens/Young Adults   Older Adults

Vocabulary

Use context clues to determine the meaning by looking back at the paragraph where the word is used (the paragraph number is in parentheses). If you need help, consult a dictionary for the definition.

A. Circle the correct meaning of each vocabulary word.

1. abreast (5)	up to date	out of date
2. precise (5)	faulty	exact
3. rudiments (14)	basic skills	advanced skills
4. banter (14)	joking	seriousness
5. inept (32)	capable	unskilled

B. Complete each sentence using the correct vocabulary word. Use each word once.

> **demographics** (5)   **hence** (14)   **utility** (31)   **pandemic** (33)   **podcast** (35)

1. I prefer to get my news as a _____; that way I can catch up on what is happening in the world while I take a walk.

2. The _____ show that most of the consumers of the Healthy Snacks brand are between the ages of 25 and 50, have an average income of $55,000, and a college degree.

3. To keep this flu strain from becoming a _____, officials around the world are urging people to avoid contact with large groups and to wash their hands often and thoroughly.

4. I have been so busy with work and school that I forgot your birthday. _____ I come bearing a belated gift.

5. I didn't at first see the _____ of having a phone in the bedroom, but now I appreciate not having to get out of bed to answer early morning calls.

C. Word parts: Create the definitions for the following words by putting the meanings of the word parts together. Add "-ing" or "-ed" to any of the roots if you need to make a definition flow. You will use two of the meanings more than once. The number of word parts contained in each word is given in parentheses. Return to pages 85–87 if you need to review the meaning of a word part.

prefixes: all   not   before

roots: people   write   say   skill

suffixes: of or relating to   tending to

1. Demographic (3 word parts): _____

2. Predictive (3 word parts): _____

3. Inept (2 word parts): _____

4. Pandemic (3 word parts): _____

The Article and You

1. Of the methods mentioned in the article, which is your preferred method to communicate with friends and family? Why do you like this method best? Do you use text messaging very often?

_____

_____

_____

2. List three advantages and three disadvantages of text messaging over making a phone call or sending an e-mail. Use information from the reading and your experiences to develop your lists.

_____

_____

_____

3. Do you think the abbreviations used in text messaging (e.g., "2moro" for "tomorrow") will influence or harm other forms of writing, such as essays written for college classes or resumes?

_____

_____

_____

4. On a separate sheet of paper, write a paragraph in which you describe how you or someone you know has had to conquer a technology phobia.

Take a Closer Look

Look at the photo again. After reading about text messaging, which of the aspects of text messaging do you think this group illustrates?

_____

_____

_____

Internet Activities

If needed, use a separate sheet of paper to fully record your responses. Include the Web address of any sites from which you gather information.

1. Go to netlingo.com. List ten text messaging terms with which you are unfamiliar. Do you think you will start using these terms now? Do you find most text messaging terms easy to understand?

_____

_____

_____

2. Checkout Eons.com or Grandparents.com. Summarize the purpose of the site and what information or activities are found at the site. Does the site look interesting? Explain why or why not.

_____

_____

Constant
Techno Communication
Brings Lack of Focus
and Loss of Privacy

by Eric Adler
and Laura Bauer

Eric Adler has covered a variety of issues for the *Kansas City Star*, including unemployment, tanning salons, and Alzheimer's. In addition to writing about topics like teen suicide, Laura Bauer contributed to an award-winning series of articles on human trafficking. The *Kansas City Star* serves the areas around Kansas City, Missouri. The writer Ernest Hemingway was a cub reporter for the paper from October 1917 to April 1918, and former president Theodore Roosevelt was a regular contributor from September 1917 until just before his death in January 1919. The following article was first printed on March 13, 2010.

Before You Read

1. Survey the first nine paragraphs. Can you relate to the story?

2. Do you feel you have lost any privacy by using new forms of communication?

3. Do you often multitask or know someone who does? Do you find it productive to do so?

4. Look at the cartoon. What does the cartoon reveal about communication today?

Vocabulary Preview

Look for these words in the reading. Exercises to reinforce the learning of new vocabulary using these words follow the reading. The paragraph number where the word appears is in parentheses.

deemed (8)	**realm** (9)
manic (16)	**commune** (18)
blanch (39)	**notion** (39)
virtual (41)	**compulsion** (45)
preoccupation (46)	**unaccustomed** (50)

The article begins on the next page.

Constant Techno Communication Brings Lack of Focus and Loss of Privacy

By ERIC ADLER
and LAURA BAUER
The Kansas City Star

1 Just days ago, Elliot Kort, 22, woke in his Lawrence apartment, yawned, brushed his teeth and greeted his girlfriend, Elyse, in the way he does most every morning.

2 "Hi, sweetie."

3 "Hi, baby," Elyse responded. "How did you sleep?"

4 "It took me a little bit to get there, but I slept OK. How about you?"

5 "Very well," she told him.

6 Intimate? Ordinary?

7 Absolutely.

8 And yet, experts said, it is the fact that such a conversation is now deemed routine—happening, as this one did, by computer, with Kort electronically chatting to his girlfriend at her apartment in Washington, D.C.—that makes it remarkable.

9 "It's our morning breakfast table in the digital realm," Kort said.

10 Cyber-savvy experts view it as far more than that, it's an example of how technology—and especially the growth in text messaging and live video chatting—is allowing people to keep in such constant communication that it has begun to radically change the sense of what it means for people to feel together, or alone, or apart.

11 Researchers even have names for it: "connected presence" or "persistent presence"—the feeling, through technology, that you are with someone when you are not.

12 "It's having this sense, this ambient awareness, of your friends or family," said Mary Madden, senior research specialist with the Pew Research Center's Internet & American Life Project. "Even if you're not communicating or interacting, they have a sense of you being there and being OK, just by you being logged on."

13 But the boom in constant connections also is raising significant concerns, from fostering poor focus and lack of independence to the real difficulty of cutting ties in an era of Facebook "friend" connections.

14 More privacy questions are sure to arise with the evolution of new phone applications. Foursquare or Gowalla now tell people where you are, using Global Positioning System satellites.

15 Some worry, too, about stalking, domestic violence and being connected to people who are truly unwanted.

16 "We are seeing persistent texting," said Parry Aftab, a lawyer and executive director of WiredSafety.org, an Internet safety organization. "People wanting to know where you are at every hour of the day, who you are with. When does it go from, 'I care about you,' to 'I'm a stalker, I'm a punching bag?' There's a thin line from what's reasonable and what's manic."

Narrowing the Gap

17 To be sure, technology's role in helping bring people closer is older than the chariot. Trains, planes, telegraphs, telephones have all played roles.

18 But social scientists said that nothing had so narrowed that gap as the unprecedented rise in technologies (text messages, Skype video chats, Twitter, cell phone access to social networking sites such as Facebook) that allow people to commune with one another as they walk through their days, at any moment and anywhere.

19 In January, a report on children aged 8 to 18 showed that 31 percent of second to fourth graders now own their own cell phones. By 18, nearly everyone has one. Some 4.1 billion texts are now sent each day in the United States, at least four times what it was in 2007.

20 Last year, users of Skype, which offers instant messaging and video conferencing, logged onto their computers to make 3.1 billion minutes of calls, up 44 percent from the year before. Of all Skype users, just over one-third were talking face to face over live video.

21 A few results of such constant connection:

22 • Going off to college no longer means kids are on their own.

23 "There are parents who are now sending their college kids wake-up calls in the morning," said Mary Chayko, a professor of sociology at New Jersey's College of St. Elizabeth and author of the

2008 book *Portable Communities: The Social Dynamics of Online and Mobile Connectedness.*

24 Maureen Baker, a teacher at Mize Elementary School in De Soto, said her daughter Hannah, a 20-year-old business major at the University of Kansas, "Probably calls me two or three times a day."

25 Hannah: "I talk to her on my way to different classes or when I'm grabbing something to eat. It's definitely comforting. Sometimes I'm a little homesick."

26 Kristopher Scott Thomas, 19, from Houston, is a freshman at Northwest Missouri State University in Maryville.

27 "I, personally, bought a webcam and got Skype just to be able to talk to my father," he said. "I Skype with my family at least once a day."

28 Nearly every Sunday, Kansas Citian Morgan Dameron, now a junior in film school at the University of Southern California, spends face time over the laptop with her mom, dad and younger sisters and brother in the metro.

29 "If it's snowing, we'll take the computer outside and show her," her mother, Lori Dameron, said.

30 • When high school friends part, the relationships don't break up.

31 Shawnee residents Emily Hodgson, 19, and Tiffany Fletcher, 19, are best friends. Hodgson went to MidAmerica Nazarene University in Olathe. Fletcher went off to Southern Nazarene University in Oklahoma.

32 They almost talk more now than when they were together.

33 "Texting is the best thing that ever happened to me," Hodgson

said. "She's even more updated on my life than some of my friends in Kansas."

34 • The perception of improved relationships.

35 "Staying in constant communication actually adds to relationships," said sociologist Barry Wellman, director of the University of Toronto's NetLab.

36 Wellman said he knew one couple, married for about three years, who text "I love you" to each other 50 times a day.

37 Kort, the student in Lawrence, attended his grandmother's funeral earlier this year. His girlfriend couldn't be there. He said that in the limousine, surrounded by grieving relatives, and driving back from the gravesite, he took out his cell phone.

38 "I missed her so much I could barely breathe," Kort said. "I wanted her there so badly."

39 He texted, "I miss you so much." She immediately texted back words of comfort. Kort understands that some people might blanch at the notion of texting at such a moment.

40 "Without knowing what is going on, it could be deemed as rude," he said. "But I did feel better. When you're dealing with your family in a situation like that, you hope that they can lift you up as much as you can lift them up. But, at that moment, I needed her to be there."

41 And in a virtual sense, he felt she was.

Loss of Focus

42 Researchers and others also recognize that such constant communication also presents difficulties—even a dark side.

43 Chayko, the New Jersey sociologist, said there existed a general sense that such constant communication, often conducted while multi-tasking in the midst of other activities, was creating a culture with a shortened attention span.

44 People talk or text while they walk or eat, watch television, sit in the movie, attend classes and, dangerously, drive. A recent poll of some 1,200 teens showed that

24 percent literally sleep with their cell phones.

45   "That is a rising trend," Chayko said. "It is a compulsion to be in contact. People actually feel nervous, uncomfortable when they are too far away from their phones."

46   It becomes a preoccupation, she said.

47   "They have trouble doing one thing at a time. When they meet friends face to face," Chayko said, "they will be texting at the same time they are with these other kids. They are used to juggling all these interactions, and they are good at it, but there is a loss.

48   "There is a loss of focus, a loss of reflection. There is a loss of depth."

49   Maureen Baker, whose daughter calls or texts her from college multiple times each day, certainly cherishes her constant contact with her daughter. But she sometimes wonders whether it comes at the price of her daughter developing greater independence.

50   Like Chayko, she also senses that repeated contact may also be an outgrowth of people being unaccustomed to exploring quiet moments.

51   Although being in constant contact helps sustain relationships, it also can make getting out of those relationships that much harder.

52   "We run into all kinds of messy situations," said Madden of the Pew Center. "I am thinking about relationships—after breakups, sometimes long after breakups when you start wading into the waters of Facebook, and the friends of all our friends in college.

53   "Suddenly you realize you are reconnected to your old boyfriend. You're seeing all these pictures of his children, all this information you did not seek out and would not have come to seek out otherwise."

54   Part of living in an age of constant communication, she said, is learning to isolate yourself from unwanted contact.

55   "You can find young people who can obsess about their exes," said University of Denver's Lynn Schofield Clark, who studies how digital media are changing family relationships. "Twenty years ago, you'd worry about passing your ex-boyfriend in the hallway at school. Now you don't know what you're going to click on and be reminded of what your ex is up to today."

56   The same goes for adults.

57   Amber Bourek, spokeswoman for Safehome, Johnson County's domestic violence agency, recalls a client who left an abusive marriage. Twenty times each day, the man continued to text her, "Miss you," and "Thinking of you."

58   One day, when she knew he would be at work, she headed to the house the couple once shared to retrieve some belongings. Once she got to the house, she heard the man's voice on the answering machine: "While you're there, let the dogs out."

59   "You can imagine how terrifying that was," Bourek said.

60   Aftab of WiredSafety.org said the constant communication could too easily lead to constant watching.

61   While dating, she said, girlfriends can check cell phones to see who their mates are texting and talking to. Boyfriends may know Facebook passwords to see who is sending messages to their girlfriends.

62   Technology "allows us to have a spy camera everywhere our significant other is," Aftab said. "And that information can do some serious damage when you no longer care about that person."

63   When you do care, Kort said, there will always exist a difference between being together through technology and in person.

64   "This is nice and cool and a means to an end," he said. "But I think we are the purest forms of ourselves when we are physically together."

Getting the Message

____ **1.** The main idea of the article is that

    a. people are texting each other too often.

    b. using new technologies can lead to problems due to continuous communication.

    c. teenagers are not learning to be independent because of regular cell phone use.

    d. technological developments need to slow down so people can improve their lives.

____ **2.** Is the main idea stated or implied?

    a. stated   b. implied

____ **3.** The article uses _____ as supporting details.

    a. personal examples and testimony

    b. statistics, testimony, and examples

    c. statistics and hypothetical examples

    d. historical examples and statistics

____ **4.** Which of the following isn't a major supporting detail?

    a. Going off to college no longer means kids are on their own.

    b. Constant communication may be creating a society with shortened attention spans.

    c. While visiting online, the Damerons will take their laptop outside to show snow to their daughter.

    d. Constant communication may lead to a loss of privacy.

____ **5.** The writers use _____ order to develop their point.

    a. chronological   c. least to most important

    b. most to least important   d. problem and solution

____ **6.** Overall, Adler and Bauer use the _____ pattern of organization.

    a. process   c. example

    b. definition   d. cause and effect

____ **7.** The following transition words—*And yet* (par. 8), *But* (par. 13 and 18), and *Like* (par. 50)—show

    a. comparison or contrast.   c. importance or example.

    b. cause and effect or contrast.   d. time and comparison.

____ **8.** The writers' purpose is to

    a. persuade people to start talking more in person.

    b. inform people about the effects of new technologies.

    c. warn people about the dangers of cell phones.

    d. entertain people with stories of how the public uses technology.

____ **9.** It can be determined from diction within the article that the original intended audience was

    a. children.

    b. teens and college students.

    c. people in technological fields.

    d. people who live in Kansas and Missouri.

_____**10.** It can be inferred from paragraph 58 that the man was

      a. ready to let his wife go.

      b. abusive to his pets.

      c. still monitoring his wife's actions.

      d. near the house.

11. List four people the writers quote. Do these people seem like credible sources? Do they reveal any bias on the writers' part?

_____

_____

_____

_____

_____

_____

_____

12. What inferences do you need to make about funerals and texting to understand the comments made in paragraphs 39 and 40? Did you consider Kort's action appropriate?

_____

_____

_____

_____

13. Give three examples (include the paragraph numbers) of information in the article that especially impressed (surprised, shocked, or disturbed) you. Briefly explain why you found each detail notable.

_____

_____

_____

_____

14. List two points you annotated in the article. Why did you pick these points?

_____

_____

15. On another sheet of paper, write a summary of the article—aim for about 300 words.

Vocabulary

Use context clues to determine the meaning of each word by referring back to the paragraph where the word is used (the paragraph number is in parentheses). If you need help, consult a dictionary for the definition.

A. Match the vocabulary word to its synonym.

> **deem(ed)** (8) **commune** (18) **notion** (39) **virtual** (41) **preoccupation** (46)

1. converse _____
2. consider _____
3. obsession _____

4. idea _____
5. simulated _____

B. Match the vocabulary words to the appropriate example. Use each word once.

> **realm** (9) **manic** (16) **blanch** (39) **compulsion** (45) **unaccustomed** (50)

1. For two weeks, Alexa has been texting me every hour to ask what I am doing. _____

2. Yoon felt the need to wash his hands 100 times a day. _____

3. When Colin pulled out Orla's chair for her at the restaurant, she was surprised by the action. _____

4. The king guarded this with an army of almost two thousand men. _____

5. Knowing about his fear of snakes, I wasn't surprised that this was Milt's reaction when I suggested he hold my pet snake. _____

C. Word parts: Circle the meaning of the underlined word part. Return to pages 85–87 if you need to review the meaning of a word part.

1. It has been great having <u>vid</u>eo (10) chats with my sister. Now I can see all of the new outfits she buys.

2. Morgan has been a <u>con</u>stant (10) friend; we have been together through good and bad times for more than 30 years.

3. I encourage inde<u>pend</u>ence (49) in my children. I do not want them to hang around the house all day expecting me to entertain them.

4. I have been married for only two months, so I am still <u>un</u>accustomed (50) to calling my husband to tell him when I will be home late. I have not had to tell anyone my schedule since I moved away from home fifteen years ago.

The Article and You

1. At what age do you think it is appropriate for kids to own a cell phone? Were you surprised by the statistic in paragraph 19? If you own a cell phone, how old were you when you first got one?

   _____

   _____

2. Have you tried video conferencing with Skype? Do you think live video conferencing will become commonplace in the next 5 years? What do you see as a plus and minus of people being able to see you while you are talking with them?

_____

_____

3. Do you leave time for "quiet moments" (par. 50) in your life? Do you think such times are important? Explain why or why not.

_____

_____

4. On a separate sheet of paper, write a paragraph in which you expand on Kort's comment that "there will always exist a difference between being together through technology and in person" (par. 63). What types of differences are there, and how significant do you consider them? To develop your point, use your experiences with family and friends or other incidents you have heard about.

Take a Closer Look

Look at the cartoon again. How does the cartoon reflect the issues brought up in paragraphs 42–48? Do you think this couple could spend a quiet evening together without their phones? Do you know people like this couple? Do you think the cartoon is funny?

_____

_____

_____

_____

Internet Activities

If needed, use a separate sheet of paper to fully record your responses. Include the Web address of any sites from which you gather information.

1. Go to facebook.com. Look at your profile and one that belongs to a friend. If you don't have a Facebook account, either create one (it's free) or use the "about" link to find two profiles to analyze (you will likely have limited access to a person's profile, but still see what you can find). List five pieces of information you learn about each person. After examining these pages, explain whether you see sites like Facebook as being a threat to one's privacy or a great way to share information with others.

_____

_____

2. Look up Foursquare or Gowalla (mentioned in par. 14). Survey the home page and other pages that explain what the application is. Write a summary on what you find. If you currently use the service, what do you like and dislike about the application? If you don't, do you think you will ever use it? Explain why or why not.

_____

_____

Happily Ever Laughter

by Peter Doskoch

Before You Read

1. Do you laugh often?
2. Survey the headings and turn them into questions.
3. What makes you laugh?
4. Look at the photo. What is your reaction to the scene?

Vocabulary Preview

Look for these words in the reading. Exercises to reinforce the learning of new vocabulary using these words follow the reading. The paragraph number where the word appears is in parentheses.

glum (2) **pathological** (3) **guffaw** (4)

incongruity (5) **physiological** (7) **mortality** (11)

astute (12) **implication** (25) **panacea** (27)

paltry (27)

Peter Doskoch is a writer and an editor who has written numerous articles for *Psychology Today*. Among the topics he has covered are perseverance, hand gestures, lying, and marriage. Since 1967, *Psychology Today* has explored health, relationship, and career issues as they relate to research in the field of psychology. The magazine is geared toward a general audience. The following article originally appeared in the July 1996 issue.

Laughter may

1 help make you happier and healthier, but not everybody benefits from humor equally. Here's how to harness laughter's powers.

2 While the humor-is-healthy viewpoint has finally gained scientific respectability, now humor's therapeutic limits become defined and its weaknesses understood. That may sound like a glum take on a cheerful subject, but it's not. For the better we understand when laughter is useful, the more effectively we can deploy it—something we can all be happy about.

3 Laughter is such an intrinsic part of our lives that we sometimes forget how very odd it is. Despite the development of newfangled imaging machines like MRI and PET scans, neuroscientists still have little idea what's happening in our brain when we laugh. Certainly the brain stem plays a role. People who've suffered strokes in this primitive brain region have been known to have prolonged bouts of pathological laughter. And some anencephalic infants—babies born missing their higher brain circuitry—will, when tickled, make faces that appear to be smiles or laughs, again implicating the primitive brain.

4 But laughing in response to something funny also calls on more sophisticated brain functions. One brain study in humor research looked at the electrical activity that occurs as we chuckle, giggle, or guffaw. About four-tenths of a second after we hear the punch line of a joke—but before we laugh—a wave of electricity sweeps through the cortex, reports Peter Derks, professor of psychology at the College of William and Mary.

5 What Derks finds most significant about this wave is that it carpets our entire cerebral cortex, rather than just one region. So all or most of

our higher brain may play a role in laughter, Derks suggests, perhaps with the left hemisphere working on the joke's verbal content while the analytic right hemisphere attempts to figure out the incongruity that lies at the heart of much humor.

In the Mood

6   That laughter is a full-cortex experience is only fitting considering the wide-ranging effects it has on us psychologically and physiologically. Perhaps the most obvious effect of laughter is on our mood. After all, with even the most intellectual brands of humor, laughter is ultimately an expression of emotion—joy, surprise, nervousness, amusement. More than a decade of research has begun unraveling the details of the laughter-mood connection:

- Stressed-out folks with a strong sense of humor become less depressed and anxious than those whose sense of humor is less well developed, according to a study by psychologists Herbert Lefcourt, of the University of Waterloo, and Rod Martin, Ph.D., now at the University of Western Ontario.

- Researchers at West Chester University in Pennsylvania found that students who used humor as a coping mechanism were more likely to be in a positive mood.
- In a study of depressed and suicidal senior citizens, the patients who recovered were the ones who demonstrated a sense of humor, reports psychiatrist Joseph Richman, professor emeritus at Albert Einstein Medical Center in the Bronx, New York.

7   All of this makes sense in light of laughter's numerous physiological effects. "After you laugh, you go into a relaxed state," explains John Morreall, president of HUMORWORKS Seminars in Tampa, Florida. "Your blood pressure and heart rate drop below normal, so you feel profoundly relaxed. Laughter also indirectly stimulates endorphins, the brain's natural painkillers."

8   In addition to its biological effects, laughter may also improve our mood through social means. Telling a joke, particularly one that illuminates a shared experience or problem, increases our sense of "belonging and social cohesion," says Richman. He believes that by

Holy Cow

psychologically connecting us to others, laughter counteracts "feelings of alienation, a major factor in depression and suicide."

9   Some of laughter's other psychological effects are less obvious. For one thing, says Morreall, it helps us think more creatively. "Humor loosens up the mental gears. It encourages out-of-the-ordinary ways of looking at things."

10   Humor guru William Fry, professor emeritus of psychiatry at Stanford University, takes this idea one step further. "Creativity and humor are identical," he contends. "They both involve bringing together two items which do not have an obvious connection, and creating a relationship."

11   Finally, humor helps us contend with the unthinkable—our mortality. Lefcourt recently found that people's willingness to sign the organ donor consent on their driver's license rises with their tendency to laugh. "Very few people are ready to think, even for a moment, about death," he says. "But those who have a sense of humor are more able to cope with the idea."

A Healthy Sense of Humor

12   The idea that laughter promotes good health first received widespread attention through Norman Cousins's 1979 best-seller, *Anatomy of an Illness*. But centuries earlier, astute observers had ascribed physical benefits to humor. Thomas Sydenham, a seventeenth-century British physician, once observed: "The arrival of a good clown into a village does more for its health than 20 asses laden with drugs."

13   Today, scientific belief in laughter's effects on health rest largely on the shoulders of Lee Berk and Stanley Tan, both of the Loma Linda School of Medicine, in Loma Linda, California. Laughter, they find, sharpens most of the instruments in our immune system's tool kit. It activates T lymphocytes and natural killer cells, both of which help destroy invading microorganisms. Laughter also increases production of immunity-boosting gamma interferon and speeds up the production of new immune cells. And it reduces levels of the stress hormone cortisol, which can weaken the immune response.

14   Meanwhile, studies by Lefcourt and others have found that levels of immunoglobulin A, an antibody secreted in saliva to protect against respiratory invaders, drops during stress—but it drops far less in people who score high on a humor scale.

15   While these findings suggest how laughter might benefit our health, nobody has yet proven that these immune effects translate into faster healing, because humor's impact on actual recovery has never been scientifically confirmed.

Laughter: The Proper Dose

16   Now that we know what laughter can do, it's important to recognize when it's most effective. Here are some things to keep in mind to live life happily ever laughter.

17   Humor may help some people more than others.

18   There's one problem with nearly all the research that links humor and mood; it's what scientists call "correlational." The fact that two things happen at the same time doesn't mean one caused the other. So if folks with a strong sense of humor are less affected by stress, "it doesn't mean laughing is what's helping them cope," says Martin. Rather, it could be that if they're coping well they can laugh a lot.

19   In Martin's view, by adulthood our sense of humor has essentially reached its final form: And for those of us whose internal humor settings are on the low side, he believes laughter may not help as much. For example, in one study, participants' levels of immunoglobulin A increased when they viewed humorous videos. But they rose most in people whose tendency to laugh was greatest to begin with. So the serious and sober among us may benefit less from laughter.

20   Others dispute this idea, asserting that humor is an equal-opportunity life-enhancer. "Anybody who has normal mental development can engage in and benefit from humor," insists Morreall. "All they have to do is put themselves in this more playful state of mind. We have to give ourselves permission to do something we did very easily when we were three years old."

21   Martin, though, remains unconvinced. "My sense is that research hasn't been as successful as people had hoped. It seems to be pretty hard to teach someone to change their sense of humor." Nonetheless, if you're a natural humor powerhouse, laughter's force may be especially at your command.

22   Control and choice may enhance laughter's benefits.

23   Numerous studies show that psychological and physical health improve when people feel a sense of control in their lives, whether over their jobs, future, relationships, or even their medical treatment. Laughter's benefits may have a similar origin, suggests Morreall.

24   "When we're stressed, we often feel like we have no control of the situation," he says. "We feel helpless. But when we laugh, at least in our minds, we assume some control. We feel able to handle it."

25   One implication of this is that the more control people have over the type of humor to which they're exposed, the more they may benefit from it. At least one study bears this out. When patients recovering from surgery at a Florida hospital were allowed to choose the humorous movies they saw, they required less painkillers than a control group that saw no movies. But a third set of patients, force-fed comedies that may not have been to their liking, did worst of all.

26   Perhaps that should come as no surprise. Humor is intensely personal. Jim Carrey's comedy has little in common with Woody Allen's. "To harness laughter's benefits, it's essential that each person is matched to his or her favorite brand of humor," says Lefcourt. Often, that's remarkably difficult, even for folks close to you.

"I'm sometimes very surprised at what people I know find funny," he says.

Prescription for Happiness

27   While laughter may not be a panacea, there's still much to be gained from it. And, truth be told, there's room for plenty of additional chortles in our lives: Fry found that by the time the average kid reaches kindergarten, he or she is laughing some 300 times each day. Compare that to the typical adult, whom Martin recently found laughs a paltry 17 times a day. (Men and women laugh equally often, Martin adds, but at different things.)

28   Fortunately, if you're attracted by the idea of using laughter to improve your spirit and health, chances are you've already got a good sense of humor. Meaning, of course, that you're just the type of person who might benefit from what Fry calls "prophylactic humor"—laughter as preventive medicine.

29   For people who want to inoculate themselves with laughter, Fry recommends this two-step process.

30   First, figure out your humor profile. Listen to yourself for a few days and see what makes you laugh out loud. Be honest with yourself; don't affect a taste for sophisticated French farces if your heartiest guffaws come from watching Moe, Larry, and Curly.

31   Next, use your comic profile to start building your own humor library: books, magazines, videos, what have you. If possible, set aside a portion of your bedroom or den as a "humor corner" to house your collection. Then, when life gets you down, don't hesitate to visit. Even a few minutes of laughter, says Fry, will provide some value.

32   "We're teaching people a skill that they can use when, say, deadline pressures are getting close," explains nurse/clown Patty Wooten, author of *Compassionate Laughter* (Commune-a-Key) and president of the American Association for Therapeutic Humor.

33   "The deadline will remain, but by taking time out to laugh, you adjust your mood, your physiology, your immune system. And then you go back to work and face what you have to do."

Getting the Message

_____ **1.** What is the main idea of the article?

    a. Laughter is the best medicine.

    b. Laughter has little influence on how people feel.

    c. Children who laugh a lot are healthier than those who rarely laugh.

    d. Not everybody benefits from humor equally.

_____ **2.** The main idea in paragraphs 22–26 is that

    a. when one feels in control, one is more likely to experience benefits from a situation.

    b. laughter improves one's immune system.

    c. comedy is a very personal matter.

    d. the benefits of laughter don't last long.

_____ **3.** What type(s) of supporting detail does Doskoch mainly use?

    a. examples

    b. statistics

    c. testimony

    d. a and c

_____ **4.** Which of the following is a major supporting detail?

    a. Norman Cousins published the best-seller *Anatomy of an Illness* in 1979.

    b. Jim Carrey's comedy is different from Woody Allen's.

    c. Laughter has a variety of effects on people.

    d. It is helpful to create a "humor corner" in one's bedroom.

_____ **5.** The sentence "'Anybody who has normal mental development can engage in and benefit from humor,' insists Morreall" (par. 20) is

    a. a fact.

    b. an opinion.

_____ **6.** _____ are the two main patterns of organization used in the article.

    a. Comparison and contrast and narrative

    b. Cause and effect and process

    c. Narrative and definition

    d. Classification and process

_____ **7.** Which type of transition word is used in paragraphs 30 and 31?

    a. time

    b. importance

    c. comparison

    d. cause and effect

_____ **8.** Doskoch's purpose is _____.

    a. to inform

    b. to persuade

    c. to entertain

_____ **9.** The tone of the article can best be labeled as _____.

      a. excited

      b. sad

      c. hopeful

      d. objective

_____ **10.** What can be inferred about the writer's audience from Doskoch's use of Jim Carrey and Woody Allen (par. 26) and Moe, Larry, and Curly (par. 30) as examples?

      a. He is aiming the article toward children.

      b. He is writing mainly for Americans.

      c. He is writing mainly for Europeans.

      d. He is writing for comedians.

11. List the five effects laughter has on people that are explained in paragraphs 6–11. How does Doskoch organize these effects?

_____

_____

12. List three of the people Doskoch quotes. Do they seem like credible sources? Explain why or why not.

_____

_____

_____

_____

13. What method does Doskoch use to define *anencephalic infants* (par. 3) and *correlational* (par. 18)? What inference can you make about his intended audience from this method? Are there other terms for which he provides definitions?

_____

_____

_____

_____

14. From your notes in the margins, write the question or comment you would most like to discuss with the class.

_____

15. On a separate sheet of paper, make a formal outline of the article.

Vocabulary

Use context clues to determine the meaning by looking back at the paragraph where the word is used (paragraph number is in parentheses). If you need help, consult a dictionary for the definition.

A. Match each word to its antonym.

> **glum** (2) **guffaw** (4) **incongruity** (5) **astute** (12) **paltry** (27)

1. stupid _____
2. cry _____
3. cheerful _____
4. sizeable _____
5. agreement _____

B. If the underlined vocabulary word is used correctly, put a *T* for true, and if it is used incorrectly, put an *F* for false.

_____ 1. My uncle is a pathological (3) liar. He tries to stop, but he can't control his urge to fib.

_____ 2. The physiological (7) benefits of swimming can most be felt in one's head.

_____ 3. In the last 100 years, the mortality (11) rate has increased in the United States due to better health care and medical developments.

_____ 4. An implication (25) of the study is that even moderate exercise will lead to better mental as well as physical health.

_____ 5. My mother considered cookies and milk a panacea (27) for all my childhood problems, and I usually did feel better after having them.

C. Word parts: Fill in the missing word part and circle the meaning of the word part found in each question. Return to pages 85–87 if you need to review the meaning of a word part.

> **mort** **path** **pan** **bene**

1. Some _____ological behaviors can be helped with therapy. A disease of the mind does not have to impact a person's life forever.

2. I'm not afraid of death. We all have to face our _____ality at some point.

3. We are lucky to have so many members willing to do good deeds for our organization. We all _____fit when they share their time and money with the community.

4. Although some people view aspirin as a _____acea, it is not a cure-all for every ache and pain.

The Article and You

1. How many of the effects of laughter mentioned in paragraphs 6–11 have you experienced? Give two examples of times you encountered at least one of these effects.

    _____

    _____

2. Were you surprised by the information in paragraph 27? How many times a day do you think you usually laugh? Name three situations that made you laugh in the last week.

    _____

    _____

3. Start creating your "humor profile" (par. 30) by listing three comedians, movies, or television shows that make you laugh. What comedy traits do these three have in common?

    _____

    _____

4. On a separate sheet of paper, write a paragraph in which you explain whether you think people can change their sense of humor as discussed in paragraphs 19–21. Use yourself and people you know as examples.

Take a Closer Look

Look at the photo again. Does the scene fit your humor profile? Explain why you do or do not find the photograph funny.

_____

_____

Internet Activities

If needed, use a separate sheet of paper to fully record your responses. Include the Web address of any sites from which you gather information.

1. Do a search for "jokes." Find one that makes you laugh. Write an explanation of why you find the joke funny. Does it show the "incongruity" mentioned in paragraph 5? Be prepared to share the joke with your classmates.

    _____

    _____

2. Look up "farce," "pun," and "slapstick." Write a definition and give an example for each word. Which of these types of humor is most likely to make you laugh?

    _____

    _____

In the Mountain Meadow

from *Gorillas in the Mist*

by Dian Fossey

Before You Read

1. Is the name Dian Fossey familiar to you?

2. What do you know about gorillas?

3. After you survey the selection, write a question that you think the reading may address:

   _____

4. Look at the photo. What is your reaction to the gorillas?

Vocabulary Preview

Look for these words in the reading. Exercises to reinforce the learning of new vocabulary using these words follow the reading. The paragraph number where the word appears is in parentheses.

sans (2)	**dire** (2)	**fortuitous** (3)	**perilous** (6)	**keen** (7)
dormant (9)	**mundane** (10)	**foliage** (10)	**coyly** (19)	**induce** (20)

Dian Fossey (1932–1985) studied mountain gorillas in Africa for almost 20 years. A 1963 safari to Africa and a meeting with the famous anthropologist Dr. Louis Leakey led to her long-term study. She received a Ph.D. in zoology from Cambridge University in 1974. She was also an activist against the poaching of and encroachment on the habitat of the mountain gorilla. Her actions made her unpopular with poachers and some government officials in Rwanda. Fossey was found murdered in her mountain cabin on December 26, 1985. Her murder has never been solved. The following excerpt is from her book *Gorillas in the Mist* published in 1983. A 1988 movie of the same name starred Sigourney Weaver as Fossey.

1 My reunion with Kabara, Sanwekwe, and the gorillas came about as a direct result of a visit by Dr. Leakey to Louisville, Kentucky, where I was continuing my work as an occupational therapist in order to pay off the huge bank loan amassed for the first safari. Vaguely remembering me as the clumsy tourist of three years earlier, Dr. Leakey's attention was drawn to some photographs and articles I had published about gorillas since my return from Africa. After a brief interview, he suggested that I become the "gorilla girl" he had been seeking to conduct a long-term field study. Our conversation ended with his assertion that it was mandatory I should have my appendix removed before venturing into the remote wilderness of the gorillas' high altitude habitat in central Africa. I would have agreed to almost anything at that point and promptly made plans for an appendectomy.

2 Some six weeks later on returning home from the hospital sans appendix, I found a letter from Dr. Leakey. It began, "Actually there really isn't any dire need for you to have your appendix removed. That is only my way of testing applicants' determination!" This was my first introduction to Dr. Leakey's unique sense of humor.

3   Eight more months passed before Dr. Leakey was able to obtain funds to launch the study. During the interim I finished paying for my 1963 safari while virtually memorizing George Schaller's two superlative books about his 1959–60 field studies with the mountain gorillas, as well as a "Teach Yourself Swahili" grammar book. Quitting my job as an occupational therapist and saying goodbye to the children who had been my patients for eleven years was difficult, as were the farewells to Kentucky friends and my three dogs. The dogs seemed to sense that this was going to be a permanent separation. I can still recall them — Mitzi, Shep, and Brownie — running after my overladen car as I drove away from my Kentucky home to head for California to say farewell to my parents. There was no way that I could explain to dogs, friends, or parents my compelling need to return to Africa to launch a long-term study of the gorillas. Some may call it destiny and others may call it dismaying. I call the sudden turn of events in my life fortuitous.

4   At the end of 1966, Leighton Wilkie, the man responsible for financially backing Jane Goodall into her long-term chimpanzee study, told Dr. Leakey that he also would be willing to initiate another long-term great ape study. Like Louis Leakey, Leighton Wilkie felt that by studying man's closest living relatives, the great apes, new light could be shed on how our ancestors might have behaved. With his support the finances of my project were assured.

5   Thus in December 1966, I was again Africa-bound. This time only gorillas were my goal. By an incredible stroke of luck, I chanced to run into Joan Root at the Heathrow airport in London while waiting for a Nairobi-bound plane. Both she and Alan were stunned that I intended to drive from Nairobi to the Congo, a distance of some 700 miles, then seek government permission to work at Kabara, and, lastly, carry out the study by myself. They shared the opinion of many friends that lone females, especially those fresh from America, should not be expected to try any one of the above "impossibilities," much less all three combined.

6   Once we were in Nairobi, Joan accompanied me on numerous shopping sprees. Because of her long experience on safaris, she saved many hours, and undoubtedly many mistakes, by helping me select functional camp supplies and equipment such as tents, lights, stoves, and bedding. Dr. Leakey purchased, after some perilous test drives through Nairobi's crowded streets, an antiquated, canvas-topped Land-Rover that I later named "Lily." Little did I know that in seven months' time Lily was going to be responsible for saving my life.

7   When all of the gear was finally assembled, Jane Goodall kindly invited me to visit the Gombe Stream Research Centre for two days to show me her methods of camp organization, data collecting, and, as well, to introduce me to her lovable chimpanzees. I fear that I was not an appreciative guest, for I was desperately keen to reach Kabara and the mountain gorillas.

8   Finally Alan Root, still doubting the sanity of myself and Dr. Leakey, said that he would accompany me in his Land-Rover during the long drive from Kenya to the Congo, nearly halfway across Africa. Without Alan I don't know if I would have

succeeded in coaxing Lily over some of the escarpment goat-trail roads prevalent in Africa at that time. Nor might I have handled with Alan's ease many of the complexities involved in obtaining the government permits necessary for working at Kabara within the Parc des Virungas.

9   On the morning of January 6, 1967, Alan and I, accompanied by some Congolese park guards and two Africans willing to stay on as camp staff, arrived at the small village of Kibumba situated at the base of Mt. Mikeno. There, exactly as I had done with my driver three years earlier, we selected several-dozen porters to carry up the camping gear to the remote Kabara meadow. Neither the porters' village nor the forest's huge, ancient, moss-laden *Hagenia abyssinica* trees seemed to have changed during my three-year absence. Elated, I climbed the nearly four thousand feet between Kibumba and Kabara, where I established my camp within the heartland of the ancient dormant volcanoes. I was thrilled to find Kabara so unchanged even to the presence of two delightfully mischievous ravens *(Corvultur albicollis)*. They absconded with every scrap of unguarded food before eventually learning to unzip the tent flap in search of concealed food.

10   Alan could stay at Kabara only for two days, but during that time he worked around the clock. At camp he supervised mundane necessities such as the digging of a latrine secluded by potato-sacking walls, placement of barrels to store water, and planning drainage ditches around my tent. To our mutual regret, we never had a visual contact with the gorillas during his two-day stay, though we did hear two groups exchanging "hootseries" from high on Mt. Mikeno's slopes. We also found fresh tracks of a gorilla group in the relatively flat saddle area adjacent to the mountain. In my excitement I promptly took off on the trail swath left by the gorillas through dense herbaceous foliage in the certainty that I would encounter the group at any moment. Some five minutes of "tracking" passed before I was aware that Alan was not behind me. Perplexed, I retraced my steps and found him patiently sitting at the very point where we had first encountered the trail.

11   With the utmost British tolerance and politeness, Alan said, "Dian, if you are ever going to contact gorillas, you must follow their tracks to where they are going rather than backtrack trails to where they've been." That was my first lesson in tracking, and one that I've never forgotten.

12   The next day I felt a sense of panic while watching Alan fade into the foliage near the descending edge of the Kabara meadow. He was my last link with civilization as I had always known it, and the only other English-speaking person on the mountain. I clung on to my tent pole simply to avoid running after him.

13   A few moments after Alan's departure one of the two Africans in camp, trying to be helpful, asked, *"Unapenda maji moto?"* Forgetting every word of Swahili memorized over the past year, I burst into tears and zipped myself into the tent to escape imagined "threats." About an hour later, feeling the fool, I asked the Congolese to repeat his statement slowly. Did I want hot water? Whether for tea or bath he didn't specify, but this seemed to be the panacea necessary for all *wazungus'* (white people's)

rough times. I accepted a couple of gallons of hot water as graciously as possible with many *asantes* (thank you's), hoping to convince the Africans that their concern was deeply appreciated.

14   The following morning it was field work, or the actual searching for gorillas, that took precedence over the endless list of camp chores such as setting up clothes-drying lines, placing the catchment barrels in optimal places to collect rainwater, and teaching the staff how to care for the kerosene lamps and stove purchased in Nairobi. Like a bored housewife, I relegated these and many more tasks to the evening hours. Daylight belonged to the gorillas. . . .

15   During the early days of the study at Kabara, it was difficult to establish contacts because the gorillas were not habituated or accustomed to my presence and usually fled on seeing me. I could often choose between two different kinds of contacts: obscured, when the gorillas didn't know I was watching them, or open contacts, when they were aware of my presence.

16   Obscured contacts were especially valuable in revealing behavior that otherwise would have been inhibited by my presence. The drawback to this method was that it contributed nothing toward the habituation process. Open contacts, however, slowly helped me win the animals' acceptance. This was especially true when I learned that imitation of some of their ordinary activities such as scratching and feeding or copying their contentment vocalizations tended to put the animals at ease more rapidly

than if I simply looked at them through binoculars while taking notes. I always wrapped vines around the binoculars in an attempt to disguise the potentially threatening glass eyes from the shy animals. With gorillas, as is often the case with humans, direct staring constitutes a threat.

17   Not only was it necessary to get the gorillas accustomed to the bluejeaned creature who had become a part of their daily lives, it was also very necessary for me to know and recognize the particular animals of each group as the amazing individuals they were. Just as George Schaller had done some seven and a half years before me, I relied heavily upon "noseprints" for identification purposes. There is a tendency for the gorillas of each group to resemble one another, especially within matrilineal lines. As no two humans have exactly the same fingerprints, no two gorillas have the same "noseprint" — the shape of the nostrils and the outstanding troughs seen on the bridges of their noses. Since the gorillas initially were unhabituated, I had to use binoculars, but even from a distance I could quickly make sketches of noseprints seen on the more curious group members peeking back at me from partially hidden positions in the dense vegetation. These sketches proved invaluable at a time when close-up photography was out of the question. Also, I would have needed a third hand in order to manage a camera, binoculars, and note taking, not to mention carrying on with the imitative routine of feeding, scratching, and vocalizing needed to relax the gorillas as well as to arouse their curiosity.

18   Occasionally I did take out my camera, especially when the sun was shining. Probably one of the most publicized pictures of gorillas in the wild was taken at Kabara during the second month of my study when the gorillas were beginning to trust me. It shows a lineup of sixteen gorillas posing like so many Aunt Matildas on a back porch. The group had been day-nesting and sunbathing when I contacted them, but upon my approach they nervously retreated to obscure themselves behind thick foliage. Frustrated but determined to see them better, I decided to climb a tree, not one of my better talents. The tree was particularly slithery and, try as I might, no amount of puffing, pulling, gripping, or clawing succeeded in getting me more than a few feet aboveground. Disgustedly, I was about to give up when Sanwekwe came to my aid by giving one mighty boost to my protruding rump; tears were running from his eyes as he was convulsed in silent laughter. I felt as inept as a baby taking its first step. Finally able to grab on to a conveniently placed branch, I hauled myself up into a respectful semislouch position in the tree about twenty feet from the ground. By this time I naturally assumed that the combined noises of panting, cursing, and branch-breaking made during the initial climbing attempts must have frightened the group on to the next mountain. I was amazed to look around and find that the entire group had returned and were sitting like front-row spectators at a sideshow. All that was needed to make the image complete were a few gorilla-sized bags of popcorn and some cotton candy! This was the first live audience I had ever had in my life and certainly the least expected.

19   That day's observation was a perfect example of how the gorillas' sense of curiosity could be utilized toward their habituation. Nearly all members of the group had totally exposed themselves, forgetting about hiding coyly behind foliage screens because it was obvious to them that the observer had been distracted by tree-climbing problems, an activity they could understand.

20   Stimulating the gorillas' curiosity was but one aspect of the habituation process learned over time. It was a while though before I realized that standing upright or walking within their view increased the animals' apprehension. That discovery marked the beginning of my knuckle-walking days. Crawling toward groups on knuckles and knees and maintaining contacts in a seated position not only kept me at the gorillas' eye level but also conveyed the impression that I was settled and not about to barge into their midst. After a contact was established I learned that if I partially concealed my celery-chomping self, their curiosity would inevitably draw them from behind thick clumps of foliage or induce them to climb trees in order to see me better. Previously when I had been completely visible throughout a contact, the gorillas were content to remain obscured and peek at me through vegetation—which did not contribute much toward my observations of their behavior. I therefore changed my tactics from climbing trees to view the gorillas to leaving the trees for the gorillas to climb to view me.

21   Initially I often had to wait for up to a half an hour, pretending to feed on foliage, before the gorillas gave in to their inquisitiveness and climbed trees surrounding me. Once their curiosity was satisfied, they would resume their usual activities, forgetting that I was there. This is what I had come to observe.

Getting the Message

____ **1.** Which is the topic of the selection?
  a. gorillas
  b. life at Kabara
  c. Fossey's life
  d. Fossey's study of mountain gorillas

____ **2.** The main idea of the excerpt is that
  a. gorillas are powerful animals.
  b. despite the difficulties, Fossey was overjoyed to be doing work she loved.
  c. Fossey didn't know enough about gorillas to do a good job observing them.
  d. Africa is a dangerous place.

____ **3.** What type of supporting detail does Fossey mainly use?
  a. personal examples
  b. testimony
  c. statistics
  d. public examples

____ **4.** After Alan Root leaves the camp, what does the Congolese man ask Fossey if she wants?
  a. food
  b. a handkerchief
  c. hot water
  d. a kerosene lamp

____ **5.** Fossey presents the information in paragraphs 1–14 using _____ order.
  a. least to most important
  b. most to least important
  c. problem and solution
  d. chronological

____ **6.** What pattern of organization does Fossey use overall?
  a. definition
  b. narrative
  c. classification
  d. comparison and contrast

____ **7.** In this excerpt Fossey's purpose is to
  a. warn people about how dangerous it can be to study wild animals.
  b. inform people about the eating habits of gorillas.
  c. amuse people with stories about human and gorilla interactions.
  d. inform people about her early experiences in studying gorillas.

____ **8.** Words that would best describe the tone of the selection are _____.
  a. funny and arrogant
  b. sad and thoughtful
  c. excited and conversational
  d. urgent and forceful

9. It can be inferred from the information in paragraphs 1–6 that part of Fossey's personality included being

    a. shy.

    b. nervous.

    c. impulsive.

    d. angry.

10. The sentence "I felt as inept as a baby taking its first step" (par. 18) uses a

    a. simile.

    b. metaphor.

11. What are three things the reader can learn about mountain gorillas from this excerpt?

_____

_____

_____

12. Give examples of three different time words or phrases Fossey uses and the paragraph number where each can be found.

_____

_____

_____

13. Why do you think Fossey uses the Swahili words in paragraph 13? Do you think it makes sense to use them?

_____

_____

_____

_____

14. List four items you circled or starred as you annotated the excerpt. Explain why you considered these items important.

_____

_____

_____

15. Paraphrase the sentence "With gorillas, as is often the case with humans, direct staring constitutes a threat" (par. 16).

_____

_____

Vocabulary

Use context clues to determine the meaning of each word by referring back to the paragraph where the word is used (the paragraph number is in parentheses). If you need help, consult a dictionary for the definition.

A. Match the word to its definition.

sans (2)	**fortuitous** (3)	**dormant** (9)	**foliage** (10)	**induce** (20)

1. as if asleep, inactive, temporarily quiet _____
2. to persuade or encourage, to cause _____
3. without, minus _____
4. plant leaves as a whole, the leaves of growing plants _____
5. happening by accident, unplanned, unexpected _____

B. Finish the reading using the vocabulary words. Use each word once.

dire (2)	**perilous** (6)	**keen** (7)	**mundane** (10)	**coyly** (19)

My sister called at 10 p.m. shouting that she was in _____ trouble, and that I needed to rush to her house. I was not too _____ on going since my sister tends to exaggerate her problems. She wouldn't say what was wrong, but that she needed me immediately. As I drove to her house, I began to envision her in some _____ situation—dangling from the roof, sloshing through a room filled with water. When I arrived, she pointed to her living room lamp and smiled _____. The light bulb was burned out. I was right; her emergency was something _____. I knew, however, that as the older sibling, I needed to be there for my 30-year-old baby sister.

C. Word parts: Match the word part to its meaning using the sample words as clues. Return to pages 85–87 if you need to review the meaning of a word part.

____ 1. -voc-: vocalizations (16), vocalizing (17) a. not

____ 2. -vis-: supervised (10), visible (20) b. to put, to place

____ 3. -pos-: positions (17), exposed (19) c. voice, call

____ 4. un-: unchanged (9), unguarded (9) d. see

The Essay and You

1. What do you think of Dr. Leakey's method of testing the "determination" of applicants (par. 2)? What are you so passionate about that you would go to great lengths to be involved in it?

_____

_____

2. List three connotations you have for the word *scientist*. How do the experiences Fossey describes match your view of a scientist?

_____

_____

3. Which of the experiences that Fossey describes in this excerpt is most memorable to you? Explain why.

_____

_____

4. Observation is a large part of Fossey's work with the mountain gorillas. Test your observational skills by sitting somewhere (such as the college cafeteria, a shopping mall, or a park) for an hour and taking notes on what you see. Once you have finished your observations, use your notes and a separate sheet of paper to write a paragraph describing what you saw.

Take a Closer Look

Look at the photo again. Now that you have read the excerpt, do you see the scene differently? Can you imagine the gorillas holding popcorn and cotton candy and watching Fossey (par. 18)? What are two steps you think people can take to protect the mountain gorilla and other endangered species?

_____

_____

_____

Internet Activities

If needed, use a separate sheet of paper to fully record your responses. Include the Web address of any sites from which you gather information.

1. Look up Jane Goodall or Biruté Galdikas. Write a summary of the woman's life including what her connection was to Dr. Louis Leakey. How is the woman's life similar to Dian Fossey's from what you learned in the excerpt?

_____

_____

2. Find four photographs of gorillas; look for photos of individuals and groups of gorillas. List three observations you can make from these photos. Print one photo to share with the class. Be prepared to explain what attracted you to this photograph. Also consider what animal you would most like to study if given the opportunity.

_____

_____

Responding to Stress

from *Mastering the World of Psychology*

by Samuel E. Wood, Ellen Green Wood, and Denise Boyd

Before You Read

1. Survey the excerpt (look at headings, subheadings, and the notes and questions in the margins). Write a question that you think the reading may address:

   _____

2. How do you respond to stress?
3. What brings about the most stress in your life?
4. Look at the photo and two figures. What clues do they give you about the reading's content?

Samuel E. Wood, Ellen Green Wood, and Denise Boyd have a combined 45 years of experience teaching psychology. They have taught in colleges in West Virginia, Missouri, and Texas. They also have numerous other experiences in education, including developing distance learning programs, teaching seminars on critical thinking, and presenting papers at professional conferences. The following excerpt comes from their introductory psychology text *Mastering the World of Psychology,* which aims to make students "active participants in the learning process."

Vocabulary Preview

Look for these words in the reading. Exercises to reinforce the learning of new vocabulary using these words follow the reading. The paragraph number where the word appears is in parentheses.

stressor (2)	**appraisal** (4)	**morale** (5)	**proactive** (8)	**menaces** (10)
attributable (12)	**sedentary** (12)	**intravenously** (13)	**cardiologists** (14)	**incessant** (15)

Responding to Stress

1   **Selye and the General Adaptation Syndrome**   Hans Selye (1907–1982), the researcher most prominently associated with the effects of stress on health, established the field of stress research. The heart of Selye's concept of stress is the general adaptation syndrome (GAS), consisting of three stages: the alarm stage, the resistance stage, and the exhaustion stage (Selye, 1956).

What is the general adaptation syndrome?

2   The body's first response to a stressor is the **alarm stage,** in which the adrenal cortex releases hormones called *glucocorticoids* that increase heart rate, blood pressure, and blood-sugar levels, supplying a burst of energy that helps the person deal with the stressful situation (Pennisi, 1997). Next, the organism enters the **resistance stage,** during which the adrenal cortex continues to release the glucocorticoids to help the body resist stressors. The length of the resistance stage depends both on the strength or intensity of the stressor and on the body's power to adapt. If the organism finally

general adaptation syndrome (GAS)
The predictable sequence of reactions (alarm, resistance, and exhaustion stages) that organisms show in response to stressors.

alarm stage
The first stage of the general adaptation syndrome, when there is emotional arousal and the defensive forces of the body are prepared to fight or flee.

resistance stage
The second stage of the general adaptation syndrome, when there are intense physiological efforts to either resist or adapt to the stressor.

"Responding to Stress," "Health and Illness," and "Try It! 10.2" from *Mastering the World of Psychology*, pages 294–299, by Samuel E. Wood, Ellen Green Wood, and Denise Boyd. Copyright © 2004 by Pearson Education, Inc. Reprinted by permission of Pearson Education, Inc., Boston, MA.

fails in its efforts to resist, it reaches the **exhaustion stage,** at which point all the stores of deep energy are depleted, and disintegration and death follow.

3   Selye found that the most harmful effects of stress are due to the prolonged secretion of glucocorticoids. Such prolonged secretion can lead to a permanent increase in blood pressure, suppression of the immune system, and weakening of muscles and can even cause damage to the hippocampus (Stein-Behrens et al., 1994). Thanks to Selye, the connection between extreme, prolonged stress and certain diseases is now widely accepted by medical experts.

4   **Lazarus's Cognitive Theory of Stress**   Richard Lazarus (1966; Lazarus & Folkman, 1984) contends that it is not the stressor itself that causes stress, but a person's perception of the stressor. According to Lazarus, when people are confronted with a potentially stressful event, they engage in a cognitive process that involves a primary and a secondary appraisal. A **primary appraisal** is an evaluation of the meaning and significance of the situation—whether its effect on one's well-being is positive, irrelevant, or negative. An event that is appraised as stressful may involve: (1) harm or loss (damage that has already occurred); (2) threat (the potential for harm or loss); or (3) challenge (the opportunity to grow or gain). An appraisal of threat, harm, or loss can occur in relation to anything important to you—a friendship, a part of your body, your property, your finances, or your self-esteem. When people appraise a situation as involving harm, loss, or threat, they experience negative emotions such as anxiety, fear, anger, or resentment (Folkman, 1984). An appraisal of a situation as involving challenge, on the other hand, is usually accompanied by positive emotions such as excitement, hopefulness, and eagerness.

exhaustion stage
The final stage of the general adaptation syndrome, occurring if the organism fails in its efforts to resist the stressor.

primary appraisal
An evaluation of the meaning and significance of a potentially stressful event according to how it will affect one's well-being—whether it is perceived as irrelevant or as involving harm or loss, threat, or challenge.

What are the roles of primary and secondary appraisal when a person is confronted with a potentially stressful event?

5　　During **secondary appraisal,** if people judge the situation to be within their control, they evaluate available resources: physical (health, energy, stamina), social (support network), psychological (skills, morale, self-esteem), material (money, tools, equipment), and time. Then, they consider the options and decide how to deal with the stressor. The level of stress they feel is largely a function of whether their resources are adequate to cope with the stressor, and how severely those resources will be taxed in the process. Figure 10.4 summarizes the Lazarus and Folkman psychological model of stress. There is research support for Lazarus and Folkman's claim that physiological, emotional, and behavioral reactions to stressors depend partly on whether the stressors are appraised as challenging or threatening.

6　　**Coping Strategies**　　**Coping** refers to a person's efforts, both action and thought, to deal with demands perceived as taxing or overwhelming. **Problem-focused coping** is direct; it consists of reducing, modifying, or eliminating the source of stress itself. If you are getting a poor grade in history and appraise this as a threat, you may study harder, talk over your problem with your professor, form a study group with other class members, get a tutor, or drop the course.

7　　**Emotion-focused coping** may involve reappraising a stressor. If you lose your job, you may decide that it isn't a major tragedy and

secondary appraisal
An evaluation of one's coping resources prior to deciding how to deal with a stressful event.

coping
Efforts, through action and thought, to deal with demands that are perceived as taxing or overwhelming.

What is the difference between problem-focused and emotion-focused coping?

problem-focused coping
A response aimed at reducing, modifying, or eliminating a source of stress.

➤ **Figure 10.4**
Lazarus and Folkman's Psychological Model of Stress

Lazarus and Folkman emphasize the importance of a person's perceptions and appraisal of stressors. The stress response depends on the outcome of the primary and secondary appraisals, whether the person's coping resources are adequate to cope with the threat, and how severely the resources are taxed in the process. (From Folkman, 1984.)

Potentially Stressful Event

Primary Appraisal
Person evaluates event as positive, neutral, or negative. Negative appraisal can involve:
· **Harm or loss** (damage has already occurred)
· **Threat** (the potential for harm or loss)
· **Challenge** (the opportunity to grow or gain)

Secondary Appraisal
If the situation is judged to be within a person's control:
1. Person evaluates coping resources (physical, social, psychological, material) to determine if they are adequate to deal with stressor.
2. Person considers options in dealing with stressor.

Stress Response
· **Physiological:** Autonomic arousal, fluctuations in hormones
· **Emotional:** Anxiety, fear, grief, resentment, excitement
· **Behavioral:** Coping behaviors (including problem-focused and emotion-focused coping strategies)

instead view it as a challenge—an opportunity to find a better job with a higher salary. Despite what you may have heard, ignoring a stressor, one form of emotion-focused coping, can be an effective way of managing stress. Researchers studied 116 people who had experienced heart attacks (Ginzburg et al., 2002). All of the participants reported being worried about suffering another attack. However, those who tried to ignore their worries were less likely to exhibit anxiety-related symptoms such as nightmares and flashbacks. But a combination of problem-focused and emotion-focused coping is probably the best stress-management strategy (Folkman & Lazarus, 1980). So, a heart patient may try to ignore her anxiety (emotion-focused coping) while conscientiously adopting recommended lifestyle changes, such as increasing exercise (problem-focused coping).

emotion-focused coping
A response aimed at reducing the emotional impact of the stressor.

8   Some stressful situations can be anticipated in advance, allowing active measures to be taken to avoid or minimize them. Such active measures are known as proactive coping (Aspinwall & Taylor, 1997). **Proactive coping** consists of actions taken in advance of a potentially stressful situation to prevent its occurrence or to minimize its consequences. Proactive copers anticipate and then prepare for upcoming stressful events and situations, including those that are certain and those that are only likely.

proactive coping
Efforts or actions taken in advance of a potentially stressful situation to prevent its occurrence or to minimize its consequences.

Health and Illness

9   **Two Approaches to Health and Illness**   For many decades, the predominant view in medicine was the **biomedical model,** which explains illness in terms of biological factors. Today, both physicians and psychologists recognize that the **biopsychosocial model** more fully explains both health and illness than the biomedical model (Engel, 1977, 1980; Schwartz, 1982). The biopsychosocial model is depicted in Figure 10.5.

How do the biomedical and biopsychosocial models differ in their approaches to health and illness?

10   Growing acceptance of the biopsychosocial approach gave rise to a subfield, **health psychology,** which is "the field within psychology devoted to understanding psychological influences on how people stay healthy, why they become ill, and how they respond when they do get ill" (Taylor, 1991, p. 6). Health psychology has become particularly important because many of today's health menaces are diseases related to unhealthy lifestyle and stress (Taylor & Repetti, 1997).

biomedical model
A perspective that focuses on illness rather than on health, explaining illness in terms of biological factors without regard to psychological and social factors.

11   **Coronary Heart Disease**   In order to survive, the heart muscle requires a steady, sufficient supply of oxygen and nutrients carried by the blood. Coronary heart disease is caused by the narrowing or blockage of the coronary arteries—the arteries that supply blood to the heart muscle. Although coronary heart disease remains the leading cause of death in the United States, responsible for 31% of all

biopsychosocial model
A perspective that focuses on health as well as illness and holds that both are determined by a combination of biological, psychological, and social factors.

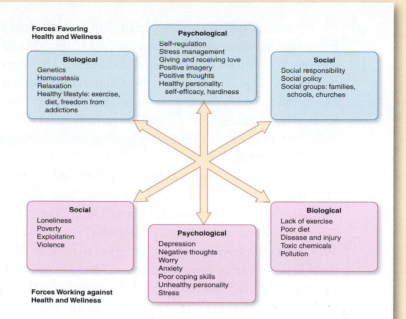

➤ **Figure 10.5**
The Biopsychosocial Model of Health and Wellness

The biopsychosocial model focuses on health and illness and holds that both are determined by a combination of biological, psychological, and social factors. Most health psychologists endorse the biopsychosocial model. (From Green & Shellenberger, 1990.)

Forces Favoring Health and Wellness

Biological
Genetics
Homeostasis
Relaxation
Healthy lifestyle: exercise, diet, freedom from addictions

Psychological
Self-regulation
Stress management
Giving and receiving love
Positive imagery
Positive thoughts
Healthy personality: self-efficacy, hardiness

Social
Social responsibility
Social policy
Social groups: families, schools, churches

Social
Loneliness
Poverty
Exploitation
Violence

Psychological
Depression
Negative thoughts
Worry
Anxiety
Poor coping skills
Unhealthy personality
Stress

Biological
Lack of exercise
Poor diet
Disease and injury
Toxic chemicals
Pollution

Forces Working against Health and Wellness

deaths, the death rate due to this cause has declined 50% during the past 30 years (National Center for Health Statistics, 2000).

12   A health problem of modern times, coronary heart disease is largely attributable to lifestyle and is therefore an important field of study for health psychologists. A *sedentary lifestyle*—one that includes less than 20 minutes of exercise three times per week—is the primary modifiable risk factor contributing to death from coronary heart disease. Other risk factors are high serum cholesterol levels, cigarette smoking, obesity, high blood pressure, and diabetes. Though not modifiable, another important risk factor is a family history. The association between family history and coronary heart disease is both genetic and behavioral. For instance, individuals whose parents have high blood pressure, but who have not yet developed the disorder themselves, exhibit the same kinds of emotional reactivity and poor coping strategies as their parents (Frazer et al., 2002).

13   High levels of stress and job strain have also been associated with increased risk for coronary heart disease and stroke (Rosengren et al., 1991; Siegrist et al., 1990). Apparently, the effects of stress can enter the bloodstream almost as if they were injected intravenously. Malkoff and others (1993) report that after an experimental group of participants had experienced laboratory-induced stress, their blood platelets (special clotting cells) released large amounts of a substance that promotes the buildup of plaque in blood vessels and may lead to heart attack and stroke. No changes were found in the blood platelets of unstressed control-group participants.

health psychology
The field concerned with the psychological factors that contribute to health, illness, and recovery.

14   Personality type is also associated with an individual's risk of heart disease. After extensive research, cardiologists Meyer Friedman and Ray Rosenman (1974) concluded that there are two types of personality: Type A, associated with a high rate of coronary heart disease, and Type B, commonly found in persons unlikely to develop heart disease. Are your characteristics more like those of a Type A or a Type B person? Before reading further, complete *Try It!* 10.2 and find out.

15   People with the Type A behavior pattern have a strong sense of time urgency and are impatient, excessively competitive, hostile, and easily angered. They are "involved in a chronic, incessant struggle to achieve more and more in less and less time" (Friedman & Rosenman, 1974, p. 84). Type A's would answer "true" to most or all of the questions in the *Try It!* In contrast, people with the Type B behavior pattern are relaxed and easygoing and do not suffer from a sense of time urgency. They are not impatient or hostile and are able to relax without guilt. They play for fun and relaxation rather than to exhibit superiority over others. Yet the Type B individual may be as bright and ambitious as the Type A, and more successful as well. Type B's would answer "false" to most or all of the *Try It!* questions.

> What are the Type A and Type B behavior patterns?

16   In a review of a number of studies, Miller and others (1991) found that 70% of middle-aged men with coronary heart disease were Type A, compared to 46% of healthy middle-aged men. Research indicates that the lethal core of the Type A personality is not time urgency but anger and hostility, which fuel an aggressive, reactive temperament (Miller et al., 1996; Smith & Ruiz, 2002; Williams, 1993). Hostility is not only highly predictive of coronary heart disease but also associated with ill health in general (Miller et al., 1996).

> What aspect of the Type A behavior pattern is most clearly linked to coronary heart disease?

Answer true (T) or false (F) for each of the statements below. (Adapted from Friedman and Rosenman, 1974.)

____ **1.** I forcefully emphasize key words in my everyday speech.

____ **2.** I usually walk and eat quickly.

____ **3.** I get irritated and restless around slow workers.

____ **4.** When talking to others, I get impatient and try to hurry them along.

____ **5.** I get very irritated, even hostile, when the car in front of me drives too slowly.

____ **6.** When others are talking, I often think about my own concerns.

____ **7.** I usually think of or do at least two things at the same time.

____ **8.** I get very impatient when I have to wait.

____ **9.** I usually take command and move the conversation to topics that interest me.

____ **10.** I usually feel guilty when I relax and do nothing.

____ **11.** I am usually too absorbed in my work to notice my surroundings.

____ **12.** I keep trying to do more and more in less time.

____ **13.** I sometimes punctuate my conversation with forceful gestures such as clenching my fists or pounding the table.

____ **14.** My accomplishments are due largely to my ability to work faster than others.

____ **15.** I don't play games just for fun. I play to win.

____ **16.** I am more concerned with acquiring things than with becoming a better person.

____ **17.** I usually use numbers to evaluate my own activities and the activities of others.

Getting the Message

____ **1.** The topic sentence in paragraph 4 is _____.
   a. sentence 1
   b. sentence 2
   c. sentence 3
   d. sentence 7

____ **2.** What is the main idea of the excerpt?
   a. Stress can be easily controlled.
   b. Stress has little impact on one's health.
   c. Stress and one's reaction to it plays a major role in one's health.
   d. Coping with stress involves both dealing with a problem and sometimes ignoring it.

____ **3.** Paragraphs _____ use hypothetical examples.
   a. 1 and 2
   b. 6 and 7
   c. 9 and 10
   d. 13 and 14

____ **4.** The following is a major detail in the excerpt:
   a. when faced with a potential stressful situation, people make a primary and secondary appraisal.
   b. losing one's job can be seen as a challenge instead of a threat.
   c. cigarette smoking and obesity can lead to coronary heart disease.
   d. a number of studies have found that 70 percent of middle-aged men with coronary heart disease were Type A.

____ **5.** The sentence "But a combination of problem-focused and emotion-focused coping is probably the best stress-management strategy"(par. 7) expresses
   a. a fact.
   b. an opinion.

____ **6.** The section Responding to Stress uses _____ order.
   a. least to most important
   b. most to least important
   c. problem and solution
   d. chronological

____ **7.** Which pattern of organization is used in paragraph 15?
   a. definition
   b. classification
   c. narrative
   d. comparison and contrast

____ **8.** The writers' purpose in this selection is to persuade.
   a. true
   b. false

_____ **9.** The words _____ describe the tone of the essay.
  a. funny and informal
  b. judgmental and formal
  c. objective and semiformal
  d. dramatic and extremely formal

_____ **10.** What can be inferred from the phrase "Growing acceptance" in paragraph 10?
  a. Most people immediately embraced the idea of biological, psychological, and social factors as having an influence on a person's health.
  b. Many people still believe that only biological factors influence one's health.
  c. Many people believe that biological and psychological factors influence one's health, but social factors don't play much of a role.
  d. The idea that biological, psychological, and social factors influence one's health was not immediately embraced by everyone in the health field.

11. List three transition words, what type each one is, and the paragraph number where it can be found.

_____

_____

_____

12. Why are the questions in the margins of the excerpt important to read?

_____

_____

_____

_____

_____

13. What can you infer about people's lives today from the last line in paragraph 10?

_____

_____

_____

14. List two questions or comments you wrote in the margins as you read the selection.

_____

_____

15. On a separate sheet of paper, write a summary (about 150 words) of the excerpt.

Vocabulary

Use context clues to determine the meaning of each word by referring back to the paragraph where the word is used (the paragraph number is in parentheses). If you need help, consult a dictionary for the definition.

A. Circle the correct meaning of each vocabulary word.

1. proactive (8)   waiting until something bad happens to deal with it   acting in advance to handle an expected problem

2. menace(s) (10)   a threat   a friend

3. attributable (12)   able to relate to a specific cause   unable to find the cause

4. sedentary (12)   active   inactive

5. intravenously (13)   through or within a vein   through the mouth

B. Write a definition and your own sentence for each word.

1. stressor (2): _____

_____

2. appraisal (4): _____

_____

3. morale (5): _____

_____

4. cardiologist (14): _____

_____

5. incessant (15): _____

_____

C. Word parts: Match the meanings on the right to the words on the left. The word parts are underlined to help you make the connections. Return to pages 85–87 if you need to review the meaning of a word part.

1. attrib<u>utable</u> (12) _____   a. not yielding

2. cardi<u>ologist</u> (14) _____   b. inclined to go all out

3. <u>incess</u>ant (15) _____   c. capable of giving credit to

4. <u>excessive</u>(ly) (15) _____   d. a person who studies the heart

The Textbook and You

1. Think of three "potentially stressful" (par. 4) events you faced in the last year. List each event and label your primary appraisal as involving harm, loss, threat, or challenge.

_____

_____

2. Think of a recent stressful situation you have faced. Now refer back to paragraphs 6–8. Did you handle the situation with problem-focused coping, emotion-focused coping, or some of both? Did you use proactive coping? Describe what you did to cope with the situation.

_____

_____

3. How many of the causes of coronary heart disease listed in paragraphs 12–14 apply to you? List two or three things you can do to change any of the "modifiable" causes that you exhibit.

_____

_____

4. On a separate sheet of paper, write a paragraph in which you use the information in Figure 10.5 to show the health benefits of looking at biological, psychological, and social influences on a person's life. To make your paragraph vivid, use two hypothetical people as examples, with one experiencing "forces favoring health and wellness" and the other living a life filled with "forces working against health and wellness."

Take a Closer Look

Look at the photo again. Pick two stressful situations the woman is faced with, and then using the information in Figure 10.4, describe three ways the woman could cope with the two stressors.

_____

_____

Internet Activities

If needed, use a separate sheet of paper to fully record your responses. Include the Web address of any sites from which you gather information.

1. Find a Type A/Type B personality quiz online and take it. Did you turn out to be the same type as your answers to the "Try It!" indicated? Do you feel your personality type is influencing your health? Explain why or why not.

_____

2. Look up "student stressors" and find a site that lists various stressors. List three that you are currently or have recently experienced. Do you feel that these stressors are hurting or have harmed your health?

_____

_____

_____

_____

Virtuoso

by Herbert Goldstone

Before You Read

1. What do you think of when you hear the word *virtuoso*?
2. Read the first six paragraphs. What are your feelings about robots?
3. What types of music do you like?
4. Look at the photo. What are two words you would use to describe the scene?

Herbert Goldstone was an English professor for nearly 50 years. He taught at Cornell University, the State University of New York at Cortland, and the University of Connecticut at Storrs. The following story was originally published in the *Magazine of Fantasy and Science Fiction* in 1953. First published in 1949, the magazine has over the last 60 years featured stories by most of the leading fantasy and science-fiction writers, including Ray Bradbury, Shirley Jackson, Harlan Ellison, and Kurt Vonnegut.

Vocabulary Preview

Look for these words in the reading. Exercises to reinforce the learning of new vocabulary using these words follow the reading. The paragraph number where the word appears is in parentheses.

supple (5) **assimilated** (10) **droned** (14)

futilely (18) **latent** (45) **coaxing** (56)

anachronisms (87) **virtuoso** (94) **repertoire** (96)

monotone (108)

1. ## "Sir?"

2. The Maestro continued to play, not looking up from the keys.

3. "Yes, Rollo?"

4. "Sir, I was wondering if you would explain this apparatus to me."

5. The Maestro stopped playing, his thin body stiffly relaxed on the bench. His long supple fingers floated off the keyboard.

6. "Apparatus?" He turned and smiled at the robot. "Do you mean the piano, Rollo?"

7. "This machine that produces varying sounds. I would like some information about it, its operation and purpose. It is not included in my reference data."

8. The Maestro lit a cigarette. He preferred to do it himself. One of his first orders to Rollo when the robot was delivered two days before had been to disregard his built-in instructions on the subject.

9. "I'd hardly call a piano a machine, Rollo," he smiled, "although technically you are correct. It is actually, I suppose, a machine designed to produce sounds of graduated pitch and tone, singly or in groups."

10. "I assimilated that much by observation," Rollo replied in a brassy baritone which no longer sent tiny tremors up the Maestro's spine. "Wires of different thickness and tautness struck by felt-covered hammers activated by manually operated levers arranged in a horizontal panel."

11 "A very cold-blooded description of one of man's nobler works," the Maestro remarked dryly. "You make Mozart and Chopin mere laboratory technicians."

12 "Mozart? Chopin?" The duralloy sphere that was Rollo's head shone stark and featureless, its immediate surface unbroken but for twin vision lenses. "The terms are not included in my memory banks."

13 "No, not yours, Rollo," the Maestro said softly. "Mozart and Chopin are not for vacuum tubes and fuses and copper wire. They are for flesh and blood and human tears."

14 "I do not understand," Rollo droned.

15 "Well," the Maestro said, smoke curling lazily from his nostrils, "they are two of the humans who compose, or design successions of notes—varying sounds, that is, produced by the piano or by other instruments, machines that produce other types of sounds of fixed pitch and tone.

16 "Sometimes these instruments, as we call them, are played, or operated, individually; sometimes in groups—orchestras, as we refer to them—and the sounds blend together, they harmonize. That is, they have an orderly, mathematical relationship to each other which results in . . ."

17 The Maestro threw up his hands.

18 "I never imagined," he chuckled, "that I would some day struggle so mightily, and so futilely, to explain music to a robot!"

19 "Music?"

20 "Yes, Rollo. The sounds produced by this machine and others of the same category are called music."

21 "What is the purpose of music, sir?"

22 "Purpose?"

23 The Maestro crushed the cigarette in an ash tray. He turned to the keyboard of the concert grand and flexed his fingers briefly.

24 "Listen, Rollo."

25 The wraithlike fingers glided and wove the opening bars of "Clair de Lune," slender and delicate as spider silk. Rollo stood rigid, the fluorescent light over the music rack casting a bluish jeweled sheen over his towering bulk, shimmering in the amber vision lenses.

26 The Maestro drew his hands back from the keys and the subtle thread of melody melted reluctantly into silence.

27 "Claude Debussy," the Maestro said. "One of our mechanics of an era long past. He designed that succession of tones many years ago. What do you think of it?"

28 Rollo did not answer at once.

29 "The sounds were well formed," he replied finally. "They did not jar my auditory senses as some do."

30 The Maestro laughed. "Rollo, you may not realize it, but you're a wonderful critic."

31 "This music, then," Rollo droned. "Its purpose is to give pleasure to humans?"

32 "Exactly," the Maestro said. "Sounds well formed, that do not jar the auditory senses as some do. Marvelous! It should be carved in marble over the entrance of New Carnegie Hall."

33 "I do not understand. Why should my definition—?"

34 The Maestro waved a hand. "No matter, Rollo. No matter."

35 "Sir?"

36 "Yes, Rollo?"

37   "Those sheets of paper you sometimes place before you on the piano. They are the plans of the composer indicating which sounds are to be produced by the piano and in what order?"

38   "Just so. We call each sound a note; combinations of notes we call chords."

39   "Each dot, then, indicates a sound to be made?"

40   "Perfectly correct, my man of metal."

41   Rollo stared straight ahead. The Maestro felt a peculiar sense of wheels turning within that impregnable sphere.

42   "Sir, I have scanned my memory banks and find no specific or implied instructions against it. I should like to be taught how to produce these notes on the piano. I request that you feed the correlation between those dots and the levers of the panel into my memory banks."

43   The Maestro peered at him, amazed. A slow grin traveled across his face.

44   "Done!" he exclaimed. "It's been many years since pupils helped gray these ancient locks, but I have the feeling that you, Rollo, will prove a most fascinating student. To instill the Muse into metal and machinery . . . I accept the challenge gladly!"

45   He rose, touched the cool latent power of Rollo's arm.

46   "Sit down here, my Rolleindex Personal Robot, Model M-e. We shall start Beethoven spinning in his grave—or make musical history."

47   More than an hour later the Maestro yawned and looked at his watch.

48 "It's late," he spoke into the end of the yawn. "These old eyes are not tireless like yours, my friend." He touched Rollo's shoulder. "You have the complete fundamentals of musical notation in your memory banks, Rollo. That's a good night's lesson, particularly when I recall how long it took me to acquire the same amount of information. Tomorrow we'll attempt to put those awesome fingers of yours to work."

49 He stretched. "I'm going to bed," he said. "Will you lock up and put out the lights?"

50 Rollo rose from the bench. "Yes, sir," he droned. "I have a request."

51 "What can I do for my star pupil?"

52 "May I attempt to create some sounds with the keyboard tonight? I will do so very softly so as not to disturb you."

53 "Tonight? Aren't you—?" Then the Maestro smiled. "You must pardon me, Rollo. It's still a bit difficult for me to realize that sleep has no meaning for you."

54 He hesitated, rubbing his chin. "Well, I suppose a good teacher should not discourage impatience to learn. All right, Rollo, but please be careful." He patted the polished mahogany. "This piano and I have been together for many years. I'd hate to see its teeth knocked out by those sledge-hammer digits of yours. Lightly, my friend, very lightly."

55 "Yes, sir."

56 The Maestro fell asleep with a faint smile on his lips, dimly aware of the shy, tentative notes that Rollo was coaxing forth.

57 Then gray fog closed in and he was in that half-world where reality is dreamlike and dreams are real. It was soft and feathery and lavender clouds and sounds were rolling and washing across his mind in flowing waves.

58 Where? The mist drew back a bit and he was in red velvet and deep and the music swelled and broke over him.

59 He smiled.

60 My recording. Thank you, thank you, thank—

61 The Maestro snapped erect, threw the covers aside.

62 He sat on the edge of the bed listening.

63 He groped for his robe in the darkness, shoved bony feet into his slippers.

64 He crept, trembling uncontrollably, to the door of his studio and stood there, thin and brittle in the robe.

65 The light over the music rack was an eerie island in the brown shadows of the studio. Rollo sat at the keyboard, prim, inhuman, rigid, twin lenses focused somewhere off into the shadows.

66 The massive feet working the pedals, arms and hands flashing and glinting—they were living entities, separate, somehow, from the machined perfection of his body.

67 The music rack was empty.

68 A copy of Beethoven's "Appassionata" lay closed on the bench. It had been, the Maestro remembered, in a pile of sheet music on the piano.

69 Rollo was playing it.

70 He was creating it, breathing it, drawing it through silver flame.

71 Time became meaningless, suspended in midair.

72 The Maestro didn't realize he was weeping until Rollo finished the sonata.

73 The robot turned to look at the Maestro. "The sounds," he droned. "They pleased you?"

74   The Maestro's lips quivered. "Yes, Rollo," he replied at last. "They pleased me." He fought the lump in his throat.

75   He picked up the music in fingers that shook.

76   "This, he murmured. "Already?"

77   "It has been added to my store of data," Rollo replied. "I applied the principles you explained to me to these plans. It was not very difficult."

78   The Maestro swallowed as he tried to speak. "It was not very difficult . . . " he repeated softly.

79   The old man sank down slowly onto the bench next to Rollo, stared silently at the robot as though seeing him for the first time.

80   Rollo got to his feet.

81   The Maestro let his fingers rest on the keys, strangely foreign now.

82   "Music!" he breathed. "I may have heard it that way in my soul. I know Beethoven did!"

83   He looked up at the robot, a growing excitement in his face.

84   "Rollo," he said, his voice straining to remain calm. "You and I have some work to do tomorrow on your memory banks."

85   Sleep did not come again that night.

86   He strode briskly into the studio the next morning. Rollo was vacuuming the carpet. The Maestro preferred carpets to the new dust-free plastics, which felt somehow profane to his feet.

87   The Maestro's house was, in fact, an oasis of anachronisms in a desert of contemporary antiseptic efficiency.

88   "Well, are you ready for work, Rollo?" he asked. "We have a lot to do, you and I. I have such plans for you, Rollo—great plans!"

89   Rollo, for once, did not reply.

90   "I have asked them all to come here this afternoon," the Maestro went on. "Conductors, concert pianists, composers, my manager. All the giants of music, Rollo. Wait until they hear you play."

91   Rollo switched off the vacuum and stood quietly.

92   "You'll play for them right here this afternoon." The Maestro's voice was high-pitched, breathless. "The 'Appassionata' again, I think. Yes, that's it. I must see their faces!

93   "Then we'll arrange a recital to introduce you to the public and the critics and then a major concerto with one of the big orchestras. We'll have it telecast around the world, Rollo. It can be arranged.

94   "Think of it, Rollo, just think of it! The greatest piano virtuoso of all time . . . a robot! It's completely fantastic and completely wonderful. I feel like an explorer at the edge of a new world."

95   He walked feverishly back and forth.

96   "Then recordings, of course. My entire repertoire, Rollo, and more. So much more!"

97   "Sir?"

98   The Maestro's face shone as he looked up at him. "Yes, Rollo?"

99   "In my built-in instructions, I have the option of rejecting any action which I consider harmful to my owner," the robot's words were precise, carefully selected. "Last

night you wept. That is one of the indications I am instructed to consider in making my decisions."

100   The Maestro gripped Rollo's thick, superbly molded arm.

101   "Rollo, you don't understand. That was for the moment. It was petty of me, childish!"

102   "I beg your pardon, sir, but I must refuse to approach the piano again."

103   The Maestro stared at him, unbelieving, pleading.

104   "Rollo, you can't! The world must hear you!"

105   "No, sir." The amber lenses almost seemed to soften.

106   "The piano is not a machine," that powerful inhuman voice droned. "To me, yes. I can translate the notes into sounds at a glance. From only a few I am able to grasp at once the composer's conception. It is easy for me."

107   Rollo towered magnificently over the Maestro's bent form.

108   "I can also grasp," the brassy monotone rolled through the studio, "that this . . . music is not for robots. It is for man. To me it is easy, yes. . . . It was not meant to be easy."

Getting the Message

_____ 1. What is the theme of the story?

    a. Robots are smarter than humans.

    b. Anyone can learn to play the piano.

    c. Some things are not meant to be done by robots or machines.

    d. Doing things the old-fashioned way is always best.

_____ 2. It takes Rollo _____ to learn to play the piano.

    a. two hours   c. 24 hours

    b. a few hours   d. two weeks

_____ 3. The story is ordered

    a. chronologically.

    b. from the least to most important point.

    c. from the most to least important point.

    d. as a problem and its solution.

_____ 4. The story uses the _____ pattern of organization.

    a. definition   c. classification

    b. narrative   d. comparison and contrast

_____ 5. What does the dialogue add to the story?

    a. It creates a sense of intimacy with the characters.

    b. It helps to show the characters' personalities.

    c. It makes the story funnier.

    d. a and b

_____ 6. Goldstone's purpose is to

    a. inform.   c. entertain and persuade.

    b. warn.   d. persuade and inform.

_____ 7. The tone of the story can be labeled as being _____.

    a. funny   c. angry

    b. sad   d. thoughtful

_____ 8. It can be inferred from the sentence "The Maestro's house was, in fact, an oasis of anachronisms in a desert of contemporary antiseptic efficiency" (par. 87) that the Maestro

    a. likes a tidy house.

    b. is the kind of person who quickly buys the latest gadgets for his house.

    c. did not delight in the developments that made other houses of his time well-organized.

    d. is too poor to afford new things.

_____ 9. What type of figurative language is used in the line "The wraithlike fingers glided and wove the opening bars of 'Clair de Lune,' slender and delicate as spider silk" (par. 25)?

    a. a simile   b. a metaphor

_____ 10. The line "The light over the music rack was an eerie island in the brown shadows of the studio" (par. 65) uses a

    a. simile.   b. metaphor.

11. List two of the Maestro's characteristics and two of Rollo's. Explain how these traits are important to the story.

_____

_____

_____

_____

_____

_____

_____

12. Explain how the following lines relate to the end of the story: "Mozart and Chopin are not for vacuum tubes and fuses and copper wire. They are for flesh and blood and human tears" (par. 13).

_____

_____

_____

_____

13. What inference can you make about when the story takes place? Give two examples from the story to show how you reached this conclusion.

_____

_____

_____

_____

14. List three lines of dialogue that you found especially revealing as you annotated the story.

_____

_____

_____

15. Paraphrase the sentence " 'I assimilated that much by observation,' Rollo replied in a brassy baritone which no longer sent tiny tremors up the Maestro's spine" (par. 10).

_____

_____

_____

Vocabulary

Use context clues to determine the meaning of each word by referring back to the paragraph where the word is used (the paragraph number is in parentheses). If you need help, consult a dictionary for the definition.

A. Match each word to its synonym.

1. urge _____
2. hidden _____
3. absorb _____
4. flexible _____
5. uselessly _____

> **supple** (5) **assimilate(d)** (10) **futilely** (18)
> **latent** (45) **coax(ing)** (56)

B. Finish the sentences using the vocabulary words. Use each word once.

> **droned** (14) **anachronisms** (87) **virtuoso** (94) **repertoire** (96) **monotone** (108)

1. The students' interest began to wane as the professor _____ on about the importance of textile mills in eighteenth-century England.

2. The _____ were easy to spot. A tractor and skyscraper were both out of place in a painting of ancient Egypt.

3. Bonnie is a cello _____; she plays with world-class symphonies.

4. It is hard to tell when Earl is excited because he always speaks in a _____.

5. The pianist's _____ is diverse. He can play classical and contemporary music.

C. Word parts: Fill in the meaning that corresponds to the underlined word part. Return to pages 85–87 if you need to review the meaning of a word part.

> **time** **to make** **one** **not**

1. My friend told me to <u>dis</u>regard (8) his e-mail. Since he was no longer free for dinner, the e-mail was _____ important any longer.

2. I wanted to quickly assimi<u>late</u> (10) to life in Japan. _____ the transition faster, I started eating a typical Japanese diet and speaking Japanese all the time.

3. I belong to a group that stages plays filled with ana<u>chron</u>isms (87). The audience loves seeing how we alter _____, such as putting alarm clocks in plays set in ancient Rome.

4. The lecturer spoke in a <u>mono</u>tone (108) for two hours. Using _____ tone made his talk really boring.

The Short Story and You

1. Reread paragraphs 21–32, and then form your own answer to Rollo's question in paragraph 21. Use two of your favorite songs or pieces of music to support your explanation.

_____

_____

2. List two activities that you feel it would be better to have humans do instead of robots. List two activities that would be preferable for robots to do. Think about a variety of fields from sports to business to medicine. Briefly explain your choices.

_____

_____

3. The Maestro's house is described as "an oasis of anachronisms in a desert of contemporary antiseptic efficiency" (par. 87). List two situations where you would prefer to see "antiseptic efficiency" and two where a more colorful or exciting inefficiency (a little chaos) would be more fun.

_____

_____

4. On a separate sheet of paper, write a paragraph where you are the Maestro when he wakes up and discovers Rollo playing the piano. Describe your reaction to Rollo's ability. Use dialogue if you want to converse with Rollo.

Take a Closer Look

Look at the photo again. Now that you have read the short story, describe your reaction to the music room.

_____

_____

Internet Activities

If needed, use a separate sheet of paper to fully record your responses. Include the Web address of any sites from which you gather information.

1. Look up Chopin, Mozart, Debussy, or Beethoven on a site where you can listen to music. Listen to and record the name of one work. Explain whether you agree with Rollo that "The sounds were well formed . . . they did not jar my auditory senses as some do" (par. 29).

_____

2. The Maestro says, "To instill the Muse into metal and machinery . . . I accept the challenge gladly!" (par. 44). Look up "Muses." Who are the Muses? How many are there? List their names and the area to which each is related.

_____

_____

_____

_____

PEARSON myreadinglab | **Objectives Check**

To check your progress in meeting chapter objectives, log in to www.myreadinglab.com, click on the Study Plan tab, and then on the Reading Skills tab. Choose Inference from the list of subtopics. Read and view the resources in the Review Materials section, then complete the Practices and Tests in the Activities section. You can check your scores by clicking on the Gradebook tab.

CHAPTER 9

In what ways do you interact with nature?

The Environment

Interacting with a Changing Planet

Skill: Critical Thinking

We live in it, we abuse it, we embrace it, and we fear it: the environment. The world around us can be a beautiful and nurturing place, but it also holds powerful forces like hurricanes, tornados, and earthquakes that threaten our homes and our lives. We need to learn how to cope with the challenges nature brings because these threats will not disappear. We also need to learn how to protect the air, water, land, and animals that make up our environment. The various interactions between the environment and humans cannot be ignored because we all depend on the planet and its resources for our survival.

Humans will need to use their critical-thinking skills to deal with environmental changes. Critical thinking is the mental ability to vigorously analyze and evaluate information to reach a conclusion. Critical thinking involves using several skills to make a wise decision about a situation. You have been using critical thinking as you approached each reading in this text and answered the various questions at the end of a reading. Deciding what the main idea is or how a reading is organized or what the writer's purpose is all take critical-thinking skills. This chapter covers two final topics where you will need to aim your critical-thinking abilities: faulty logic and figurative language. In analyzing the following four essays or articles, textbook excerpt, and short story you will continue to develop your critical-thinking skills as you explore the changes and challenges our planet faces.

- Spot faulty logic.
- Recognize a few common fallacies.
- Interpret figurative language in the forms of similes and metaphors.

Critical Thinking

Critical thinking is an essential skill to help one through college and life. **Critical thinking** is the ability to logically and vigorously analyze and evaluate information in order to reach a conclusion. For example, at a party you meet a man, Ted, who is quite charming and intelligent. He tells you about an investment opportunity that with just two hundred dollars he can guarantee you will make fifty-thousand dollars in one year, but he needs your money by ten the following morning. Emotionally you may want to give Ted the two hundred dollars right there. You think, "Wow, I could make fifty-thousand dollars without spending much money!" He seems honest, his business card looks impressive, and he has called over a past client who tells you how much money she made. But before you hand over the money, it would be wise to use critical thinking. Analyze the situation (Why does he need the money by ten?), evaluate the information he has given you (How do you know that the woman he introduced you to is really a former client?), and consider what he hasn't told you (How can this investment guarantee such a high return?). By taking the time to look closely at a situation, to ask questions, and to find answers to those questions, you are using critical-thinking skills. Using these skills can provide for more rewarding experiences whether in your work or personal life, or when reading an article, essay, textbook, or short story.

Faulty Logic

Occasionally the points a writer makes are not well thought out or developed. Part of your job as an active and critically thinking reader is to be aware of these flaws in thinking, or faulty logic. Sometimes faulty logic is accidental. The writer gets carried away by the topic and doesn't take the time to carefully think out his or her points. At other times, writers intentionally use flawed arguments to manipulate the reader, especially when they don't have a strong argument to begin with. One way to be aware of faulty logic is to learn a few common fallacies.

A **fallacy** is an idea that is based on faulty logic or perception. More than a hundred types of formal fallacies exist. You don't need to know the names of all of them to be able to detect a flaw in the logic used by a writer, but being aware of the existence of fallacies and knowing the details about a few commonly used ones can prompt you to look for faulty thinking. You may come across faulty logic in a letter to the editor in your local paper, on a television ad, and even, at times, in your own thinking. Below are a few basic steps to follow in your search for faulty logic.

- **Check that the evidence used to support a proposal is relevant to the argument.**
- **Decide whether enough support is given to make a strong case.**

- **See if the organization clearly shows how one action leads to another and will produce the result the writer asserts.**
- **Look closely at the words chosen to support an argument. Ask yourself if they show any bias or try to manipulate the reader through emotional appeals.**
- **Decide if there are other possible outcomes besides the one(s) the writer presents.**

Examples

Listed below are four common fallacies with their definitions and a tip on what "To look for" to help you recognize the fallacy.

- **Appeal to emotion:** The arguer uses words or images to appeal to people's feelings instead of their minds. The appeal can be to any number of emotions, including anger, fear, envy, pity, or hatred.

  To look for: See if there are emotionally charged words or images that work to obscure the lack of a logical argument.

- **False dilemma or black and white thinking:** The writer presents a situation as having only two choices when there are other possibilities.

  To look for: Ask yourself if there are other alternatives than the two presented, and question why they weren't offered as choices.

- **Hasty generalization or leaping to a conclusion:** The arguer reaches a conclusion (usually a sweeping one) based on too small of a sample, too few situations, or an uncommon situation.

  To look for: Consider whether the sample size is sufficient or if the circumstance is a regular one. Also look for words that show all-encompassing conclusions, such as "never" or "always." If a writer uses qualifiers, such as "usually" or "sometimes," the statement probably doesn't fit as a hasty generalization.

- **Slippery slope:** The arguer reasons that one action will lead to a chain reaction with the outcome usually being something horrible, but the path from action A to result D isn't clearly shown.

  To look for: Check the chain of events in the argument and see if it is a reasonable one, or whether there is even evidence to show how the situation would move from point A to the conclusion D.

Identify the type of fallacy that each example illustrates, and briefly explain how the example fits the characteristics of the fallacy.

1. After three days of searching for a parking space at noon during the first week of the semester, Primo declares, "There are never enough parking spots on this campus!"

    _____

    _____

_____

_____

_____

2. If we ban handguns, the United States will become completely defenseless and be invaded by a ruthless dictator in a matter of months.

_____

_____

_____

_____

3. The kids dashed to the car excited to be going to Grandma's house. Mom carefully buckled up her treasures and merrily started the car. It was a rainy day and the roads were slick. The curve was sharper than she had realized. Smash! She could faintly hear her children's cries and the sound of the ambulance. If only Mom had had Suretread tires, they would have all seen Grandma's smiling face that afternoon.

_____

_____

_____

_____

_____

4. Either cut up your credit cards or go into debt.

_____

_____

_____

_____

_____

Read the following paragraphs and identify the fallacies and sentence(s) you find them in for each of the paragraphs. There is more than one fallacy in each paragraph.

1. Mayor Thomson's latest proposal to make the city more environmentally friendly will never work.[1] Do you want to see your job disappear when another factory closes because it causes too much pollution according to the mayor's plan?[2] Picture the thousands of families forced out of their homes when they can't pay their mortgages.[3] Think about the business you run and the customers you will no longer have.[4] Our storefronts will be boarded up, our houses empty, our beloved city will become a ghost town.[5] After talking to half a dozen citizens who agree that Mayor Thomson doesn't know what is best for our city, it is easy to conclude that voting "no" on Proposition Q is the only way to keep jobs in our city.[6]

    _____

    _____

2. We either build a light rail system or traffic will continue to get worse on our freeways.[1] The congestion on our roads today has most commuters stuck in traffic for an average of 15 minutes each evening.[2] As the county continues to grow, traffic will only get worse, and before you know it, you will be sitting in traffic for two hours for what should be a 20-minute commute.[3] As traffic backs up, road rage will increase, and we can expect to see hundreds of people wounded or dead from shootings.[4] Just last week, I observed the start of such road rage when a woman screamed obscenities at a man after he cut in front of her in a long line of traffic.[5] His response was an unfriendly hand gesture.[6] Without a doubt, this kind of behavior happens hundreds of times a week throughout the county.[7] Act now and write your state representative demanding action be taken on getting a light rail system started before the bloodshed begins.[8]

    _____

    _____

Figurative Language

Figurative language creates vivid images for the reader between unlike items by using direct or implied comparisons. The two most common types of figurative language are similes and metaphors. By using similes and metaphors, a writer can create vivid pictures of a person, a place, an experience, or a feeling. Figurative language can also help to create a mood or tone. Figurative language is most often found in fiction—short stories, novels, plays, and poetry—but it can also be found in nonfiction, such as essays and articles.

Examples

Simile: a figure of speech that compares two unlike things, introduced by the word *like* or *as*

> Howard can be <u>as</u> prickly as a cactus.

> My bedroom is <u>like</u> a cup of cocoa.

Metaphor: a figure of speech that makes a direct comparison between things that are not literally alike

> Life <u>is</u> an ocean.

An overused simile or metaphor is called a **cliché** (e.g., Gerry is as cool as a cucumber). Clichés don't add the freshness to writing that an original simile or metaphor does. In fact, clichés are such commonplace expressions that they usually make a piece of writing dull. Original uses of figurative language, however, make writing fresh and offer the reader new perspectives.

To understand a simile or metaphor, follow the steps below:

Determine what two items are being compared. In the examples above: Howard and a cactus, a bedroom and a cup of cocoa, life and an ocean.

Consider the various meanings or qualities associated with the item to which the first thing is being compared. Sometimes the meaning of a comparison can be hard to understand, and that is when the reader needs to use critical thinking to analyze the simile or metaphor. Use inference to help decide what the writer means. Explore the connotations of a word.

In the example above, what are the qualities of a cactus? It has sharp needles that can hurt a person, it isn't something one wants to touch, and it doesn't need much water. What associations are there with cocoa? It is usually considered a comforting drink. It may have connections to childhood: something kids drink to warm up on cold days or that people enjoy as they sit by the fire sharing family stories. What are the qualities of an ocean? The following list provides a few connections: huge, scary, dangerous, filled with beautiful creatures, mysterious, wet, blue, and one can play in it, swim in it, or drown in it.

Connect the pertinent meanings or qualities to the item to which it is being compared. Now you need to evaluate the qualities you came up with to see which ones best apply. It makes more sense to apply the not-wanting-to-touch quality of the cactus to Howard than the not-needing-much-water. The comparison then creates a vivid picture of Howard as a person who isn't always easy to be around. The bedroom is probably a comforting place where the owner feels safe since it is like a cup of cocoa. The ocean metaphor could have several interpretations from a single sentence. If the metaphor is seen in a larger context, the reader would likely be able to make stronger connections. For now, the reader might decide that the ocean metaphor means that life involves both beautiful and scary elements.

ACTIVITY 3

Identify which type of figurative language each of the following examples shows, which two items are being compared, and what the comparison means.

1. Though Sid is biscuits and gravy and Gloria pate and caviar, their marriage has been a happy one for 25 years.

   _____

   _____

   _____

2. Our quilts were rolled around us, like two thick cocoons, very warm.

   —from *The Kitchen God's Wife* by Amy Tan

   _____

   _____

3. Getting an "A" in Professor Ramsey's chemistry class is as easy as climbing Mount Everest.

   _____

   _____

   _____

4. I was the page from yesterday's calendar crumpled at the bottom of the waste basket.

   —from *The Little Sister* by Raymond Chandler

   _____

   _____

   _____

5. Laurene will be back with our coffee as quick as a wink.

   _____

   _____

ACTIVITY 4

Try making a few of your own similes and metaphors by finishing the following comparisons. If you get stuck, common items to make comparisons to are animals, food, and nature (flowers, trees, bodies of water).

1. The moon rose like _____

2. The movie was as boring as _____

3. Life is like _____

4. My friend is _____

5. Happiness is _____

Critical Thinking Checklist

Faulty Logic

✓ Check that the evidence used to support a proposal is relevant to the argument.

✓ Determine whether enough support is given to make a strong case.

✓ See if the organization clearly shows how one action leads to another and will produce the result the writer asserts.

✓ Look closely at the writer's words to determine if they show any bias or try to manipulate the reader through emotional appeals.

✓ Decide if there are other possible outcomes besides the one(s) the writer presents.

✓ Be aware of fallacies as a way to look for faulty logic.

Figurative Language

✓ Determine what two items are being compared.

✓ Consider the various meanings or qualities associated with the item to which the first thing is being compared.

✓ Connect the pertinent meanings or qualities to the item to which it is being compared.

Where to Hide from Mother Nature

by Brendan I. Koerner

Brendan I. Koerner is a journalist and contributing editor for *Wired* magazine. He is also a columnist for *Slate* magazine and the *New York Times*. He is a fellow at the New American Foundation, a think tank in Washington, D.C., created to promote "innovative political solutions" that reach across traditional party lines. He wrote *Now the Hell Will Start: One Soldier's Flight from the Greatest Manhunt of World War II*. The book tells about Herman Perry's experience as a fugitive in Southeast Asia during World War II. The following article originally appeared in *Slate* in September 2005.

Before You Read

1. What types of natural disasters occur most often in your state?
2. How safe do you consider yourself in relation to these natural disasters?
3. Where do you think would be the safest place to live in the United States? Refer to the map to help you narrow your choices.
4. Look at the photo. What do you think happened here?

Vocabulary Preview

Look for these words in the reading. Exercises to reinforce the learning of new vocabulary using these words follow the reading. The paragraph number where the word appears is in parentheses.

lethal (1)	**nil** (2)	**skewed** (4)	**fatality** (5)	**prolific** (6)
frigid (6)	**slew** (7)	**affluent** (8)	**dicey** (11)	**boonies** (12)

Wyoming? Nope. West Virginia? Think again.

1   # Human beings are self-absorbed creatures, so the response to Hurricane Katrina has naturally included some hand-wringing over the question: "Could this happen to my hometown?" Depending on the worrywart's location the theoretical catastrophe could be a flash flood, a wildfire, or an earthquake rather than a hurricane; no corner of the United States is immune to lethal natural disasters.

2   Still, some corners are safer than others. If an American wants to minimize his chances of dying at Mother Nature's hands, where should he set up house? *Slate* crunched the numbers—and did some educated guesswork—to find the U.S. city where the odds of perishing in a natural disaster are closest to nil.

3   We started by taking a look at every presidential disaster declaration from 1965 through 2004. The Eastern half of the nation has had the most officially declared disasters, although North Dakota, Washington, and California have endured more than their share of woe. Going by presidential decrees alone, then, Western states such as Nevada or Wyoming appear safest.

4   But the data are skewed by the fact that disasters are more likely to be declared in populated areas. Disasters are declared in order to make funds available to people and businesses affected by a catastrophe. So, a severe storm in the Milwaukee suburbs is a lot likelier to be declared a federal disaster than a severe storm in an unpopulated expanse of southwestern Wyoming.

5   The declared disasters list was useful, however, in helping to eliminate the obvious noncontenders. Like, say, California. The state's massive population gives it a low per-capita fatality rate for natural disasters, but no one would consider it a safe haven from nature's worst: it's susceptible to earthquakes, mudslides, wildfires, torrential rains, rip currents, and even volcanoes. Unsurprisingly, then, California has had more declared disasters than any other state but Texas, which is frequently hammered by tornadoes, thunderstorms, and floods.

6   For simplicity's sake—*Slate* still lacks a supercomputer to handle massive number-crunching assignments—we automatically eliminated the 30 states with the most declared disasters. Most were no-brainers, such as the hurricane-prone states of the Gulf Coast and the heartland states that lie in Tornado Alley. Sparsely populated North Dakota has regular problems with severe flooding, as do Virginia, Tennessee, and New York. (Flooding, tornadoes, and tropical storms/hurricanes have been the most prolific killers in recent years, although heat waves often take significant tolls.) Illinois and Pennsylvania didn't make the grade because their cities can get lethally hot. Also disqualified were some notably frigid members of the union, such as Wisconsin and Minnesota; blizzards and icy conditions are frequently deadly, especially for motorists. And seemingly placid West Virginia? It has some issues with landslides, particularly in the counties that border Ohio.

7   That left 20 states, two of which we knocked out immediately on common-sense grounds: Hawaii, since islands are inherently at the ocean's mercy (plus there's a slew of volcanoes), and Alaska, where severe winter storms are the norm. For the remaining 18 states, then, we looked at year-by-year fatalities resulting from severe weather, dating back to 1995, as recorded by the National Weather Service. The NWS statistics cover 27 different types of weather events, including such relative rarities as deaths due to volcanic ash, fog, dust devils, and "miscellaneous." (Since California had been eliminated at this stage, we ignored earthquake fatalities, which the NWS does not track.) We then used the total number of fatalities from each state to arrive at a deaths-per-thousand figure, based on population numbers taken from the 2000 Census.

8   Of the 18 states, only three had a fatality rate lower than 0.01 per thousand for the last decade: Connecticut (0.00587 per thousand), Massachusetts (0.00299), and Rhode Island (0.00286). These figures are somewhat surprising, given that all three of these New England states have ample coastlines and are thus susceptible to fierce storms. But they are also more immune to hurricanes than their southerly counterparts, virtually free of tornadoes, and blessed with relatively cool summers and winters that, although cold, aren't quite North Dakota cold. They're also affluent—all three boast family median incomes above

the national average—and, as Hurricane Katrina reminded us, socioeconomics matter when it comes to preserving life during natural disasters.

9   For the three finalists, we looked at the county-by-county breakdowns of presidential-disaster declarations since 1995. Rhode Island only had one, during the Blizzard of '96. Connecticut was hit by that storm, too, as well as by Tropical Storm Floyd in 1999, which affected Litchfield, Hartford, and Fairfield counties. Massachusetts, meanwhile, had five major declared disasters, mostly associated with heavy rains and flooding in its seven easternmost counties.

10   Based solely on the numbers, then, Rhode Island would seem to be the winner. But the tiny state's cities are clustered around bays and rivers, which means a major hurricane could cause flooding. During the Great New England Hurricane of 1938, for example, a violent storm surge hit Providence.

11   Eastern Massachusetts is dicey because its long coastline is exposed to the unforgiving Atlantic Ocean. The rural west has proven statistically safer, but winter in the Berkshires can be snowy and harsh.

12   That leaves Connecticut, whose coastline faces the Long Island Sound rather than the open ocean. Still, living near the water is not recommended for the truly tense; a safer bet is somewhere inland, away from rivers and lakes, but not too deep in the boonies. The state's winters aren't tropical, but they tend to be not quite as snowbound as those in western Massachusetts.

13   After much debate, then, we settled on *Slate's* "America's Best Place to Avoid Death Due to Natural Disaster": the area in and around Storrs, Conn., home to the University of Connecticut. It lies in Tolland County, which was not part of the 1999 federal disaster declaration for Tropical Storm Floyd. It's a safe 50 miles from the sound and not close to any rivers. It also has relatively easy access to a major city (Hartford) in the event an evacuation or hospitalization becomes necessary.

14   This conclusion is by no means scientific, nor can safety ever be completely guaranteed; as moviegoers and Rick Moody fans are already aware, Connecticut does have its share of dangerous ice storms. And we're open to suggestions about other candidates for the title. If you want to make a case for your hometown, please drop us a line. In the meantime, the parents of UConn students can sleep a little easier tonight.

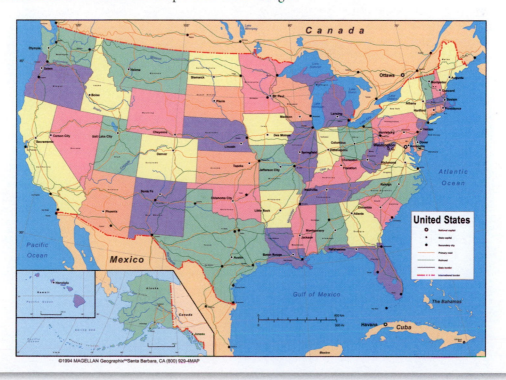

Getting the Message

____ **1.** The topic of the article is
- a. Hurricane Katrina.
- b. natural disasters.
- c. the dangers of living in California.
- d. a safe place to live.

____ **2.** Which sentence expresses the central idea of paragraph 6?
- a. sentence 1
- b. sentence 2
- c. sentence 4
- d. sentence 7

____ **3.** What is the main idea of the article?
- a. People are more likely to die in the Gulf Coast states than anywhere else in the United States.
- b. Connecticut can have dangerous ice storms.
- c. Natural disasters kill thousands of people each year.
- d. Though no place is guaranteed safe from natural disasters, some cities are safer than others.

____ **4.** Two types of supporting details used in the article are
- a. testimony and facts.
- b. examples and statistics.
- c. reasons and testimony.
- d. personal examples and hypothetical examples.

____ **5.** The sentence "Unsurprisingly, then, California has had more declared disasters than any other state but Texas, which is frequently hammered by tornadoes, thunderstorms, and floods" expresses
- a. a fact.
- b. an opinion.

____ **6.** The article is ordered using the _____ format.
- a. chronological
- b. least to most important
- c. most to least important
- d. problem and solution

____ **7.** The article uses the _____ pattern of organization.
- a. comparison and contrast
- b. cause and effect
- c. narrative
- d. definition

____ **8.** Paragraph 9 uses _____ transition words.
- a. addition and time
- b. time and cause and effect
- c. comparison and contrast
- d. importance and addition

____ **9.** Koerner's purpose is to
- a. convince people to move to Storrs.
- b. amuse people by describing different types of natural disasters.
- c. inform people about the risks of living in different states.

____ **10.** It can be inferred from paragraphs 3 and 4 that Nevada
- a. is heavily populated.
- b. is not heavily populated.
- c. has only one major city: Las Vegas.
- d. has never had a major natural disaster.

11. What can you infer from the phrase "After much debate, we settled on . . ." (par. 13)?

_____

_____

_____

_____

12. Is the tone of the article formal or informal? Give three examples of words or phrases that helped you make your decision.

_____

_____

_____

13. Has Koerner made a hasty generalization in reaching his conclusion about the city safest from natural disasters in the United States?

_____

_____

_____

_____

14. Look at your annotations of the article. List two of the questions or comments you wrote in the margins that you would most like to discuss with the class.

_____

_____

_____

_____

15. On a separate sheet of paper, write a summary of the article.

Vocabulary

Use context clues to determine the meaning by looking back at the paragraph where the word is used (the paragraph number is in parentheses). If you need help, consult a dictionary for the definition.

A. Match each vocabulary word to its antonym.

> **nil** (2)   **skewed** (4)   **prolific** (6)   **frigid** (6)   **slew** (7)

1. few _____
2. everything _____
3. hot _____
4. unbiased _____
5. limited _____

B. Match each word to the appropriate example.

> **lethal** (1)   **fatality** (5)   **affluent** (8)   **dicey** (11)   **boonies** (12)

1. After three hours of driving, we pulled into a town with one gas station, one restaurant, and a corner market. _____
2. We tried to cross a rickety bridge suspended above a deep canyon. _____
3. The likely result if a person takes a whole bottle of sleeping pills. _____
4. The couple drives a Ferrari, she often wears a diamond necklace, and they own a mansion. _____
5. The man's body was taken to the morgue after the car accident. _____

C. Word parts: Use the words to help you connect the word part to its meaning. Return to pages 85–87 if you need to review the meaning of a word part.

1. un-: unpopulated, unsurprisingly, unforgiving ____
2. -ist: motorist, finalist, survivalist ____
3. -y: dicey, snowy, icy ____
4. -clar-: declaration, declared, clarify ____

a. a person who
b. clear
c. not
d. being, having

The Article and You

1. What is the most severe weather condition or weather-related event you have ever faced? Was the situation scary?

_____

_____

2. What state wouldn't you want to live in because of the natural disasters it may or does face (such as California for earthquakes)? Refer to the article for natural disasters common to certain areas. Use the map on page 381 to help you make your decision. Explain your reasoning.

_____

_____

_____

3. Would you rather be faced with surviving a heat wave or a blizzard? Why?

_____

_____

_____

4. On a separate sheet of paper, write a paragraph in which you agree or disagree with the statement "socioeconomics matter when it comes to preserving life during natural disasters" (par. 8). Think about the kinds of evidence you would want to gather to support or counter this statement.

Take a Closer Look

Look at the photo again. The photo is of Highway 90 ruined by Hurricane Katrina. Does it surprise you that the damage is from a hurricane? What are two actions you think humans can take to protect themselves from the violence of nature?

_____

_____

_____

Internet Activities

If needed, use a separate sheet of paper to fully record your responses. Include the Web address of any sites from which you gather information.

1. Look up the Federal Emergency Management Administration (FEMA) site at fema.gov. Once there click on the "Declared Disasters and Emergencies" page. Find the number of declared disasters for your state. What were the major causes of these disasters? Write a summary of the information you find for your state.

_____

_____

2. Look up "Sperling's Best Places." Here you can compare cities in various areas including crime, cost of living, and climate. Compare your city to another city in three different categories and create a chart or other visual that shows how these two cities differ.

by Janet Eastman
and Bettijane Levine

Stuffing a Lifetime into a Suitcase

Before You Read

1. What are three items you would grab if you had to evacuate your home?

2. Are your choices practical or emotional?

3. Would these items be easy or hard to find and pack?

4. Look at the photograph. What do you think of the women's choice as an item to save?

Vocabulary Preview

Look for these words in the reading. Exercises to reinforce the learning of new vocabulary using these words follow the reading. The paragraph number where the word appears is in parentheses.

irreplaceable (3)	**inconsequential** (3)	**reign** (4)
emeritus (5)	**frenzy** (8)	**cherish** (8)
indispensable (9)	**inadvertently** (11)	**combustible** (18)	**hypothetical** (19)

Janet Eastman and Bettijane Levine are reporters for the *Los Angeles Times*. They often cover design, homes, fashion, and relationship topics. The following article was written at the time of the 2007 wildfires in southern California. The fires burned at least 1,500 homes and destroyed more than 500,000 acres of land. One million people were forced to evacuate their homes, resulting in the largest evacuation in U.S. history. The fires began on October 20 and were fully contained 19 days later on November 9. The article appeared in the October 25 issue of the *Los Angeles Times*.

The article begins on the next page.

Stuffing a Lifetime into a Suitcase

By JANET EASTMAN and BETTIJANE LEVINE
Los Angeles Times

1 LOS ANGELES—The decisions are made in a scary, smoky instant. A wildfire is blazing toward the front door: What to take to safety? What to leave behind?

2 One woman in Malibu grabbed her old wedding ring and divorce papers. A Santa Clarita man showed up at an evacuation center with four suitcases but little memory of what he and his wife threw into them. "Probably not what we need," he said, clutching his pillow. An Escondido woman, her head cloudy with panic, rescued her $1,000 Christian Louboutin shoes.

3 Practical or sentimental, irreplaceable or as inconsequential as a carton of orange juice, the belongings that fire evacuees packed up before fleeing home speak to the daunting task of distilling a life into a backpack, a suitcase or the trunk of a car.

4 In the chaos of disaster, logic doesn't always reign. Los Angeles psychologist Helen Lena Astin said there's no predicting what people see as essential in times of crisis. She remembers a friend doubling back to his house during a 1978 fire to retrieve his tuxedo. He later explained that it was difficult to find a tuxedo that fit him well.

5 "That's crazy, but it's interesting," said Astin, a researcher and professor emeritus at the University of California, Los Angeles. "Of all the things to worry about. But people make snap decisions, not always about what is practical, but what's valuable to them at the time."

6 Some people save photographs, but in the neighborhoods threatened by fires this week, evacuees also were loaded down with high-school yearbooks, college dissertations, tax returns, concert tickets, skateboards.

7 After a night of watching the flames creep closer to her driveway, Alyson Dutch was told Monday morning to leave her home in Malibu. All she remembered was flinging open her wardrobe closet, stuffing a pair of cowboy boots and a down jacket into a bag, tossing her computer and insurance papers into a box, then corralling her dog and cat into her Porsche.

8 Hours later, at her brother's house, she reached into her pocket and was surprised to find a feline-shaped piece of jade that she kept by her nightstand. In the frenzy to pack, she apparently had thought to grab a jewelry box that holds a childhood rosary, charms her mother gave her and an old postcard from her late father. "I cherish these things," she said. "If the rest burns, it's all replaceable."

9 The California Department of Forestry and Fire Protection recommends that people not only devise an evacuation plan but also draw up a list of indispensable belongings to take in the event of a disaster: medications, identification, vital documents and valuables. At one evacuation center, some of the Santa Clarita Valley residents forced to leave their homes had thought to take birth certificates and ATM cards.

10 Those with extra minutes and extra space in their cars took advantage of both.

11 Under a glowing sky, Dawn Elder packed her mother's ashes but inadvertently left home without the family's three cats. "We had to run back and get them and bring them to a friend," said Elder, a mother of two.

12 Ken Zachary and Dallas Blair had stashed food and supplies in case of an earthquake but were unprepared for fire. When sheriff's officials told them to evacuate, they debated what to take. Blair focused on clothes; Zachary hunted for paperwork they might need later. "We wound up with four suitcases," he said, "and we still don't know exactly what's in them."

13 Police told John and Cruz Gingiloski to leave their Rancho Santa Fe house Monday, and in the 20-minute dash to pack, Cruz left her jewelry and the contents of the couple's vault—and grabbed her scarves. "I don't know why I thought I needed them," she said. "It's 90 degrees outside, but for some reason I wanted them, too."

14 She also packed a box of cards from her grandchildren, a cross that had belonged to her mother and the American flag that had been draped on her father's coffin.

15 Therapist Gary Bell of San Bernardino-based Counseling Team International, which provides support services to police and fire departments, remembers one man who tried to push his great-grandfather's piano out of a house during a blaze. The man wasn't merely saving the piano, Bell said. He was rescuing a reminder of family.

16 "The keepsake that leads them to the memory of a loved one is the thing that will go with them," Bell said.

17 Malibu resident Rory Crowder and wife Shannon Rubicam volunteer for a neighborhood arson-watch program and coincidentally plotted an escape plan two weeks ago. They had an evacuation packing list prepared.

18 "We were well aware of the risk of fire with these high winds, dry conditions and combustible brush," Crowder said.

19 "I'm grateful we thought about it when it was just hypothetical, and our brain cells weren't oozing out of our ears in a panic," Rubicam said.

20 They packed lightly, leaving the commercially valuable art on the wall. Instead, they packed photographs their daughter had taken, the 1890s artwork of Rubicam's grandmother, and paintings formerly owned by Crowder's late father.

21 Left behind: boxes of family photographs that were too large to fit into the cars.

22 "I remembered someone saying that they would rather have the things that someone did than pictures of that person," Rubicam said.

23 "What we have with us now are pieces of the person in action, which means more to us."

24 When the couple drove north on Las Flores Canyon Road, on the way to safety in the San Fernando Valley, they stopped on a ridge where neighbors had gathered to see the canyon burn below. A woman stood nearby, her eyes fixed on the scene, her hands gripped to the cherished possession she had spirited away from home: an urn holding the ashes of her dog.

Getting the Message

_____ **1.** Where is the topic sentence in paragraph 12 located?

    a. sentence 1   c. sentence 3

    b. sentence 2   d. sentence 4

_____ **2.** The main idea of the article is that people

    a. react logically during an emergency.

    b. do not always react logically when faced with the decision of what to take during an evacuation.

    c. people have a clear of idea of what to take when they have to evacuate their homes.

    d. usually take sensible items when they are forced to evacuate.

_____ **3.** What types of supporting details do the writers use?

    a. examples and statistics   c. examples and testimony

    b. examples and reasons   d. testimony and personal examples

_____ **4.** The article contains _____ examples.

    a. short

    b. extended

    c. both short and extended

_____ **5.** The article uses the following patterns of organization:

    a. process and narrative.   c. comparison and contrast and definition.

    b. classification and definition.   d. cause and effect and examples.

_____ **6.** Which type of transition word is used most often in the article?

    a. order of importance   c. contrast

    b. example   d. addition

_____ **7.** Eastman and Levine's purpose is to

    a. inform.   c. entertain and persuade.

    b. persuade.   d. inform and persuade.

_____ **8.** The intended audience for the article is most likely

    a. children.   c. people over 50.

    b. southern Californians.   d. women.

_____ **9.** The tone of the article is _____.

    a. objective   c. sad

    b. mad   d. scary

_____ **10.** It can be inferred that the items the women in paragraphs 8 and 14 take with them are worth saving because they

    a. are worth a lot of money.   c. relate to family members.

    b. were given as presents.   d. are old.

11. Do the writers use the appeal to emotion fallacy? Explain why or why not.

_____

_____

_____

_____

12. In paragraph 11, Dawn Elder packs "under a glowing sky." Use this image to create your own similes.

Under a sky glowing like _____

Under a sky glowing as _____

13. What can be inferred about the economic status of several of the people mentioned in the article? Give three examples that helped you come to this conclusion.

_____

_____

_____

_____

_____

_____

14. List two points you annotated in the article. Why did you pick these points?

_____

_____

_____

15. Paraphrase the following sentence: "Ken Zachary and Dallas Blair had stashed food and supplies in case of an earthquake but were unprepared for fire" (par. 12).

_____

_____

_____

Vocabulary

Use context clues to determine the meaning of each word by referring back to the paragraph where the word is used (the paragraph number is in parentheses). If you need help, consult a dictionary for the definition.

A. Match each vocabulary word to its synonym.

> **inconsequential** (3) **frenzy** (8) **indispensable** (9) **inadvertently** (11) **hypothetical** (19)

1. unintentionally _____   4. rush _____

2. unimportant _____   5. supposed _____

3. essential _____

B. If the sentence uses the underlined vocabulary word correctly, put a *T* for true, and if the word is used incorrectly, put an *F* for false.

_____ 1. This pencil is <u>irreplaceable</u> (3); I just bought it at the drug store.

_____ 2. Olivia usually lets her serious side <u>reign</u> (4) even when the situation calls for some silliness.

_____ 3. Professor Remsburg is a professor <u>emeritus</u> (5). It is her first year of teaching.

_____ 4. I <u>cherish</u> (8) the glass elephant my favorite aunt gave me when I was seven.

_____ 5. Water is a highly <u>combustible</u> (18) substance, and it must be watched carefully in times of dry weather.

C. Word parts: Fill in the missing word part for each word. Return to pages 85–87 if you need to review the meaning of a word part.

> **il**   **im**   **in**   **ir**

1. The vase was made by my great-grandmother. It is _____ replaceable.

2. I can't find a thing in my office without Janice's help. She is _____ dispensable.

3. It did not make sense for her to take frozen meat to the evacuation center; she was being _____ logical.

4. Trying to save the piano was _____ practical. It would never fit in his car.

5. The word parts "il," "im," "in," and "ir" all mean _____.

The Article and You

1. After reading the article, would you still take the three items you thought about in the Before You Read section? Explain why or why not.

_____

_____

2. List four items you would definitely want to bring now that you have read the article, and briefly state why each item is important.

_____

_____

3. What do you need to do to make these items readily available in case you need to evacuate quickly?

_____

_____

4. On a separate sheet of paper, write a paragraph in which you envision yourself evacuating due to a natural disaster. You have been given 30 minutes' notice that you need to get out. What do you do in that time?

Take a Closer Look

Look at the photo again. List three reasons the women might be trying to save the painting. Refer back to the article to help you generate ideas.

_____

_____

_____

_____

_____

Internet Activities

If needed, use a separate sheet of paper to fully record your responses. Include the Web address of any sites from which you gather information.

1. Search for "what to save in a fire" or "tips on evacuating." Find two articles or sites with recommendations on what to save or on what people have taken. Were items mentioned that you hadn't already considered bringing? Write a summary of your findings. In the summary include a list of a few items common to the sites and a few unexpected, distinctive, or personal objects.

_____

_____

_____

_____

_____

2. Look up "disaster preparedness" or "go bag." List 10 items that are suggested you have ready to go at a moment's notice. Do you have such a bag prepared? Do you think you will assemble one now?

_____

_____

_____

_____

Mayors Take the Lead

by Anne Underwood with Matthew Phillips

Before You Read

1. How environmentally aware do you think your city is, with 10 being "extremely" to 1 being "not at all"?

2. Survey the article, and write your own question that you think the article may address:

   _____

3. How serious of a problem do you consider global warming?

4. Look at the cartoon and photos. What comment about the environment is the cartoon making? What environmental trends do the photos show?

Anne Underwood has been a writer for *Newsweek* for 24 years. She specializes in health, fitness, and science. She is a co-writer of *The Color Code*, a book about the benefits of eating different colors of fruits and vegetables. Underwood has degrees in Russian studies and international relations from Yale and Columbia. She is also a part-time musician and has two CDs out featuring music from the 18th and 19th centuries. Matthew Philips has been a reporter for *Newsweek* since 2006; he mainly covers business and finance. He has a degree from the Graduate School of Journalism at Columbia University. The following article initially appeared in the April 16, 2007, issue of *Newsweek*.

Vocabulary Preview

Look for these words in the reading. Exercises to reinforce the learning of new vocabulary using these words follow the reading. The paragraph number where the word appears is in parentheses.

emissions (2)	**maverick** (3)	**sustainability** (4)	**initiative** (4)	**tote** (5)
windfall (6)	**audits** (9)	**accrue** (9)	**hybrids** (10)	**dither** (19)

1 # Sometimes
great ideas are born of born of desperation. For Seattle Mayor Greg Nickels, that sense of urgency developed in the winter of 2004–05, when the annual snowfall failed to materialize in the neighboring Cascade Mountains. That's a serious issue in Seattle, where melting snow feeds the city's reservoirs in the springtime and swells the river that supplies its hydroelectric energy. Nickels's advisers were coming to him weekly with reports that the snow pack was just 1 percent of normal. "I don't think 'normal' exists anymore," Nickels remembers saying, having endured a succession of unusually warm winters. "Normal would be cause for popping champagne corks."

2 Nickels wasn't the only one who was starting to worry about climate change. In February 2005, 141 nations worldwide were preparing to put the Kyoto Protocol into effect—aiming to reduce global warming by cutting greenhouse-gas emissions 7 percent below 1990 levels by 2012. The United States was notably not one of them, so Nickels decided to "show the world there was intelligent life in the United States after all" by getting American cities to commit to Kyoto's targets. He drafted a document called the U.S. Mayors Climate Protection Agreement and

presented it along with eight fellow mayors at the U.S. Conference of Mayors in March 2005. Their goal: to have 141 of their colleagues sign within a year, equaling the number of foreign countries that were party to Kyoto.

3   Two years later, a maverick idea has blossomed into a movement. To date, 435 mayors have signed on, Republican and Democratic, in Red States and Blue, from the crunchy coasts to the conservative heartland. Some of them govern cities with longstanding records of environmental activism, such as Chicago, San Francisco and Portland, Ore. But their ranks also include recent converts like conservative Republican Robert Cluck of Arlington, Texas, and Tom Barrett of Milwaukee, who just two years ago said it would be hard for him to join because of his city's commitment to promoting industry. Their combined efforts are now far more than symbolic. "These cities represent 61 million people," says Nickels. "That's equivalent to the population of France and larger than the United Kingdom."

4   The resources they bring to the task vary widely. In San Francisco, the city's Department of the Environment tackles sustainability with a staff of 70 people and a budget of $20 million. In Fayetteville, Ark., Mayor Dan Coody just hired his city's first sustainability director. Still, a remarkable patchwork of programs is emerging, from the creation of car-sharing schemes on the West Coast to a new initiative in Cambridge, Mass., that aims to green at least half the buildings in town. In the process, city officials are discovering that these measures save money, reduce demands on overstretched utilities and make cities more pleasant places to live and work. "We're not talking about some broad international policy that doesn't trickle down," says Coody. "Cities are where the rubber meets the road." Here are some ways they're taking action:

Energy Efficiency

5   Embarking on an environmental program sounds like a great idea. But if you're a mayor trying to cut greenhouse gases, where do you begin? How do you even know how to measure your current levels? That's where an organization called ICLEI—Local Governments for Sustainability can help. Founded in 1991, ICLEI provides computer software that walks city officials through the calculation one step at a time, helping tote up emissions from buildings (based on energy-consumption data from utilities) and vehicles (based on volume of traffic—that's what those little black strips on roads are for). The software even takes into account emissions from landfills, which generate methane, a potent greenhouse gas. ICLEI presents officials with a menu of energy-saving measures and helps calculate the reductions they can achieve from each. "We show them the low-, medium- and high-hanging fruit," says executive director Michelle Wyman.

6   One of the easiest measures is also one of the most cost effective. That's converting stoplights from incandescent bulbs to LEDs. On the downside, the conversion demands a major investment upfront. "When I found out the cost, it scared me," says Cluck in Arlington, Texas, noting that the new lights will cost his city $1.35 million. But since LEDs use 80 percent less energy than standard lights—and last six to 10 times longer—they pay for themselves in several years. After that, cities reap the savings. For Arlington, that's a projected windfall of more than $250,000 a year. In a larger city like New York, it's even more. The Big Apple—which has replaced 80,000 incandescent bulbs in 12,000 intersections—will realize savings of $6.3 million a year once the initial investment of $28 million is paid off.

7   There are dozens of other ways for a city government to cut its power use. Buildings themselves can be made more energy efficient with good insulation, tight ducts and efficient air-conditioning systems. "In cities, buildings account for 50 to 70 percent of energy consumption and, therefore, greenhouse-gas emissions," says Rob Pratt, head of the climate-change initiative at the Henry P. Kendall Foundation in Boston. Many municipalities now require that new government buildings meet the certification standards of the U.S. Green Building Council.

8   But to achieve ambitious energy-reduction targets, a city needs to get private developers and citizens onboard, too. One of the best examples is Austin, Texas, home to the nation's first green building program. A major citywide energy-conservation program in the 1990s allowed the city-owned utility to

avoid construction of a new 500-megawatt power plant that would have been needed by 2000. Now Mayor Will Wynn has an even more ambitions program: to make all new homes in Austin "zero-energy-capable" by 2015. That means they will draw 65 percent less energy than a new home built today—so little that the rest of their energy needs could be supplied by solar panels on the roof, if the homeowners installed them. "Houses like this are possible today," says Roger Duncan, deputy general manager of Austin Energy. But they require every energy-saving trick in the green builder's book.

9   The city of Cambridge is hoping for a more immediate impact with a sweeping $100 million initiative announced two weeks ago to cut the energy consumption of every neighborhood in town—municipal, university, commercial and residential alike. "Energy audits" of buildings will be provided free to those who want them, along with recommendations on how to cut energy use. To help owners make the suggested upgrades, low- or zero-interest loans will be available, to be repaid as savings accrue from the new efficiencies. Realistically, the organizers hope for a 50 percent participation rate, which would cut emissions an estimated 10 percent by 2012. The same program will soon roll out in Boston and four other Massachusetts cities.

Transportation

10   After buildings and lighting, the next obvious issue for a city to address is motor vehicles. As their fleets age, many towns are gradually converting their cars, garbage trucks, salt spreaders, tow trucks and fire engines to hybrids or alternative-fuel vehicles that use ethanol, compressed natural gas or biodiesel. In San Francisco, officials are going the extra mile, so to speak, and will soon use recaptured fat, oil and grease from restaurants to make biodiesel fuel for the city's garbage trucks. These fleet

Carbon Offset
The process of balancing a unit of carbon dioxide emissions with a product that saves or stores an equivalent amount of CO_2. Carbon credits are typically bought and sold through a number of online retailers and trading platforms.

upgrades "aren't quite as cost effective as lighting changes," says Garrett Fitzgerald, director of programs at ICLEI. "But they're simple to do, and they provide a great opportunity to reduce emissions."

11   Many cities are also encouraging private individuals and taxi companies to switch to hybrids and other high-efficiency vehicles by offering a variety of incentives. In Salt Lake City, says Mayor Rocky Anderson, "the transportation department will put a decal in your rear window, and you can park at any city meters without ever having to pay." And in Boston the Massachusetts Port Authority, which runs Logan airport, is about to start giving hybrid taxis two passes per shift allowing them to cut to the front of the passenger-pickup line. But the very existence of a program for hybrid taxis in Boston is due at least in part to a private initiative by architect John Moore, who last year got permission to follow a standard cab around town for a day in a borrowed Ford Escape hybrid. At the end of the day, the hybrid had used just 3.5 gallons of gas, versus 10.2 for the cab—and with fewer emissions. Moore's experiment helped persuade the city to approve hybrid cabs, a shift that could ultimately translate into greater reductions of greenhouse gases than for most autos, since cabs are on the road all day.

12   Better yet are trips not taken at all—at least not in privately owned cars. Des Moines, Iowa, has installed bike racks on the front of buses to make longer, car-free commutes more practical, and it has sponsored contests to design artistic bike racks for public spaces. In addition, a growing number of cities have seen the arrival of car-sharing programs like Flex-car in Seattle. For a $35 annual fee, you can go online and reserve cars parked at convenient locations. "Like a cash machine, there should always be one within a couple blocks," says spokesman John Williams. You pay $9 per hour, but the company covers gas, insurance and parking in designated spots. It's so convenient that about half the members end up selling an existing car or avoid buying a new one.

Vibrant Downtowns

13   New York is the most energy-efficient city in the nation, since millions of residents live in densely packed apartment buildings and rely on walking or public transit for most of their transportation needs. "New Yorkers use half the energy per capita as residents of other cities," says Deputy Mayor Dan Doctoroff.

14   No wonder cities across the country are trying to attract residents back downtown to live, not just work. In Miami, the city code and zoning laws are being overhauled for that very purpose. "Miami was developed haphazardly by engineers whose only interest was in making it easier for cars, so they built broad roads and narrow sidewalks," says Mayor Manny Diaz. "We want to change that, to have wide sidewalks, with shade trees and parks that create a pedestrian feel." Admittedly, the plan will take decades to implement, but Diaz seems committed to a broad range of shorter-term changes, too, including cleaning up city waterways and building green buildings. "We're on the front line of global climate change here," he says. "The water level doesn't have to rise too much for us to be riding around Miami in canoes."

15   The greening of city centers isn't just metaphorical. In Chicago, city officials have mapped the "heat islands," where asphalt and black roofs absorb heat and raise the city's overall temperature. These areas are then planted with trees—400,000 to date. "Trees are like big air conditioners," says Environment Commissioner Sadhu Johnston.

Carbon Neutral
Involves calculating your total carbon emissions, reducing them where possible, and balancing your remaining emissions by purchasing carbon offsets. In essence, you neutralize your personal footprint so as not to contribute to global warming.

They lower the temperature, filter air, remove carbon dioxide, absorb storm water and provide shade and beauty. (They even boost the economy. "Research has shown that people are willing to spend up to 12 percent more on a product if they're shopping in a district with mature trees," thanks to the pleasant ambience of the neighborhood, says Johnston.)

16   At Chicago's Center for Green Technology, the city also runs free programs on topics like planting green roofs, which are actual plots of grass on roofs. They absorb storm water, reduce heat loss in winter and help cool buildings in summer. "We run green-roof test plots to see how much they bring down the temperature," says Johnston. The verdict: a green roof can reduce the surface temperature of a summer-sundrenched roof from 170 degrees to just 80 to 90 degrees. Chicago has 300 such roofs already built or under development.

The Small Things

17   Then there are the little things we can all do. "If every household in America switched out one compact fluorescent bulb, it would reduce energy consumption as much as taking a million cars off the road," says Des Moines Mayor Frank Cownie. We could also start drinking tap water rather than the bottled variety. "Production of the bottles alone consumes over 1.5 million barrels of oil a year," says Rocky Anderson in Salt Lake City.

Even worse is the energy squandered on shipping water halfway around the world. As a result, he says, "you pay more for a bottle of water than an equivalent amount of gasoline." And we could carry our own mesh shopping bags. Two weeks ago, San Francisco grabbed headlines for banning nonbiodegradable plastic bags, which were costing the city $8 million a year to clear from streets, storm drains and recycling machines.

18   In the future, there will no doubt be more amazing ways of contributing.

San Francisco has major plans for renewable energy from solar, wind and even tidal power, which would be created by harnessing the tides flowing in and out through the narrow channel below the Golden Gate Bridge. Giant bidirectional blades would spin in the current, fueling generators. "And unlike solar and wind power, which are unpredictable, tidal power is incredibly reliable," says Jared Blumenfeld, director of the San Francisco Department of the Environment.

19   While the U.S. government continues to dither on climate change, foreign countries are sending representatives to San Francisco to study its green policies. "The Danish, Irish and French environment ministers have come to meet with us in the last six months," says Blumenfeld. "When we asked why, they said, 'Our governments are taking action at the federal level, but we have no idea what to do at the local level.'" America's green mayors could teach them a thing or two.

Getting the Message

___ 1. What is the topic?

    a. things mayors do   c. changes in American cities

    b. finding one's carbon footprint   d. the environment

___ 2. The topic sentence in paragraph 11 is located in

    a. sentence 1.   c. sentence 5.

    b. sentence 2.   d. sentence 6.

___ 3. What is the main idea?

    a. Mayors in the United States are the only ones trying to protect the environment.

    b. It is easy for a city to calculate its creation of greenhouse gases.

    c. Efforts to protect the environment at the local level are growing.

    d. Using solar, wind, and tidal power will make a major difference in improving the environment.

___ 4. All of the following points are major supporting details except that

    a. buildings and lighting can be made more energy efficient to help the environment.

    b. finding alternatives to traditional motor vehicle use can help the environment.

    c. making a city's downtown more pleasant helps save energy.

    d. drinking tap water instead of bottled water helps the environment.

___ 5. The article contains uses _____ as supporting details.

    a. testimony   c. statistics

    b. examples   d. all of the above

___ 6. The sentence "Des Moines, Iowa, has installed bike racks on the front of buses to make longer, car-free commutes more practical, and it has sponsored contests to design artistic bike racks for public spaces" (par. 12) is

    a. a fact.   b. an opinion.

___ 7. The article uses the _____ patterns of organization.

    a. comparison and contrast and process   c. cause and effect and definition

    b. classification and example   d. narrative and cause and effect

___ 8. What is the writers' purpose?

    a. to inform   c. to entertain

    b. to persuade   d. to inform and persuade

___ 9. The tone of the article is best labeled as _____.

    a. depressed   c. humorous

    b. upbeat   d. angry

___ 10. It can be inferred from the lines "In a larger city like New York, it's even more. The Big Apple— which has replaced 80,000 incandescent bulbs in 12,000 intersections—will realize savings of $6.3 million a year once the initial investment of $28 million is paid off" (par. 6) that

    a. New York is the second largest city in the United States.

    b. incandescent bulbs cannot be recycled.

    c. the Big Apple is a nickname for New York.

    d. New York has replaced bulbs in about half of its intersections.

11. List three minor details used in the Transportation section of the article.

_____

_____

_____

_____

_____

_____

12. What can be inferred from the lines "'Normal would be cause for popping champagne corks'" (par. 1)?

_____

_____

_____

_____

13. Identify the transition words used in paragraph 17 and what type each one is?

_____

_____

14. From your notes in the margins, write the question you would most like to discuss with the class.

_____

15. Finish the informal outline of the article.

Thesis: _____

1. Several mayors are banding together to find ways to protect the environment. par. _____

2. _____

_____ par. 5–9

3. _____ par. 10–12

4. _____ par. 13–16

5. _____ par. 17

6. The innovations used by American cities will continue to grow, and the spread of green ideas is moving to other countries as officials come to see what America's mayors are doing. par. _____

Vocabulary

Use context clues to determine the meaning by looking back at the paragraph where the word is used (the paragraph number is in parentheses). If you need help, consult a dictionary for the definition.

A. Match each word to its definition.

> **emissions** (2) **maverick** (3) **sustainability** (4) **tote** (5) **audit** (9)

1. independent in thought or behavior _____
2. an inspection of a building _____
3. a substance discharged into the air, especially by cars _____
4. to add up _____
5. capable of being continued with minimal lasting effect on the environment _____

B. Complete each sentence with the appropriate vocabulary word.

> **initiative** (4) **windfall** (6) **accrue** (9) **hybrid(s)** (10) **dither** (19)

1. By ignoring my debt, it didn't go away. I continued to _____ more bills each month until my sister sat down with me and helped me budget my money.
2. I'm glad I drive a _____. The combination of the car's electric and gas features is saving me a lot of money on my 50-mile roundtrip commute to work.
3. If you continue to _____, you won't get any cleaning done. You need to decide what to give away and what to keep.
4. When a thirty-thousand dollar check from his great-aunt's will arrived, Apolo considered it an amazing _____ since he had just been laid off from work.
5. The _____ calls for the city to provide more bike racks and lockers downtown since many people now commute to work by bicycle.

C. Word parts: Circle the meaning of the underlined word part found in each question. Return to pages 85–87 if you need to review the meaning of a word part.

1. Because the car was old, the mechanic told me that its e<u>mis</u>sions would send harmful chemicals into the air.
2. The plastic bottle is nonbiode<u>grad</u>able, so it will not go through a step by step process of breaking down naturally.
3. We plan to turn the garage into a family room. Once the con<u>vers</u>ion is done, we can get a ping pong table.
4. Because <u>bio</u>diesel is made from renewable plant sources, it may be a better source of fuel for the life of the planet.

The Article and You

1. Which of the energy reduction methods mentioned in paragraphs 6–12 have been implemented in your city or could be done easily?

   _____

   _____

   _____

2. Describe your city's downtown. Would the word *vibrant* fit in your description? Do you enjoy being downtown? Explain why or why not.

   _____

   _____

   _____

3. Which of the "small things" in paragraph 17 could you do or have you done? Explain how one of these changes would impact or has impacted your life.

   _____

   _____

4. On a separate sheet of paper, write a paragraph in which you explain how you do or could use transportation alternatives, instead of a car, to get around during an average week. In your supporting details tell where you would go and how you would get to each place.

Take a Closer Look

Look at the cartoon again. How effective do you find the cartoon? Would the addition of a caption help or hinder its message?

Look at the photos again. Can these green innovations be found in your city or life? Do you think they could easily be implemented?

   _____

   _____

   _____

Internet Activities

If needed, use a separate sheet of paper to fully record your responses. Include the Web address of any sites from which you gather information.

1. Look up "carbon footprint calculator." Pick one site (you might want to try two sites to compare the results), and estimate your carbon footprint. What was your score/result? What can you do to lower it?

   _____

   _____

2. Search for "simple green ideas." List three ideas to make the world greener that you could easily put into practice.

   _____

   _____

   _____

Surface Waters and Underground Seas

by Rachel Carson

from *Silent Spring*

Before You Read

1. After reading the first two paragraphs, write your own question that you think the reading may address:

   _____

2. Do you feel your drinking water is safe? Do you use some kind of filter for your tap water or do you drink bottled water?

3. Do you feel that fish are safe to eat?

4. Look at the photo and chart. What is your reaction to the river? Does the information in the chart change your reaction at all?

Rachel Carson (1907–1964) was a marine biologist, writer, and naturalist. She graduated from John Hopkins University with a master's degree in zoology. She worked for the U.S. Bureau of Fisheries as a scientist and editor. She also wrote articles and books about nature. In 1952, her book *The Sea Around Us* became a best seller. She then began writing full time. The excerpt below is from *Silent Spring*, which was published in 1962 and caused quite a stir at the time. Carson died at age 56 after battling breast cancer for several years.

Vocabulary Preview

Look for these words in the reading. Exercises to reinforce the learning of new vocabulary using these words follow the reading. The paragraph number where the word appears is in parentheses.

paradox (1)	**pesticides** (2)	**mélange** (2)	**augment** (2)	**synthetic** (3)
inextricably (3)	**residues** (4)	**insecticide** (5)	**derived** (10)	**catalyzing** (13)

1 Of all our natural resources water has become the most precious. By far the greater part of the earth's surface is covered by its enveloping seas, yet in the midst of this plenty we are in want. By a strange paradox, most of the earth's abundant water is not usable for agriculture, industry, or human consumption because of its heavy load of sea salts, and so most of the world's population is either experiencing or is threatened with critical shortages. In an age when man has forgotten his origins and is blind even to his most essential needs for survival, water along with other resources has become the victim of his indifference.

2 The problem of water pollution by pesticides can be understood only in context, as part of the whole to which it belongs—the pollution of the total environment of mankind. The pollution entering our waterways comes from many sources: radioactive wastes from reactors, laboratories, and hospitals; fallout from nuclear explosions; domestic wastes from cities and towns; chemical wastes from factories. To these is added a new kind of fallout— the chemical sprays applied to croplands and gardens, forests and fields. Many of the chemical agents in this alarming mélange imitate and augment the harmful effects of radiation, and within the groups of chemicals themselves there are sinister and little-understood interactions, transformations, and summations of effect.

3   Ever since chemists began to manufacture substances that nature never invented, the problems of water purification have become complex and the danger to users of water has increased. As we have seen, the production of these synthetic chemicals in large volume began in the 1940's. It has now reached such proportions that an appalling deluge of chemical pollution is daily poured into the nation's waterways. When inextricably mixed with domestic and other wastes discharged into the same water, these chemicals sometimes defy detection by the methods in ordinary use by purification plants. Most of them are so stable that they cannot be broken down by ordinary processes. Often they cannot even be identified. In rivers, a really incredible variety of pollutants combine to produce deposits that the sanitary engineers can only despairingly refer to as "gunk." Professor Rolf Eliassen of the Massachusetts Institute of Technology testified before a congressional committee to the impossibility of predicting the composite effect of these chemicals, or of identifying the organic matter resulting from the mixture. "We don't begin to know what that is," said Professor Eliassen. "What is the effect on the people? We don't know."

4   To an ever-increasing degree, chemicals used for the control of insects, rodents, or unwanted vegetation contribute to these organic pollutants. Some are deliberately applied to bodies of water to destroy plants, insect larvae, or undesired fishes. Some come from forest spraying that may blanket two or three million acres of a single state with spray directed against a single insect pest—spray that falls directly into streams or that drips down through the leafy canopy to the forest floor, there to become part of the slow movement of seeping moisture beginning its long journey to the sea. Probably the bulk of such contaminants are the waterborne residues of the millions of pounds of agricultural chemicals that have been applied to farmlands for insect or rodent control and have been leached out of the ground by rains to become part of the universal seaward movement of water.

5   Here and there we have dramatic evidence of the presence of these chemicals in our streams and even in public water supplies. For example, a sample of drinking water from an orchard area in Pennsylvania, when tested on fish in a laboratory, contained enough insecticide to kill all of the test fish in only four hours. Water from a stream draining sprayed cotton fields remained lethal to fishes even after it had passed through a purifying plant, and in fifteen streams tributary to the Tennessee River in Alabama the runoff from fields treated with toxaphene, a chlorinated hydrocarbon, killed all the fish inhabiting the streams. Two of these streams were sources of municipal water supply. Yet for a week after the application of the insecticide the water remained poisonous, a fact attested by the daily deaths of goldfish suspended in cages downstream.

6   For the most part this pollution is unseen and invisible, making its presence known when hundreds or thousands of fish die, but more often never detected at all. The chemist who guards water purity has no routine tests for these organic pollutants and no way to remove them. But whether detected or not, the pesticides are there, and as might be expected with any materials applied to land surfaces on so vast a scale, they have now found their way into many and perhaps all of the major river systems of the country.

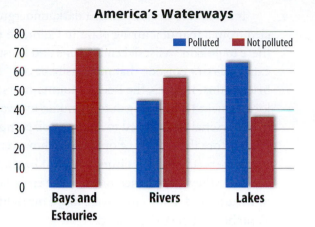

America's Waterways

Polluted means too contaminated for fishing, swimming, and other water activites.

Adated from data from the Environmental Protection Agency, 2004.

7   If anyone doubts that our waters have become almost universally contaminated with insecticides he should study a small report issued by the United States Fish and Wildlife Service in 1960. The Service had carried out studies to discover whether fish, like warm-blooded animals, store insecticides in their tissues. The first samples were taken from forest areas in the West where there had been mass spraying of DDT for the control of the spruce budworm. As might have been expected, all of these fish contained DDT. The really significant findings were made when the investigators turned for comparison to a creek in a remote area about 30 miles from the nearest spraying for budworm control. This creek was upstream from the first and separated from it by a high waterfall. No local spraying was known to have occurred. Yet these fish, too, contained DDT. Had the chemical reached this remote creek by hidden underground streams? Or had it been airborne, drifting down as fallout on the surface of the creek? In still another comparative study, DDT was found in the tissues of fish from a hatchery where the water supply originated in a deep well. Again there was no record of local spraying. The only possible means of contamination seemed to be by means of groundwater.

8   In the entire water-pollution problem, there is probably nothing more disturbing than the threat of widespread contamination of groundwater. It is not possible to add pesticides to water anywhere without threatening the purity of water everywhere. Seldom if ever does Nature operate in closed and separate compartments, and she has not done so in distributing the earth's water supply. Rain, falling on the land, settles down through pores and cracks in soil and rock, penetrating deeper and deeper until eventually it reaches a zone where all the pores of the rock are filled with water, a dark, subsurface sea, rising under hills, sinking beneath valleys. This groundwater is always on the move, sometimes at a pace so slow that it travels no more than 50 feet a year, sometimes rapidly, by comparison, so that it moves nearly a tenth of a mile in a day. It travels by unseen waterways until here and there it comes to the surface as a spring, or perhaps it is tapped to feed a well. But mostly it contributes to streams and so to rivers. Except for what enters streams directly as rain or surface runoff, all the running water of the earth's surface was at one time groundwater. And so, in a very real and frightening sense, pollution of the groundwater is pollution of water everywhere.

9   It must have been by such a dark, underground sea that poisonous chemicals traveled from a manufacturing plant in Colorado to a farming district several miles away, there to poison wells, sicken humans and livestock, and damage crops—an extraordinary episode that may easily be only the first of many like it. Its history, in brief, is this. In 1943, the Rocky Mountain Arsenal of the Army Chemical Corps, located near Denver, began to manufacture war materials. Eight years later the facilities of the arsenal were leased to a private oil company for the production of insecticides. Even before the change of operations, however, mysterious reports had begun to come in. Farmers several miles from the plant began to report unexplained sickness among livestock; they complained of extensive crop damage. Foliage turned yellow, plants failed to mature, and many crops were killed outright. There were reports of human illness, thought by some to be related.

10   The irrigation waters on these farms were derived from shallow wells. When the well waters were examined (in a study in 1959, in which several state and federal agencies participated) they were found to contain an assortment of chemicals. Chlorides, chlorates, salts of phosphonic acid, fluorides, and arsenic had been discharged from the Rocky Mountain Arsenal into holding ponds during the years of its operation. Apparently the groundwater between the arsenal and the farms had become contaminated and it had taken 7 to 8 years for the wastes to travel underground a distance of about 3 miles from the holding ponds to the nearest farm. This seepage had continued to spread and had further contaminated an area of unknown extent. The investigators knew of no way to contain the contamination or halt its advance.

11   All this was bad enough, but the most mysterious and probably in the long run the most significant feature of the whole episode was the discovery of the weed killer 2,4-D in some of the wells and in the holding ponds of the arsenal. Certainly its presence was enough to account for the damage to crops irrigated with this water. But the mystery lay in the fact that no 2,4-D had been manufactured at the arsenal at any stage of its operations.

12   After long and careful study, the chemists at the plant concluded that the 2,4-D had been formed spontaneously in the open basins. It had been formed there from other substances discharged from the arsenal; in the presence of air, water, and sunlight, and quite without the intervention of human chemists, the holding ponds had become chemical laboratories for the production of a new chemical—a chemical fatally damaging to much of the plant life it touched.

13   And so the story of the Colorado farms and their damaged crops assumes a significance that transcends its local importance. What other parallels may there be, not only in Colorado but wherever chemical pollution finds its way into public waters? In lakes and streams everywhere, in the presence of catalyzing air and sunlight, what dangerous substances may be born of parent chemicals labeled "harmless"?

Getting the Message

_____ **1.** Which is/are the topic sentence(s) in paragraph 8?

a. sentence 1
b. sentence 4
c. sentence 6
d. sentences 1 and 9

_____ **2.** What is the main idea of the reading?

a. Chemists have created perfect substances to rid the world of pests.
b. Pesticides are poisoning the Earth's water.
c. Fish can't live in polluted water.
d. Groundwater can move almost a tenth of a mile in a day.

_____ **3.** The following is a minor detail:

a. chemicals are polluting America's waterways.
b. most water pollution from chemicals is invisible.
c. in fifteen streams that lead to the Tennessee River, the runoff from chemically treated fields killed all the fish in the streams.
d. groundwater is an essential way of spreading pollutants.

_____ **4.** Carson uses testimony in paragraph _____.

a. 1
b. 3
c. 7
d. 12

_____ **5.** What kind of supporting details are used in paragraph 5?

a. statistics
b. testimony
c. hypothetical examples
d. public examples

_____ **6.** The following is an extended example in the essay:

a. the orchard in Pennsylvania.
b. the manufacture of synthetic chemicals to a larger degree in the 1940s.
c. DDT found in the tissues of fish from a hatchery.
d. the Rocky Mountain Arsenal.

_____ **7.** "For example, a sample of drinking water from an orchard area in Pennsylvania, when tested on fish in a laboratory, contained enough insecticide to kill all of the test fish in only four hours" (par. 5). The previous sentence expresses

a. a fact.
b. an opinion.

_____ **8.** The order used to present the information in the essay is

a. least to most important point.
b. most to least important point.
c. problem and solution.
d. chronological.

_____ **9.** Words that describe the tone of the essay are _____.

a. sad and thoughtful
b. funny and sentimental
c. concerned and passionate
d. friendly and objective

_____**10.** It can be inferred from the information in paragraphs 3 and 4 that

    a. only a few areas were using pesticides in the 1950s.

    b. the development of synthetic chemicals led to a wide use of pesticides in the 1950s.

    c. pesticide use was tightly controlled by the government.

    d. people didn't care if the water was polluted as long as insects weren't around.

11. What was so unsettling about what happened at the Rocky Mountain Arsenal?

_____

_____

_____

_____

12. What is Carson's purpose? Give three examples of words, phrases, or examples that show Caron's purpose.

_____

_____

_____

_____

_____

_____

13. Which of the fallacies introduced in this chapter might Carson's essay be said to exhibit? Explain whether you think it does contain this fallacy.

_____

_____

_____

_____

_____

_____

14. List three items you circled, starred, or otherwise highlighted as you annotated the essay. Explain why you marked these points.

_____

_____

15. On a separate sheet of paper, write a summary of the essay in about 200 words.

Vocabulary

Use context clues to determine the meaning of each word by referring back to the paragraph where the word is used (the paragraph number is in parentheses). If you need help, consult a dictionary for the definition.

A. Circle the correct definition for each vocabulary word.

1. paradox (1):   exhibiting contradictory parts   in agreement

2. mélange (2):   a lone ingredient   mixture

3. augment (2):   to make larger   to make smaller

4. inextricably (3):   completely   partially

5. derived (10):   lost   obtained

B. Write a definition and your own sentence for each word. Use the words either as given in the reading, or change plurals to singulars and "ing" forms to the base form, such as catalyze instead of catalyzing.

1. pesticide(s) (2) _____

2. synthetic (3) _____

3. residue(s) (4) _____

4. insecticide (5) _____

5. catalyze(ing) (13) _____

C. Word parts: Use the definition and sample word to help you to write another word that uses the word part. Return to pages 85–87 if you need to review the meaning of a word part.

1. -cide: killing; pesticide (2): a chemical for killing troublesome plants or animals. _____ cide

2. com-: with, together; composite (3): to put together. com _____

3. trans-: across; transcend (13): to go across usual limits. trans _____

4. para-: almost, beyond, beside; parallel (13): beside but not meeting, almost like. para _____

The Essay and You

1. Though Carson's book, from which this excerpt was taken, was published in 1962, do you feel that some of her points are still relevant to today's environment? If you do, list three points that you think are a concern. If you don't feel the essay is relevant, explain why.

_____

_____

2. What are three important bodies of water (lakes, rivers, oceans) near your city? Have measures been taken to keep them free from pollutants?

_____

_____

3. What changes do you see around you as a result of greater awareness about the dangers of pesticides and other chemicals? For example, think about when you go to the grocery store or work on the yard.

_____

_____

4. On a separate sheet of paper, write a paragraph in which you examine your reaction to Carson's essay. Explain whether it excites you to action or whether her concerns seem exaggerated. Explain why you feel this way.

Take a Closer Look

Look at the photo and chart again. Now that you have read the excerpt, do you see the river in a different light? Are you surprised by the information in the chart? Did you expect America's waterways to be cleaner?

_____

_____

Internet Activities

If needed, use a separate sheet of paper to fully record your responses. Include the Web address of any sites from which you gather information.

1. Search for "dirty rivers" or "polluted rivers." List six of the most polluted rivers in the world. How many are in the United States? Which country has the most polluted river?

_____

_____

_____

_____

2. Look up the book *Silent Spring* from which the excerpt was taken. What was the initial reaction to the book? What influences did the book have?

_____

_____

_____

_____

What Makes Cities Livable?

by Richard T. Wright

from *Environmental Science*

Before You Read

1. Survey the reading. Look at the subheadings and words in italics. Read the To the Point section. Then consider three qualities a livable city should contain.

2. What city have you enjoyed living in or visiting? What did you like about it?

3. What are three qualities that can make a city unpleasant?

4. Look at the photos. Do these cities look like you would want to live in them?

Richard T. Wright is Professor Emeritus of Biology at Gordon College in Massachusetts. He taught environmental science there for 28 years. He received his master's and doctorate degrees from Harvard University. He is a member of several groups including the Audubon Society, the Nature Conservancy, and Habitat for Humanity. He continues to write and speak about environmental issues. The excerpt is from the 9th edition of his textbook *Environmental Science: Toward a Sustainable Future.*

Vocabulary Preview

Look for these words in the reading. Exercises to reinforce the learning of new vocabulary using these words follow the reading. The paragraph number where the word appears is in parentheses.

urban (1)	**sprawl** (1)	**blight** (1)	**density** (3)	**heterogeneity** (3)
vagrancy (5)	**curtail** (6)	**hydroponic** (9)	**co-opting** (10)	**biosphere** (10)

1 **The environmental** consequences of urban sprawl and the social consequences of urban blight are two sides of the same coin. A sustainable future will depend on both reining in urban sprawl and revitalizing cities. The urban blight of cities in the developing world requires deliberate policies to address the social needs of the people flocking to the shantytowns. The only possible way to sustain the global population is by having viable, resource-efficient cities, leaving the countryside for agriculture and natural ecosystems. The key word is *viable,* which means *livable.* No one wants to, or should, be required to live in the conditions that have come to typify urban blight.

2 *Livability* is a general concept based on people's response to the question "Do you like living here, or would you rather live somewhere else?" Crime, pollution, recreational, cultural, and professional opportunities, as well as many other social and environmental factors, are summed up in the subjective answer to that question. Although many people assume that the social ills of the city are an outcome of high population densities, crime rates and other problems in U.S. cities have climbed while populations dwindled as a result of the exurban migration.

3 Looking at livable cities around the world, we find that the common denominator is (1) maintaining a high population density; (2) preserving a heterogeneity of residences, businesses, stores, and shops; and (3) keeping layouts on a human dimension, so that people can meet, visit, or conduct business incidentally over coffee at a sidewalk café or stroll on a

promenade through an open area. In short, the space is designed for, and devoted to, people. In contrast, development of the past 50 years has focused on accommodating automobiles and traffic. Two-thirds of the land in cities that have grown up in the era of the automobile is devoted to moving, parking, or servicing cars, and such space is essentially alien to the human psyche. William Whyte, a well-known city planner, remarked, "It is difficult to design space that will not attract people. What is remarkable is how often this has been accomplished."

4 **A Matter of Design** The world's most livable cities are not those with "perfect" auto access between all points. Instead, they are cities that have taken measures to reduce outward sprawl, diminish automobile traffic, and improve access by foot and bicycle in conjunction with mass transit. For example, Geneva, Switzerland, prohibits automobile parking at workplaces in the city's center, forcing commuters to use the excellent public transportation system. Copenhagen bans all on-street parking in the downtown core. Paris has removed 200,000 parking places in the downtown area. Curitiba, Brazil, with a population of 1.6 million, is cited as the most livable city in all of Latin America. The achievement of Curitiba is due almost entirely to the efforts of Jaime Lerner, who, serving as mayor since the early 1970s, has guided development with an emphasis on mass transit rather than cars. The space saved by not building highways and parking lots has been put into parks and shady walkways, causing the amount of green area per inhabitant to increase from 4.5 square feet in 1970 to 450 square feet today.

5 **Charinkos** In Tokyo, millions of people ride *charinkos,* or bicycles, either all the way to work or to subway stations from which they catch fast, efficient trains, including the "bullet train," to their destination. By sharply restricting development outside certain city limits, Japan has maintained population densities within cities and along metropolitan

corridors that ensure the viability of commuter trains. Japan's cities have maintained a heterogeneous urban structure that mixes small shops, professional offices, and residences in such a way that a large portion of the population meets its needs without cars. In maintaining an economically active city, it is probably no coincidence that street crime, vagrancy, and begging are virtually unknown in the vast expanse of Tokyo, despite the seeming congestion.

6 **Portland** Portland, Oregon, is a pioneering U.S. city that has taken giant steps to curtail automobile use. The first step was to encircle the city with an urban growth boundary, a line outside of which new development was prohibited. Thus, compact growth, rather than sprawl, was ensured. Second, an efficient light-rail and bus system was built, which now carries 45% of all commuters to downtown jobs. (In most

U.S. cities, only 10% to 25% of commuters ride public transit systems.) By reducing traffic, Portland was able to convert a former expressway and a huge parking lot into the now-renowned Tom McCall Waterfront Park. Portland is now ranked among the world's most livable cities.

7   **The Big Dig**   Other U.S. cities are discovering hidden resources in their inner core areas. Expressways, which were built with federal highway funds to speed vehicles through the cities, frequently dissected neighborhoods, separating people from waterfronts and consuming existing open space. Now, with federal help from TEA-21 programs, many cities are removing or burying the intruding expressways. Boston, for example, is in the closing stages of its "Big Dig," a $15 billion project that has moved its central freeway below ground, added parks and open space, and reconnected the city to its waterfront. The waterfronts themselves are often the neglected relics of bygone transportation by water and rail. In recent years, cities such as Cleveland, Chicago, San Francisco, and Baltimore have redeveloped their waterfronts, turning rotting piers and abandoned freight yards into workplaces, high-rise residences, and public and entertainment space.

8   It turns out that the U.S. economic boom of the 1990s contributed immeasurably to urban renewal, filling the federal coffers and at the same time boosting employment in the inner cities. Retail businesses and manufacturers are discovering that inner-city neighborhoods can provide a valuable labor pool, as well as customers for their goods and services.

Livable Equals Sustainable

9   The same factors that underlie livability also lead to sustainability. The reduction of auto traffic and a greater reliance on foot and public transportation reduce energy consumption and pollution. Urban heterogeneity can facilitate the recycling of materials. Housing can be retrofitted with passive solar space heating and heating for hot water. Landscaping can provide cooling. A number of cities are developing vacant or cleared areas into garden plots and rooftop hydroponic gardens are becoming popular. Such gardens will not make cities agriculturally self-sufficient, but they add to urban livability, provide an avenue for recycling compost and nutrients removed from sewage, give a source of fresh vegetables, and have the potential to generate income for many unskilled workers. If urban sprawl is curbed, relatively close-in farms could provide most of the remaining food needs for the city.

10   **To the Point**   The preceding discussion of urban issues may seem to have strayed far from nature and environmental science. However, there is a close connection between the two: The decay of our cities is hastening the

degradation of our larger environment. As the growing human population spreads outward from the old cities in developed countries, we are co-opting natural lands and prime farmlands and ratcheting up the rate of air pollution and greenhouse gases. Similarly, as increasing numbers in the developing world stream *into* the cities, they are degrading the human and social resources that are vital to all environmental issues. Thus, without the creation of sustainable human communities, there is little chance for the sustainability of the rest of the biosphere.

11   By making urban areas more appealing and economically stable, we not only improve the lives of those who choose to remain or must remain in cities, but also spare surrounding areas. Our parks, wildernesses, and farms will not be replaced by exurbs and shopping malls, but rather, will be saved for future generations. In the last decade, some remarkable developments have begun to accelerate the movement toward building sustainable communities.

Getting the Message

____ **1.** The topic is
   a. decaying cities.
   b. cites that cater to automobile traffic.
   c. livable cities.
   d. environmental problems.

____ **2.** The main idea of the excerpt can be found in paragraph _____.
   a. 1
   b. 3
   c. 5
   d. 8

____ **3.** Where is the topic sentence located in paragraph 6?
   a. sentence 1
   b. sentence 2
   c. sentence 4
   d. sentence 7

____ **4.** Which of the following is a minor supporting detail?
   a. Creating livable cities means working to reduce urban sprawl.
   b. Geneva, Switzerland, prohibits automobile parking at workplaces in the city's center.
   c. Livable cities are those that rely less on automobiles.
   d. Livable cities equal sustainable cities.

____ **5.** Wright uses _____ as supporting details.
   a. examples and testimony
   b. testimony and personal examples
   c. statistics
   d. a and c

____ **6.** The sentence "Japan's cities have maintained a heterogeneous urban structure that mixes small shops, professional offices, and residences in such a way that a large portion of the population meets its needs without cars" (par. 5) expresses
   a. a fact.
   b. an opinion.

____ **7.** How does Wright order his information?
   a. chronologically
   b. least to most important point
   c. problem and solution
   d. most to least important point

____ **8.** Wright's purpose is to
   a. share information on urban sprawl.
   b. warn people about the environmental consequences of depending on cars.
   c. entertain with stories about how some cities are working to become more livable.
   d. persuade people of the importance of making cities more livable.

____ **9.** The tone of the reading is _____.

    a. pessimistic

    b. encouraging and urgent

    c. humorous

    d. dramatic and hopeful

____ **10.** What can be inferred from the examples in paragraphs 4–6?

    a. Creating livable cities is only a problem for Europe.

    b. Australia has no problems with making cities livable.

    c. The move to create livable cities pertains to more than one continent.

    d. Cars will be obsolete in the next 20 years.

11. Create a slippery slope assertion by completing Wright's statement "without the creation of sustainable human communities . . . " (par. 10). For example: Without the creation of sustainable human communities, people will not last another twenty years on Earth.

_____

_____

12. Give an example of a sentence that expresses a fact, one that expresses an opinion, and one that contains both. Give the paragraph number where the sentence is located.

_____

_____

_____

_____

_____

13. Create your own similes based on topics in the reading.

    a. Residing in a livable city is like _____

    b. Portland's waterfront park is as _____

    c. Picking vegetables from my rooftop garden is like _____

14. List two questions or comments you wrote in the margins as you read the selection.

_____

_____

15. Paraphrase the following sentence: "The achievement of Curitiba is due almost entirely to the efforts of Jaime Lerner, who, serving as mayor since the early 1970s, has guided development with an emphasis on mass transit rather than cars" (par. 4).

_____

_____

_____

Vocabulary

Use context clues to determine the meaning of each word by referring back to the paragraph where the word is used (the paragraph number is in parentheses). If you need help, consult a dictionary for the definition.

A. Match each vocabulary word to its definition.

> **sprawl** (1)   **heterogeneity** (3)   **hydroponic** (9)   **co-opt(ing)** (10)   **biosphere** (10)

1. the growing of plants by putting the roots in liquid instead of soil _____
2. the part of the earth's crust, waters, and atmosphere that support life _____
3. to take or assume for one's own use; appropriate _____
4. unplanned growth or extension outward _____
5. the quality of being different; diverseness _____

B. Finish the reading with the appropriate missing words. Use each word once.

> **urban** (1)   **blight** (1)   **density** (3)   **vagrancy** (5)   **curtail** (6)

I like _____ life. The _____ of people and buildings found downtown turns some away from living in the city, but I appreciate the benefits, such as the museums and theaters. I find that the concentration of people excites me. However, the _____ that is increasing in the neighborhood just a few blocks from my apartment worries me. Many of the residents of that area have been facing economic problems in the past few years, causing people to move out and leave houses and apartments abandoned. The departures have led to a problem with _____ as homeless people move in and out of these buildings and make the neighbor even more undesirable. The city council has done nothing to _____ the decay in this area. I am going to start attending city council meetings to voice my concern.

C. Word parts: Fill in the missing meanings for the underlined word parts. Use one word twice. Return to pages 85–87 if you need to review the meaning of a word part.

> **life**   **make**   **put**   **city**

1. I don't like <u>urban</u> life. Living in the _____ is too crowded for me.
2. In an enclosed <u>bio</u>sphere in Arizona, scientists spent 2 years studying _____ in a variety of environments.
3. It isn't currently <u>vi</u>able for humans to live on the moon. For _____ to be sustainable there, we need to create special buildings.
4. I am happy to <u>fac</u>ilitate at the conference. It will _____ registration easier if there are four of us helping at check-in.
5. We just bought a com<u>post</u> bin. We _____ the remains of our fruits and vegetables in it and then use the decayed material as fertilizer for our garden.

The Textbook and You

1. Provide an answer for the question "Do you like living here, or would you rather live somewhere else?" (par. 2). Explain your response.

_____

_____

2. How livable would you rate your city or town, with 10 being "super" and 1 being "a disaster area"? List three factors that helped you reach your decision. Do any of these factors match the characteristics of a livable city mentioned in the excerpt?

_____

_____

_____

_____

3. Is mass transit used much in your area or are cars still the main form of transportation? Could your area become less auto dependent by using any of the ideas mentioned in paragraphs 4–7?

_____

_____

4. On a separate sheet of paper, write a paragraph that contrasts two spaces in your city—one that attracts people and one that does not. Use William Whyte's quotation in paragraph 3 as a starting point. The spaces can be neighborhoods, shopping malls, parks, or any other place where people come together.

Take a Closer Look

Look at the photos again. How does each photograph present one or more livable aspects of a city?

_____

_____

_____

_____

Internet Activities

If needed, use a separate sheet of paper to fully record your responses. Include the Web address of any sites from which you gather information.

1. Look for photos of the redeveloped waterfront of one of the five cities mentioned in paragraph 7. For example, try typing "Boston waterfront photos." Pick a photo, print it, and add a caption that conveys the people-friendly atmosphere of the waterfront.

_____

2. Go to walkscore.com. This site calculates how walking friendly a neighborhood is. Type in your address or zip code, and see how your area rates. Do you agree with the score for your neighborhood?

_____

The Phoenix

by Sylvia Townsend Warner

Before You Read

1. What do you think of when you hear the word *phoenix*?

2. Do you think that humans as a whole treat animals well?

3. Think of two words that describe how people should treat animals.

4. Look at the artwork. What do you think is special about this bird?

Vocabulary Preview

Look for these words in the reading. Exercises to reinforce the learning of new vocabulary using these words follow the reading. The paragraph number where the word appears is in parentheses.

aviary (1)   **affable** (3)   **ornithologists** (3)

rancour (3)   **chivied** (23)   **capricious** (28)

languorous (28)   **quiver** (30)   **wearily** (30)

pyre (33)

Sylvia Townsend Warner (1893–1978) was a British writer. She wrote novels, short stories, poetry, and essays. She was also an excellent musician, and she worked for 10 years as an editor of the 10-volume *Tudor Church Music.* Her first novel, *Lolly Willowes,* was published in 1926. She contributed short stories to the *New Yorker* for more than 40 years. She had a total of eight volumes of collected short stories. The following story was first published in 1940.

1 Lord Strawberry, a nobleman, collected birds. He had the finest aviary in Europe, so large that eagles did not find it uncomfortable, so well laid out that both humming-birds and snow-buntings had a climate that suited them perfectly. But for many years the finest set of apartments remained empty, with just a label saying: "PHOENIX. *Habitat: Arabia.*"

2 Many authorities on bird life had assured Lord Strawberry that the phoenix is a fabulous bird, or that the breed was long extinct. Lord Strawberry was unconvinced: his family had always believed in phoenixes. At intervals he received from his agents (together with statements of their expenses) birds which they declared were the phoenix but which turned out to be orioles, macaws, turkey buzzards dyed orange, etc., or stuffed cross-breeds, ingeniously assembled from various plumages. Finally Lord Strawberry went himself to Arabia, where, after some months, he found a phoenix, won its confidence, caught it, and brought it home in perfect condition.

3 It was a remarkably fine phoenix, with a charming character—affable to the other birds in the aviary and much attached to Lord Strawberry. On its arrival in England it made a great stir among ornithologists, journalists, poets, and milliners, and was constantly visited. But it was not puffed by these attentions, and

when it was no longer in the news, and the visits fell off, it showed no pique or rancour. It ate well, and seemed perfectly contented.

4   It costs a great deal of money to keep up an aviary. When Lord Strawberry died he died penniless. The aviary came on the market. In normal times the rarer birds, and certainly the phoenix, would have been bid for by the trustees of Europe's great zoological societies, or by private persons in the U.S.A.; but as it happened Lord Strawberry died just after a world war, when both money and bird-seed were hard to come by (indeed the cost of bird-seed was one of the things which had ruined Lord Strawberry). The London *Times* urged in a leader that the phoenix be bought for the London Zoo, saying that a nation of bird-lovers had a moral right to own such a rarity; and a fund, called the Strawberry Phoenix Fund, was opened. Students, naturalists, and school-children contributed according to their means; but their means were small, and there were no large donations. So Lord Strawberry's executors (who had the death duties to consider) closed with the higher offer of Mr. Tancred Poldero, owner and proprietor of Poldero's Wizard Wonderworld.

5   For quite a while Mr. Poldero considered his phoenix a bargain. It was a civil and obliging bird, and adapted itself readily to its new surroundings. It did not cost much to feed, it did not mind children; and though it had no tricks, Mr. Poldero supposed it would soon pick up some. The publicity of the Strawberry Phoenix Fund was now most helpful. Almost every contributor now saved up another half-crown in order to see the phoenix. Others, who had not contributed to the fund, even paid double to look at it on the five-shilling days.

6   But then business slackened. The phoenix was as handsome as ever, and as amiable; but, as Mr. Poldero said, it hadn't got Udge. Even at popular prices the phoenix was not really popular. It was too quiet, too classical. So people went instead to watch the antics of the baboons, or to admire the crocodile who had eaten the woman.

7   One day Mr. Poldero said to his manager, Mr. Ramkin: "How long since any fool paid to look at the phoenix?"

8   "Matter of three weeks," replied Mr. Ramkin.

9   "Eating his head off," said Mr. Poldero. "Let alone the insurance. Seven shillings a week it costs me to insure that bird, and I might as well insure the Archbishop of Canterbury."

10   "The public don't like him. He's too quiet for them, that's the trouble. Won't mate nor nothing. And I've tried him with no end of pretty pollies, ospreys, and Cochin-Chinas, and the Lord knows what. But he won't look at them."

11   "Wonder if we could swap him for a livelier one," said Mr. Poldero.

12   "Impossible. There's only one of him at a time."

13   "Go on!"

14   "I mean it. Haven't you ever read what it says on the label?"

15   They went to the phoenix's cage. It flapped its wings politely, but they paid no attention. They read:

16   "Pansy. *Phoenix phoenixis-sima formosissima arabiana.* This rare and fabulous bird is UNIQUE. The World's Old Bachelor. Has no mate and doesn't want one. When old, sets fire to itself and emerges miraculously reborn. Specially imported from the East."

17   "I've got an idea," said Mr. Poldero. "How old do you suppose that bird is?"

18   "Looks in its prime to me," said Mr. Ramkin.

19   "Suppose," continued Mr. Poldero, "we could somehow get him alight? We'd advertise it beforehand, of course, work up interest. Then we'd have a new bird, and a bird with some romance about it, a bird with a life-story. We could sell a bird like that."

20   Mr. Ramkin nodded.

21   "I've read about it in a book," he said. "You've got to give them scented woods and what not, and they build a nest and sit down on it and catch fire spontaneous. But they won't do it till they're old. That's the snag."

22   "Leave that to me," said Mr. Poldero. "You get those scented woods, and I'll do the ageing."

23   It was not easy to age the phoenix. Its allowance of food was halved, and halved again, but though it grew thinner its eyes were undimmed and its plumage glossy as ever. The heating was turned off; but it puffed out its feathers against the cold, and seemed none the worse. Other birds were put into its cage, birds of a peevish and quarrelsome nature. They pecked and chivied it; but the phoenix was so civil and amiable that after a day or two they lost their animosity. Then Mr. Poldero tried alley cats. These could not be won by manners, but the phoenix darted above their heads and flapped its golden wings in their faces, and daunted them.

24   Mr. Poldero turned to a book on Arabia, and read that the climate was dry. "Aha!" said he. The phoenix was moved to a small cage that had a sprinkler in the ceiling. Every night the sprinkler was turned on. The phoenix began to cough. Mr. Poldero had another good idea. Daily he stationed himself in front of the cage to jeer at the bird and abuse it.

25   When spring was come, Mr. Poldero felt justified in beginning a publicity campaign about the ageing phoenix. The old public favourite, he said, was nearing its end. Meanwhile he tested the bird's reactions every few days by putting a few tufts of foul-smelling straw and some strands of rusty barbed wire into the cage, to see if it were interested in nesting yet. One day the phoenix began turning over the straw. Mr. Poldero signed a contract for the film rights. At last the hour seemed ripe. It was a fine Saturday evening in May. For some weeks the public interest in the ageing phoenix had been working up, and the admission charge had risen to five shillings. The enclosure was thronged. The lights and the cameras were trained on the cage, and a loud-speaker proclaimed to the audience the rarity of what was about to take place.

26   "The phoenix," said the loud-speaker, "is the aristocrat of bird-life. Only the rarest and most expensive specimens of oriental wood, drenched in exotic perfumes, will tempt him to construct his strange love-nest."

27   Now a neat assortment of twigs and shavings, strongly scented, was shoved into the cage.

28   "The phoenix," the loud-speaker continued, "is as capricious as Cleopatra, as luxurious as la du Barry, as heady as a strain of wild gypsy music. All the fantastic pomp and passion of the ancient East, its languorous magic, its subtle cruelties . . ."

29   "Lawks!" cried a woman in the crowd. "He's at it!"

30   A quiver stirred the dulled plumage. The phoenix turned its head from side to side. It descended, staggering, from its perch. Then wearily it began to pull about the twigs and shavings.

31   The cameras clicked, the lights blazed full on the cage. Rushing to the loud-speaker Mr. Poldero exclaimed:

32   "Ladies and gentlemen, this is the thrilling moment the world has breathlessly awaited. The legend of centuries is materializing before our modern eyes. The phoenix . . ."

33   The phoenix settled on its pyre and appeared to fall asleep.

34   The film director said:

35   "Well, if it doesn't evaluate more than this, mark it instructional."

36   At that moment the phoenix and the pyre burst into flames. The flames streamed upwards, leaped out on every side. In a minute or two everything was burned to ashes, and some thousand people, including Mr. Poldero, perished in the blaze.

Getting the Message

____ **1.** Which of the following are characters in the story?
  a. Mr. Poldero, Lord Strawberry, and la du Barry
  b. Mr. Poldero, Mr. Ramkin, and the phoenix
  c. Lord Raspberry, the phoenix, and Mr. Poldero
  d. the phoenix, a television director, and Mr. Tancred Poldero

____ **2.** The story is set in _____.
  a. London
  b. Paris
  c. New York
  d. Rome

____ **3.** What is the theme of the story?
  a. Birds should not be kept in cages.
  b. Circuses and zoos are harmful to animals.
  c. Animals should be treated with respect.
  d. Birds aren't interesting to watch.

____ **4.** _____ best describe the phoenix's personality.
  a. Mean and loud
  b. Greedy and disagreeable
  c. Wild and unpleasant
  d. Friendly and agreeable

____ **5.** What order does Warner use to present her story?
  a. chronological
  b. problem and solution
  c. most to least important
  d. least to most important

____ **6.** Warner uses a _____ pattern of organization to tell the story.
  a. definition
  b. narrative
  c. classification
  d. comparison and contrast

____ **7.** Warner's purpose is to
  a. inform.
  b. persuade.
  c. entertain.
  d. entertain and persuade.

____ **8.** The tone of the story can best be labeled as _____.
  a. sad
  b. ironic
  c. excited
  d. cheerful

9. It can be inferred from the line "but as it happened Lord Strawberry died just after a world war" (par. 4) that Lord Strawberry likely died in

    a. 1815 or 1915.

    b. 1901 or 1922.

    c. 1919 or 1946.

    d. 1946 or 1990.

10. "'The phoenix,' the loud-speaker continued, 'is as capricious as Cleopatra, as luxurious as la du Barry, as heady as a strain of wild gypsy music'" (par. 28). The previous line uses _____ to describe the phoenix.

    a. similes

    b. metaphors

11. What is the main conflict in the story? How does it reveal the writer's purpose?

_____

_____

_____

_____

12. What is ironic about the end of the story?

_____

_____

_____

13. What can be inferred about Mr. Poldero's priorities from his statements in paragraphs 19 and 22?

_____

_____

14. List three points you highlighted, circled, or starred. Why did you consider these points important?

_____

_____

_____

15. On a separate sheet of paper, make a sketch of a key scene in the story and under the sketch briefly explain why this scene is important. Be prepared to share your sketch with classmates and discuss why the chosen scenes are important.

Vocabulary

Use context clues to determine the meaning of each word by referring back to the paragraph where the word is used (the paragraph number is in parentheses). If you need help, consult a dictionary for the definition.

A. Match each word to its synonym.

1. unpredictable   _____
2. harassed   _____
3. pleasant   _____
4. bitterness   _____
5. dreamy   _____

> **affable** (3)   **rancour***(3)   **chivied** (23)
>
> **capricious** (28)   **languorous** (28)

*British spelling; American spelling: rancor.

B. If the sentence uses the vocabulary word correctly, put a *T* for true, and if the word is used incorrectly, put an *F* for false.

____ 1. Elephants are kept in aviaries (1).

____ 2. An ornithologist (3) could have an interest in emus, woodpeckers, or swans.

____ 3. The man wearily (30) made his way back to camp as he neared the end of the 25-mile hike.

____ 4. The woman was all a quiver (30) when she heard her name called as the winner of the poetry contest.

____ 5. One would almost certainly enjoy sleeping on a funeral pyre (34).

C. Word parts: Fill in the missing word part from the list, and circle the meaning of the word part found in each question. One word uses two word parts. Return to pages 85–87 if you need to review the meaning of a word part.

> ex   or   vert   sub   ist   able

1. I would like to be a person who studies birds, so I am taking courses to become an ornitholog_____.

2. Vicky likes to think she is ami_____. However, from what I've seen she isn't capable of being friendly.

3. To be the _____ecut_____ of my will, I am looking for a person who will carry out all of the conditions of my will and who will be supportive of my family during their time of grief.

4. My cousin was _____tle in his campaign to take over the company. He kept his plans under the radar of the top executives.

5. If we ad_____ise in the paper, people will know where to turn for their gardening needs.

The Short Story and You

1. What was your reaction to the treatment of the phoenix by Mr. Poldero?

_____

_____

2. What did you think of the ending? Was it appropriate for what happened in the story? Did it surprise you?

_____

_____

_____

3. List four ways humans use animals. After each, note whether you think the treatment is humane or not.

_____

_____

_____

4. On a separate sheet of paper, write a paragraph where you explore the idea of whether people need a spectacle to be impressed by nature. As a starting point, refer to paragraph 6 where the phoenix is called "too quiet, too classical" to continually attract the public's interest. Use various aspects of nature, from animals and plants to rivers and mountains, to support your view.

Take a Closer Look

Look at the photo again. Now that you have read the short story, describe your reaction to the phoenix.

_____

_____

Internet Activities

If needed, use a separate sheet of paper to fully record your responses. Include the Web address of any sites from which you gather information.

1. Look up "phoenix mythological bird" and find a site with additional information on the bird. Write a summary of your findings.

_____

2. Look up "endangered animals." Pick two animals and write a summary which explains why the animals are endangered.

_____

 **Objectives Check**

To check your progress in meeting chapter objectives, log in to www.myreadinglab.com, click on the Study Plan tab, and then on the Reading Skills tab. Choose Critical Thinking from the list of subtopics. Read and view the resources in the Review Materials section, then complete the Practices and Tests in the Activities section. You can check your scores by clicking on the Gradebook tab.

CHAPTER 10

Do maps or globes inspire you?

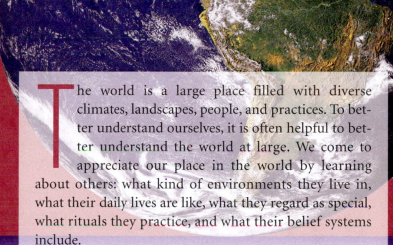

The World

Glimpses of Different Places and Perspectives

Mastering the Reading Skills

The world is a large place filled with diverse climates, landscapes, people, and practices. To better understand ourselves, it is often helpful to better understand the world at large. We come to appreciate our place in the world by learning about others: what kind of environments they live in, what their daily lives are like, what they regard as special, what rituals they practice, and what their belief systems include.

As you come to a greater mastery of understanding the world, you can show how you have come to master the reading process. This chapter gives you a chance to put all the skills you have been learning to a final test. The checklists for each of the skills you have reviewed in the previous chapters are presented here as reminders. Use them as guides as you read about different aspects of the world. The nearly two hundred countries that make up the world are too numerous to cover here, but the readings do represent places on each continent. Enjoy the four essays and articles, textbook excerpt, and folktales that introduce you to the diversity of planet Earth.

- Judge your mastery of the reading skills.
- Enjoy the benefits of being an active reader.

Checklist Review

Look over the following checklists before you tackle the final readings in this text. How many of these steps have become an automatic part of your reading process?

SQ4R Method

✓ **Survey:** Skim the pages you have been assigned to read, looking at the title, headings and subheadings, bold and italicized words, visual aids, and any concluding sections.

✓ **Question:** Ask questions about the reading to help you connect with the material and generate interest in the reading.

✓ **Read:** Have your pen ready to annotate, reread confusing sections, and base your reading speed on the difficulty of the material.

✓ **Record:** Write down what you have learned.

✓ **Recite:** Repeat aloud what you have learned.

✓ **Review:** Review your annotations, summaries, and other notes often. Reflect on what you have just read, and think of ways to relate the new knowledge to your life.

Main Idea

✓ Determine the topic of the reading.

✓ Establish the point of each paragraph, using topic sentences if provided, to uncover the main idea.

✓ Find a thesis statement or express an implied main idea in your own words.

Supporting Details

✓ Look for major and minor supporting details.

✓ Be able to identify the four main types of supporting details: examples, statistics, testimony, and reasons. Remember that examples can be personal, public, hypothetical, and facts.

- ✓ Determine if a statement is a fact by asking yourself whether you can find reliable information to verify the statement.

- ✓ Determine if a statement is an opinion by asking yourself whether another view or side to the statement is possible.

- ✓ Decide if the types of supporting details used are effective for the writer's purpose.

- ✓ Determine if there are enough details to make or prove the writer's point.

- ✓ Determine if a supporting detail is relevant to the point being made.

- ✓ Establish if a supporting detail is accurate or credible.

Organization

Ch. 6
Ch. 1

- ✓ Determine the order of the information presented.

- ✓ Look for common patterns of organization.

- ✓ Identify transition words and phrases to help you verify the order of the information and patterns of organization.

Purpose and Tone

- ✓ Decide on the writer's main purpose: to inform, to persuade, or to entertain.

- ✓ Establish the tone by noting the diction, choice of words, used by the writer.

- ✓ Pay attention to two general tones: formal and informal.

- ✓ Determine the writer's intended audience.

- ✓ Look for irony and exaggeration, two techniques that can show tone and purpose.

- ✓ Label the writer's tone using one or two words.

Inference

- ✓ Look for evidence in the reading to support your reasoning.

- ✓ Use your prior knowledge about a subject.

- ✓ Look at the organization of a reading.

- ✓ Pay attention to the writer's tone and diction.

- ✓ Watch for a writer's bias toward the topic.

✳ Critical Thinking

✳ Faulty Logic

✔ Check that the evidence used to support a proposal is relevant to the argument.

✔ Determine whether enough support is given to make a strong case.

✔ See if the organization clearly shows how one action leads to another and will produce the result the writer asserts.

✔ Look closely at the writer's words to determine if they show any bias or try to manipulate the reader through emotional appeals.

✔ Decide if there are other possible outcomes besides the one(s) the writer presents.

✔ Be aware of fallacies as a way to look for faulty logic.

✳ Figurative Language

✔ Determine what two items are being compared.

✔ Consider the various meanings or qualities associated with the item to which the first thing is being compared.

✔ Connect the pertinent meanings or qualities to the item to which it is being compared.

Short Story

✔ Determine what happens in the story to comprehend the plot.

✔ Know who the characters are and establish their personality traits through their actions and dialogue.

✔ Decide what kind or kinds of conflict the protagonist faces.

✔ Establish what impact the setting—time and place—has on the story, and how the tone may be developed through the setting.

✔ Decipher any symbols found in the story.

✔ Use the various literary elements to decide on the theme.

Journey to the Seven Wonders

by Tony Perrottet

Before You Read

1. Survey the headings. How many of the Seven Wonders have you heard of?
2. What do you think made these seven architectural works "Wonders"?
3. What would you consider an architectural wonder of the last 200 years?
4. Look at the photos and drawing. What do they reveal about time?

Vocabulary Preview

Look for these words in the reading. Exercises to reinforce the learning of new vocabulary using these words follow the reading. The paragraph number where the word appears is in parentheses.

antiquity (6)	**erudite** (8)	**peripatetic** (9)	
enclave (10)	**pellucid** (12)	**ostentatious** (15)	
svelte (15)	**apogee** (18)	**ziggurats** (19)	**transience** (31)

Tony Perrottet was born in Australia, and as a youth enjoyed traveling. While in school, he journeyed to India, Sumatra, and Australia's outback, among other places. After getting a history degree, he headed to South America where he worked as a journalist. Eventually, he ended up in New York City. He has written four books and numerous articles (many on travel), and he often appears as a guest on the History Channel. Among the publications his articles have appeared in are *Smithsonian Magazine*, the *New York Times*, the *London Sunday Times, Outside*, and *National Geographic Adventure*. The following article appeared in the *Smithsonian* in June 2004.

1 Visitors to the lobby of the Empire State Building in Midtown Manhattan are often surprised to find a series of pictorial stained-glass panels. Added in the 1960s, they were meant to link the great skyscraper to other engineering triumphs. These triumphs, however, are not the great symbols of American modernity you might expect—other massive steel-and-concrete structures like the Hoover Dam or the Panama Canal—but the Seven Wonders of the Ancient World.

2 The colorful lobby paintings make no attempt at accuracy. Rather, they echo fantasies of the ancient monuments that have been current since the Renaissance—but they are mysteriously inspiring all the same: the Pyramids of Giza, the Pharos of Alexandria, the Temple of Artemis in Ephesus, the Mausoleum at Halicarnassus, the Colossus of Rhodes, the Hanging Gardens of Babylon, the Statue of Zeus at Olympia.

"Though only one of the ancient marvels still stands, they still engage our imagination—and launch a thousand tours—more than two millennia later"

3 Why should a collection of monuments more than two millennia old still capture the imagination—especially when six of the seven are no longer standing?

4 "It's that word 'wonder,'" says David Gilman Romano, professor of classics at the University of Pennsylvania. "If you just called them the Seven Architectural Marvels, it wouldn't have the same impact." Then, too, the one that does survive—the Pyramids of Giza—is sufficiently stunning to convince us that the ancients weren't exaggerating the splendor of the other six.

5 It's also our passion for ordering the world. "We are living in a time very much like that of the Hellenic period," says Larissa Bonfante, professor of classics at New York University. "The Greeks loved to have things categorized—they loved anything out of the ordinary—and so do we." In our chaotic age, bombarded as we are with new technologies and rapid cultural change, we still seem to yearn for the security of mutually acknowledged "greats"—whether it be Impressionist painters, *Citizen Kane,* the Washington Monument, Cartier-Bresson photographs or the Hanging Gardens of Babylon.

6 One of the first-known lists of wonders was drawn up in the third century B.C., when a Greek scholar at the Library of Alexandria, Callimachus of Cyrene (305–240 B.C.), wrote a treatise called "A collection of wonders in lands throughout the world." The essay has been lost, but his choices may have become the basis for later selections, such as the famous list attributed to the engineer Philo of Byzantium around 250 B.C. Of course, the whole idea of Seven Wonders started with antiquity's fondness for the number seven: being indivisible, it gave each of its elements equal status and so enjoyed a privileged position in numerology.

7 The list also reflected a shift in Western attitudes toward the world, as thinkers began to celebrate man-made creations along with those of the gods. In the wake of Alexander the Great's conquests of the Persian Empire and parts of India (334–325 B.C), Greeks marveled at their own achievements. "Like the sun," raves Philo of the Hanging Gardens, "beauty dazzling in its brilliance."

8 From their inception, the ancient Wonders were also rooted in human curiosity. In fact, the sites, originally, were not called "Wonders" at all, but *theamata,* "things to be seen," preferably in person. In the Hellenic era, wealthy and erudite Greeks traveled by land and sea around the cultural centers of the eastern Mediterranean, broadening their education firsthand. Although the lands conquered by Alexander the Great had dissolved into separate kingdoms by the time Philo compiled his list, they were still ruled by Greek-speaking dynasties, and while travel was not yet as safe as it would become under the Roman Empire, the network of Greek culture extended far and wide, offering an open invitation to explore.

9 Today one can follow the itinerary of an ancient traveler as he—a peripatetic Greek scholar of that time was almost always

male—sought out the magnificent Seven. Along the route, he would find passable highway inns and cheap roadside restaurants. At the sites themselves, professional tour guides called *exegetai*, or "explainers," jostled for commissions ("Zeus protect me from your guides at Olympia!" prayed one first-century B.C. antiquarian worn down by their harangues). There were papyrus guidebooks to consult before departing and vendors with whom to haggle over souvenirs: a cheap glass vial engraved with an image of the Pharos of Alexandria has been found by archaeologists as far away as Afghanistan.

The Statue of Zeus at Olympia

10 Departing in the shadow of the Acropolis from Athens, the traditional center of ancient learning, a scholar-tourist of 250 B.C. would likely have set off on his grand tour with a couple of servants and a pair of pack mules to carry the luggage. The first and easiest Wonder to visit was the great sculptor Phidias' (c. 485–425 B.C.) Statue of Zeus (completed around 435 B.C.) at Olympia, a religious sanctuary in southern Greece and the site of the Olympic Games. An energetic walker could cover the 210 miles in ten days. Arriving at Olympia, visitors beheld a walled enclave where a trio of Doric temples, 70 altars and hundreds of statues of past Olympic victors created a dazzling garden. The most impressive of the structures was the Temple of Zeus, built between 466 and 456 B.C. and resembling the Parthenon in Athens. Through its grand bronze doors a constant stream of travelers passed into the flickering torchlight, there to behold a glowering, 40-foot-high, gold-and-ivory figure of the King of the Gods seated on a throne, his features framed by a leonine mane of hair.

11 "It seems that if Zeus were to stand up," wrote the Greek geographer Strabo, who visited the statue early in the first century B.C., "he would unroof the temple." Beyond its stunning size, viewers were struck by the majesty of the image's expression—even stray dogs were said to be cowed. The sculptor had captured both Zeus' invincible divinity and his humanity. Roman general Aemilius Paullus (c. 229–160 B.C.), an earlier visitor, "was moved to his soul, as if

he had beheld the god in person," while the Greek orator Dio Chrysostom wrote that a single glimpse of the statue would make a man forget his earthly troubles.

The Colossus of Rhodes

12 From Olympia, our intrepid traveler would have caught a merchant ship from the isthmus of Corinth, sailing eastward some 300 miles across the pellucid waters of the Aegean. Since there was no exclusive passenger service, one simply negotiated a price with the ship's captain and took a place on deck. One's servants would arrange the creature comforts, leaving the traveler to enjoy the view and make small talk with fellow passengers.

13 Arriving a few days later at their destination, the bustling island of Rhodes, the travelers would have been greeted with a breathtaking sight. There, towering majestically above the island's port, so crowded with ships' masts that it was said to resemble a field of wheat, stood a 110-foot-high Colossus—a gleaming bronze statue of the Greek sun god Helios. It was long believed that the statue straddled the harbor entrance, but modern archaeologists say this would not have been possible with the bronze-casting techniques available to the sculptor, Chares of Lindos, when he erected it between 294 and 282 B.C.

14 While not even a drawing of the statue survives, scholars theorize the Colossus was an upright figure holding a torch aloft in one hand not unlike the Statue of Liberty; Helios' face was quite possibly modeled after Alexander the Great's. Yet, for all its majesty the Colossus turned out to be the most fragile Wonder of them all—standing for only 56 years before collapsing in an earthquake in 226 B.C. "Even lying on the ground, it is a marvel," wrote Roman scholar Pliny the Elder in the first century A.D. "Few people can even put their arms around the figure's thumb, and each of its fingers is larger than most statues."

The Temple of Artemis in Ephesus

15 The Colossus would have made an appropriate introduction to the opulence of Asia Minor (modern Turkey), where the Temple of Artemis mixed Oriental splendor and Hellenic artistry. Size mattered in the ancient world, and in the ostentatious port

of Ephesus, citizens built their greatest temple to tower above the city skyline. Though the Parthenon of Athens was regarded as the most perfectly proportioned of all buildings, the Temple of Artemis overwhelmed it in scale. Estimates suggest the interior was about 425 feet long and 255 feet wide, making it nearly as cavernous as New York City's Grand Central Terminal. One hundred twenty-seven columns, painted in gaudy colors, supported its huge ceiling; some visitors felt lost in the dizzying forest of pillars, as imposing as sequoia trunks. Guides warned tourists not to stare at the temple's polished white-marble walls lest they be struck blind by their brilliance. Swathed in clouds of incense, a statue of the mother goddess beckoned with open arms. This was not the svelte, athletic huntress Artemis of Greek lore but a majestic, maternal creation from the East, whose multiple breasts hung like papayas from her torso. Among eunuch priests offering sacrifice at the statue's feet, silversmiths peddled souvenir miniatures of the temple and goddess for the pagan faithful. "Only in Heaven has the Sun ever looked upon its equal," gushed Greek author Antipater around 100 B.C.

The Mausoleum at Halicarnassus

16 No less splendor graced the Mausoleum, rising 140 feet into the air like a gigantic wedding cake above the turquoise harbor of Halicarnassus, now the modern port of Bodrum on the so-called Turkish Riviera, about 60 miles from the Colossus. Built, legend has it, around 350 B.C. for King Mausolos, the ruler of Caria, by his grief-stricken sister-wife, Artemisia, the Mausoleum was an art lover's fantasy whose tiers teemed with more than a hundred statues of heroes, kings and Amazon warriors, carved by the five greatest Greek sculptors of the day. "Even today," noted Pliny the Elder in 75 A.D., "the hands of the sculptors seem to vie with one another in artistry." The glittering confection was topped with a statue believed to be of the dead king and his wife riding a golden chariot.

The Lighthouse of Alexandria

17 Sailing south to Egypt, a journey of several days, travelers up to 50 miles out to sea could spot the fifth—and the only practical—ancient Wonder: the Pharos, or lighthouse, of Alexandria, whose orange flame guided ship pilots along the Nile

Delta's treacherous coastline. Looming above Alexandria's busy Eastern Harbor and surrounded by palm trees and statues of the Pharaohs, the 445-foot, three-tiered limestone tower was taller than the Statue of Liberty. At its pinnacle, a giant burning brazier topped by a statue of Zeus provided a suitably theatrical arrival to the city where Europe, Africa and Asia met. Once ashore, visitors hastened to Alexandria's Great Library to observe the scientists, astronomers and geographers who labored in what amounted to the first government-funded think tank, the Mouseion. It was these learned men who had produced the lighthouse.

The Pyramids of Giza

18 Eventually, our Seven Wonders tourist would likely have torn himself away from Alexandria's pleasures to sail up the Nile and gaze upon the oldest and most impressive Wonder of them all—the Pyramids of Giza, three pyramids that rise, even to this day, from the undulating sands of the Giza Plateau. (For thousands of years, the Great Pyramid of Giza was the tallest and most precise stone building in the world.) The pyramids were especially dazzling in the Greek era when they were still sheathed in white limestone and covered by hieroglyphics and graffiti, glistening brilliantly in the desert sun. Surrounding the pyramids, the remains of ancient temples dating back to the Old Kingdom—the apogee of Egyptian military power and artistic skill circa 2500 B.C.—dotted the landscape. Shaven-headed priests, acting as tour guides, pretended to translate the pyramids' hieroglyphics, which they said described the construction of the monuments, including even what the Egyptian workmen who built them, between around 2580 and 2510 B.C., ate on the job.

The Hanging Gardens of Babylon

19 The final site on our traveler's itinerary would have been the most difficult to visit. He would have had to sail to Antioch, in Syria, then follow 500 miles of desert tracks, either on horseback or by carriage, to gaze upon the gardens' splendor. Babylon, lying some 45 miles south of modern Baghdad, was once widely regarded as the most intoxicating urban center in the world. Travelers entered the city through the Ishtar Gates, inlaid with blue glazed bricks bearing images of lions, bulls and dragons, only to behold a forest of towering ziggurats,

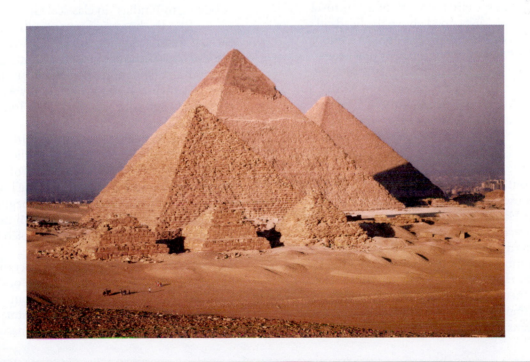

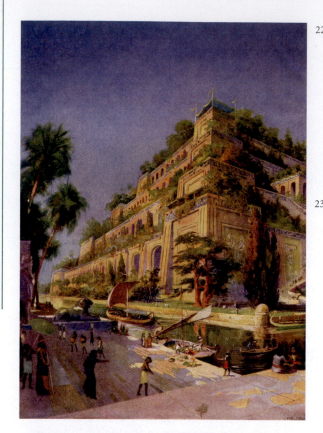

obelisks and smoking altars by the Euphrates River.

20   The Hanging Gardens—a rooftop paradise of sculpted terraces, shade, and perfumed flowers—rose majestically above the human sprawl, watered by a hydraulic irrigation system. ("A work of art of royal luxury . . . suspended above the heads of spectators," noted Greek engineer Philo around 250 B.C.) The gardens had been built by King Nebuchadnezzar II (604–562 B.C.) for his wife, a princess from Media, a fertile kingdom by the southern Caspian Sea, who was homesick for greenery; it was said Alexander the Great gazed upon them from his deathbed in the royal palace in 323 B.C.

21   But much about the gardens is unknown, including their exact location. "The Hanging Gardens, by their very nature, cannot be definitively found," says Richard A. Billows, professor of history at Columbia University. "They would not leave a very clear footprint that says 'this must have been the spot.' This isn't helped by the fact that there is no clear idea of what the gardens looked like."

22   Though only one of the Seven Wonders survives, it and the sites of the six others still launch a thousand package tours each year. Fascination with the Pyramids of Giza is certainly understandable; even stripped of their gleaming limestone—Arab conquerors used it as building material in the Middle Ages—the pyramids' majesty, antiquity and bulk continue to astonish visitors, even if their first glimpse is from a crowded Cairo suburban highway.

23   But our fascination with the "missing" Wonders is harder to explain. Two of them exist only as fragments on display in museums; others have been scorched entirely from the earth. And yet, they remain curiously compelling. Phidias' Statue of Zeus at Olympia was taken to Constantinople in the fourth century A.D. and was later destroyed in a palace fire, but the sanctuary itself—near the first Olympic stadium through overgrown ruins buzzing with bees—remains one of the most visited attractions in Greece. All that is left of the Temple of Zeus is its foundation, but the spot where the statue stood has been identified. In 1958, archaeologists found, some 50 yards from the temple ruins, the workshop in which the artist Phidias sculpted the statue in the fifth century B.C.—including pieces of ivory and the base of a bronze drinking cup engraved with the words "I belong to Phidias" in classical Greek.

24   In Rhodes, hordes of tourists cluster each summer at Mandraki Harbor, where the Colossus is thought to have stood. Around A.D. 650, more than eight centuries after its collapse, it was broken up by Arab plunderers and sold as scrap metal. Today, not a toenail remains, though local entrepreneurs peddle souvenir T-shirts, spoons and cups emblazoned with the statue's image. (In 1999, the citizens of Rhodes announced a memorial to be built on the site, though work has yet to begin.)

25   As for the two Wonders of Asia Minor— the Temple of Artemis and the Mausoleum— they were devastated by earthquakes, barbarians and vengeful Christians. Scraps of both lie in the British Museum in London, but their sites are hauntingly bare. In an ironic genuflection to the cycles of history, chunks of the Mausoleum's original masonry

were used to refortify the Castle of St. Peter at Bodrum, which was restored in the 1970s as a museum dedicated to underwater archaeology.

26 And, as the city of Alexandria reminds us, there is always hope for finding "lost" Wonders. In 1994, Asra el Bakri, an Egyptian filmmaker creating a documentary about Alexandria's Eastern Harbor, noticed some huge stone blocks just below the water's surface off Fort Qaitbey, on a promontory at the heart of the old city. Within a year, French marine archaeologists had catalogued just under 3,000 chunks of masonry, some of which is thought to be the lighthouse, scattered about the ocean floor. Soon they were raising the magnificent statues that once stood by its side. The sculptures are believed to have fallen there during earthquakes that struck the region from late antiquity to the 14th century A.D.

27 "As a news story, it was definitely very sexy," says Colin Clement, spokesman for the Centre d'Etudes Alexandrines (CEA), the French organization leading the work. "It seemed like everyone wanted to film or photograph what we were doing." More recently, marine archaeologists discovered the frame of a nearly 40-foot-high double door that was once part of the lighthouse. Using computer graphics, CEA archaeologists are now piecing together how the edifice would have looked and functioned. "Little by little, from campaign to campaign, we have more results," says Jean-Yves Empereur, director of the CEA, emphasizing that he is attempting to reconstruct all of ancient Alexandria graphically, not just a single monument.

28 One tour company, ignoring warnings that the harbor's untreated sewage may cause typhoid, offers recreational diving to the lighthouse stones as well as to two dozen fragmented sphinxes on the sea bottom. For its part, the Egyptian government has floated plans for an underwater marine park, which tourists would visit in glass-bottomed boats. "Why not?" says Clement. "What's the point of doing the work if it's just for a few academics reading fusty, obscure journals?"

29 Of course, one Wonder has dropped off today's grand tour entirely—the Hanging Gardens. "Things have been going very badly for Babylon over the last 20 years," says Harriet Crawford, chairman of the British School of Archaeology in Iraq. Saddam Hussein's "reconstruction" program, begun in 1987, devastated the Mesopotamian city's venerable ruins. As a self-styled new Nebuchadnezzar, Hussein built a luxurious palace on a hill above the excavations of the original royal palace, then ordered the ancient edifice rebuilt using bricks stamped with his name. The Hanging Gardens—Babylon's trademark feature—played a key role in this farce: courtyards and passageways were built to integrate the supposed site of the gardens into the reconstruction. Ironically, new research carried out by Stephanie Dalley and others of the Oriental Institute at Oxford University suggests the gardens may not have been in Babylon at all, but in Nineveh, the ancient capital of Assyria in what is now northern Iraq. Nor are they thought to have been built by Nebuchadnezzar, but an Assyrian king, Sennacherib.

30 Misguided though it was, the work in Babylon shows the power of the past to shape the present. In seeking to connect himself to Iraq's most glorious era, "Hussein saw the significance of Babylon," says Crawford. "He used it as a symbol of national identity and triumph, to unite all the factions in Iraq."

31 The fate of the original Seven Wonders has long provoked a wide spectrum of reactions, from melancholy meditations on human vanity to the transience of man's achievements. But if their most obvious lesson is that our finest creations will one day turn to rubble, it is a lesson that we resolutely refuse to learn. Which is only as it should be, as the ancient Wonders' durability—if only in our imagination—so eloquently testifies.

Getting the Message

_____ 1. What is the topic?

    a. the Empire State Building   c. large buildings

    b. ancient Greece   d. the Seven Wonders

_____ 2. The topic sentence in paragraph 8 can be found in

    a. sentence 1.   c. sentence 3.

    b. sentence 2.   d. sentence 4.

_____ 3. The following sentence best expresses the main idea:

    a. We can journey to the Seven Wonders exactly as the ancient Greeks did.

    b. Though only one of the Seven Wonders still exists, they still continue to amaze us.

    c. Modern architectural achievements will never match the Seven Wonders.

    d. Seeing the Seven Wonders at their height was an amazing experience.

_____ 4. What types of supporting detail does Perrottet use?

    a. examples and facts   c. facts and statistics

    b. reasons and testimony   d. a and b

_____ 5. Which of the following is a minor supporting detail?

    a. It's also our passion for ordering the world. (par. 5)

    b. An energetic walker could cover the 210 miles in ten days. (par. 10)

    c. Shaven-headed priests, acting as tour guides, pretended to translate the pyramids' hieroglyphics. . . . (par. 18)

    d. b and c

_____ 6. Perrottet uses the _____ pattern of organization for paragraphs 9–21.

    a. definition   c. classification

    b. process   d. comparison and contrast

_____ 7. The transition word _Eventually_ that begins paragraph 18 shows

    a. comparison.   c. time.

    b. addition.   d. order of importance.

_____ 8. Perrottet's purpose is to

    a. inform people about the significance of the Seven Wonders.

    b. warn people about the transience of human creations.

    c. amuse people with descriptions of the Seven Wonders.

    d. persuade people to see the Seven Wonders.

_____ 9. It can be inferred from the line "Today one can follow the itinerary of an ancient traveler as he—a peripatetic Greek scholar of that time was almost always male—sought out the magnificent Seven" (par. 9) that women in ancient Greece

    a. didn't have much interest in travel.

    b. were not treated as equals.

    c. were not very curious individuals.

    d. were not allowed on ships.

_____**10.** Does the following line contain a simile or metaphor? "No less splendor graced the Mausoleum, rising 140 feet into the air like a gigantic wedding cake above the turquoise harbor of Halicarnassus . . ." (par. 16).

a. simile   b. metaphor

11. Perrottet uses testimony from modern and historic sources. Give an example from each time period and explain whether you find these sources effective in supporting Perrottet's main idea.

_____

_____

_____

_____

_____

12. Perrottet looks at the effects the Seven Wonders have had on people from the time they were built to today. List three effects he mentions and give the paragraph number where you find the information.

_____

_____

_____

13. For each Wonder list a word that Perrottet uses to describe it. Are any of the same words used to describe more than one of the Wonders? How does Perrottet's diction help to capture the magnificence of the Wonders?

_____

_____

_____

_____

14. List two questions or comments you wrote in the margins.

_____

_____

15. Paraphrase the sentence "From their inception, the ancient Wonders were also rooted in human curiosity" (par. 8).

_____

_____

Vocabulary

Use context clues to determine the meaning by looking back at the paragraph where the word is used (the paragraph number is in parentheses). If you need help, consult a dictionary for the definition.

A. Match each vocabulary word below to its synonym.

> **erudite** (8)   **peripatetic** (9)   **pellucid** (12)   **svelte** (15)   **apogee** (18)

1. peak _____
2. wandering _____
3. clear _____
4. educated _____
5. slim _____

B. Complete each sentence using the correct vocabulary word. Use each word once.

> **antiquity** (6)   **enclave** (10)   **ostentatious** (15)   **ziggurat** (19)   **transience** (31)

1. The _____ of a culture's accomplishments can be seen in the Roman-era ruins scattered throughout Italy.

2. I enjoyed standing on the top terrace of the _____, admiring the river below.

3. Suzy never worried about being _____; wearing diamonds and rubies to a picnic was just her style.

4. For some, _____ holds a certain romance with stories of the Greek and Roman gods and goddesses, noble architecture, and ancient warfare.

5. The _____ of rooms, restaurants, and tourist facilities in the jungle was amazing.

C. Word parts: Fill in the missing word part from the list, and circle the meaning of the word part found in each question. Return to pages 85–87 if you need to review the meaning of a word part.

> **trans**   **cis**   **ology**   **lect**   **or**

1. I don't rely on numer_____, but many cultures have used the study of numbers to predict a person's future.

2. I had a lot to choose from. Among the se_____ions were two of my favorites: salmon and pork.

3. The orat_____ spoke for four hours. I wish I was one who could talk to crowds.

4. The dropping of leaves each fall reflects the _____ience of life. We all go across new bridges and leave familiar places behind.

5. I want to be pre_____e when I measure where to cut the wood.

The Article and You

1. Which of the Seven Wonders seems the most wondrous to you? Explain why.

_____

_____

2. Pick seven modern structures (from the last 2000 years) that you would put on a list of "Modern Wonders of the World."

_____

_____

3. Would you have undertaken the journey to see the Seven Wonders? Explain why or why not.

_____

_____

4. On a separate sheet of paper, write a paragraph where you create your own wondrous structure. Describe what it will look like, where it will be located, and why you would build it. Make a sketch of it to further help your readers visualize your creation.

Take a Closer Look

Look at the photos and drawing again. After reading about the Wonders and looking at the visuals, why do you think they have captured people's imaginations? Look at the map on page 434 again, and circle the Mediterranean region where the Seven Wonders were located.

_____

_____

Internet Activities

If needed, use a separate sheet of paper to fully record your responses. Include the Web address of any sites from which you gather information.

1. Pick two of the Seven Wonders and search for sketches or paintings that show what people think the buildings or statues might have looked like in their prime. Pick one image to print and share with the class. What struck you about this depiction of the Wonder?

_____

_____

2. Go to new7wonders.com, and list the sites voters chose as the Seven New Wonders of the World. Did any of the places you picked for question 2 in The Article and You win? Do you agree that the sites qualify as Wonders?

_____

_____

_____

Country of Longitudinal Essences

by Isabel Allende

from *My Invented Country: A Nostalgic Journey through Chile*

Before You Read

1. Skim the first few paragraphs. Could you find Chile on a map?

2. What do you know about Chile?

3. What qualities do you think make a country special?

4. Look at the photos. What impressions do they give you about Chile?

Vocabulary Preview

Look for these words in the reading. Exercises to reinforce the learning of new vocabulary using these words follow the reading. The paragraph number where the word appears is in parentheses.

cordillera (2)	**formidable** (2)	**voraciously** (3)	**pampa** (5)	**inclement** (6)
esoteric (7)	**usurped** (7)	**libation** (7)	**labyrinth** (9)	**junta** (13)

Isabel Allende has written six novels, including *The House of the Spirits* and *Eva Luna*; children's books; a collection of short stories; and the memoirs *Paula* and *Aphrodite: A Memoir of the Senses*. She was born in Peru, grew up in Chile, and now lives in California. Her book *My Invented Country: A Nostalgic Journey through Chile* was first published in 2003. In the book she tells about her experiences in Chile as a child and an adult, and she explores various aspects of Chile's history and people.

1 Let's begin at the beginning, with Chile, that remote land that few people can locate on the map because it's as far as you can go without falling off the planet. *Why don't we sell Chile and buy something closer to Paris?* one of our intellectuals once asked. No one passes by casually, however lost he may be, although many visitors decide to stay forever, enamored of the land and the people. Chile lies at the end of all roads, a lance to the south of the south of America, four thousand three hundred kilometers of hills, valleys, lakes, and sea. This is how Neruda describes it in his impassioned poetry:

> *Night, snow and sand compose the form*
> *of my slender homeland,*
> *all silence is contained within its length,*
> *all foam issues from its seaswept beard,*
> *all coal fills it with mysterious kisses.*

2 This elongated country is like an island, separated on the north from the rest of the continent by the Atacama Desert—the driest in the world, its inhabitants like to say, although that must not be true, because in springtime parts of that lunar rubble tend to be covered with a mantle of flowers, like a wondrous painting by Monet. To the east rises the cordillera of the Andes, a formidable mass of rock and eternal snows, and to the west the abrupt coastline of the Pacific Ocean. Below, to the south, lie the solitudes of Antarctica. This nation of dramatic topography and diverse climates, studded with capricious obstacles and shaken by the sighs of hundreds of volcanoes, a geological miracle between the

heights of the cordillera and the depths of the sea, is unified top to tail by the obstinate sense of nationhood of its inhabitants.

3   We Chileans still feel our bond with the soil, like the campesinos we once were. Most of us dream of owning a piece of land, if for nothing more than to plant a few worm-eaten heads of lettuce. Our most important newspaper, *El Mercurio*, publishes a weekly agricultural supplement that informs the public in general of the latest insignificant pest found on the potatoes or about the best forage for improving milk production. Its readers, who are planted in asphalt and concrete, read it voraciously, even though they have never seen a live cow.

4   In the broadest terms, it can be said that my long and narrow homeland can be broken up into four very different regions. The country is divided into provinces with beautiful names, but the military, who may have had difficulty memorizing them, added numbers for identification purposes. I refuse to use them because a nation of poets cannot have a map dotted with numbers, like some mathematical delirium. So let's talk about the four large regions, beginning with the *norte grande,* the "big north" that occupies a fourth of the country; inhospitable and rough,

guarded by high mountains, it hides in its entrails an inexhaustible treasure of minerals.

5   I traveled to the north when I was a child, and I've never forgotten it, though a half-century has gone by since then. Later in my life I had the opportunity to cross the Atacama Desert a couple of times, and although those were extraordinary experiences, my first recollections are still the strongest. In my memory, Antofagasta, which in Quechua means "town of the great salt lands," is not the modern city of today but a miserable, out-of-date port that smelled like iodine and was dotted with fishing boats, gulls, and pelicans. In the nineteenth century it rose from the desert like a mirage, thanks to the industry producing nitrates, which for several decades were one of Chile's principal exports. Later, when synthetic nitrate was invented, the port was kept busy exporting copper, but as the nitrate companies began to close down, one after another, the pampa became strewn with ghost towns. Those two words—"ghost town"—gave wings to my imagination on that first trip.

6   I recall that my family and I, loaded with bundles, climbed onto a train that traveled at a turtle's pace through the inclement Atacama Desert toward Bolivia. Sun, baked

rocks, kilometers and kilometers of ghostly solitudes, from time to time an abandoned cemetery, ruined buildings of adobe and wood. It was a dry heat where not even flies survived. Thirst was unquenchable. We drank water by the gallon, sucked oranges, and had a hard time defending ourselves from the dust, which crept into every cranny. Our lips were so chapped they bled, our ears hurt, we were dehydrated. At night a cold hard as glass fell over us, while the moon lighted the landscape with a blue splendor. Many years later I would return to the north of Chile to visit Chuquicamata, the largest open-pit copper mine in the world, an immense amphitheater where thousands of earth-colored men, working like ants, rip the mineral from stone. The train ascended to a height of more than four thousand meters and the temperature descended to the point where water froze in our glasses. We passed the silent salt mine of Uyuni, a white sea of salt where no bird flies, and others where we saw elegant flamingos. They were brush strokes of pink among salt crystals glittering like precious stones.

7   The so-called *norte chico,* or "little north," which some do not classify as an actual region, divides the dry north from the fertile central zone. Here lies the valley of Elqui, one of the spiritual centers of the Earth, said to be magical. The mysterious forces of Elqui attract pilgrims who come there to make contact with the cosmic energy of the universe, and many stay on to live in esoteric communities. Meditation, Eastern religions, gurus of various stripes, there's something of everything in Elqui. It's like a little corner of California. It is also from Elqui that our *pisco* comes, a liquor made from the muscatel grape: transparent, virtuous, and serene as the angelic force that emanates from the land. *Pisco* is the prime ingredient of the *pisco* sour, our sweet and treacherous national drink, which must be drunk with confidence, though the second glass has a kick that can floor the most valiant among us. We usurped

the name of this liquor, without a moment's hesitation, from the city of Pisco, in Peru. If any wine with bubbles can be called champagne, even though the authentic libation comes only from Champagne, France, I suppose our *pisco,* too, can appropriate a name from another nation. The *norte chico* is also home to La Silla, one of the most important observatories in the world, because the air there is so clear that no star—either dead or yet to be born—escapes the eye of its gigantic telescope. Apropos of the observatory, someone who has worked there for three decades told me that the most renowned astronomers in the world wait years for their turn to scour the universe. I commented that it must be stupendous to work with scientists whose eyes are always on infinity and who live detached from earthly miseries, but he informed me that it is just the opposite: astronomers are as petty as poets. He says they fight over jam at breakfast. The human condition never fails to amaze.

8   The *valle central* is the most prosperous area of the country, a land of grapes and apples, where industries are clustered and a third of the population lives in the capital city. Santiago was founded in 1541 by Pedro de Valdivia. After walking for months through the dry north, it seemed to him that he'd reached the Garden of Eden. In Chile everything is centralized in the capital, despite the efforts of various governments that over the span of half a century have tried to distribute power among the provinces. If it doesn't happen in Santiago, it may as well not happen at all, although life in the rest of the country is a thousand times calmer and more pleasant.

9   The *zona sur,* the southern zone, begins at Puerto Montt, at 40 degrees latitude south, an enchanted region of forests, lakes, rivers, and volcanoes. Rain and more rain nourishes the tangled vegetation of the cool forests where our native trees rise tall, ancients of thousand-year growth now threatened by the timber industry. Moving south, the traveler crosses pampas lashed by furious winds, then

the country strings out into a rosary of unpopulated islands and milky fogs, a labyrinth of fjords, islets, canals, and water on all sides. The last city on the continent is Punta Arenas, wind-bitten, harsh, and proud; a high, barren land of blizzards.

10   Chile owns a section of the little-explored Antarctic continent, a world of ice and solitude, of infinite white, where fables are born and men die: Chile ends at the South Pole. For a long time, no one assigned any value to Antarctica, but now we know how many mineral riches it shelters, in addition to being a paradise of marine life, so there is no country that doesn't have an eye on it. In the summertime, a cruise ship can visit there with relative ease, but the price of such a cruise is as the price of rubies, and for the present, only rich tourists and poor but determined ecologists can make the trip.

11   In 1888 Chile annexed the Isla de Pascua, mysterious Easter Island, *the navel of the world,* or Rapanui, as it is called in the natives' language. The island is lost in the immensity of the Pacific Ocean, 2,500 miles from continental Chile, more or less six hours by jet from Valparaíso or Tahiti. I am not sure why it belongs to us. In olden times, a ship captain planted a flag, and a slice of the planet became legally yours, regardless of whether that pleased its inhabitants, in this case peaceful Polynesians. This was the practice of European nations, and Chile could not lag behind. For the islanders, contact with South America was fatal. In the mid-nineteenth century, most of the male population was taken off to Peru to work as slaves in the guano deposits, while Chile shrugged its shoulders at the fate of its forgotten citizens. The treatment those poor men received was so bad that it caused an international protest in Europe, and, after a long diplomatic struggle, the last fifteen survivors were returned to their families. Those few went back infected with small pox, and within a brief time the illness exterminated eighty percent of the natives on the island. The fate of the remainder was not much better. Imported sheep ate the vegetation, turning the landscape into a barren husk of lava, and the negligence of the authorities—in this case the Chilean navy—drove the inhabitants into poverty. Only in the last two decades, tourism and the interest of the world scientific community have rescued Rapanui.

12   Scattered across the Easter Island are monumental statues of volcanic stone, some weighing more than twenty tons. These *moais* have intrigued experts for centuries. To sculpt them on the slopes of the volcanoes and then drag them across rough ground, to erect them on often-inaccessible bases and place hats of red stone atop them, was the task of titans. How was it done? There are no traces of an advanced civilization that can explain such prowess. Two different groups populated the island. According to legend, one of those groups, the Arikis, had supernatural mental powers, which they used to levitate the *moais* and transport them, floating effortlessly, to their altars on the steep slopes. What a tragedy that this technique has been lost to the world! In 1940, the Norwegian anthropologist Thor Heyerdahl built a balsa raft, which he christened *Kon Tiki,* and sailed from South America to Easter Island to prove that there had been contact between the Incas and the Easter Islanders.

13   I traveled to Easter Island in the summer of 1974, when there was only one flight a week and tourism was nearly nonexistent. Enchanted, I stayed three weeks longer than I had planned, and thus happened to be on the spot when the first television broadcast was celebrated with a visit by General Pinochet, who had led the military junta that had replaced Chile's democracy some months earlier. The television was received with more enthusiasm than the brand-new dictator. The general's stay was extremely colorful, but this isn't the time to go into those details. It's enough to say that a mischievous little cloud strategically hovered above his head every time he wanted to speak in public, leaving him wringing wet and limp as a dishrag. He had come with the idea of delivering property titles to the islanders, but no one was terribly interested in receiving them, since from the most ancient times everyone has known exactly what belongs to whom. They were afraid, and rightly so, that the only

use for that piece of government paper would be to complicate their lives.

14   Chile also owns the island of Juan Fernández, where the Scots sailor Alexander Selkirk, the inspiration for Daniel Defoe's novel *Robinson Crusoe,* was set ashore by his captain in 1704. Selkirk lived on the island for more than four years—without a domesticated parrot or the company of a native named Friday, as portrayed in the novel—until he was rescued by another captain and returned to England, where his fate did not exactly improve. The determined tourist, after a bumpy flight in a small airplane or an interminable trip by boat, can visit the cave where the Scotsman survived by eating herbs and fish.

Getting the Message

____ **1.** The central idea of paragraph 3 is expressed in

    a. sentence 1   c. sentence 3.

    b. sentence 2.   d. sentence 4.

____ **2.** Which sentence best states the main idea of the selection?

    a. Chile is a huge country.   c. Chile is not a very interesting place.

    b. Chile is far from Paris.   d. Chile is filled with diverse landscapes.

____ **3.** Allende uses _____ as supporting details in paragraphs 5 and 6.

    a. facts   c. personal examples

    b. statistics   d. testimony

____ **4.** Which types of supporting details are used in the excerpt?

    a. personal examples and testimony   c. statistics and historical examples

    b. public examples and facts   d. all of the above

____ **5.** Paragraph 11 presents the information in _____ order.

    a. chronological   c. problem and solution

    b. most to least important   d. least to most important

____ **6.** The overall pattern of organization used in the selection is

    a. process.   c. cause and effect.

    b. classification.   d. definition.

____ **7.** The transition word *after* as used in the sentence "After walking for months through the dry north, it seemed to him that he'd reached the Garden of Eden" (par. 8) shows

    a. time.   c. comparison.

    b. addition.   d. contrast.

____ **8.** The tone of the essay is _____.

    a. formal   b. informal

____ **9.** It can be inferred from the line "It's like a little corner of California" (par. 7) that

    a. Californians like to drink pisco sours.

    b. a lot of former Californians live in Elqui.

    c. in California people participate in various spiritual practices.

    d. California has valleys that look like Elqui.

____ **10.** Which type of figurative language does the following sentence illustrate: "They [the flamingos] were brush strokes of pink among salt crystals glittering like precious stones" (par. 6)?

    a. simile   b. metaphor

11. Give two examples of words Allende uses to describe the shape of Chile. After looking at a map—use the map on page 434, your atlas, or check the Internet—do these words seem appropriate? Circle Chile on the map on page 434.

_____

_____

12. Allende uses several similes. List three of them and the paragraph number where each is located. Which one do you like best? Why? What do they add to the reading?

_____

_____

_____

_____

_____

13. What can be inferred about Allende's opinion of the military? Give examples of two passages that helped you reach this conclusion.

_____

_____

_____

_____

14. Look at your annotations. Pick two questions or comments you made that you would like to discuss in class.

_____

_____

15. Finish the informal outline of the essay.

Thesis: _____.

1. Chile is _____. par. 1–2

2. Chileans _____. par. 3

3. Chile can be _____. par. 4

4. _____. par. 5–6

5. _____. par. 7

6. _____. par. 8

7. _____. par. 9

8. Chile's _____. par. 10

9. Chile's _____. par. 11–13

10. Chile's _____. par. 14

Vocabulary

Use context clues to determine the meaning of each word by referring back to the paragraph where the word is used (the paragraph number is in parentheses). If you need help, consult a dictionary for the definition.

A. Match the vocabulary word to its definition.

> cordillera (2)   pampa (5)   esoteric (7)   usurp(ed) (7)   junta (13)

1. to take; to seize_____

2. a chain of mountains or mountain ranges_____

3. a small group running a country, especially after a coup and before a legally formed government has been established_____

4. a large treeless grassland area_____

5. cryptic; mysterious_____

B. Replace the underlined synonym in each sentence with the related vocabulary word.

> formidable (2)   voraciously (3)   inclement (6)   libation (7)   labyrinth (9)

1. The <u>bad</u> weather forced us to reschedule our picnic._____

2. My grandmother's favorite <u>drink</u> was a Cosmopolitan. I don't know if she liked it for the taste or because she considered the pink color pretty._____

3. It took me four hours to make it through the <u>maze</u> of procedures that had to be completed before I could attend the college._____

4. Tony reads books <u>avidly</u>. He often finishes fifteen in a week._____

5. The research paper looked like a <u>difficult</u> project, but when I broke it into small parts, it wasn't so hard to complete._____

C. Word parts: Use the words to match the word part to its meaning. Return to pages 85–87 if you need to review the meaning of a word part.

____1. -ist: ecologist (10), anthropologist (12), sociologist   a. feeling, disease

____2. -able: formidable (2), unquenchable (6), interminable (14)   b. a person who

____3. -pas-, -pat-, -path-: impassioned (1), compassion, sympathy   c. capable of, is, can be

____4. -lev-: levitate (12), elevator, relevant   d. lift, light, rise

The Essay and You

1. Allende talks about pisco sour as being "our sweet and treacherous national drink" (par. 7). What would you nominate as the national drink for the United States? Defend your choice with a couple of reasons.

_____

_____

2. The essay is mainly about Chile's landscape, but Allende mentions other aspects of life in Chile. List three other bits of information you learned about Chile from this selection.

_____

_____

3. Would you like to travel to Chile after reading Allende's account of the country? Give examples of three points she mentions that either attracted you to the area or that dissuaded you from visiting.

_____

_____

_____

4. On a separate sheet of paper, write a paragraph in which you pick a place and divide it into regions as Allende does with Chile. You may want to pick your state or city. Limit the number of regions to no more than five so that you can make your descriptions of each area vivid. As Allende does, try to capture the essence of each region.

Take a Closer Look

Look at the photos again. Has your impression of any of the areas in the photographs changed now that you have read more about Chile? Which four areas do you think the photos present? Which area looks most interesting? Why?

_____

_____

Internet Activities

If needed, use a separate sheet of paper to fully record your responses. Include the Web address of any sites from which you gather information.

1. Look up one of the following people Allende mentions and write a short biography of the person: Pablo Neruda (par. 1), Pedro de Valdivia (par. 8), Thor Heyerdahl (par. 12), General Pinochet (par. 13), or Alexander Selkirk (par. 14).

_____

_____

2. Pick three of the regions or cities Allende mentions and find photos of each place. Using the photographs, pick the place you would most want to visit. Select one photo to print and explain why this photo attracted you to the place.

_____

_____

_____

Mongolia: Dancing in the Village of Delight

Before You Read

1. What do you know about Mongolia?

2. Have you ever considered working in a foreign country?

3. Write your own question you think the reading might address: _____
_____

4. Look at the photos. Would you like to live in such a structure or milk a horse?

Louisa Waugh worked with homeless young people in London for 5 years. She then decided to indulge an urge to travel and discovered Mongolia. After a brief visit there in the early 1990s, she returned 3 years later to work as a journalist in Ulaanbaatar, the capital, for 2 years. She then moved to the isolated village of Tsengel, which means "village of delight" in Mongolian. On her return to Britain, she wrote a book about her time in Mongolia published in 2003 as *Hearing Birds Fly: A Nomadic Year in Mongolia*. The following essay appeared in *The Rough Guide Women Travel 4* in 1999.

Vocabulary Preview

Look for these words in the reading. Exercises to reinforce the learning of new vocabulary using these words follow the reading. The paragraph number where the word appears is in parentheses.

raucous (2)	**nomads** (3)	**steppe** (3)	**resilient** (6)	**conscripted** (12)
eked (13)	**cosseted** (14)	**epicenter** (15)	**dung** (17)	**basked** (21)

1 **"Gansukh,"** I **said,** beaming helplessly, "I'm completely drunk." Smiling, Gansukh tutted and reprimanded me affectionately, her own eyes glinting from the numerous bowls of local vodka we'd knocked back to toast the bride and groom.

2 Gansukh and I had been working together for several months, teaching English at the small Tsengel village school, in the remote far west of Mongolia. When the school year finished she and her husband, Sansar-Huu, had invited me to spend the summer with them, in the Altai mountains beyond Tsengel, where nomads celebrate their weddings with raucous laughter, heartbreaking song and home-distilled vodka. This time with my nomadic friends was supposed to be the culmination of my six-month stay in the village, but I didn't want to leave at the end of summer: there was too much to experience, learn and write about life in the mountains.

3 I'd already spent two years learning Mongolian and working as a journalist and editor in the dilapidated Mongolian capital, Ulaanbaatar, where, after a bloodless revolution, democracy had been secured in 1990. Following 75 years of rigorously enforced socialism and Russian domination, the market economy was now being

pursued with an almighty vengeance. I was both fascinated and appalled by the political and economic implications of the reforms: the homeless children, the young entrepreneurs with their mobile phones and recently acquired American accents, and the dislocated older people, who told me they longed to return to a collective past they understood and felt part of. I wondered how these upheavals were affecting life in the countryside, where three-quarters of a million nomads are still living in their felt *ger* tents, herding their livestock across the arid steppe. I decided to find out by spending several months in the countryside, collecting anecdotes for a book about life in rural Mongolia after democracy.

4   Most of my friends in Ulaanbaatar thought I'd last about a week in the countryside, where there's still only very erratic electricity, and no night life. But, almost in spite of myself, I'd made my mind up, although I didn't have a clue where to go. It was a Kazak friend of a friend who first told me about Tsengel. Late one night, as we sat drinking beer in a dark, dank bar pulsating with Mongolian rock music, he described an isolated village, more than 80km from the nearest town, which was home not only to Mongolian herders, but also Shamanic Tuvan and Muslim Kazak nomads from the neighbouring central Asian republics. Tsengel, he explained, is built on the banks of the wide, treacherous Hovd river and has a small clinic and a school where children from nomadic settlements in the surrounding mountains board twelve to a dormitory. Their parents pay the fees in meat and wood.

5   Intrigued, I wrote to the village governor, Abbai, and offered to teach English classes at the school in return for accommodation and food. Ten days later I received a brief telex, saying the school was drawing up a schedule for me and asking that I come as soon as I could. I had a sleepless night, took a very deep breath and bought a one-way ticket to the airport nearest Tsengel, which was almost 2000km from Ulaanbaatar. "It's OK," I told my sceptical friends. "I'll be back in three or four months. That's plenty of time to research my book." It was almost a year before they saw me again.

6   Within days of arriving in the village in mid-February, the naivety of my self-imposed timetable made me laugh out loud. Tsengel had no electricity or running water. I had never chopped wood, fetched water from a river or well, lit a fire, or cooked on a wood-burning stove in my life. I would have to learn to fend for myself, before I could even begin to unravel these resilient people and the traditions that bound them to their unlit wooden cabins, defiantly carved amid these barren, windswept mountains.

7   At first I was housed alone at the clinic, in a spooky, dark, freezing ward with faded Cyrillic UN posters on the chilly walls and a continual audience of schoolchildren banging on my window. After ten days I begged Abbai to move me and was offered a *ger,* one of the circus top-shaped felt tents which provide shelter for Mongolia's

nomads. My *ger* was situated in one of the Tuvan teachers' *hashas* (fenced yards) and thus began my life with Gansukh, her husband Sansar-Huu and their two young children. They became my greatest friends. We shared the outside trench toilet, did our washing, sawed logs and fetched water together and spent our evenings relaxing in their candle-lit cabin, sharing stories and songs. Gansukh had taught herself a little English, but, in the absence of any other Anglophiles, my Mongolian was finally flourishing.

8   International Women's Day was celebrated just a few weeks after my arrival. Gansukh and I were invited "for tea" to the house of our neighbour Handaa, and found ourselves at a riotous, all-day party. The men had been sent out for the day and the house taken over by Handaa and her friends, their children, mothers and grandmothers. Every woman had brought a platter of meat and a bottle of vodka. We ate and drank, toasted each other for Women's Day, recited poetry, sang, laughed and hugged each other. By ten o'clock that evening I was waltzing round the room with a 55-year-old mother of eight and wondering why it had taken me so long to move west.

9   During the spring many of the village men travelled to the mountains to tend to their families' livestock, while the women remained in the village with the children. This was a particularly brutal spring for Tsengel, as dust and snow storms battered the village and weakened the herds after a long, freezing winter. Thousands of animals died. While Sansar-Huu was away, digging calves and lambs out of snow drifts, Gansukh and her friends, Tuya and Amraa, patiently taught me how to chop wood, light and keep my wood-burning stove going and cook dried meat. I also learnt to brew Mongolian milk tea dosed with salt and to gut fish freshly hooked from the Hovd River.

10   After acquiring a babysitter and a red lipstick, the four of us would storm off to the village disco. Held in a crumbling, generator-powered theatre and with an amazing, tilted dance floor that was almost a hillside, I have many fond memories of ancient, distorted dance records and practising my Mongolian waltz! At first the village men were too intimidated to ask me to dance (although the women waltzed happily with me and each other), but people were gradually becoming used to me living in their small, intimate community. Nomads who lived in settlements outside Tsengel would still gape open-mouthed at me as they rode through the village, but locals now visited my *ger* for tea, updated me on local gossip and shyly asked about life in England: whether we kept camels and sheep, how many children people had and what kind of food we ate. After so long away, I gradually realised my own perceptions of England were receding—I began to recall a perpetually warm country, where it never snowed and everyone lived as part of a nuclear family and next door to a cosy, oak-beamed village pub.

11   At the end of April, it was my thirtieth birthday. People greeted me all day, calling to me from their yards and doorways and presenting me with numerous bags of glistening boiled sweets and armfuls of plastic flowers. Two hundred people turned up to my party at the disco and I was finally cajoled into mounting the narrow, dark stage and crooning the Beatles. Gansukh, Tuya, Amraa and new friends from the school and disco cooked me a glorious, garlicky midnight feast and we sang and danced in my *ger* till we keeled over.

12   It was just after my birthday that I tasted the only true fear I ever felt in Tsengel. At the end of spring a mass of young herders were conscripted into military service for a year and poured into the village from their mountain settlements. Bored with waiting for trucks to transport them to the provincial capital, they drank vodka all day, brawled

in the streets and broke into *hashas* at night. My cosy *ger* with its latticed wooden walls suddenly felt flimsy and vulnerable, as I dozed without sleeping properly and was warned by my friends to barricade my door. After the weekend disco, which for once Gansukh and I decided not to attend, four of the conscripts tried to break in to my *ger*. Sansar-Huu was away and I sat upright in my narrow bed, too rigid and intimidated to light a candle, or even scream for help. But anger finally triumphed over fear, as I rose to my feet, brandished my axe and swore venomously into the darkness. One man lingered at my door, pleading with me to let him in, until, feigning more confidence than I felt, I told him I was going back to sleep and he could visit for tea the next afternoon. I never saw or heard from him again.

13   By the beginning of May, people were waiting for rain to drench the parched steppe. But the elements threw down yet more snow and dust and the grasslands remained resolutely white and yellow. Vegetables had long run out and, like all the villagers, I was living on rice, dried meat and home-made bread. Gansukh and I slowly eked out my Ulaanbaatar-bought provisions. There was hardly anything to buy in the few kiosks in Tsengel. People usually bartered, exchanging sheep and goat skins for shoes, flour for salt, vodka for beef. When Sansar-Huu returned from the mountains for a few days, we shared fresh milk and yoghurt. But yields were low. This had been the harshest spring for a decade.

14   I'd gradually realised that Gansukh and Sansar-Huu had an unusually equal marriage. Gansukh taught at the school while Sansar-Huu, when he wasn't assisting his parents, did the housework and looked after their two children. Cosseted by tradition, most of the men I met in Tsengel did no housework, no cooking, cleaning or washing, and the women always rose first, to rekindle the cold stove. When I visited herders in their isolated settlements, halfway up mountains and accessible only by camel or horse, the women often looked exhausted, their dry faces prematurely aged by constant child rearing and the daily struggle to scrape a living from the unyielding terrain.

15   It wasn't until the beginning of June that the rains finally lashed down. My *ger* obligingly leaked, the felt walls were sodden, the canvas roof saturated. I had to live in the epicentre for several days, constantly mopping up streams that coursed through my home and ruined sacks of flour. But it was worth it, to see smiles unwrapping on people's faces and the steppe and valleys surrounding us erupt into green, moist pasture for the emaciated cows and camels to gorge themselves on at last.

16   Around this time Gansukh and Sansar-Huu suggested I spend the summer in the mountains west of Tsengel with them and Sansar-Huu's parents. Summer is the only kindness this climate bestows on the herders; people live on milk, cream and cheese, literally fattening themselves up for the lean winter ahead. When we moved to our summer camp at the end of June, the weather was glorious and I was looking forward to a long, warm rest, milking the odd yak or goat and learning to curdle cheese. But my blissful ignorance about the pace of summer nomadic life was shattered on impact.

17   We worked fifteen hours a day. Rising at dawn we milked the goats and yaks twice a day and the horses every two hours, fetched water, collected dung for fuel, sheared sheep with scissors, curdled thick cheeses, churned cream and butter and distilled our own vodka. I was totally wrecked by the end of the first week. While the men rode off on lengthy hunting trips, I helped to herd the families' 350 goats and sheep with

Sansar-Huu's little sister and was immersed in the extended household led by his statuesque mother, Dere-Huu. But it wasn't all about work. After we'd completed the evening milking and rounded up the animals for the night, we would all curl up together on the grass *ger* floor and sip hot, frothing yak's milk. We bathed together in the freezing river and rode over the mountains to drink tea with Amraa and Tuya in their "nearby" valleys. There were resplendent weddings when the nomads' *gers* resounded with applause as well-fed guests, elegantly attired in their calf-length embroidered tunics and brilliant silk sashes, chorused yet another ode to

love, the mountains, horses or everyone's mothers. Parties lasted till dawn, although people couldn't afford to lie in for the morning—there was too much to do. After a particularly memorable celebration (which involved the women whipping the men), we mounted our patient horses as the sunrise washed over us, and blearily cantered across the wild flower-drenched valley to our own settlement, where we spent the morning tethering and milking sixty frisky goats.

18   Gansukh and Dere-Huu escorted me on a visit to the formidable female shaman, Enkhtuya. This powerful young woman came from a lineage of female shamans stretching back nine generations. She had a smooth face, but the bearing of a much older, more tired woman. "I am," she told me quietly, "the link between people and the spirits. I speak with animals and the mountains and I offer people the wisdom I receive from the spirits." I was a little afraid of Enkhtuya—and I believed every word she said.

19   By the end of summer I knew how to milk goats, yaks, cows and horses. I could tell by looking at a piece of dung if it would burn or just smother the flames. I could ferment my own milk, saddle my own horse and herd sheep. I also knew how to beat and roll sheep's wool into sheets of fresh felt for the *ger* walls. Dere-Huu, Gansukh and their family had taught me well. They had shared their lives with me that summer, teased and encouraged me, offered to find me a husband with a huge herd of his own, and taken me on a four-day, breakneck horse-riding trip to the most beautiful places I have ever seen.

20   I looked around me and knew with a quiet certainty that I wanted to stay in Tsengel until winter—until the river froze two metres thick and drivers and horsemen used the marble ice as a flat road across the valley. I wanted to witness a full cycle of the seasons and the work they dictated; to help slice hay for winter fodder with a crude hand-held scythe; to wake up to the burnished autumn colours Mongolians call "the short golden season"; to visit the sacred mountain where the legendary Ibex sheep roamed; and to go to Tuya's wedding. I sat down with Gansukh outside our *ger* and bluntly told her I longed to stay. I could train her to take over my classes when I left, I

brokered, but I would have to move to a wooden house, it would be too cold for a *ger*. Would she help me to stay, talk to the school director and Abbai, the governor? Gansukh stared at me intently, frowning, and then laughed out loud. "Yes, yes! If you help me I can be an English teacher after you leave, then we don't have to wait for another foreigner to come . . . and I know Abbai has a house in his *hasha*. I will talk to him, but also to the school director because you'll need coal in winter and we can talk to Tuya and Amraa, they'll help and . . . Sansar-Huu, come here . . ."

21   I sat back against the warm felt walls and basked in the brilliant afternoon sunshine, because now time was on my side.

Getting the Message

_____ **1.** What is the topic of the essay?

    a. life in Mongolia's capital   c. life with nomads in Mongolia

    b. Mongolia's diverse landscape   d. learning how to milk a horse

_____ **2.** The topic sentence in paragraph 15 can be found in

    a. sentence 1.   c. sentence 3.

    b. sentence 2.   d. sentence 4.

_____ **3.** What is the main idea of the essay?

    a. Life in Mongolia is difficult.

    b. Mongolia's nomads would be better off if they moved to the city.

    c. Living in an isolated village in Mongolia is difficult, but it has its rewards.

    d. Women in Mongolia make great friends.

_____ **4.** Waugh mainly uses _____ as supporting details.

    a. statistics   c. testimony

    b. personal examples   d. public examples

_____ **5.** How old is Waugh for most of her time in Tsengel?

    a. 25   c. 38

    b. 30   d. The essay doesn't say.

_____ **6.** The sentence "Tsengel had no electricity or running water" (par. 6) is

    a. a fact.   b. an opinion.

_____ **7.** The essay uses the _____ pattern of organization.

    a. comparison and contrast   c. narrative

    b. cause and effect   d. classification

_____ **8.** Look at the phrases that begin paragraphs 11, 13, and 15. What do they show?

    a. time   c. addition

    b. comparison   d. contrast

_____ **9.** Waugh's two most likely purposes are to _____.

    a. inform and persuade   c. entertain and persuade

    b. entertain and inform

_____ **10.** It can be inferred from the line "Nomads who lived in settlements outside Tsengel would still gape open-mouthed at me as they rode through the village" (par. 10) that

    a. some nomads don't have the best manners.

    b. Waugh was dressed inappropriately for the area.

    c. Waugh was making funny faces as people walked by her.

    d. some nomads rarely, if ever, saw a foreigner.

11. Choose two words to describe the nomads Waugh meets and give an example of a sentence or paragraph that shows how each word applies to the people.

_____

_____

_____

_____

_____

_____

12. Give three examples of what you think makes life in Tsengel appealing for Waugh.

_____

_____

_____

_____

13. Waugh states that "Cosseted by tradition, most of the men I met in Tsengel did no housework, no cooking, cleaning or washing, and the women always rose first, to rekindle the cold stove" (par. 14). Is this statement an example of a hasty generalization? Explain why or why not.

_____

_____

_____

_____

14. What is a question or comment you wrote in the margins as you annotated the essay that you would like to discuss with the class?

_____

_____

15. On a separate sheet of paper, make a Venn diagram that shows chores or tasks you perform daily (or monthly) and chores Waugh performs in Mongolia (at her _ger_ or in the mountains). In the center put chores or tasks that overlap. For example, Waugh needs to chop wood to light a fire to cook, while you need to turn on the stove or microwave, and the overlapping area is need to cook food.

Vocabulary

Use context clues to determine the meaning by looking back at the paragraph where the word is used (the paragraph number is in parentheses). If you need help, refer to a dictionary for the definition.

A. Match the word to its antonym.

> **raucous** (2)   **resilient** (6)   **conscript(ed)** (12)   **cosset(ed)** (14)   **epicentre*** (15)

1. neglect _____
2. volunteer_____
3. orderly_____
4. weak_____
5. edge_____

* British, American spelling: epicenter

B. Finish the reading by inserting the missing words. Use each word once.

> **nomads** (3)   **steppes** (3)   **eke** (13)   **dung** (17)   **bask** (21)

In the _____ of central Asia many find joy in the vast open plains. For most people it would be a difficult life to move whenever one's animals needed new grazing land, but for many _____ the wandering life is what they prefer. They have to work hard to _____ out a living from their animals and the treeless landscape. They endure cold winters and hot summers, but it is the life they know, and many wouldn't want to change it. They _____ in the warmth of family ties and the knowledge that they have worked hard. At the end of the day, families can be found rejoicing around their stoves, powered with the _____ of their animals, as they share stories and songs.

C. Word parts: Match each word to its appropriate definition. The word part is underlined to help you make the connection. Return to pages 85–87 if you need to review the meaning of a word part.

> **collective** (3)   **Anglophile** (7)   **receding** (12)   **epicentre** (15)

1. upon or at the center _____
2. yielding; diminishing _____
3. to choose to be together; combined _____
4. one who loves England, its people, and traditions _____

The Essay and You

1. Do you think you could handle the life in Mongolia that Waugh experiences? Explain why or why not.

_____

_____

2. List three skills Waugh learned while in Mongolia. What three skills have you learned from an experience? Do you still use those skills?

_____

_____

_____

3. Briefly tell how your perceptions of a place changed when you were gone from it for some time, as happens to Waugh in paragraph 10. This feeling can even occur with some place in your town that you haven't visited in a long time, such as a restaurant or your elementary school.

_____

_____

_____

4. On a separate sheet of paper, write a paragraph about a people, place, or experience that excited you.

Take a Closer Look

Look at the photos again. What do they reveal about life in Mongolia? What would be the benefits and the disadvantages of living in a *ger*? Circle Mongolia on the map on page 434.

_____

_____

Internet Activities

If needed, use a separate sheet of paper to fully record your responses. Include the Web address of any sites from which you gather information.

1. Do a search for "Mongolia photos" to find photographs of traditional Mongolian life. You might look for photos of sheep shearing, horseback riding, or the Naadam sports festival. Find three photos that interest you and sum up what they show about Mongolian life. Pick one photo to print and share with the class.

_____

_____

2. Look up a country where you would be interested in living for a year or two. Find out information on the customs, food, clothing, and occupations of the people. Write a summary of your findings.

_____

_____

Uluru

from *In a Sunburned Country*

by Bill Bryson

Before You Read

1. Survey the first three paragraphs. Have you heard of Uluru or Ayers Rock?
2. Is there a natural wonder (for example, canyon, rock, or mountain) that has fascinated you?
3. What do you know about Australia?
4. Look at the photo. What is your reaction to the rock?

Vocabulary Preview

Look for these words in the reading. Exercises to reinforce the learning of new vocabulary using these words follow the reading. The paragraph number where the word appears is in parentheses.

sumptuously (3)	**hubbub** (5)	**hied** (11)
dismay (31)	**doleful** (34)	**inert** (44)
monolith (44)	**eminence** (46)	**agog** (46)
happenstance (47)		

Bill Bryson was born in Des Moines, Iowa. He moved to England in his early twenties, met his wife there, and they lived there for 20 years. He wrote for *The Times* and *The Independent* newspapers in England. He also supplemented his income writing travel articles. He moved back to the United States in 1995. While in the States, he wrote *A Walk in the Woods,* which became a best seller, about his adventures hiking the 2,100-mile Appalachian Trail. He returned to England in 2003. He has written several other books including *The Life and Times of the Thunderbolt Kid,* which chronicles his growing up years in Des Moines in the 1950s. The following selection is from *In a Sunburned Country* about his travels in Australia, published in 2000.

1   **And so in** the morning we rose early and set off for mighty Uluru. Alice Springs could wait.

2   Uluru and Alice Springs are so inextricably linked in the popular imagination that nearly everyone thinks of them as cozily proximate. In fact, it is almost three hundred miles across a largely featureless tract to get from the one to the other. Uluru's glory is that it stands alone in a boundless emptiness, but it does mean that you have to really want to see it; it's not something you're going to pass on the way to the beach. That is as it should be, of course, but it is equally a fact that when you have just completed a thousand-mile passage through barren void, you don't really require another five hours of it to confirm your impression that much of central Australia is empty.

3   Well into the 1950s Ayers Rock was inaccessible to all but the most dedicated sightseers. As late as the late 1960s, the number of annual visitors was no more than ten thousand. Today Uluru gets that many every ten days on average. It even has its own airport, and the resort that has sprung up to serve it, called Yulara, is the third largest community in the Territory when full. Yulara stands a discreet and respectful dozen or so miles from the rock itself, so we stopped there first to get rooms. It consists essentially of a lazy loop road along which are tucked a range of accommodations, from campgrounds and a youth hostel up to the most sumptuously deluxe of resort hotels.

4   With nothing better to do, we had passed much of the five-hour drive working out a program for ourselves for our stay. Essentially this had established that we would spend the afternoon studying the rock in a calm and reflective manner, then divide whatever remained of the day between a cooling dip in the hotel pool, drinks on a terrace while watching the setting sun gorge the rock with the red glow for which it is famed, a little stroll through the desert to stretch our legs and look for dingoes, wallabies, and kangaroos, and finally a dinner of refinement and quality beneath a sky of twinkling stars. We had, after all, just driven thirteen hundred miles in two and a half days. If ever anyone was entitled to a little desert R&R it was us. So there was a certain real excitement as we turned off the highway and entered the cosseted confines of Yulara.

5   We went first to the Outback Pioneer Hotel, which sounded moderately priced, if dangerously likely to have chandeliers made of wagon wheels and an all-you-can-eat buffet for people in baseball caps. In fact, it proved on approach to be rather grand and clearly very nice, but unexpectedly busy. Stacks of luggage were being unloaded from two tour buses out front and there were people everywhere, nearly all white-haired and pear-shaped, standing around squinting or fiddling with cameras and video recorders. Allan dropped me out front and I trotted inside to inquire about rates. I was amazed at the amount of hubbub in the lobby. It was early afternoon on a weekday out of season and the place was a circus. The check-in area brought to mind a mustering station on a foundering cruise ship. I asked a guy at the concierge desk what was going on.

6   "Nothing in particular," he said, joining me in considering the unattractive chaos. "It's always like this."

7   "Really?" I said. "Even out of season?"

8   "There is no out of season here now."

9   "Are there any rooms here, do you know?"

10   "Afraid not. The only place with rooms left is the Desert Gardens."

11   I thanked him and hied back to the car.

12   "Problem?" said Allan as I climbed in.

13   "Very poor dessert selection," I said, not wishing to alarm him. "Let's try the Desert Gardens Hotel. It's much nicer."

14   The Desert Gardens was vastly more swank than the Pioneer Outback, and mercifully less crowded. Only one person, a man of about seventy, stood between me and the check-in clerk. I arrived just in time to hear the clerk say to him, "It's three hundred and fifty-three dollars a night."

15   I swallowed hard at this.

16   "We'll take it," said the man in an American accent. "How big is it?"

17   "I beg your pardon?"

18   "How big is the room?"

19   The clerk looked taken aback. "Well, I'm not sure of its dimensions exactly. It's a fair size."

20   "What's that mean? 'Fair size.'"

21   "It's amply proportioned, sir. Would you like to see the room?"

22   "No, I want to sign in," the man said shortly, as if the clerk were needlessly delaying him. "We want to get to the rock."

23   "Very good, sir."

24   As he signed in he asked a million subsidiary questions. Where was the rock exactly? How long did it take to get there? Was there a cocktail lounge in this hotel? Where was that exactly? What time was dinner served? Could you see the rock from the dining room? Was it worth seeing the rock from the dining room? Where was the pool? Through which doors? *Which* doors? And what about the elevator—where was that? *Where?*

25   I looked at my watch unhappily. It was getting on for two o'clock, and we didn't even have rooms yet. Time was speeding away.

26   "So is it good, this rock?" the man was saying in what might have been an attempt at levity.

27   "I beg your pardon, sir?"

28   "The rock. Is it worth coming all this way?"

29   "Well, as rocks go, sir, I think you could say it's first-class."

30   "Yeah, well it'd better be," the man said darkly.

31   Then his wife joined him and to my dismay *she* began asking questions. Was there a hairdresser's? How late was it open? Where could they mail postcards? Did the gift shop accept traveler's checks? These were U.S. dollars traveler's checks; was that okay? And how much are postage stamps for America? Is there an iron and ironing board in the room? Where'd you say the gift shop is? And what about my brain? Have you seen that anywhere? It's about the size of a very small walnut and never been used.

32   Eventually they shuffled off and the clerk turned to me. With a regretful air, he informed me that the gentleman ahead of me had taken the last room. "There might be dormitory space at the youth hostel," he said, and allowed this deeply unappealing proposition to sit there for a moment. "Shall I check?"

33   "Yes, please," I murmured.

34   He consulted his computer and looked suitably doleful. "No, I'm afraid even that's full now. I'm sorry."

35   I thanked him and went out. Allan was leaning against the car with a hopeful face, which fell when he saw mine. I explained to him the situation. He looked crushed.

36   "So no swim?" he said.

37   I nodded.

38   "No wine on the terrace? No sunset over the rock? No elegant room with downy pillows? No complimentary fluffy bathrobe and tinkling minibar?"

39   "The bathrobes never fit anyway, Allan."

40   "Not quite the point." He fixed me with a frank gaze. "And instead of these things we will be . . .?"

41   "Driving back to Alice Springs."

42   He removed his focus to the wider world while he allowed this thought to settle. "Well," he said at last, "I suppose we'd better go and see if this bloody rock is worth a six-hundred-mile roundtrip."

43   It was.

44   The thing about Ayers Rock is that by the time you finally get there you are already a little sick of it. Even when you are a thousand miles from it, you can't go a day in Australia without seeing it four or five or six times—on postcards, on travel agents' posters, on the

cover of souvenir picture books—and as you get nearer the rock the frequency of exposure increases. So you are aware, as you drive to the park entrance and pay the ambitiously pitched admission fee of A$15 a head and follow the approach road around, that you have driven thirteen hundred miles to look at a large, inert, loaf-shaped object that you have seen photographically portrayed a thousand times already. In consequence, your mood as you approach this famous monolith is restrained, unexpectant—pessimistic even.

45   And then you see it, and you are instantly transfixed.

46   There, in the middle of a memorable and imposing emptiness, stands an eminence of exceptional nobility and grandeur, 1,150 feet high, a mile and a half long, five and a half miles around, less red than photographs have led you to expect but in every other way more arresting than you could ever have supposed. I have discussed this since with many other people, nearly all of whom agreed that they approached Uluru with a kind of fatigue, and were left agog in a way they could not adequately explain. It's not that Uluru is bigger than you had supposed or more perfectly formed or in any way different from the impression you had created in your mind, but the very opposite. It is exactly what you expected it to be. You *know* this rock. You know it in a way that has nothing to do with calendars and the covers of souvenir books. Your knowledge of this rock is grounded in something much more elemental.

47   In some odd way that you don't understand and can't begin to articulate you feel an acquaintance with it—a familiarity on an unfamiliar level. Somewhere in the deep sediment of your being some long-dormant fragment of primordial memory, some little severed tail of DNA, has twitched or stirred. It is a motion much too faint to be understood or interpreted,

but somehow you feel certain that this large, brooding, hypnotic presence has an importance to you at the species level—perhaps even at a sort of tadpole level—and that in some way your visit here is more than happenstance.

48   I'm not saying that any of this is so. I'm just saying that this is how you feel. The other thought that strikes you—that struck me anyway—is that Uluru is not merely a very splendid and mighty monolith but also an extremely distinctive one. More than this, it is an extremely recognizable one—very possibly the most immediately recognizable natural object on earth. I'm suggesting nothing here, but I will say that if you were an intergalactic traveler who had broken down in our solar system, the obvious directions to rescuers would be: "Go to the third planet and fly around till you see the big red rock. You can't miss it." If ever on earth they dig up a 150,000-year-old rocket ship from the galaxy Zog, this is where it will be. I'm not saying I expect it to happen; not saying that at all. I'm just observing that if I were looking for an ancient starship this is where I would start digging.

49   Allan, I noted, seemed similarly affected. "It's weird, isn't it?" he said.

50   "What is?"

51   "I don't know. Just seeing it. I mean, it just feels weird."

52   I nodded. It does feel weird. Quite apart from that initial shock of indefinable recognition, there is also the fact that Uluru is, no matter how you approach it, totally arresting. You cannot stop looking at it; you don't want to stop looking at it. As you draw closer, it becomes even more interesting. It is more pitted than you had imagined, less regular in shape. There are more curves and divots and wavelike ribs, more irregularities of every type, than are evident from even a couple of hundred yards away. You realize that you could spend quite a lot of time—possibly a worryingly large amount of time; possibly a sell-your-house-and-move-here-to-live-in-a-tent amount of time—just looking at the rock, gazing at it from many angles, never tiring of it. You can see yourself in a silvery ponytail, barefoot, and in something jangly and loose-fitting, hanging out with much younger visitors and telling them, "And the amazing thing is that every day it's different, you know what I am saying? It's never the same rock twice. That's right, my friend—you put your finger on it there. It's awesome. It's an awesome thing. Say, do you by any chance have any dope or some spare change?"

53   We stopped at several places to get out and have a look, including the spot where you can climb up it. It takes several hours and much exertion, which comfortably eliminated it from our consideration, and in any case the route was closed for the afternoon. So many people have collapsed and died on the rock that they close it to climbers when the weather is really warm, as it was this day. Even when it's not too hot, lots of people get in trouble from fooling around or taking wrong turns. Just the day before, a Canadian had had to be rescued after getting himself onto some ledge from which he could not get either up or down. Since 1985, ownership of the rock has been back in the hands of the local Aboriginal people, the Pitjantjatjara and Yankunyjatjara, and they deeply dislike visitors (whom they call *minga*, or ants) clambering all over it. Personally I don't blame them. It is a sacred site to them. I think it should be for everyone, frankly.

54   We stopped at the visitors' center for a cup of coffee and to look at the displays, which were all to do with interpretations of the Dreamtime—the Aborigines' traditional conception

of how the earth was formed and operates. There was nothing instructive in a historical or geological sense, which was disappointing because I was curious to know what Uluru is doing there. How do you get the biggest rock in existence onto the middle of an empty plain? It turns out (I looked in a book later) that Uluru is what is known to geology as a bornhardt: a hunk of weather-resistant rock left standing when all else around it has worn away. Bornhardts are not that uncommon—the Devils Marbles are a collection of miniature bornhardts—but nowhere else on earth has one lump of rock been left in such dramatic and solitary splendor or assumed such a pleasing smooth symmetry. It is a hundred million years old. Go there, man.

Getting the Message

____ **1.** Which is the topic sentence in paragraph 4?

    a. sentence 1

    b. sentence 2

    c. sentence 3

    d. sentence 5

____ **2.** The main idea of the selection is that

    a. Uluru is a long way from anywhere.

    b. Uluru does not meet one's expectations.

    c. Uluru is worth seeing.

    d. It is important to make reservations.

____ **3.** Uluru is _____ from Alice Springs.

    a. a respectful dozen or so miles

    b. almost 300 miles

    c. 1000 miles

    d. 1300 miles

____ **4.** The sentence "Bornhardts are not that uncommon—the Devils Marbles are a collection of miniature bornhardts—but nowhere else on earth has one lump of rock been left in such dramatic and solitary splendor or assumed such a pleasing smooth symmetry" (par. 54) mainly expresses

    a. a fact.

    b. an opinion.

____ **5.** How is the information in the essay ordered as a whole?

    a. chronologically

    b. least to most important

    c. problem and solution

    d. most to least important

____ **6.** What patterns of organization does Bryson use?

    a. comparison and contrast

    b. classification and process

    c. examples and definition

    d. narrative and cause and effect

____ **7.** The word *but* in paragraph 54 shows _____.

    a. contrast

    b. addition

    c. importance

    d. time

____ **8.** To _____ would best describe Bryson's main purpose.

    a. inform

    b. persuade

    c. entertain

_____ 9. The tone of the essay can best be labeled as
  a. sad.
  b. objective.
  c. angry.
  d. humorous.

_____ 10. It can be inferred from Bryson's description at the end of paragraph 52 that the rock could turn a person into _____.
  a. a business tycoon
  b. a lunatic
  c. a hippie
  d. an environmentalist

11. How does Bryson use irony in the scene where they look for a room in Yulara?

_____

_____

_____

_____

12. Explain two of the effects the rock has on Bryson. What is your reaction to these effects?

_____

_____

_____

_____

13. Give two examples of exaggeration that Bryson uses in paragraphs 24–42. Did you find his use of exaggeration funny?

_____

_____

_____

_____

14. Look back at your annotations of the essay. List three items that you starred, circled, or otherwise marked as important sections.

_____

_____

15. On a separate sheet of paper, write a summary of the essay in approximately 200 words.

Vocabulary

Use context clues to determine the meaning by looking back at the paragraph where the word is used (the paragraph number is in parentheses). If you need help, refer to a dictionary for the definition.

A. Match the vocabulary word to the corresponding example.

> **hubbub (5)**   **hied (11)**   **doleful (34)**   **inert (44)**   **agog (46)**

1. A person in a coma._____

2. How the kids reacted when they heard the ice cream truck. _____

3. Leo's response when the dog that he has had since he was ten dies. _____

4. The scene when a thousand passengers from a cruise ship start disembarking and the dockside vendors begin to call out to them. _____

5. Elizabeth's behavior as she eats lunch with her favorite movie star. _____

B. Finish the sentences with the correct vocabulary word. Use each word once.

> **sumptuously (3)**   **dismay (31)**   **monolith (44)**   **eminence (46)**   **happenstance (47)**

1. Juanita's behavior continues to _____ me. She is such a bright student, but she keeps turning her assignments in late, which is bringing down her grade.

2. When I bumped into my future wife at a crowded baseball game, I knew it was more than _____ that I had knocked her hot dog to the ground.

3. The house was _____ decorated for the ball. There were large flower arrangements in every room, hundreds of balloons in the entry, and yards of silk flowing down the stairway.

4. The _____ was so huge and imposing that I understood why it impressed so many people.

5. The mayor was a man of such _____ in the community that even children recognized him as he walked down the streets.

C. Word parts: Fill in the missing meaning for the underlined word part. Return to pages 85–87 if you need to review the meaning of a word part.

> **not**   **between**   **one**   **light**

1. The rock is now <u>in</u>ert; it is _____ moving down the hill anymore, so the house should be safe.

2. That <u>mono</u>lith is _____ big rock! I am so glad I travelled all this way to see it.

3. I would be thrilled to go on an <u>inter</u>galactic voyage. Traveling _____ galaxies sounds exciting.

4. The <u>lev</u>ity from Shonali's humorous stories created a _____ mood in the room, which was appreciated by most people after having listened to Francisco describe diseases for 20 minutes.

The Essay and You

1. If you "were looking for an ancient starship" (par. 48), where would you start looking? Why? How good do you consider Bryson's choice of a location?

   _____

   _____

2. Think about a place that has greatly impressed you. Tell what the place is and list five descriptive words to convey the impact of the place, as Bryson does in paragraph 46: imposing, eminence, nobility, grandeur, arresting.

   _____

   _____

3. List four places (e.g., a country, a city, or a national park) you would like to visit and briefly explain what attracts you to these destinations.

   _____

   _____

4. On a separate sheet of paper, write a paragraph that relates a humorous scene. You can use an experience you have had, one you have observed, or make one up. Use exaggeration to develop the scene. Refer to paragraphs 16–31 in the essay for inspiration. Try using dialogue if it fits in your scene.

Take a Closer Look

Look at the photo again. Has your impression of the rock changed after reading Bryson's descriptions of it? Pick three words of your own to describe Uluru. Circle Australia on the map on page 434.

_____

_____

Internet Activities

If needed, use a separate sheet of paper to fully record your responses. Include the Web address of any sites from which you gather information.

1. Look up "Uluru photos." Find photos of the rock taken at different times of the day and from different distances. Summarize your opinion of the rock after studying six different photos. Pick one photograph that particularly appeals to you and print it to share with the class. Be prepared to explain why you picked this photo.

   _____

2. Pick one of the places you chose for question 3 in The Essay and You and find out how many people visit each year and what tourist facilities are available. Then write a paragraph similar to paragraph 3 in Bryson's essay.

   _____

Gestures

by James M. Henslin

from *Essentials of Sociology: A Down-to-Earth Approach*

Before You Read

1. Think of three gestures you often use. What do they mean?

2. How often do you see people communicating by using gestures?

3. Have you ever been confused by a gesture someone has used?

4. Look at the photos and cartoon. Do you know what the gestures mean?

James M. Henslin is Professor Emeritus of Sociology from Southern Illinois University, Edwardsville. He was born in Minnesota, attended colleges in California and Indiana, and earned his master's and doctorate degrees in sociology from Washington University in St. Louis, Missouri. His specialties are in the sociology of everyday life, deviance, and international relations. He has written several books and articles for sociology journals. He enjoys traveling and visiting people in other cultures to see "sociological principles come alive." The following excerpt is from the sixth edition of his book *Essentials of Sociology: A Down-to-Earth Approach*.

Vocabulary Preview

Look for these words in the reading. Exercises to reinforce the learning of new vocabulary using these words follow the reading. The paragraph number where the word appears is in parentheses.

convey (1)	**culture** (1)	**succinct** (1)	**internalized** (2)	**extent** (2)
retaliated (3)	**facilitate** (4)	**indicate** (4)	**provoke** (5)	**associated** (7)

Gestures, using

1 one's body to communicate with others, are shorthand ways to convey messages without using words. Although people in every culture of the world use gestures, a gesture's meaning may change from one culture to another. North Americans, for example, communicate a succinct message by raising the middle finger in a short, upward-stabbing motion. I stress "North Americans," for that gesture does not convey the same message in most other parts of the world.

2 I once was surprised to find that this particular gesture was not universal, having internalized it to such an extent that I thought everyone knew what it meant. When I was comparing gestures with friends in Mexico, however, this gesture drew a blank look from them. After I explained its intended meaning, they laughed and showed me their rudest gesture—placing the hand under the armpit and moving the upper arm up and down. To me, they simply looked as if they were imitating monkeys, but to them the gesture meant "Your mother is a whore," absolutely the worst possible insult in that culture.

3 With today's U.S. political, military and cultural dominance, "giving the finger" is becoming well known in other cultures. Following 9/11, the United States began to photograph and fingerprint foreign

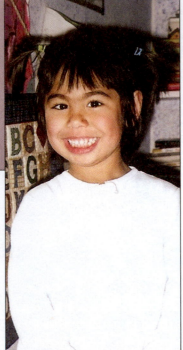

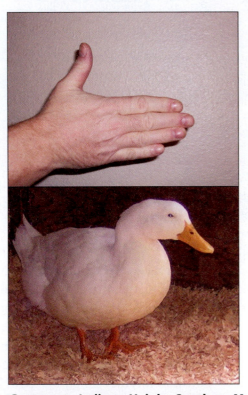

Gestures to Indicate Height, Southern Mexico

travelers. Feeling insulted, Brazil retaliated by doing the same to U.S. visitors. Angry at this, a U.S. pilot raised his middle finger while being photographed. Having become aware of the meaning of this gesture, Brazilian police arrested him. To gain his release, the pilot had to pay a fine of $13,000 ("Brazil Arrests" . . . 2004).

4   Gestures not only facilitate communication but also, because their meanings differ around the world, they can lead to misunderstanding, embarrassment, or worse. One time in Mexico, for example, I raised my hand to a certain height to indicate how tall a child was. My hosts began to laugh. It turns out that Mexicans

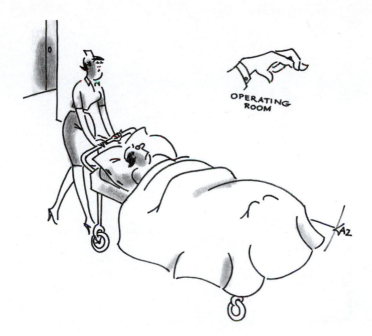

use three hand gestures to indicate height: one for people, a second for animals, and yet another for plants. They were amused because I had ignorantly used the plant gesture to indicate the child's height.

5   To get along in another culture, then, it is important to learn the gestures of that culture. If you don't, not only will you fail to achieve the simplicity of communication that gestures allow, but also you will miss much of what is happening, run the risk of appearing foolish, and possibly offend people. In some cultures, for example, you would provoke deep offense if you were to offer food or a gift with your left hand, because the left hand is reserved for dirty tasks, such as wiping after going to the toilet. Left-handed Americans visiting Arabs, please note!

6   Suppose for a moment that you are visiting southern Italy. After eating one of the best meals of your life, you are so pleased that when you catch the waiter's eye, you smile broadly and use the standard U.S. "A-OK" gesture of putting your thumb and forefinger together and making a large "O." The waiter looks horrified, and you are struck speechless when the manager asks you to leave. What have you done? Nothing on purpose, of course, but in that culture this gesture refers to a part of the human body that is not mentioned in polite company (Ekman et al. 1984).

7   Some gestures are so associated with emotional messages that the gesture itself, even when demonstrated out of context, summons up emotions. For example, my introduction to Mexican gestures took place at a dinner table. It was evident that my husband-and-wife hosts were trying to hide their embarrassment at using their culture's obscene gesture at their dinner table. And I felt the same way—not about *their* gesture, of course, which meant nothing to me, but about the one I was teaching them.

Getting the Message

____ **1.** The topic sentence in paragraph 5 can be found in sentence _____.

    a. 1

    b. 2

    c. 3

    d. 4

____ **2.** What is the main idea of the excerpt?

    a. Gestures universally have the same meaning.

    b. Gestures can be helpful to know when interviewing for a job.

    c. Most gestures have obscene meanings.

    d. Gestures are a convenient way to convey information, but they can lead to problems because they do not mean the same thing in all cultures.

____ **3.** To support his point, Henslin uses a _____ in paragraph 6.

    a. personal example

    b. public example

    c. hypothetical example

    d. fact

____ **4.** What types of supporting details does Henslin use in paragraphs 2 and 3?

    a. testimony and reasons

    b. personal and public examples

    c. public examples and statistics

    d. statistics and facts

____ **5.** The sentence "Following 9/11, the United States began to photograph and fingerprint foreign travelers" (par. 3) is

    a. a fact.

    b. an opinion.

____ **6.** As a whole, the information in the excerpt is ordered using the _____ method.

    a. problem and solution

    b. chronological

    c. most to least important

    d. least to most important

____ **7.** Which pattern of organization does the excerpt use overall?

    a. narrative

    b. definition

    c. series of examples

    d. process

____ **8.** In paragraph 4, the word _____ shows a cause and effect relationship.

    a. but

    b. also

    c. because

    d. for example

____ **9.** The tone of the excerpt is
  a. serious.
  b. friendly.
  c. sad.
  d. funny.

____ **10.** Can it be inferred from paragraphs 1 and 2 that Henslin does not consider Mexico to be a part of North America?
  a. yes
  b. no

11. Henslin writes that "Gestures . . . are shorthand ways to convey messages without using words" (par. 1). Give two examples of how someone could convey a message using a gesture.

_____

_____

_____

12. Henslin gives four reasons for learning the gestures of another culture. List them and explain which one you think is the most important.

_____

_____

_____

_____

13. List the countries or cultures Henslin shows the gestures of or how their meaning of a gesture differs from what it does in the United States. Do you feel these are enough examples to make his point?

_____

_____

_____

14. List two questions you wrote in the margins of this selection.

_____

_____

15. On a separate sheet of paper, make an outline of the excerpt. You can decide if an informal or formal outline would best help you remember the information in the excerpt.

Vocabulary

Use context clues to determine the meaning by looking back at the paragraph where the word is used (the paragraph number is in parentheses). If you need help, consult a dictionary for the definition.

A. Put a *T* if the underlined vocabulary word is used correctly and an *F* if it is used incorrectly.

_____ 1. Luckily, I was able to <u>convey</u> (1) my meaning to the man through gestures because the music was too loud for him to clearly hear me.

_____ 2. I find that there is something interesting about every <u>culture</u> (1), but I am currently most interested in studying the Aborigines in Australia and the Laplanders in Finland.

_____ 3. Toni kept her answers <u>succinct</u> (1); it took her 15 pages to complete the four questions on the application form.

_____ 4. The <u>extent</u> (2) of the flood damage wasn't very much. Only one bedroom had a soggy carpet.

_____ 5. Kris tried to <u>provoke</u> (5) a fight by telling Luis how sorry he was about breaking the window.

B. Write the definition and a sentence for each of the words below. Try to use context clues in your sentences that help to show what the vocabulary word means.

1. internalize(d) (2) _____

_____

2. retaliate(d) (3) _____

_____

3. facilitate (4) _____

_____

4. indicate (4) _____

5. associated (7) _____

_____

C. Word parts: Circle the meaning found in the question for the underlined word part. Return to pages 85–87 if you need to review the meaning of a word part.

1. I am sure Zack wanted to pro<u>vok</u>e a fight when he called me a cheapskate.

2. I need you to tell me what I should bring for Sunday's family reunion. If you in<u>dic</u>ate what you need by Friday, I can go shopping on Saturday.

3. It will <u>fac</u>ilitate the unpacking process if you make it clear what items a box contains by writing a list on the outside of the box.

4. I was <u>compar</u>ing grocery bills with my friends and found that I was spending a lot more money than they were.

The Textbook and You

1. Has using a gesture ever gotten you in trouble or led to miscommunication with someone as happens in paragraphs 3 and 6 in the excerpt?

_____

_____

2. Do you often use gestures or know someone who does? Describe two common gestures you use or see being used often. Do you agree that gestures can "facilitate communication" (par. 4)?

_____

_____

_____

3. Brainstorm at least seven gestures with which you are familiar. Then get together with two classmates and compare your lists. How many gestures were common to your lists? How many were different?

_____

_____

4. On a separate sheet of paper, write a narrative that shows a person using six gestures throughout a day's activities.

Take a Closer Look

Look at the photos again. Were you surprised or confused by the hand signals from Mexico? Is the cartoon funny if you don't know what the gesture means? Do these images show why it is important to learn the gestures of a culture or "you will miss much of what is happening" (par. 5)? Using the map on page 434, circle two of the regions mentioned in the excerpt.

_____

_____

_____

Internet Activities

If needed, use a separate sheet of paper to fully record your responses. Include the Web address of any sites from which you gather information.

1. Look up "international gestures." Find two gestures that are either different from ones used in the United States or ones used in the United States but with different meanings in another culture. Explain what the gestures look like and what they mean.

_____

_____

2. Find a photo of a person using a gesture and explain what the gesture means. Bring in a photo of the gesture to share with the class. See if people can guess what the gesture means.

_____

Folktales from Around the World

Before You Read

1. Survey the four folktales. What traits do you think the tales might have in common?
2. Can you recall any folktales you may have heard while growing up?
3. Write a question that you think the folktales might address:

   _____

4. Look at the photos. What kind of luck do you think the man has? What traits do you associate with cats?

Folktales are stories that have been passed down in a culture through oral traditions. Every culture has some form of these tales. The stories may go by other names, such as legends or tall tales. Fables are similar to folktales, but they usually have a moral and often use animals or inanimate objects as characters. The writer of a fable may be known, but due to the oral nature of the folktale, the original creator is unknown.

Vocabulary Preview

Look for these words in the readings. Exercises to reinforce the learning of new vocabulary using these words follow the readings. The paragraph number where the word appears is in parentheses.

malicious ("Snake's" 1) **ploys** ("Snake's" 3) **eloquently** ("Snake's" 4)

despondent ("Roaming" 1) **yearned** ("Roaming" 3) **mandatory** ("Roaming" 4)

haughtily ("Crossing" 4) **grave** ("Crossing" 9) **jovially** ("Cat" 1)

weather ("Cat" 2)

Snake's Promise

an Apache tale from the southwest United States

1 Early one especially cold morning a young woman left the village to gather herbs. After walking nearly a mile, she spied a snake in the middle of the path. Aware that snakes were often malicious, she carefully approached it, but it didn't move.

2 Suddenly the snake spoke to her, "Help me! It is oh so cold, and I will die without heat. Please pick me up and warm me."

3 The woman hesitated. Finally she said, "You are a rattlesnake. I am sure this is one of your wily ploys. If I pick you up, you will bite me."

4 "No, I won't. I will be so grateful for your assistance that I could never hurt you. We will be friends forever," the snake eloquently replied.

5 The young woman still hesitated, but, having a kind heart, she picked up the snake.

6 She pressed the snake against her body to warm it. A few minutes later, she felt a twinge as the snake's fangs pierced her skin.

7 "Snake," she screamed, "why did you bite me? You promised you wouldn't."

8 "You knew my traits when you picked me up," the snake hissed as it jumped out of her arms and slithered off.

The Roaming Horse
from China

1 One day in a small village in China, a young man's prized horse ran off. The young man was despondent, and his friends tried to cheer him up. His father, however, asked, "How do you know this isn't a good event?"

2 Two months later, the horse returned with a fine stallion running beside it. The young man was filled with joy. His father, on the other hand, asked, "How do you know this isn't a bad event?"

3 The young man couldn't see how that was possible. He merrily took to riding the stallion around the countryside. One day he fell off the horse and broke his leg. The young man was depressed; he yearned to be back on both feet. But his father asked, "How do you know this isn't a good event?"

4 Three days later word came to the village that it was mandatory for all healthy men to join the army to fight invaders from the north. The young man, however, couldn't go because of his broken leg. The battles were fierce, and most of the men from the village didn't return home.

5 Father smiled and said, "We can never know for certain what fate has planned for us."

Crossing the Lake
from the Middle East

1 A scholar from a distinguished university hired a boatman to take him across the Caspian Sea. The sun was shining and a gentle breeze was blowing as he boarded the small boat. Since he was the only passenger, he engaged the boatman in conversation.

2 "Boatman, have you studied much grammar?" he asked.

3 "No," replied the boatman, "I haven't had the need to."

4 The scholar haughtily told the boatman, "Then you have wasted a third of your life."

5 The wind began to pick up, and the skies darkened as the boat sailed on.

6 "What about philosophy? Surely, you have studied philosophy."

7 "No, I haven't had the need to," the boatman replied.

8 "Then you have wasted another third of your life," the scholar declared.

9 The skies grew darker, rain began to fall, and the wind blew hard. The little boat tossed from side to side. The situation was looking grave.

10 "Hold on Scholar! The ride is going to get rocky. Do you know how to swim?" the boatman called above the wind.

11 "No, I haven't had the need to," the scholar answered.

12 Suddenly the boat tipped over, and both men were thrown into the lake.

13 "Then you have wasted your whole life," shouted the boatman.

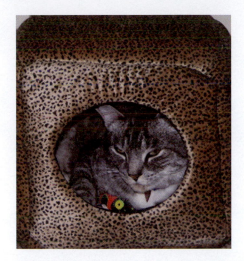

Cat and Fox in the Forest
from several European countries

1   Cat and Fox were strolling through the forest. They were jovially discussing a variety of topics. When they came to talk about the growing problems in the world, Fox began to brag.

2   "I'm not worried about surviving any disasters or other misfortunes. I have hundreds of tricks to weather any situation. What about you, Cat?"

3   "I admit I only have one trick. If it doesn't work, I'd be in trouble."

4   Fox started to laugh at Cat, but he stopped when they heard the blow of a horn, the barking of dogs, and the trample of hoofs. The hunt was on!

5   Cat quickly climbed a nearby tree and hid among the leaves. Fox couldn't decide which of his tricks to use. The hounds were getting closer. Fox hid in a hollow log, but the hounds sniffed him out. He ran into the river to cover his scent, but the hounds found him. Fox was shooting everywhere like fireworks in the sky. He ran over rocks and weaved through the trees, but none of his tricks worked. The dogs caught him.

6   Cat looked down from her perch in the tree and thought: All one really needs is one good trick.

Getting the Message

____ **1.** Paragraph _____ expresses the theme in "Cat and Fox in the Forest."

    a. 1

    b. 4

    c. 5

    d. 6

____ **2.** In "Crossing the Lake" the theme is that

    a. swimming is an essential skill for everyone to learn.

    b. knowing how to swim is more important than knowing about grammar.

    c. the information worth knowing depends on the circumstances.

    d. it is impolite to be rude to boatmen.

____ **3.** In "The Roaming Horse," _____ are used as supporting details.

    a. statistics

    b. facts

    c. testimony

    d. examples

____ **4.** In "Crossing the Lake," a detail that reveals the scholar's personality is that he

    a. is "from a distinguished university."

    b. hired a boat "to take him across the Caspian Sea."

    c. replies to the boatman "haughtily."

    d. asks the boatman if he has "studied much grammar."

____ **5.** What aspect of the setting is especially important in "Snake's Promise"?

    a. It is a cold morning.

    b. The snake is found on a path.

    c. There is a village.

    d. The events in the story take place within an hour.

____ **6.** In "The Roaming Horse," the conflict shows the protagonist against _____.

    a. himself

    b. another character

    c. society

    d. nature

____ **7.** What type of order do all of the tales use?

    a. chronological

    b. problem and solution

    c. most to least important

    d. least to most important

____ **8.** All four tales use the _____ pattern of organization.

    a. definition

    b. narrative

    c. classification

    d. comparison and contrast

___ **9.** Which word in "Snake's Promise" shows contrast?

      a. after

      b. but

      c. suddenly

      d. finally

___ **10.** In "Cat and Fox in the Forest" the line "Fox was shooting everywhere like fireworks in the sky" uses a

      a. simile.

      b. metaphor.

11. Put the themes of "The Roaming Horse" and "Snake's Promise" into your own words.

_____

_____

_____

_____

12. Which of the folktales would you label as having a humorous tone? Explain why. If you don't find any of the tales amusing, explain why.

_____

_____

_____

13. List three characteristics that three or four of the tales share. Possible areas to consider include organization, purpose, and diction.

_____

_____

_____

14. For any of the tales, list two lines of dialogue that you found especially important as you annotated the work.

_____

_____

15. On a separate sheet of paper, make a sketch of a scene from one of the folktales and write under it how it shows an important point in the tale.

Vocabulary

Use context clues to determine the meaning of each word by referring back to the paragraph where the word is used (the paragraph number is in parentheses). If you need help, consult a dictionary for the definition.

A. Match each word to its synonym.

> **malicious** ("Snake's" 1)   **eloquently** ("Snake's" 4)   **despondent** ("Roaming" 1)
> **haughtily** ("Crossing" 4)   **jovially** ("Cat" 1)

1. evil _____

2. sad _____

3. conceitedly _____

4. movingly _____

5. pleasantly _____

B. Finish the sentences using the vocabulary words. Use each word once.

> **ploys** ("Snake's" 3)   **yearned** ("Roaming" 3)   **mandatory** ("Roaming" 4)
> **grave** ("Crossing" 9)   **weather** ("Cat" 2)

1. I can _____ the hard times if my car keeps running for a few more years.

2. The meeting on Friday is _____. Everyone must be there.

3. The news was _____; seven students were suspended for cheating on the test.

4. Daisy's _____ to "accidentally" run into Hiroshi at the mall and the movies worked.

5. Adele _____ to return to her hometown each spring when the tulips were in bloom.

C. Word parts: Fill in the meaning that corresponds to the underlined word part. Return to pages 85–87 if you need to review the meaning of a word part.

> **send**   **down**   **love**   **bad**

1. My friend was <u>de</u>pressed over losing her diamond ring. I too would be _____ if I lost something that expensive.

2. My neighbor is <u>mal</u>icious. He enjoys saying _____ things about people on the block.

3. I ad<u>mit</u> that I was wrong. I will _____ my friend a text to apologize.

4. I am taking a <u>phil</u>osophy class because I _____ to study different ideas and beliefs.

The Folktales and You

1. Pick one of the folktales and explain one or two ways you can relate the theme to your life.

_____

_____

2. Which folktale did you like best? Why?

_____

_____

3. Which folktale did you like least? Why?

_____

_____

4. What would you want people to learn from a folktale? On a separate sheet of paper, write your own folktale that teaches a lesson. Use people or animals in your tale and dialogue if it fits the situation.

Take a Closer Look

Look at the photos again. Do you now have a different perspective on the man's broken legs? Does the cat's expression strike you differently? Did the cat in the folktale fit any traits you connect with cats? Circle the places on the map on page 434 from which the four folktales come.

_____

_____

Internet Activities

If needed, use a separate sheet of paper to fully record your responses. Include the Web address of any sites from which you gather information.

1. Look up "_____ folktales." Fill in the blank with a country from your cultural background or a country you are interested in learning about. Find a folktale you enjoy and print it. Bring it to class to share. Discuss how the tales people picked are similar and different.

_____

2. Go to storyarts.org/classroom/retelling and read about "Becoming a Storyteller." Pick one of the folktales in this chapter and practice retelling it. Then tell it to a friend, a child, or a classmate. Your instructor may ask you to share the story with a small group in class. After you have told your tale, write a summary of the experience including what information you found especially useful on the storyarts Web site.

PEARSON myreadinglab | Objectives Check

To check your progress in meeting chapter objectives, log in to www.myreadinglab.com, click on the Study Plan tab, and then on the Reading Skills tab. Choose Combined Skills and Reading Skills Diagnostic Post-Test from the list of subtopics. Read and view the resources in the Review Materials section, then complete the Practices and Tests in the Activities section. You can check your scores by clicking on the Gradebook tab.

PART 3

Additional Resources

Using the Internet

Skimming and Scanning
SKIMMING
SCANNING

Forms for Photocopying
READING REVIEW FORM
EVIDENCE CHART
CHECKLISTS
SQ4R METHOD
MAIN IDEA
SUPPORTING DETAILS
EVALUATING SUPPORTING DETAILS
ORGANIZATION
PURPOSE AND TONE
INFERENCE
CRITICAL-THINKING
SHORT STORY

Using the Internet

As you do the Internet Activities in this book and use the Internet for your classes and personal needs, there are a few points to keep in mind.

1. **Survey a Web site when you open it to see if the information is relevant to your purpose.**

   A. Decide on your purpose for using the Internet.

   Your purpose will aid in determining your search parameters.

   Are you looking up information for fun or out of curiosity?

   Examples: the year a celebrity was born, the writer of a popular song, where your favorite fruit is grown

   Are you looking up the information for a specific need?

   Examples: to keep the plants in your garden from dying, to find the closest pizza parlor, to get a cake recipe for your friend's birthday

   Are you looking up information for an academic situation?

   Examples: a class project, a research paper, a speech

   If you are looking up the information out of curiosity and likely to forget it in the next few days, then you don't have to be as picky in your source material. For example, you could use Wikipedia, "The Free Encyclopedia" site with entries written collaboratively by people with an interest on the topic. These entries are not necessarily checked for accuracy as a published paper encyclopedia would be, so an entry could be filled with misinformation. Some Wikipedia articles are skillfully written and researched, and they do have the advantage that they can be updated in a matter of minutes instead of months or years as it would take for a paper encyclopedia. On the other hand, some of the articles are not well researched, and some malicious people have been known to purposely put misleading information on such sites. It is up to you to decide how you will use the information from your sources, and what the consequences may be if you use inaccurate information. Even if you are only going to share the trivia or "fun facts" you find on the Web with friends, it is best to give them the most reliable information you can find.

   If you are looking up information for a specific purpose, such as to save your garden or make a healthy meal, you want the information to be reliable. You don't want to kill your plants because someone posted a "good suggestion" on how to deal with fungus on your zucchini. There are a lot of sites on the Web where people can ask questions and other people can post responses. Sometimes these people have valid advice to give, and other times these people know nothing special about the topic but still weigh in with their advice or opinion. You must use your critical-thinking skills to decide if this information is useful. It is a good idea to check the information you find on a Web site with a few other sites on the same topic to make sure the information is dependable.

Finally, if you are looking up the information for academic reasons, you definitely want the information to be reliable since you will be sharing it with others and likely putting it in writing. For these situations, you want to carefully study the sites you visit and use the information below on how to check a site for reliability. You also want to use multiple sources for your academic work. You do not want all of your sources to come from the Internet. Visit the library to check out books, journals, and other sources related to your subject.

B. Look at the main components of the Web site.

First survey the home page, the main page that usually appears when you open a Web site. See what topics are covered on this page. Look at any tabs at the top of the page that indicate other sections of the Web site. Scroll down and see what other information the page contains. Read any headings and subheadings on the page. If the Web site looks helpful, continue to read the information on the home page and open tabs and other links on the site. If the site does not look helpful, return to your search.

2. **Check to see if the Web site is reliable.** Use your critical-thinking and inference skills to decide if the information on a site is accurate and credible.

    A. Discover where the Web site originated by checking its address.

    Every Web site has an address called a URL (uniform resource locator). For example, the Web address for the publisher of this text is www.pearsonhighered.com. Part of the address contains the domain name. Common domain names are *edu, gov, com,* and *org.* By being aware of the domain type and its purpose, you can decide how reliable a site will be. Education (.edu) and government (.gov) sites are usually credible. Some government sites, however, may show a preference for the political views of those currently in charge of the government. Many commercial (.com) and organization (.org) sites are also credible, but remember that a commercial site is trying to sell something, and an organization may have a specific agenda it is promoting.

Below are the addresses for a few Web sites. Visit each site and determine whether the purpose of the site is to inform, to persuade (to get you to buy something, go some place, or do something), or entertain. If you feel the site has more than one purpose, indicate that too. Note the domain designator for each site.

1. Stanford University at standford.edu: _____

2. National Weather Service at nws.noaa.gov: _____

3. The Australian government at australia.gov.au (The "au" indicates that the site is from Australia. Each country has a two-letter code. For the United States it is "us."):

    _____

4. Chicago Convention and Tourism Bureau at choosechicago.com: _____

    _____

5.   American Red Cross at redcross.org: _____

_____

_____

6.   Bored at bored.com: _____

B. Look for a site's credentials.

Search the site for any information that explains who wrote it and what makes the person or group qualified to present this information. If the site represents the views of one person, see if there is a biography or resume on the site. A reputable site should give the educational background and life experiences that make the person an expert on the topic. Remember anyone can set up a Web site.

C. Discover how up-to-date the site is.

If you need current information on a topic, it is important to realize that some Web sites never get updated. Scroll to the bottom of the Web site where you may find a line that states when the Web site was last updated or revised. If you don't find such a statement, try to use information on the site that indicates how up-to-date the site is. There may be an announcement of an upcoming event that shows that the site is current. Or there may be an announcement of "an upcoming event" that happened two years ago showing that the site is far from current. Articles on a site often have a date attached to them. Sometimes your topic will be one that hasn't changed in some years, so it is not essential to find Web sites that have been updated in the last year. Let your topic guide your decision on how current a Web site needs to be.

Just as information on the Web can remain the same for years, it can also change in minutes. Information that may have been on a site when you wrote a paper may not be there by the time you submit the paper. For this reason, you want to indicate the date you visited a site. Your readers will then have a rough idea of when the information changed and understand why they can't gather the same information from the Web site. For example, does the Australian government site still list "Swine Flu Outbreak" information under the "Features" section as it did in November 2009 when this text was in production? Don't be surprised if a site even disappears from the Web. Because the Web can change so dramatically, record the URL of a site you used or want to investigate again in a notebook or other secure place. It may be hard to find the site any other way, and if the site has disappeared, you will at least know you were using the right address to try to find it.

D. Search for bias on the site.

Look at the diction used on the page. Does the site use words with strong connotations or emotionally charged language or images? Are multiple sides of an issue presented? It is understandable that an organization will present only its side, but it is your job to be aware that there is another side or multiple sides to the issue. Check the opposition's site (the Web site you are on may clearly indicate who the opposition is) to see how either side may be manipulating examples, statistics, or visuals. You should also check multiple sites if you are buying a product or going to be hiring a company based on Web research. The company's Web site may present a different view of itself than you will find at the Better Business Bureau's site.

3. **Use your time wisely.**

It is easy to get sidetracked as you click on links taking you from one site to another. Or you may become so involved in finding "the best" site that you spend hours on the Internet. Keep an eye on the clock as you work, or set a timer for a specified time, such as 45 minutes, to keep you from devoting hours and hours to searching when you have other tasks that need your attention. If you get frustrated in searching for a piece of information, it is a good idea to take a break and come back to the Internet later with a fresh perspective.

Remember that the Internet can be an excellent tool for finding information, but it can also be a great source of misinformation. One of the benefits of doing the Internet Activities in this text is developing your critical-thinking skills as you determine whether a Web site will be helpful for your needs.

Look up the following Web sites to practice using the Internet. Note how long it takes you to look at all five sites.

1. The Web site for your college or university.

   What is its address? _____

   List one piece of interesting information on the site.

   _____

2. The Web site for the local government in your area (city, town, county).

   What is its address? _____

   List two services that you can access via this site.

   _____   _____

3. A .com Web site that you use often or one for a product that you are interested in buying.

   What is the company's address? _____

   List two items the company sells.

   _____   _____

4. The Web site of an organization you admire.

   What is its address? _____

   What is the goal of the organization as stated on the site?

   _____

5. A Web site for a foreign country, such as its tourism bureau or a government site.

What is the address? What is the two-letter country code?

_____ _____

List something interesting you noticed as you surveyed the site (e.g., a heading or photo).

_____

In what language was the information written? Could you pick other languages in which to display the information, and, if so, what languages were available?

_____

_____

Skimming and Scanning

Sometimes you will not need to or have the time to read an entire article, essay, or text-book chapter. For these situations you want to use skimming and scanning.

Skimming

Skimming means to read through quickly. Use skimming when it is not essential that you know all the details of a reading. Follow the steps below to skim a reading:

1. Read the title, subheadings, and any words in bold or italics or words defined in the margins.
2. Read the first and last paragraphs and any sections with headings such as "In summary."
3. Read the first sentence of each paragraph.
4. Using the information you have gathered from this brief reading of the material, determine the writer's main idea.

Skimming can be a real time-saver. Situations where skimming is appropriate include with the newspaper to catch up on world or local events, while doing preliminary research to see if an article or essay is appropriate for your topic, when going over a text-book chapter you have already read to remind yourself of key points, and when searching the Internet for information.

For newspaper articles, the skimming process usually works well because reporters know that people often skim articles so the first sentence in a paragraph is typically the topic sentence. Skimming does not tend to work well with fiction. Reading only the first sentence in a short story could leave a reader quite confused as to what happens. Think about the importance of the reading material to your life (will you be tested on the reading, is it essential to your job, are you reading for fun) when you decide whether to skim or read the entire work.

ACTIVITY 1

To test your skimming skills, try the above steps on the reading on page 111. Then read the entire article. Did the main idea you decided on in step four of the skimming process match the main idea you found when you read the entire article?

Scanning

Scanning means to look over quickly, but it also has a second meaning of close examination. You want to use scanning when you are looking for a specific piece of information. Use the following steps to scan for information:

1. In a longer work like a textbook, search for the term you want in the Table of Contents located in the front of the book or look in the Index at the back of the book.

2. If you cannot find the term you are looking for, think of synonyms for the term and then search for those. For example, if you are looking for "supporting details" but you can't find the term in a book, try "evidence" instead. Also remember that people with pseudonyms could be listed under their real names, such as Mark Twain being under Samuel Clemmons in an index.

3. If you find the term, turn to the page (or sometimes pages) where it is located. Move your eyes across the page looking for just that term. When you find the term, read the sentence or paragraph where it is located to get the information you need.

4. If the work is shorter, an article or essay, look down the page for the key word or words that relate to your area of interest. You may want to quickly run your fingers across the page to help guide your scanning. Once you find the word, read the area around it to see if the information is useful to you.

Scanning can save you lots of time. It is especially helpful when you are researching a topic. By scanning a book, you can quickly tell whether it has the information you need for your paper, talk, or project. Other situations when you can use scanning include looking for the name of your favorite team in the sports section of the newspaper to see how it did in a recent game or when searching for the definition of a word you want to review in a textbook.

ACTIVITY 2

To test your scanning skills look up the word *summary* in this book and answer the questions below.

1. Did you find the word in the Table of Contents or the Index? _____

2. On what page is *summary* defined? _____
   _____

3. What does *summary* mean? _____
   _____

Pick one of the words or names below, search for it in this textbook, and answer the following questions.

| irony | word choice | Mongolia | Zora Neale Hurston | simile | Poe |

1. Did you find the word or name in the Table of Contents or the Index? _____
   _____

2. Did you need to use a synonym to find the word? _____

3. On what page(s) did you find the word or name? _____

4. Summarize the information you found about the word or name. _____
   _____
   _____

Forms for Photocopying

The following forms can be photocopied as you or your instructor find necessary. Make sure you always keep one blank form as you may return to using a form several times. Carefully filling out the forms will help you to internalize the various reading skills.

You may want to use the Reading Review Form for each reading. The Evidence Chart is especially helpful for evaluating persuasive readings. Use the SQ4R Method form with the earliest readings to remind yourself of the steps in this process. You can use the other forms as you work with the chapters that focus on the skill related to the form. Of course, the short story form should be used with the short stories and folktales. Also feel free to use a form for any skill that you think you need to concentrate on or that you don't feel comfortable using.

Reading Review Form

Name _____

Class _____ Date _____

1. **Title** and **writer** of the reading: _____

2. Reading **topic:** _____

3. **Main idea**—put it in your own words or use the thesis statement (Circle: stated or implied):

   _____

   _____

4. List the major **supporting details.** If there are more than four, write them on the back of this form.

   A. _____

   B. _____

   C. _____

   D. _____

5. List the major pattern or patterns the writer uses to **organize** the reading:

   _____

   _____

6. State the writer's **purpose** and list a word (or two) that describes the **tone** of the reading:

   _____

   _____

7. Explain your **impressions of** or **reactions to** the reading and why you feel this way. (For example, did you find the reading interesting or dull, informative or amusing, persuasive or weak?)

   _____

   _____

8. List three of the **vocabulary** words you especially want to learn along with a definition for each.

   A. _____

   B. _____

   C. _____

9. Additional comments on items you want to **reflect on, remember,** or **share** about this reading:

   _____

   _____

Evidence Chart

Name _____ Class _____ Date _____ Title of the Reading _____

In the first column, list the evidence (supporting details) found in the reading. In the second column, identify the type of supporting detail (such as statistics, testimony, personal example) for each piece of evidence. In the third column, state whether the evidence is relevant to the writer's point. In the fourth column, assess how accurate or credible the evidence is. In the fifth column, rate the effectiveness or strength of the support. For the fourth and fifth columns you can use a five-point scale with 5 being extremely convincing and 1 being not convincing at all or use plus (+), checkmark (✓), and minus signs (–) to indicate strong, average, and weak evidence.

Support from the Reading	Type of Detail	Relevant (yes or no)	Accurate or Credible	Effectiveness of

Circle your overall assessment (based on the above elements as well as there being **enough** evidence to convince the reader):

Strong Support   Passable Support   Weak Support

SQ4R Method Checklist

Name _____

Class _____ Date _____

✓ **Survey:** Skim the pages you have been assigned to read, looking at the title, headings and subheadings, bold and italicized words, visual aids, and any concluding sections.

✓ **Question:** Ask questions about the reading to help you connect with the material and generate interest in the reading.

✓ **Read:** Have your pen ready to annotate, reread confusing sections, and base your reading speed on the difficulty of the material.

✓ **Record:** Write down what you have learned.

✓ **Recite:** Repeat aloud what you have learned.

✓ **Review:** Review your annotations, summaries, and other notes often. Reflect on what you have just read, and think of ways to relate the new knowledge to your life.

1. Did you survey the reading? Did you find it helpful to do so?

   _____

2. List two questions you asked before you started reading.

   _____

   _____

3. Did you annotate as you read? Was there a confusing section in the reading that you had to reread? Give the paragraph numbers for any confusing sections.

   _____

4. How did you record what you read (e.g., writing a summary or making a chart)? Where are you keeping your recorded materials?

   _____

5. List two points you recited.

   _____

   _____

6. How many times do you plan to review your annotations, summaries, or notes in the next week? Provide a reflection you made about the reading. List two ways you related the reading to your life.

   _____

   _____

   _____

Main Idea Checklist

Name _____

Class _____ Date _____

✓ Determine the topic of the reading.

✓ Establish the point of each paragraph, using topic sentences if provided, to uncover the main idea.

✓ Find a thesis statement or express an implied main idea in your own words.

1. What is the topic of the reading?

_____

2. List the point of each paragraph. Use topic sentences if they are in the reading. If you need more space, continue your list on the back of this sheet.

_____

_____

_____

_____

_____

_____

_____

_____

3. Provide the main idea either by quoting the thesis statement (indicate which paragraph the thesis statement is in) or by putting an implied main idea into your own words.

_____

_____

_____

Supporting Details Checklist

Name _____

Class _____ Date _____

✔ Look for major and minor supporting details.

✔ Be able to identify the four main types of supporting details: examples, statistics, testimony, and reasons. Remember that examples can be personal, public, hypothetical, and facts.

✔ Determine if a statement is a fact by asking yourself whether you can find reliable information to verify the statement.

✔ Determine if a statement is an opinion by asking yourself whether another view or side to the statement is possible.

1. List the supporting details. If you need more space, continue your lists on the back of this sheet.

   Major details:

   _____

   _____

   _____

   _____

   Minor details:

   _____

   _____

   _____

   _____

2. List the types of supporting details in the reading.

   _____

   _____

3. Give an example of a fact in the reading. How could you verify this statement?

   _____

   _____

4. Give an example of an opinion in the reading. What would another view or side be?

   _____

   _____

Evaluating Supporting Details Checklist

Name _____

Class _____ Date _____

✔ Decide if the types of supporting details used are effective for the writer's purpose.

✔ Determine if there are enough details to make or prove the writer's point.

✔ Determine if a supporting detail is relevant to the point being made.

✔ Establish if a supporting detail is accurate or credible.

1. List the supporting details found in the reading. If you need more space, continue your list on the back of this sheet.

_____

_____

_____

_____

_____

2. Are the supporting details effective for the writer's purpose? Explain why or why not.

_____

_____

3. Are there enough details to make or prove the writer's point? Explain why or why not.

_____

_____

4. Are all the supporting details relevant to the point being made? Explain why or why not.

_____

_____

5. Are all the supporting details accurate or credible? Explain why or why not.

_____

_____

Organization Checklist

Name _____

Class _____ Date _____

✔ **Determine the order of the information presented.**

✔ **Look for common patterns of organization.**

✔ **Identify transition words and phrases to help you verify the order of the information and patterns of organization.**

1. In what order is the information presented: chronological (time order), least to most important point, most to least important point, a problem and its solution or solutions?

   _____

   _____

2. What pattern or patterns of organization does the reading use? The seven common types are cause and effect, classification, comparison and contrast, definition, example, narrative, and process.

   _____

   _____

3. List five transition words or phrases in the reading and explain what type of transition each shows (e.g., addition, contrast, or importance). See either page 11 or 206 for a list of transition words and phrases. Do several of the transition words correspond to the order of the information or pattern(s) of organization in the reading?

   _____

   _____

   _____

   _____

   _____

   _____

   _____

Purpose and Tone Checklist

Name _____

Class _____ Date _____

✓ Decide on the writer's main purpose: to inform, to persuade, or to entertain.

✓ Establish the tone by noting the diction, choice of words, used by the writer.

✓ Pay attention to two general tones: formal and informal.

✓ Determine the writer's intended audience.

✓ Look for irony and exaggeration, two techniques that can show tone and purpose.

✓ Label the writer's tone using one or two words.

1. What is the writer's main purpose?

_____

2. List three words in the reading that seem key to you in establishing the tone of the reading.

_____

_____

3. Is the general tone of the reading formal or informal? List three words or phrases in the reading that helped you reach this decision.

_____

_____

4. Who is the writer's intended audience? Is it the general public or a more specific group? Areas to consider in making your decision include the reader's age, gender, knowledge about the subject, and geographic location.

_____

5. If the writer uses irony, give an example of an ironic statement or situation.

_____

_____

6. If the writer uses exaggeration, give an example of where it is used.

_____

_____

7. Use one or two words from the list of tone words on page 256 or use your own words to label the tone of the reading.

_____

Inference Checklist

✔ **Look for evidence in the reading to support your reasoning.**

✔ **Use your prior knowledge about a subject.**

✔ **Look at the organization of a reading.**

✔ **Pay attention to the writer's tone and diction.**

✔ **Watch for a writer's bias toward the topic.**

1. Find a passage where you need to make an inference. Quote the passage (it might be a sentence or a paragraph).

   _____

   _____

   _____

   _____

2. What is your inference?

   _____

   _____

3. What evidence in the reading supports your reasoning?

   _____

   _____

4. What prior knowledge do you have about the subject that supports your reasoning?

   _____

   _____

5. Does the organization of the reading help in making your inference?

   _____

6. What is the writer's tone? Does the tone have an influence on the inference you have made (e.g., irony in the reading)?

   _____

7. Can you detect any type of writer bias in the reading? Does the bias have any connection to the inference you have made?

   _____

   _____

Name _____

Class _____ Date _____

Faulty Logic

✓ Check that the evidence used to support a proposal is relevant to the argument.

✓ Determine whether enough support is given to make a strong case.

✓ See if the organization clearly shows how one action leads to another and will produce the result the writer asserts.

✓ Look closely at the writer's words to determine if they show any bias or try to manipulate the reader through emotional appeals.

✓ Decide if there are other possible outcomes besides the one(s) the writer presents.

✓ Be aware of fallacies as a way to look for faulty logic.

1. Is the evidence in the reading relevant to the argument?

    _____

2. Is there enough support to make a strong case?

    _____

3. Does the organization clearly show how one action leads to another to produce the result the writer asserts? If not, explain where the problem is.

    _____

4. Does the writer use any words that show a bias or does the writer try to manipulate the reader through emotional appeals? If so, give two examples.

    _____

    _____

5. Can you list any other possible outcomes besides the one(s) the writer presents?

    _____

    _____

6. Does the writer use any of the four following fallacies: appeal to emotion, false dilemma (or black and white thinking), hasty generalization (or leaping to a conclusion), slippery slope? If so, explain where.

    _____

    _____

Critical-Thinking Checklist

Figurative Language

✓ Determine what two items are being compared.

✓ Consider the various meanings or qualities associated with the item to which the first thing is being compared.

✓ Connect the pertinent meanings or qualities to the item to which it is being compared.

1. Give an example of figurative language used in the reading. Is it a simile or metaphor?

   _____

   _____

2. What two items are being compared?

   _____

   _____

3. List two to four meanings or qualities associated with the item to which the first thing is being compared.

   _____

   _____

   _____

   _____

4. Which of the meanings or qualities seems most pertinent to the item to which it is being compared? What does the connection reveal about the first item/person/place?

   _____

   _____

   _____

   _____

   _____

Short Story Checklist

✓ Determine what happens in the story to comprehend the plot.

✓ Know who the characters are and establish their personality traits through their actions and dialogue.

✓ Decide what kind or kinds of conflict the protagonist faces.

✓ Establish what impact the setting—time and place—has on the story, and how the tone may be developed through the setting.

✓ Decipher any symbols found in the story.

✓ Use the various literary elements to decide on the theme.

1. Summarize what happens in the story. Use the back of this sheet if you need more room.

   _____

   _____

   _____

   _____

2. List the major characters and their personality traits.

   _____

   _____

   _____

3. What kind or kinds of conflict does the protagonist face?

   _____

   _____

4. What is the setting—time and place—of the story? Does the setting have an impact on what happens in the story? Is the tone shown through the setting?

   _____

   _____

5. List one or two symbols found in the story. What does each symbol mean?

   _____

   _____

6. What is the theme of the story?

   _____

Glossary

A

annotate *v.* to make notes on what you read, usually in the margins

antagonist *n.* the character who works against the main character

antonym *n.* a word that means the opposite of another word

B

bias *n.* a preference or prejudice that can hinder one's objective decision making

C

cause and effect *n.* a pattern of organization that looks at why something happened or the results related to an event or both

characters *n.* the people (or beings) who populate a story; besides being humans, characters can, for example, be animals, robots, or ghosts

chronological *adj.* arranging information using time order

classification *n.* a pattern of organization that puts items into categories to clarify the characteristics of each item

cliché *n.* an overused simile; a commonplace expression or idea

climax *n.* the turning point or the point of highest intensity in a story

comparison *n.* a pattern of organization that looks at similarities between subjects or items, often combined with contrast

conflict *n.* a struggle; in a work of fiction, the battle between the protagonist and either the self, another character, society, or nature

connotation *n.* the suggestive or associative meaning of a word beyond its literal definition; the emotional associations connected to a word

context *n.* the words surrounding a specific word

contrast *n.* a pattern of organization that looks at differences between subjects or items, often combined with comparison

critical thinking *n.* the ability to logically and vigorously analyze and evaluate information in order to reach a conclusion

D

definition *n.* 1. a pattern of organization that attempts to give the meaning of a term 2. the meaning of a word

denotation *n.* the explicit or direct meaning of a word

dialogue *n.* a vocal exchange between two or more characters

diction *n.* choice of words

E

etymology *n.* the history of a word

exaggeration *n.* a technique, often used for humorous effect, where the writer enlarges or overstates a situation to usually unbelievable proportions

example *n.* 1. a type of supporting detail used by writers; examples come in four types: personal experiences, public (media sources), hypothetical (imaginary situations), and facts; 2. a pattern of organization that uses one extended example or a series of examples to prove a point

F

fact *n.* a piece of information regarded as true or real; a fact can be verified through research

fallacy *n.* an argument that is based on faulty logic or perception

figurative language *n.* words used to create images between unlike items by using direct or implied comparisons

flashback *n.* a looking back on events that happened before the time of the current narration in a story

foreshadowing *n.* a technique where a writer subtly suggests what will happen later in a story

G

guide words *n.* two words at the top of a page in a dictionary that signal that the words on that page will come alphabetically between these two words

H

hypothetical example *n.* an example created by the writer's imagination, but it represents a situation that could happen to real people

I

implied main idea *n.* the point the writer wants to make conveyed indirectly or suggested

inference *n.* a technique that uses reasoning to figure out what a writer means when the point is not directly stated; deduction

irony *n.* 1. the use of words to state the opposite of their precise meaning; 2. a clash between what is expected to happen and what really does, often used for humorous effect

L

least to most important a method of ordering information that starts with points that are not as important and builds up to the most important point

M

main idea *n.* the point the writer wants to make; the main idea can be stated (see thesis statement) or implied (see implied main idea)

metaphor *n.* a figure of speech that makes a direct comparison between things that are not literally alike

most to least important a method of ordering information that starts with the most important point and then adds points that the writer does not consider as important

N

narrative *n.* a pattern of organization that tells a story

O

opinion *n.* a view or feeling a person has about something that cannot be supported by objective measures

organization *n.* how something is put together; order

outline *n.* a numbered or lettered summary of a piece of writing that illustrates its major points

P

paraphrase *n.* a sentence where a writer's words are put into one's own words and the writer's original point is retained *v.* to express in other words

personal example *n.* an example that comes from observations the writer provides from events he or she has experienced

plot *n.* the storyline or the plan of a story

prefix *n.* a word part added to the beginning of a word that changes the meaning of the root

problem and solution a method of ordering information that presents a problem and then offers one or more solutions

process *n.* a pattern of organization that explains how to do something or how something is done

protagonist *n.* the main character; the character the action revolves around in a work of fiction

public example *n.* an example that comes from sources the writer has read or seen, such as newspaper articles, books, movies, and television shows

purpose *n.* why the writer wrote the piece; the writer's intention; the three main purposes are to inform, to persuade, and to entertain

R

reason *n.* a sensible explanation that answers the question "Why?" used as a supporting detail

resolution *n.* the outcome or closure to the events in a story

root *n.* a word's basic part with its essential meaning

S

setting *n.* the time and place in which a story takes place

simile *n.* a figure of speech that compares two unlike things, introduced by the word *like* or *as*

statistic *n.* a numerical comparison

suffix *n.* a word part added to the end of a word, which also indicates the part of speech

summary *n.* a condensing of a reading into a shorter version than the original

supporting details *n.* the proof or evidence a writer uses to make a point

symbol *n.* an item that on the surface appears to be what it literally is, but which also has another meaning or many meanings

synonym *n.* a word with a similar meaning to another word

T

testimony *n.* the opinion or statement of an expert on a subject often given in his or her own words (also known as a quotation)

thesaurus *n.* a book that lists synonyms and antonyms

theme *n.* the main idea the writer wants to convey in a work of fiction

thesis statement *n.* one or two sentences that explain the writer's point in a work of nonfiction

tone *n.* the writer's attitude toward the subject; the mood of the reading

topic *n.* what a reading is about in general

topic sentence *n.* a sentence that expresses the point of a paragraph

transition words (or phrases) *n.* words or phrases that help a writer move from one point to another

V

visual aids *n.* photographs, cartoons, diagrams, graphs, charts, tables, sketches, and maps used to convey or enhance the meaning of a reading; they can also be created by readers to aid in comprehending a piece of writing

Credits

Text Credits

p. 20 From FAREWELL, MY LOVELY by Raymond Chandler. New York: A. A. Knopf, 1940.; p. 25 "Writing Tips" from ACTIVE VOCABULARY: GENERAL AND ACADEMIC WORDS, 4TH EDITION by Amy Olsen. Copyright © 2010 by Pearson Education, Inc. Reprinted by permission of Pearson Education, Glenview, IL.; p. 35 "What defines a sport? Like a ping-pong match, the debate goes back and forth" by David Andriesen from THE SEATTLE POST-INTELLIGENCER, January 17, 2008. Reprinted by permission of Hearst Communications, Inc., Hearst Newspapers Division.; p. 49 "Memory as a Reconstruction" and "Eyewitness Testimony" from MASTERING THE WORLD OF PSYCHOLOGY, pp 155–157, by Samuel E. Wood, Ellen Green Wood, and Denise Boyd. Copyright © 2004 by Pearson Education, Inc. Reprinted by permission of Pearson Education, Inc., Boston, MA.; p. 61 "The Stolen Party" by Liliana Heker, Copyright © 1982, which appeared in OTHER FIRES: SHORT FICTION BY LATIN AMERICAN WOMEN edited and translated by Alberto Manguel, Copyright © 1985. Reprinted by permission of Westwood Creative Artists, Ltd; p. 78 From *Merriam-Webster's Collegiate Dictionary*, Eleventh Edition. Copyright © 2010 by Merriam-Webster, Incorporated (www.Merriam-Webster.com.) Reprinted by permission of Merriam-Webster, Inc.; p. 91 From MASTERING THE WORLD OF PSYCHOLOGY by Samuel E. Wood, Ellen Green Wood, and Denise Boyd. Copyright © 2004 by Pearson Education, Inc. Reprinted by permission of Pearson Education, Inc., Boston, MA.; p. 92 From PLANNING YOUR FUTURE: KEYS TO FINANCIAL FREEDOM by Stephan Konowalow. Copyright © 2003 by Pearson Education, Inc. Reprinted by permission of Pearson Education, Inc., Boston, MA.; p. 93 From MASTERING THE WORLD OF PSYCHOLOGY by Samuel E. Wood, Ellen Green Wood, and Denise Boyd. Copyright © 2004 by Pearson Education, Inc. Reprinted by permission of Pearson Education, Inc., Boston, MA.; p. 98 "Get Time On Your Side" by Jennifer Nichols from CAREERS AND COLLEGES MAGAZINE, March/April 2004. Copyright © 2004 by Alloy Education. Reprinted by permission of Alloy Education.; p. 105 "The Blessed Bean: There's Nothing on Earth like Coffee" by Grem Lee and Slim Randles from NEW MEXICO MAGAZINE, September 2005. Reprinted by permission of New Mexico Magazine.; p. 111 "Professor delves into odd culture of freshman" by Michelle Roberts from THE ASSOCIATED PRESS, August 26, 2005. Used with permission of The Associated Press Copyright © 2010. All rights reserved.; p. 117 "Behind Every Grad..." by Thomas L. Friedman from THE NEW YORK TIMES, Copyright © June 10, 2005 by The New York Times. All rights reserved. Used by permission and protected by the Copyright Laws of the United States. The printing, copying, redistribution, or retransmission of the Material without express written permission is prohibited. Reprinted by permission of PARS International.; p. 123 "Socialization into Gender" pp. 65–67 from *Essentials of Sociology: Down-to-Earth Approach* by James Henslin. Copyright © 2006 by Pearson Education, Inc. Reprinted by permission of Pearson Education, Inc., Boston, MA. p. 131 "Thank You, M'am" from SHORT STORIES by Langston Hughes. Copyright © 1996 by Ramona Bass and Arnold Rampersad. Reprinted by permission of Hill and Wang, a division of Farrar, Straus and Giroux, LLC.; p. 141 From ACCESS TO HEALTH, 10TH EDITION by Rebecca J. Donatelle and Patricia Ketcham. Copyright © 2008 by Pearson Education. Printed and Electronically reproduced by permission of Pearson Education, Inc., Upper Saddle River, New Jersey.; p. 142 From PLANNING YOUR FUTURE: KEYS TO FINANCIAL FREEDOM by Stephan Konowalow. Copyright © 2003 by Pearson Education, Inc. Reprinted by permission of Pearson Education, Inc., Boston, MA.; p. 151 "We need to get smart about marijuana" by Rick Steves from THE SEATTLE POST-INTELLIGENCER, March 25, 2008. Reprinted by permission of Hearst Communications, Inc., Hearst Newspapers Division.; p. 157 "Have gun, will show it" by Nicholas Riccardi from the LOS ANGELES TIMES, June 7, 2008. Copyright © 2008 by the Los Angeles Times. Reprinted by permission of the Los Angeles Times.; p. 165 "Under Whom?" written by the Los Angeles Times Editorial Staff from the LOS ANGELES TIMES, September 18, 2005. Copyright © 2005 by the Los Angeles Times. Reprinted by permission of the Los Angeles Times.; p. 171 "Complexion" from HUNGER OF MEMORY: THE EDUCATION OF RICHARD RODRIGUEZ by Richard Rodriguez. Copyright © 1982 by Richard Rodriguez. Reprinted by permission of David R. Godine, Publisher, Inc.; p. 181 "Identity in Contemporary America" from CREATED EQUAL: A SOCIAL AND POLITICAL HISTORY OF THE UNITED STATES, SINGLE VOLUME EDITION, FIRST EDITION by Jacqueline Jones, Peter H. Wood, Elaine Tyler May, Thomas Borstelmann, and Vicki L. Ruiz. Copyright © 2003 by Pearson Education, Inc. Printed and Electronically reproduced by permission of Pearson Education, Inc., Upper Saddle River, New Jersey.; p. 191 "Harrison Bergeron" from WELCOME TO THE MONKEY HOUSE by Kurt Vonnegut, Jr. Copyright © 1961 by Kurt Vonnegut, Jr. Used by permission of Dell Publishing, a division of Random House, Inc.; p. 209 "Life stages of debt" by Sheyna Steiner from BANKRATE.COM, February 25, 2008. Reprinted by permission of Bankrate, Inc.; p. 217 "How to Buy Happiness" by Cynthia G. Wagner originally published in THE FUTURIST. Used with permission from the World Future Society, 7910 Woodmont Avenue, Suite 450, Bethesda, MD 20814, USA. Telephone: 301-565-8274; www.wfs.org.; p. 223 "For love or money: Workers weigh passion against the need to make a living" by Michelle Goodman from NW JOBS (CAREER ADVICE), March 28, 2010. Reprinted with permission by Michelle Goodman.; p. 229 "School Again" from DUST TRACKS ON A ROAD by Zora Neale Hurston. Copyright © 1942 by Zora Neale Hurston; renewed © 1970 by John C. Hurston. Reprinted by permission of HarperCollins Publishers.; p. 237 "Becoming Financially Independent" (pp 17–22) from PLANNING YOUR FUTURE: KEYS TO FINANCIAL FREEDOM by Stephen Konowalow. Copyright © 2003 by Pearson Education, Inc. Reprinted by permission of Pearson Education, Inc., Boston, MA.; p. 245 "Hot Dog Grotto" by Katy Tallorin. Reprinted by permission of author.; p. 259 "The Great Awakening" by Catherine Price from OUTSIDE, June 2008. Reprinted by permission of Outside Magazine.; p. 265 "Sun Savvy: Myth or Reality? From blistering to bronze, the truth about tanning" by Tracy Davis from the ANN ARBOR (MICHIGAN) NEWS. Copyright © 2007 by The Ann Arbor News. All rights reserved. Used with permission of The Ann Arbor News.; p. 273 "Cross Train Your Brain" by Kate Hanley. Copyright © 2007 by Martha Stewart Living Omnimedia, Inc. All rights reserved. As first seen in the June, 2007 issue of WHOLE LIVING BODY + SOUL MAGAZINE. www.wholeliving.com. Reprinted by permission of Martha Stewart Living Omnimedia, Inc.; p. 281 "How We Eat Reflects and Defines Our Personal and Cultural Identity" from EATING WELL FOR OPTIMUM HEALTH by Andrew Weil, M.D. Copyright © 2000 by Andrew Weil, M.D. Used by permission of Alfred A. Knopf, a division of Random House, Inc.; p. 291 "Healthy Relationships" from ACCESS TO HEALTH, 10TH EDITION by Rebecca J. Donatelle and Patricia Ketcham. Copyright © 2008 by Pearson Education, Inc. Printed and Electronically reproduced by permission of Pearson Education, Inc., Upper Saddle River, New Jersey.; p. 315 "Kids led the way, but texting's GR8 for all" by Kevin Simpson from THE SEATTLE POST-INTELLIGENCER, December 10, 2007. Reprinted by permission of Hearst Communications, Inc., Hearst Newspapers Division.; p. 323 "Constant techno communication brings lack of focus and loss of privacy" by Eric Adler and Laura Bauer from THE KANSAS CITY STAR, March 13, 2010. Reprinted by permission of The Kansas City Star.; p. 331 "Happily Ever Laughter" by Peter Doskoch from PSYCHOLOGY TODAY, July 1996. Reprinted by permission of Sussex Publishers, Inc.; p. 339 From GORILLAS IN THE MIST by Dian Fossey. Copyright © 1983 by Dian Fossey. Reprinted by permission of Houghton Mifflin Harcourt Publishing Company. All rights reserved.; p. 349 "Responding to Stress," "Health and Illness," and "Try It! 10.2" from MASTERING THE

Photo Credits

Index

Reading Review Form

Name _____

Class _____ Date _____

1. **Title** and **writer** of the reading: _____

2. Reading **topic:** _____

3. **Main idea**—put it in your own words or use the thesis statement (Circle: stated or implied):

   _____

   _____

4. List the major **supporting details.** If there are more than four, write them on the back of this form.

   A. _____

   B. _____

   C. _____

   D. _____

5. List the major pattern or patterns the writer uses to **organize** the reading:

   _____

   _____

6. State the writer's **purpose** and list a word (or two) that describes the **tone** of the reading:

   _____

   _____

7. Explain your **impressions of** or **reactions to** the reading and why you feel this way. (For example, did you find the reading interesting or dull, informative or amusing, persuasive or weak?)

   _____

   _____

8. List three of the **vocabulary** words you especially want to learn along with a definition for each.

   A. _____

   B. _____

   C. _____

9. Additional comments on items you want to **reflect on, remember,** or **share** about this reading:

   _____

   _____

Reading Review Form

1. **Title** and **writer** of the reading: _____

2. Reading **topic:** _____

3. **Main idea**—put it in your own words or use the thesis statement (Circle: stated or implied):

   _____

   _____

4. List the major **supporting details.** If there are more than four, write them on the back of this form.

   A. _____

   B. _____

   C. _____

   D. _____

5. List the major pattern or patterns the writer uses to **organize** the reading:

   _____

   _____

6. State the writer's **purpose** and list a word (or two) that describes the **tone** of the reading:

   _____

   _____

7. Explain your **impressions of** or **reactions to** the reading and why you feel this way. (For example, did you find the reading interesting or dull, informative or amusing, persuasive or weak?)

   _____

   _____

8. List three of the **vocabulary** words you especially want to learn along with a definition for each.

   A. _____

   B. _____

   C. _____

9. Additional comments on items you want to **reflect on, remember,** or **share** about this reading:

   _____

   _____

Reading Review Form

Name _____

Class_____ Date _____

1. **Title** and **writer** of the reading: _____

2. Reading **topic:** _____

3. **Main idea**—put it in your own words or use the thesis statement (Circle: stated or implied):

    _____

    _____

4. List the major **supporting details.** If there are more than four, write them on the back of this form.

    A. _____

    B. _____

    C. _____

    D. _____

5. List the major pattern or patterns the writer uses to **organize** the reading:

    _____

    _____

6. State the writer's **purpose** and list a word (or two) that describes the **tone** of the reading:

    _____

    _____

7. Explain your **impressions of** or **reactions to** the reading and why you feel this way. (For example, did you find the reading interesting or dull, informative or amusing, persuasive or weak?)

    _____

    _____

8. List three of the **vocabulary** words you especially want to learn along with a definition for each.

    A. _____

    B. _____

    C. _____

9. Additional comments on items you want to **reflect on, remember,** or **share** about this reading:

    _____

    _____